The Golden Age Remembered

THE
GOLDEN
AGE

Appolo souchek

Remembered

*He flew me from
Korea to Japan
my last flight
in 1953.*

U.S. NAVAL AVIATION, 1919–1941

EDITED BY E. T. WOOLDRIDGE

NAVAL INSTITUTE PRESS • ANNAPOLIS, MARYLAND

Library of Congress Cataloging-in-Publication Data

The golden age remembered : U. S. naval aviation, 1919–1941 / edited by E. T. Wooldridge.
    p.   cm.
   Includes bibliographical references (p.   –   ) and index.
   ISBN 1-55750-938-7 (acid-free paper)
   1. United States.   Navy—Aviation—History.   I. Wooldridge, E. T.
VG93.G657 1998   97-41901
359.9'4'0973—dc21

Printed in the United States of America on acid-free paper ∞
05 04 03 02 01 00 99 98   9 8 7 6 5 4 3 2
First printing

Unless otherwise indicated, all photographs are official U.S. Navy photographs and were obtained from the U.S. Naval Institute.

Frontispiece: Lt. Apollo Soucek in a Wright Apache. He set a new world altitude record for Class C land planes, reaching 39,140 feet over NAS Anacostia, D.C.

*To the pioneers of the golden age
of U.S. naval aviation*

Contents

Preface

My personal memories of naval aviation during the period between the wars—the "golden age" of aviation—go back to the late 1930s in Annapolis, Maryland. Like many local kids, I hung out at the U.S. Naval Academy, soaking up the lore, enjoying the activities—and watching airplanes. The personal plane of Rear Adm. Wilson Brown, superintendent of the Naval Academy, was usually parked near the seawall along the Severn River. The admiral's plane was a Grumman J2F-3 Duck, an amphibian with the dark-glossy-blue fuselage of a command airplane. The two stars of a rear admiral were painted on the side, and there was silver trim on the wing floats. It was a gorgeous airplane. A small boy could touch it, peak inside the window, and live vicariously. For diversion, PBY Catalina flying boats could usually be seen cavorting on and over the Severn River on indoctrination flights for midshipmen. These sights and sounds were the stuff of lasting memories.

The ultimate happening for a twelve-year-old occurred some months later and an ocean away during a visit to the aircraft carrier *Saratoga* in Hawaii, just a year or so before the attack on Pearl Harbor. I explored the ship from stem to stern and sat in the cockpit of another classic airplane of the 1930s—the Curtiss SBC Helldiver. A look through the Aldis telescopic sight in the windscreen, a cursory cockpit check, and a complementary set of miniature navy wings of gold completed a day that I will remember for the rest of my life. Not long thereafter, I had my first flight in an airplane—a Douglas Sleeper Transport (DST), the sleeper version of the DC-3. It was a slow, noisy trip across the continent with many stops along the way. But at least it was flying—and what better way to start than in the airplane that revolutionized air transportation in the golden age.

The introduction that follows and the short essays preceding the three parts of this book are intended to set the scene for the reader and to place the oral history narratives in the context of historical aviation events and developments around the world. The essays are not definitive or complete by any means, and the reader is encouraged to expand his or her knowledge of the golden age by reading some of the truly scholarly works listed in the bibliography.

I extend my sincere thanks to the staff of the U.S. Naval Institute (USNI) for their continuing support of this and similar projects that have made extensive use of USNI oral history and photo collections. Paul Stillwell, director of history, again very graciously placed the oral history collection at the disposal of the National Air and Space Museum (NASM); Mary Beth Straight-Kiss, former USNI manager of library services and photo archivist, provided an outstanding service in the selection of photographs that has become her stock in trade; and Ann Hassinger, administrative assistant, willingly helped me select the oral history transcripts for editing. Dr. John T. Mason, founding father of the USNI oral history collection, oversaw the work involved in about 130 volumes of oral history and was ably assisted in the interviewing process by Paul Stillwell and Comdr. Etta-Belle Kitchen, USN (Ret.).

I am indebted to many members of the NASM staff who provided advice, encouragement, and assistance during the project: Nadya Makovenyi, associate director for exhibits and public services, most likely a golden age carrier pilot in another life; Mark Avino and Carolyn Russo of the museum's lab, who provided timely and highly professional support; Dana Bell, Dan Hagedorn, Melissa Keiser, and Kristine Kaske of the archives division, who were particularly generous in providing the invaluable assistance and expert guidance to which thousands of serious aviation researchers have become accustomed over the years; and Mary Pavlovich, circulation librarian, always particularly generous and understanding in making available the considerable resources of the NASM's branch of the Smithsonian Institution libraries.

I am particularly indebted to Vice Adm. Donald D. Engen, USN (Ret.), director, National Air and Space Museum. Without his enthusiastic interest in preserving our naval aviation heritage at NASM, this book would not have been possible.

Introduction

With the passage of time, aviation writers and enthusiasts have come to view the years between the two world wars with nostalgia and affection. Those were the good old days, when new aircraft performance records were daily occurrences, heroes were made overnight, and companies boomed (and busted) in the blink of an eye. Some memories have dimmed over the years: dreadful accident rates; dangerous, grueling cross-country flights in atrocious weather; flimsy, open-cockpit biplanes with primitive instruments, no radios, and unreliable motors.

Despite those growing pains, we now call the period the golden age of aviation—and with good reason. Viewed in absolute terms, it was an era of great achievement in practically every phase of aviation, both civil and military. There were astounding advances in aviation technology, innumerable record flights made possible by these technological improvements, heroic efforts to explore remote regions of the world, and the intense interest of the public in aviation events.

Viewed from a modern-day perspective, there can be little argument that, for aviation, those years were the golden age of the rugged individualists— courageous and often foolhardy men and women who were unfettered by convention, regulations, or restrictions, and who eagerly faced a world of unlimited opportunity, adventure, and challenge. Records of every kind begged to be broken—time and again—and racing and aerobatic pilots, explorers, and adventurers became household names. Their mystique was nourished and perpetuated in newspaper headlines and dramatized by commentator Lowell Thomas in Fox Movietone newsreels and his evening radio broadcasts, heard by millions.

From the first air race held in 1909 in Rheims, France, the affairs had evolved into major spectacles of entertainment by the 1930s. The American public was attracted by the drama and the showmanship, as well as the opportunity to see many of the leading aviation personalities of the day, all gathered in one place at the same time. The National Air Races offered everything a worshiping public could wish for—aerobatic teams, wing walkers, pylon races, and spectacular aerial maneuvers by squadrons of the U.S. Navy and the Army Air Corps. Under the inspired leadership of managing director Cliff Henderson, the Nationals matured in the 1930s into an annual event that guaranteed astonishing performances and shattered records.

Maj. Al Williams, U.S. Marine Corps, renowned aerobatic pilot and former navy racing pilot of the 1920s, thrilled the crowd as he performed his repertoire of incomparable precision flying in the orange-and-white *Gulfhawk II*. Swashbuckling dandy Roscoe Turner, replete with powder-blue uniform, boots, and waxed mustache, posed with his traveling companion Gilmore the Lion. Jimmie Doolittle and the infamous Gee Bee, Tony LeVier and the Keith Rider *Fire Cracker*, Steve Wittman and *Chief Oshkosh*—all were nearby, preparing for the next event. Frank Hawks passed through with his red-and-white *Texaco Mystery Ship* on his way to establishing one of his more than two hundred intercity speed records.

The air shows and the exploits of long-distance flyers and explorers provided excitement, drama, and pathos on a daily basis and were the essence of the golden age. But as entertaining and impressive as these performances were for the public, they were often a means to an end for the emerging air arms of the U.S. Navy and the Army Air Corps. The air shows and the public recognition of each new record flight provided unprecedented opportunity for favorable publicity and visibility for the military services, the pilots, and their machines. Of equal importance, the races were testing grounds and showcases for the latest advances in engines and airplanes. Military and civilian demands for improved air-craft performance stimulated the need for airplanes that could fly faster, farther, and higher than the wood-and-fabric biplanes of an earlier era. As a result, between 1919 and 1941, the United States made extraordinary progress in aviation technology. The airplane was transformed from a rudimentary machine with an uncertain future into an established, yet developing commodity.

"My God, he's going to England with only a candy bar!" As the sound of Douglas Corrigan's tired old Curtiss Robin faded away to the east, it occurred to aviation photographer Rudy Arnold that the quiet, reticent Irishman was not really heading for California. Arnold had gone to Floyd Bennett Field on Long Island that day in July 1938 to photograph Corrigan when he departed for a nonstop flight to California. Instead, "Wrong Way" Corrigan headed east to Ireland—and to a place in aviation history. By 1938 Corrigan was just one of hundreds of pilots and daredevils who had become afflicted with what has been called Atlantic fever.

It had all started in the aftermath of World War I, when far-sighted leaders in the U.S. Navy and the Army Air Service realized that future wars would require the deployment far from the United States of long-range aircraft to fill a wide range of military missions, ranging from convoy escort and antisubmarine warfare to strategic bombardment and recon-naissance. The navy led the way across the Atlantic with the Navy-Curtiss NC-4 flying boat in May 1919, followed several years later by the eighteen hundred–mile record-breaking flight of the PN-9 flying boat en route from San Francisco to Honolulu. These flights stood as highlights amid scores of long-range flights flown by U.S. Navy flying boat crews during the twenties and thirties.

The dramatic improvements in flying boat design and increases in engine performance and reliability by the mid-1930s reaped enormous benefit for the navy, as well as making the prospect of safe, efficient air transportation across the oceans of the world a reality. The era of the big commercial flying boats began in August 1931 with the arrival of the German-built Do X flying boat over the Hudson River after an inaus-picious ten-month odyssey from Friedrichshafen, Germany. The Dornier Do X—ponderous and ungainly with its three decks, twelve engines, and accommodations for sixty-six passengers—was hardly the answer to the challenge of transatlantic travel. But by the end of the decade, in June 1939, Pan American Airway's president Juan Trippe had initiated the first sustained scheduled passenger service with the most luxurious flying machines of the day, the Boeing 314 Clippers.

Countless heroic deeds, historic flights, and sensational events caught and held the public's attention, but few received such international acclaim or so monopolized the aviation spotlight as the mass formation flight of Italian general Italo Balbo and his twenty-four flying boats across the Atlantic to the United States in 1933. The astounding flight was a source of intense national pride for all Italians and clearly demonstrated the potential of mass long-distance flying.

The vast expanses of the Atlantic and Pacific Oceans challenged the pilots and risk takers of the golden age. The Polar regions, the jungles of New Guinea, the Amazon, the Yucatan, and the desert of northern Africa were virtually inaccessible until they were reached by airplane. Pilots turned explorer, and with the backing of foundations, museums, wealthy patrons, and, in some cases, with what money they themselves could raise, these adventurers went to far-off lands and brought back invaluable photographic records of the amazing sights they had seen.

With a national interest in exploration, navy pilots also stretched their legs, routinely flying survey flights outside the continental United States to remote locations, searching for advance base sites to support military operations. These survey flights ranged from single-plane photographic surveys of relatively short duration and objective to large-scale operations involving a squadron of aircraft, tender ships, and maintenance crews to support sustained flight operations under the most arduous conditions.

Speed seekers Jimmie Doolittle and Roscoe Turner with their sleek racers; distance flyers Charles Lindbergh, Amelia Earhart, and Wrong Way Corrigan; daredevil stunt pilots, such as Rumanian captain Alex Papana, Major Al Williams, and Lt. Tommy Tomlinson, U.S. Navy—all these memorable, great aviation personalities—left their names and deeds indelibly imprinted on the record books and on the American consciousness. They were heroes who represented everything that was exciting, romantic, and glamorous in the era. But there was yet another chapter in the saga—a bloody and tragic one—without which any remembrance of the age would be incomplete. The period of the 1920s and 1930s was also the era of the rigid airship.

The U.S. Navy envisioned rigid airships as strategic scouts for the fleet, especially in the Pacific, where distances were vast and American outposts widely scattered. The airship era began for the navy in September 1923 with the maiden flight of the USS *Shenandoah* (ZR-1). In 1924, Lt. Comdr. Zachary Lansdowne took the airship on an extended transcontinental flight of some 235 hours in the air. Though the flight was hailed as the forerunner of a commercial passenger airship service, the euphoria was short lived. The *Shenandoah* was destroyed in a fierce storm over Ohio on 3 September 1925.

Despite the loss of the *Shenandoah*, three more airships entered the skies: the USS *Los Angeles* (ZR-3), the *Akron* (ZR-4), and the *Macon* (ZR-5). The three airships, while demonstrating some potential as scouting ships for the fleet, nonetheless suffered additional setbacks, as both the *Akron* and the *Macon* perished in bad weather. With the loss of the *Macon* on 12 February 1935 off Point Sur, California, the navy concluded that the airship had "failed to demonstrate its usefulness," and that "further expenditure of public funds for this type of vessel is not justified."

Despite the navy's failures with rigid airships, they continued to play a role in commercial air transportation until the spring of 1937. By then, the magnificent airship *Hindenburg* had finished a successful year of commercial operation between Europe and the United States, carrying a full load of fifty passengers in each direction during many safe Atlantic crossings. No other form of transportation could carry passengers so swiftly, reliably, and comfortably between the two continents. Airship travel, it was said, was an idea whose time had finally come.

That is, until the evening of 6 May 1937, when the *Hindenburg* arrived from Europe and approached its mooring at the Naval Air Station, Lakehurst, New Jersey. Without warning, flames erupted from the ship's hull, and within seconds the ship's charred remains lay on the ground. Thirty-five people died in the inferno, while ninety-seven miraculously survived. The tragedy of the *Hindenburg* marked the end of the commercial airship era, just as the disasters of the *Shenandoah*, *Akron*, and *Macon* years before had precipitated the end of the U.S. Navy's brief experiments with rigid airships.

For all intents and purposes, the golden age came to an end with the advent of war in Europe in 1939 and the U.S. entry into the conflict in 1941. Commercial transoceanic clipper service would become a thing of the past in the postwar era as the venerable clippers were replaced by four-engine land planes of equal range and greater speed. The rigid airship had seen its heyday, although nonrigid blimps would be used for long-range patrol operations until the end of naval airship operations in 1961. For the navy, the era of biplanes on aircraft carriers had finally come to a glorious end, with the Grumman F3F-3 laying claim to the best biplane fighter ever built, and the Curtiss SBC Helldiver retiring as the last combat biplane built in the United States. As the biplanes took their final bows, most of the airplanes that would fight the war for the navy were either operational or well into their development cycle. The war in the Pacific would be won by the Catalina, Wildcat, Dauntless, Avenger, and the Corsair—all products of the golden age. The best fighter of them all, the Hellcat, was on the drawing board as war approached.

On the racing circuit, the 1939 National Air Races were the last of the era. With the beginning of the war in Europe, air races vanished for its duration. They returned after the war, with the indestructible Steve Wittman at the top of a short list of old crowd pleasers still in the cockpit—Earl Ortman, Art Chester, and Jackie Cochran—all of whom raced for a few more years. Events of the war had shaped the lives of many performers in ways they could not possibly have imagined during their earlier air show days. Doolittle became a general after leading the first bombing raid on Japan from the carrier *Hornet;* LeVier became a leading test pilot for Lockheed, heading a list of air show pilots who migrated to test pilot jobs with aircraft manufacturers.

With the advent of the jet age, records became meaningless, as military jet aircraft flew out of sight at speeds that were unimaginable just a few short years before. Aside from dedicated aviation enthusiasts and aviation professionals, it became difficult for the general public to relate to the rapidly improving innovations—and many essentially lost interest. Sadly, with a few exceptions now and again, aviation heroes became a thing of the past. The romance was gone; things just weren't the way they used to be.

The U.S. Navy took aviation to sea during the golden age in the face of problems, frustrations, and challenges without precedent. Regulations, traditions of the service, and the biases of hidebound members of the "gun club" made difficult tasks even more formidable. However, the navy attracted its own share of free spirits, visionaries, and leaders who met the challenges head on. Naval officers—aviators, tacticians, planners, engineers, and a handful of enlightened and farsighted "blackshoes"—structured naval aviation, developed doctrine and tactics, and designed, tested, and operated aircraft and carriers during the interwar years. During World War II, many of these officers became squadron and air group commanders, department heads, and commanding officers of carriers. Dozens of flag officers who earned their spurs in the early days led naval aviation into combat at sea and managed the shore establishment throughout the war.

Following World War II, these veterans provided the strong, effective leadership that carried the navy through the turmoil of demobilization, the creation of the Department of Defense, hot wars and cold wars, and the critical transition of naval aviation into the jet age—and beyond. For seven decades, these pioneers of the golden age of naval aviation were the heart and soul, the bedrock, of naval aviation, from its inception in 1911 until 1976, when the last golden age warrior, Adm. Noel A. M. Gayler, retired.

The Golden Age Remembered

PART ONE

PRELUDE TO THE GOLDEN AGE

IN AUGUST 1909, almost six years after the Wright brothers made their first successful flight in 1903, the Aero Clubs of France, England, and the United States staged the world's first International Air Meet near Rheims, France. For the first time, premier aviators of the day from Europe and the United States came together. Enormous crowds came to see the likes of Louis Bleriot, who just one month earlier had become the first man to fly the English Channel, and Glenn Curtiss, the lone American entry with his small pusher biplane, the *Golden Flyer*. Thirty-six aircraft of every description flew during the meet, most of them underpowered, unstable, and with primitive forms of lateral control. A height of 503 feet won the altitude prize; Curtiss came through for the United States to win top honors in the first James Gordon Bennett Cup speed race with an average speed of 47 mph.

New aircraft performance records were set the following year when the International Air Meet was held in the United States. U.S. Army and Navy officers attended the meet, took note of the impressive records, and at least began to become aware of the potential offered by the airplane.

The French, however, with their Deperdussin monoplanes, soon dominated the annual Bennett Cup races, and by 1913 they had raised the speed mark to 124.5 mph. After Glenn Curtiss's win in 1909, the United States was not a factor in the Bennett Cup race or in the two International Schneider Trophy races for hydroaeroplanes held before World War I.

As the U.S. public grew more interested in aviation, a handful of officers within the navy foresaw the possibilities of aircraft as offensive weapons, and they recognized the need for a central point of contact for aviation matters in the Navy Department. In September 1910 a keen-minded engineer named Washington Irving Chambers was given that responsibility. During his three years on the job, Captain Chambers became interested in the scientific and technical aspects of aviation, devoting all his energies and intellect to generating interest in aviation in the navy and to stimulating research in aerodynamics.

Naval aviation soon took its first tentative steps toward going to sea: Glenn Curtiss and Eugene Ely showed the world that airplanes could operate from a man-of-war; the first cadre of pilots were trained; and naval officers flew airplanes from catapults. In 1913 Captain Chambers could report to the navy's General Board that eight airplanes were in commission: three Curtiss and two Wright hydroaeroplanes, one Burgess and two Curtiss flying boats. There was an airfield near the Naval Academy at Annapolis, and thirteen officers held pilot's licenses. They had flown 2,118 flights for a total of more than 500 hours in the air, covering just fewer than 28,000 miles.

Despite these signs of progress, Chambers described the navy as being in an "embryonic and chaotic state." Equipment was scant, men were all too few. In Europe, France still had the lead in the air and, with England and Italy, was moving out front in seaplane development; Germany had superiority in dirigibles. During the war, Great Britain accelerated development of early aircraft carriers, including the *Furious,* the *Vindictive,* and the *Argus.* From all appearances, the United States was far behind and showing few signs of catching up in the international race to develop aviation.

Despite Captain Chambers's pessimism, there were signs of progress. By the end of 1914, Capt. Mark Bristol, an officer of strong character and recognized ability, became the first "director of naval aeronautics"; the first aeronautic station was established at Pensacola, Florida; and aviation detachments from Pensacola were operating from battleships in Mexican waters in support of military operations at Vera Cruz. Pioneer aviators such as Mustin, Whiting, Towers, Rodgers, and Bellinger played vital roles in these early milestone events in naval aviation history and during the events to follow in the next two decades.

Whatever progress had been made in naval aviation, it was nonetheless poorly equipped to fight a war in Europe and the North Atlantic. One naval air station, several dozen airplanes, about fifty aviators and students, and almost two hundred enlisted men were not enough. As requirements for naval and air forces overseas increased dramatically, so too did aircraft procurement, naval air stations at home and abroad, and ground and flight schools to handle the influx of thousands of officers and enlisted personnel. Naval aviation was the first on the scene overseas when Lt. Kenneth Whiting led the first military detachment to reach France in June 1917. Others soon followed, and U.S. Navy airmen flying Curtiss flying boats contributed in great measure to the antisubmarine warfare effort. Naval aircraft flew more than three million miles of war patrols and attacked twenty-five submarines, sinking or damaging a dozen of them. From their experiences came a requirement for a flying boat of greatly increased range and combat capability. What followed was the first great long-distance flight of the postwar era—the transatlantic flight of the NC-4.

When Joe Cline reported to Pensacola for flight training in the spring of 1917, he found the training command disorganized and unprepared to meet the sudden increase in training workload. The solution to his dilemma was to volunteer for overseas duty with the First Aeronautical Detachment, commanded by Lieutenant Whiting. In a wonderful example of the enthusiasm and resiliency of youth, Cline and other Americans learned to fly French aircraft with French instructors, assembled their aircraft, which had been shipped over from the United States, and built their own living quarters with the leftover packing crates. Although most of their missions were boring, arduous antisubmarine patrols over the English Channel, airmen of the First Aeronautical Detachment were killed in action, as well as in numerous operational accidents. Contrary to popular perception, all the aerial combat in Europe was not confined to the skies over the western front.

Aldred K. Warren reported to Pensacola for his flight training in the summer of 1917 "young and foolish," and anticipating the glamour and freedom of flying through the air with the greatest of ease. All the glamour disappeared in the noise and vibration of his first flight, the most disappointing of his aviation career. Flying Curtiss floatplanes off Pensacola Bay soon revived his spirit of adventure, stimulated some latent ingenuity and resourcefulness, and taught him the niceties of seamanship. Performing a loop in the only trainer that was equipped with an airspeed indicator whet his appetite for stunt flying, which he enjoyed throughout his brief flying career. Warren later flew Curtiss flying boats from NAS North Island, San Diego, the site of Glenn Curtiss's old 1911 aviation camp, where the flying was fun, full of adventure, and always a challenge to his considerable flying skills—and to his sense of humor.

I

THE LOST DETACHMENT

Ens. Joseph Charles Cline

JOSEPH CHARLES CLINE *was born on 1 March 1893 in Chicago, Illinois, and graduated from Hyde Park High School in Chicago in 1910. After serving four years in the Illinois Naval Militia, he enlisted as landsman for quartermaster (aviation) in the U.S. Navy on 3 April 1917. He was a member of the First Aeronautic Detachment, the first U.S. armed forces sent to Europe during World War I, and was transported to Europe on board the USS* Neptune *(AC-8). He received ground and flight training at various French naval air stations, was designated French naval aviator no. 346, and later U.S. naval aviator no. 1832. He flew combat missions over the English Channel until the end of World War I, at which time he returned to the United States for duty at NAS Bay Shore, Long Island, New York. After his release from active duty on 13 January 1919, he was subsequently promoted to ensign, U.S. Naval Reserve Force, to date from 7 June 1918, and recalled to active duty. Ensign Cline served in several shore duty assignments until resigning from the navy on 22 May 1922.*

At eight o'clock in the morning on the third of April 1917, three days before war was declared, I was down at the recruiting station in Chicago.

By ten o'clock I had finished the physical examination, and at four-thirty that afternoon, I was on my way to Pensacola for flight training. All of us who were selected for flight training at that time were enlisted as landsman for quartermaster; the lowest rank in the navy was landsman— landsman for anything—and the pay was $17.60 a month.

When we arrived at Pensacola, they didn't know exactly what to do with us. There were no ground school provisions for us; they just dumped us down there. "Here we are, here are some students of aviation for you." They scurried around a little bit to find out what they could do for us, so we started getting some navy indoctrination. I was very fortunate in that I had had four years training in the naval reserve. I knew how to roll up my clothes, salute an officer, stand at attention, and I knew the *Manual of Arms*.

That almost turned out to be my "Waterloo." They made me company commander, and I didn't want to do that. They wanted me to stay at Pensacola and train and instruct recruits. Meantime, scuttlebutt got around that the first people who asked would get to go overseas. I wanted to go overseas and stay with my crowd, so I didn't become very efficient from then on, and somehow, I eventually got over with the first detachment.

In 1917, there were about a hundred men, perhaps a little less, at Pensacola for training. Fifty of them would be trained as machinist mates for maintenance, motor mechanics, and so forth, and fifty of them would be quartermasters, who were trained as pilots. We were down there about three weeks. Our flight commander was Lt. Comdr. R. W. Cabaniss (naval aviator no. 36), who would later be killed in a plane crash in 1927.

We didn't get any training whatsoever; we never sat in an American airplane, even though they had all types of old airplanes at that time, such as Curtiss F-boats and N-9s. We didn't know the theory of flight, and they had no facilities for training us in the theory of flight. Most of us never even drove an automobile. We'd wander through the hangars in our leisure hours when we weren't drilling or studying. We'd take a cylinder of an OX-5 engine and draw a sketch. That would be our afternoon's work as far as ground school was concerned.

One day Mr. Cabaniss came out during the morning formation and said that he wanted volunteers for duty aboard the colliers *Neptune* and *Jupiter* (AC-3). Everybody gazed at one another and said, "We're down here for aviation. We don't want to go to sea. We want to learn to fly." And nobody volunteered. So finally he said, "If nobody volunteers, we will take you anyway." I looked at a friend of mine, Mac Weddell of Chicago, and I said, "Mac, we'd better step forward." So we stepped forward, along with some of the others. Finally they all stepped forward and volunteered. We had no idea what it was all about.

They split the group. One group went aboard the *Jupiter*, at Hoboken, while the group I was in went to Baltimore to pick up the *Neptune*, which had been lying there loading flour and grain for over a week for starving allies. After a stop in Norfolk, we were off for France, escorted by two destroyers, the *Jarvis* (DD-38) and the *Perkins* (DD-26). After a twelve-day crossing, we arrived at St. Nazaire on 5 June 1917, and we just waited to find out what they were going to do with us. Lt. Kenneth Whiting, our commanding officer, rushed off to Paris to see the American ambassador, the naval attaché, the French minister, and a few others. There was a conference at Paris, I understand, and it was agreed that the French would train us. They would supply us with airplanes, motors, armaments, bombs and accessories, and so forth, in which the United States was woefully lacking, and would construct air stations for us while we were in training.

The French were waiting for the Americans since we had declared war. I understand the French had requested American troops immediately in order to bolster the morale of the French army and the French nation. We were the first Americans to set foot on French soil after the declaration of war in 1917, the First Aeronautic Detachment.

In a few days we left for Brest, a small fishing village near the Bay of Camerae. There were now fifty of us, because the mechanics had gone to Pauillac. We were under the command of Lt. Virgil Griffin. We slept in barracks that Napoleon slept in, on straw mattresses and what not, and ate French rations. The barracks were just old-fashioned brick buildings that had been through the wars—just natural grey color, unattractive French barracks; but we didn't care, we were there, and we were having fun. We were going to war. We were twenty-two years old, we didn't care about anything. It was just a lark, as far as we were concerned.

After about two weeks, we had orders to get a train for Paris. With ten loaves of French potato bread and fifteen bottles of red wine, we got on a train on our way to Tours, with Chief Petty Officer Charles O'Connor in charge of our group. We sat up all night in compartments, about eight of us in each, and we were quite comfortable. We were wearing sailor uniforms, regular dress blues. We had only one suit each of dress blues and dungarees; that was it.

We got there about three o'clock on a rainy morning and were met by Lt. Grattan C. Dichman, who arrived from the United States on the *Jupiter* and was sent on ahead to take command of the detachment at Tours. We were loaded into trucks and driven about twelve miles outside of Tours to the *Ecole d'Aviation Militaire de Tours*. When we arrived at Tours, they didn't expect us either. The only place for us to sleep was one barracks that was occupied by a lot of French Senegalese soldiers up from the front. They routed out the Senegalese soldiers. They climbed out of their bunks on one side, and we got in on the other. There was no changing of sheets; we slept on just plain straw with no blankets. It really was a lark. These Senegalese soldiers with the tribal marks on their faces with the Zouave uniform didn't care much about that.

The next day we lined up in formation and the French officials came in from the school. They took our names and lined us up and tried to tell us what they expected of us. They spoke very little English—the assistant chief pilot a little, the instructor none. They grouped us up in eight or ten people in one class to one instructor. Each class would push the plane out in the morning on different parts of this great aviation field; *place d' aviation* it was called. This one instructor would take your name and introduce himself.

We had one leather flying coat, one pair of goggles, one crash helmet, and that was our flight uniform for the whole class—one for all of eight or ten of us. There were also four, five, or six French students going through the class with us. We'd pass the flight gear down. We'd come down from a flight every fifteen or twenty minutes, and then pass it on to the next man who was going on a flight.

 We were flying the French Caudron G-3 with warping wings and a ninety-horsepower Anzani or LeRhone engine. Our instruments consisted of an oil gauge, an altimeter, and a tachometer. We sat in the front seat, and the instructor would take us around and give us dual instruction. If your nose was too high, he'd push on your helmet. If your nose was too low, he'd pull on your helmet. If your right wing was up, he'd tap you on the right shoulder. If your left wing was up, he'd tap you on the left shoulder. In the meantime, you were handling the stick. That was the extent of your instruction.

The instructor also had a length of cardboard with a line drawn down the center. One half was in French, and the other half was in English.

When you came back from your flight with the instructor, whatever you did wrong he would show you in French and then you'd look in English to see what he meant—warped too much, climbed too much, too slow, too fast, left wing down, land too high. That went on until he thought we were good enough to solo and fly alone.

On the first solo flight, you'd rev the engine up. It was a dual throttle, air and gas. The ship had longerons and a nacelle, in which you sat. The mechanic would adjust the throttle wide open for you, while the rest of the students hung on to the wings to keep the airplane from moving forward. Then when the mechanic got out, the instructor would say, "Everybody let go," and you shot off into the air. You were supposed to go up to about five hundred feet, cut the switch, and make a landing at the end of the field. That was your first flight alone. You'd soloed, you were an aviator.

During landing, you just rolled. You were supposed to gauge your distance from the fence in front of you and land before you hit the fence. That was the idea. There was no such thing as brakes; you just floated along and gauged your distance. A lot of the students cracked up. They'd misjudge their landing, the wheels would go off, and they'd go over on their nose. The French instructor would say, "Students, students, what am I going to do with you? Another landing like an omelet!" In other words, a landing all mixed up.

After you soloed, then they'd let you go alone on a turn of the airfield. After you made the turn of the airfield, then you put in time. Then you were checked by your French instructor, followed by a tour of three fields, from Tours to Bois, from Bois to Vendome, and then back. It was a cross-country flight, about eighty or ninety miles total. If you completed all that satisfactory, then you went to what they called a landing class. The landing class consisted of going up to about 8,000 feet, cutting the engine, making a complete circle in a glide, and landing to the right of a "T."

With the landing class, we went about five miles from the main airdrome in a truck every morning at daylight. They would let us fly at daylight because the air was not rough until ten o'clock, when the sun came out and the air got turbulent. We'd knock off until about three in the afternoon, and then we'd continue flying until about nine or ten at night, while it was still light and the air was smooth again. In our landing class, our instructor, named Benaush, would come over with a piece of canvass cut like a "T," about three feet in diameter. He rolled it out on the ground simply as an indication of the direction of the wind. The head of the "T" was into the wind and you landed to the right of the "T."

There was one little meadow that we called the "salad patch," with an orchard on one side and a stone wall on three sides. When you got to your altitude, this looked very, very small. A mechanic on the ground would lay the canvass "T" out into the wind. Benaush was a very temperamental and excitable sort of a Frenchman. He had quite a record on the front, with seventeen or eighteen Germans to his credit. They sent him back to this school as a monitor, which they called the instructor, to sort of relieve him of the tension. He was in pretty bad shape.

Before you'd take off, he'd have to see that this "T" was perfect. He would take a handful of clover and throw it in the air to see the direction of the wind. He had a sort of a cane, the top of which spread out into a seat [for the instructor]. That took about fifteen minutes to make sure the wind was right, and that the "T" was in the direction of the wind. When he was sure of this, you could take off.

The student, at the correct altitude, would cut the switch at the right of the "T." Then he would go into a glide and make a left 180-degree turn and come around and land to the right of the "T." Some of the students would cut the switch and stretch their glide and get in trouble. Benaush would stand there and throw his hat on the ground. In the meantime, he'd talk to this guy who was 3,000 or 4,000 feet in the air. He'd get very excited, throw his cane, jump up and down, and scream at the man in the air. We would turn our faces and laugh because he was very, very funny.

After the first day at the landing class, at the canteen back at the school at Tours, I was speaking to a Frenchman who had spent a lot of time in England and spoke good English. I said, "This Benaush is a very excitable individual. He gets all excited, yelling at a man 6,000 or 8,000 feet in the air, and you can't hear him."

He said, "Benaush is an excellent pilot. He knows everything a student should do. When a student cuts the motor and goes into his glide for his landing and he's in trouble, Benaush throws away his hat. The next time, if the student is getting worse, Benaush will throw away his cane. If at last he throws away his pipe, the man is dead!"

So I told him, "I can understand that."

Mingling with the French instructors and the French student pilots, we got to know their idiosyncrasies and ways. Everybody carried a talisman of some kind. One of their superstitions was that you had to wear your sweetheart's, your fiancée's, or your wife's stocking under your helmet. You put that stocking, which had to be taken off the left leg, on your head and roll it around with the foot under your chin and up the side. Then you put your helmet on top of that. It was like a scarf, but concealed by your helmet. It was on your head and that was a memento of good luck. You couldn't perish with that on.

Then they had another little talisman—two little dolls that your fiancée or someone would knit for you. They were made of different colored yarn sewed together, about two inches high and about two inches wide. You put that on the outboard strut of your plane. The dolls were named Nannette and Rattatin. They were supposed to be the good luck charms of the aviators. Legend also had it that when the Germans started bombing Paris with the big Bertha guns, Nannette and Rattatin went down in the cellar to get away from the big guns and went to sleep on the coal. The next morning Radadu was born, and became a third talisman, made of black yarn. So we had Nannette, Rattatin, and Radadu, all for good luck.

On the fourth of July 1917 they gave us liberty, so we all proceeded to Tours to find some ladies' stockings. We had to be in the barracks by midnight, and a lot of us didn't get in until four in the morning. Lieutenant Chevalier made a bed check and found us all up. The people that were missing were all given a summary court martial the next day. So we lined up and took our picture with our stockings and were proud of it. We were restricted to the base for awhile, but it was worth it.

About two-thirds of that first class of fifty qualified to solo. Flying under those conditions with French instructors that didn't speak English, no ground school, no theory of flight, we soloed in less than four hours of dual instruction, which shows the ingenuity of the American youth. I soloed at three hours and twenty-eight minutes dual instruction, and the planes were harder to fly because they had no instruments to speak of. It was all by the seat of your pants; you just had to feel your way around. Yet we were very much thrilled. I look back now and think of things that I did in aviation, and it scares me to death.

We were at Tours about two months for our preliminary land plane training. The first ten or fifteen of us that completed the course there were sent on to the next phase while the rest of them were getting instruction. We were sent to *Ecole d'Aviation Maritime de Hourtin* on a small lake outside of Bordeaux, which was the preliminary seaplane school for the French navy. When we arrived there, there was no place for us, so we got hold of some tents, which we put together in the pine woods alongside the lake. Our mess hall consisted of planks put on gasoline drums out in the woods. The galley was an all French galley with French cabbage soup and red wine, which was alright with us, and potato bread.

Our instructors were noncommissioned French navy men, comparable to our chief petty officers. We were taken out and taught to maneuver the FBA [Franco-British Aviation] seaplane, a small two-seater seaplane with a pusher engine. After about an hour of dual instruction in that, we soloed those French seaplanes. We were there a little over a month because the weather was bad, then as the other class came in, we shoved off and went to *Ecole d'Aviation de St. Raphael* on the Mediterranean Sea, the Pensacola of the French navy, located between Toulon and Cannes.

There we had our aerial gunnery, navigation, and bombing instruction in all types of French seaplanes—Donnet-Denhauts, Telliers, FBAs, and Salmsons. Our instruction there was bombing and machine-gun runs, using the old Lewis light machine gun with only one barrel. They sent a lot of the mechanics' group, whom they didn't have any work for, to the aerial gunnery school of the French army at Caseaux, where they became observers and bombardier gunners. They flew with the French, the British, the marines, all of the allies.

We took an altitude test there, where we had to stay up at a high altitude for an hour. There was a small barograph box that they hung around your neck on rubber bands to record your altitude and duration of flight so you couldn't cheat them on it. Then you came down, and that completed your course. The first day that I went up to take my altitude test the clouds came down the coast of Toulon, and I couldn't make my altitude so I had to come down without completing my test. The weather was bad for about three days. On the fourth day I reached my altitude alright. It took me thirty-five or forty minutes to get up there. Then the clouds started coming down the coast again, and I thought to myself, "I'm not going to do this all over again."

I'd fly to the edge of the clouds that were pushing down the coast, then I'd go away from them, make a circle, and come back to the edge of the clouds. In the meantime, the clouds kept moving down the coast. I was still going south, waiting for my time, watching my clock on the dashboard.

Then I saw Monte Carlo in the distance, so I stayed over fifteen minutes to compensate for the variation in the barograph. I didn't want to try it again, so I stayed up an hour and fifteen minutes.

I was right over Monte Carlo, which is way down the coast from San Rafael. So I cut the engine and started my long glide to come down about five miles off the port of Monte Carlo, not knowing my motor cooled on the way down. It took me so long in a very light glide that, when I put my throttle back on, the engine was so cold she stopped on me. The ground swell was in one direction, the wind swell in another direction, and here I am out in the open sea in the Mediterranean five miles off the city of Monte Carlo. I was undecided what to do, and meantime, I was losing altitude.

I finally plopped on top of a ground swell, made about two bounces, and came down pretty heavy. I opened the back of the compartment to see whether the bottom was still on my airplane, which was a Donnet-Denhaut. I was alright, and I floated there awhile. The first thing I knew, from the beach, which was right on the Italian border, a gunboat came out and made a circle around me a couple of times and saw the colors. I started yelling, "American, American." They put a small boat over with two French sailors, who came up to me and sort of looked me over. One of the sailors said, "You're an American; hey, Johnny, I was in New York." Then he yelled to the skipper, "American, American," so they took me in tow into the harbor at Monte Carlo.

I moored the plane inside the harbor, and they brought the secretary to the director of the casino at Monte Carlo down. He spoke English, naturally. I told him I wanted to get in touch with St. Raphael and let them know where I was. He said, "We'll arrange that, sir, we'll arrange that." That was the first "sir" I ever got since I was still a quartermaster.

He said, "We'll have a carriage here for you in a minute, Mr. Cline."

I said, "What did the people in San Raphael say?"

He said, "They told you to stay here tonight. They will send somebody over tomorrow." I had told them I had engine trouble. I didn't know what it was. It had stopped, that was all I knew.

Then a beautiful pair of horses came down with a carriage. The director of the casino got in beside me and said, "The *Hotel des Anglais*." I didn't know what that meant. Right across from the casino was the greatest hotel in Monte Carlo, the *Hotel des Anglais.*

I said, "Look, I can't stay here. I don't have any money on me, I don't have ten francs."

He said, "Money is nothing, sir, money is nothing, sir."

It was a convalescent quarters they had taken over for all the allied officers who were under rehabilitation and what not. They gave me a beautiful room, then they ushered me into the main dining room and set me a place. I had two generals, three French army captains, and several other allied officers there who were convalescing, and some spoke a little English. It had gotten so warm that I had taken off my fur-lined flying clothes, and I had torn dungarees and an old army khaki shirt on under my flying suit, so I was quite a curiosity there—a quartermaster in dungarees and an old khaki shirt.

I didn't know what to do; I was flabbergasted, with all this rank around me. They were asking me questions, some I could answer and some I couldn't. We were all instructed not to say anything to anybody, who we were or what it was all about. The director of the casino wanted to know if I wanted to go over and see the casino. Monte Carlo was neutral, supposedly. I said, "No, I don't want to go to the casino. I just want to go to bed. Wake me at daybreak in the morning," and I turned in.

In the morning about daybreak the light came into the room from the shutters, and this nun came in with a little receptacle containing oil with a wick burning in it. She said, in a very broad Irish brogue, "What time do you want to get up?"

I said, "What time is it now, sister?"

She said, "It's five after four."

I said, "That will be fine. I'll get up now."

She said, "I saw you come in last night, and I said to myself, 'He's not an Englishman, he surely must be an American.'"

They sent a mechanic down from St. Raphael. He explained to me the best he could that it was just that the engine was cold. It started right up, then we flew back to St. Raphael. After completing our course there, on 17 October 1917, we got our certificate and our French *brevet*, with quite a bit of ceremony. The captain congratulated us, signed our certificates, and gave us our French navy wings. Mine was no. 346, indicating that I was the 346th aviator in the French navy. There weren't too many. Naval aviation at that time was not too much. Everything was concentrated on the land planes at the front. I never got my U.S. naval aviators wings (no. 1832) until I came back home over two years later.

I think in that first class there were about ten or twelve of us. Were we proud! We were something! We were aviators, heroes of the day! It called for a big party, which we had—champagne and nothing else but.

Then we were assigned to a place outside of Bordeaux called Moutchic, which was to be the training area for the navy fliers who were coming over for indoctrination and training in French boats. They had already finished at Pensacola and gone through MIT. Then they were assigned to the different air stations that the French were to build, or we were to take over on the French coast for submarine patrol.

When we got to Moutchic, it was about the end of November and it was very cold. There was nothing there. There were no hangars. We had these tents again and no mess hall. They sent us crates of FBA seaplanes but we had no hangars to put them in. We took the airplanes out and started assembling them, and made a mess hall out of the crates. We drew some picks, shovels, and wheelbarrows from the French and started digging sand and building our hangars.

After we assembled three FBAs, we started flying them until the air got rough, then we went back to building hangars. Of course we griped, everybody griped. The chow was bad, there was no liberty, no this, no that. It was cold, rainy, and murky along the coast of Brittany. We did that for about three weeks, until they finally sent some work parties over who took over the hangar construction.

In the meantime, some of the Yale unit came over. When they arrived, we instructed them in French boats and then turned them loose. Ens. Robert A. Lovett came over as the commanding officer in October 1917; he later became secretary of war for air from 1942 to 1945, and still later secretary of defense in 1951. Ens. Artemus L. Gates was commander of our first groups that went down to St. Raphael. He became under secretary of the navy in 1945. He was a hell of a nice guy.

Finally, they decided then they wanted to get us on active duty. They wanted to get us flying. They sent us to Le Croisic, on the northern coast of Brittany, a naval air station still operated by the French then. We went up in a group of twelve to Le Croisic, still serving as quartermasters. We slept in a hospital that was only partially constructed; it was all open. In the meantime, we slept in hammocks on the concrete floor in that place.

Lt. William M. Corry (naval aviator no. 23) took command of the station for the United States. Everybody stood at attention the day the

French flag came down and the American flag went up. So we were all ready for war. They had some Tellier seaplanes, which we immediately flew on submarine patrol. They were bringing convoys down from Quiberon Bay into St. Nazaire. When the convoys were coming over from the United States, they all rendezvoused at Quiberon for the stretch down through what they called "the slot" on the Bay of Biscay on the northern coast of Brittany. We patrolled for submarines in that sector. The submarines would go in there at night and lay mines. When the convoy was about to come down the coast, the sweepers would go out and sweep the channel. The convoy would take the inner channel while they swept the outer channel, and vice versa.

In the meantime, we would patrol all the time. Our sector was about 250 miles from Quiberon to St. Nazaire. We would go as far as Belle Ile, about forty miles off the coast of Brittany. We were all circling the convoy all the time. We'd fly out from the convoy and come back, go astern of it, go forward again, on the right side, on the left side. We always flew in two's, two planes on patrol at one time, sixty or seventy miles off the coast until we closed in on St. Nazaire. We had the capacity for four hours patrol, and we did this in all kinds of weather, if we could see! But, there was no night flying at all in those days.

We always had carrier pigeons with us. There was a Frenchman who controlled the pigeon loft with the carrier pigeons. I got to know him pretty well. I used to give him cigarettes and gum. One of the older pigeons was named Nancy, and every time I'd go out on patrol, he'd give me Nancy because she would always come home. We had two pigeons in a little basket. Any time we had a forced landing, or sighted a submarine, we'd write a note and put it in the little vial on the pigeon's leg, giving them our location, what our trouble was, how we were—and then Nancy would beat it for Le Croisic. When she went to the pigeon loft, she went through a little slot that rang a bell, then the pigeon master would go up and get the note.

The pigeons would never fly at night or in a fog. One time I had a forced landing off of Belle Ile, and I got Nancy out and told her to fly home. She flew around the plane and perched on the outboard wing. I started throwing tools at her and everything else, but Nancy wouldn't go. She stayed there all night. As dawn broke, she beat it for Le Croisic. We picked up our French patrol boat halfway in, and we made our way in together.

* * *

I was in Le Croisic about fifteen months, doing patrol duty there. I felt at this time that I was really in the war. In the meantime, though, we were still answering to quartermaster, even though we had finished four flight schools and been on patrol for ten or twelve months. One day the bugle started blowing, bells started ringing, and three staff touring cars drove up to the island across a small bridge from the mainland. Who should get out of the car but Adm. William Benson and Adm. William S. Sims, commander of U.S. Naval Forces in Europe, with their staff on an inspection tour.

Everybody got in dress blues as fast as we could and lined up for inspection. We had been wearing dungarees all the time. Admiral Sims and Admiral Benson came down the line. Mac Weddell, Paul Gillespie, and I were standing together with our French wings on.

Admiral Sims looked at Mac Weddell and said, "What's that you're wearing, young man?"

Mac said, "That's the French *brevet,* sir."

"French *brevet?* What does it signify?"

"That's a designation by the French government."

"Oh, why, what for?"

He said, "For flying."

He said, "Are you an aviator?"

"Yes sir.

"Do you fly airplanes here at Le Croisic?"

"Yes sir."

"Go out on patrol with the convoys?"

"Yes sir."

"How long have you been doing that?"

"About twelve months, sir."

All his staff was behind the two admirals, and Corry, of course.

So he said, "Lieutenant Corry, why aren't these men commissioned?"

Corry said, "Admiral, I have so recommended three or four different times to the Navy Department. I have yet to hear from it."

He called his aide and took our names. In two weeks, we got orders to take examinations to be commissioned for ensign. The exam didn't mean anything though. We got in the pilots' room and answered a few questions. Corry convened a board, and they gave us flight questions that we all knew. We had an oral and a written examination, and he sent in his recommendations to Paris, which was the aviation headquarters. And we had our commissions.

The First Aeronautic Detachment was all split up around the different air stations. Both observers and pilots went with the Northern Bombing Group, some went with the British and all the different allies. Three of our detachments were stationed up at Dunkerque, up off the English Channel. That station was taken over from the French by the Americans. It had been bombed from the sea and also quite often from the German air station at Ostend. So the French had given up the idea of trying to patrol out of there. Submarines were all coming in to the pens at Zeebrugge and Ostend from the channel. So they decided to turn that over to the Americans.

Kenneth Whiting knew the situation up there. He refused to send the pilots up there or take over the station unless they had fighter cover. We had no fighter planes. The class that had just finished about that time, the third or fourth class at St. Raphael, consisting of about twelve or fourteen people, was sent over to England to take up fighter plane training and acrobatics with the Royal Air Force. Then they went to Ayr, Scotland, with the Royal Air Force, and got their combat training, and following that, they were stationed at Dunkerque. As soon as Whiting was assured that we were going to have fighter cover for our seaplanes out of Dunkerque, we took the station over.

One day on patrol Julian F. "Pee Wee" Carson, Pete Parker, and Franklin Young, all First Aeronautic Detachment members, were on patrol from Dunkerque in the English Channel off Zeebrugge. They caught a German submarine on the surface going into Zeebrugge. Carson attacked with his bombs, but he was driven off by fire from the deck guns of the submarine. Pete Parker and Franklin Young were covering him in fighters. They attacked the submarine and killed all the deck crew. In the meantime, Carson was laying off and as soon as they wiped out the guns on the submarine, he returned and dropped his bombs and sank the submarine. He was credited with a sinking by the French government and awarded a *Croix de Guerre.*

On 4 March 1918, at Le Croisic, my observer, Fred Lovejoy, and I were on alert duty. We always had an alert or stand-by duty at the station ready to go out. We had a message from a tanker that was being shelled by a German submarine on the surface within our sector. So everybody rushed up to get the alert over the side. We had to lift the planes off on a crane and put them over the seawall. There were two Mark IV bombs, each one next to the fuselage under each wing. In the hustle and bustle and excitement of getting the plane over the side in a hurry, whoever hung the bombs on neglected to hang them on properly.

After they put the plane in the water, the tide was out, so I had to go outside of the seawall to take off. I'd just warmed up my engine, headed into the wind, got on the step, and was about to pull it off when the bombs dropped off into nine feet of water! By the time it took to drop the nine feet and to detonate, one bomb set off the other bomb and blew the plane in half! There was a lighthouse on the end of the seawall, about eighty-five feet high. They told me later that my whole tail section and half the airplane went up about fifteen feet beyond the top of the lighthouse! I cut the switches, and the plane started sinking. Lovejoy, my observer, was in the front cockpit. I said to him, "Get off your clothes Lovey, we've got to swim." I let the pigeons go, and we took off our clothes. By the time we got our clothes off, which was very, very quickly, the forward half of the plane settled on the bottom. Lovejoy climbed on the nose and didn't even get his feet wet, and I just got wet to my knees. The crash boat came out and picked us up. That was a close one!

Lieutenant Corry was transferred to Brest, to take command of the new air station up there. He had always been an inspiration to me, and I think he was one of the greatest fellows I ever met. I always wanted to serve under him again. I was sorry to see him go, so I put in for a transfer to Brest, and it was granted. So I went up with Corry, which was fine, and I was there until the armistice was signed.

After that I came home and reported to Bay Shore, Long Island, and from there I went to Great Lakes as a flight instructor until about March 1919. Then I was transferred out to North Island with Air Squadrons Pacific Fleet with some famous names in naval aviation—Marc Mitscher, Henry Mustin, and Jack Towers.

I had a bad crash out there in December 1921. It killed a chief AP named McLain. I had him up on a test flight in a Jenny. We were coming in for a landing; Mac was flying the ship. There were two courses, a two-ball course and a one-ball course. On the two-ball course, you were not to land toward the hangars, you had to land away from the hangars. Just for about twenty minutes, a terrific Santa Ana wind came up. I looked at the administration building, and the flags were sticking straight out.

Mac was flying the ship, and we were coming down for a landing with the wind because we couldn't land toward the wind. I yelled to Mac, "Go around again, Mac, you can't make it." So he gave it the gun to go around again to make a landing. When he got in his turn, he lost flying speed. I think what he did was he misjudged his flying speed for his ground speed; we had the wind on our tail, and he was going across the ground so fast, he thought he had adequate flying speed. But he didn't have sufficient power on, and he got into a half spin and nosed into the ground.

He smashed the plane all to pieces. He was in the front seat, and the engine came back in his lap and broke every bone in his body. He was killed instantly. They pulled me out and got me over to the hospital. I was there about eight months with internal injuries, arm injuries, and so forth. Then I came back to active duty, but I decided I wanted to go to San Francisco and get married, which I did, and I resigned from the navy in 1922.

In the First Aeronautic Detachment a lot of people were killed. They lost about twenty-two, I think, during the war. We lost a lot of observers— mechanics who were sent down to do maintenance work but became observers and machine gunners flying all the time with the British, with the French, with everybody.

After the war was over, the original detachment broke up, and served all over Europe or returned to the United States. In the First Aeronautic Detachment a lot of people were killed. They lost about twenty-two, I think, during the war. I remember names such as T. W. Barrett, G. E. Manley, T. M. Weddell, E. C. Kenep, H. G. Velie, F. W. Hough, J. Ganster, M. J. Chapin, D. Marshborn, M. E. O'Gorman, J. L. Goggins, and C. A. Nelson. They never came back. We lost a lot of observers, mechanics who were sent down to do maintenance work, but became observers and machine gunners flying all the time with the British, with the French, with everybody.

A lot of them stayed in the navy after the war and made life careers out of it. Several of them became captains and commanders. A lot of them went into commercial aviation. Harold A. Elliott became vice president and general manager of Eastern Airlines. Paul Gillespie was managing director of the Roosevelt Flying School on Long Island for many years.

Later, he was with the Civil Aeronautics Administration and was a captain in the navy in command of NAS New Orleans during World War II. Erlon H. "Pete" Parker was division operations manager for Eastern Airlines. Franklin Young was a captain pilot for TWA for many years until he retired. Duke Jernigan was head of the aviation department for Texaco, Inc. and was the first man to tow a glider across the United States. Eddie Nirmaier flew for a radio corporation for years. Charlie Boyland had a flight school in New Orleans and was killed in a crash. A lot of them stayed on in aviation because they loved it. I have no idea what happened to many of the others that I haven't mentioned. If any of them are still around and kicking, I hope they keep her nose down and fly straight. They were a great gang.

We were the lost battalion. Nobody knew where we were. They didn't know about us. Even today, naval aviation as big and as expansive as it is, nobody ever heard of the First Aeronautic Detachment. They forgot all about us. We were there, and we were doing our job. If Admiral Sims hadn't come along and found us, I don't think we'd have gotten anywhere.

2

WE WERE THE BEGINNING

Lt. Aldred K. Warren

ALDRED K. WARREN *was born in Staten Island, New York, in 1897. He attended high school in New York City, but in 1916 he passed up college to join the 101st Massachusetts Field Artillery—the famous Knickerbocker Greys— and went out on the Mexican border. After his discharge from the National Guard, he enlisted in the Massachusetts Naval Militia, and in the summer of 1917 he reported to the Massachusetts Institute of Technology (MIT) for avia-tion ground training. He began flight training at Pensacola on 24 September 1917 and qualified as a naval aviator two months later, after twenty practice flights. Warren reported to the Naval Air Station, San Diego, California, in January 1918 for duty as a primary flight instructor. He concluded his naval service as an advanced flight instructor at Pensacola, leaving the service as a lieutenant (jg) in 1919.*

I became interested in aviation in the first place because I was young and foolish. I was intrigued with the thought of flying, and I wanted to do that. About February 1917, when I was twenty years old, I was looking around to see where I could get some aviation training. I had only had a high school education. I thought aviation would be glamorous; I thought it would be marvelous to fly through the air with the greatest of ease, enjoy the freedom, and everything that might go with that concept. I didn't have any idea that there would be any danger involved.

My father had met Franklin Delano Roosevelt on a Caribbean cruise, about 1910, and they seemed to enjoy each other's company, pacing the deck together and talking about one thing and another. Because of that, my father took it upon himself, when he saw that I was really anxious to get in aviation, to write to a man he had known and ask if there were anything he could do to get me out of the Field Artillery. This man said no, but he sent the request through channels, and it was signed by Franklin Delano Roosevelt.

So they accepted me in the Massachusetts Naval Militia, and I signed up after I got my discharge from the National Guard. About the middle of July I got orders to report on 23 July 1917 to the navy yard in Boston, and there we were given sea bags, seaman's whites, a little underwear, and then sent over to the Massachusetts Institute of Technology, where there was to be a ground school. It so happened that those of us at that time were in the first flight, which was flight A. Lt. (jg) Edward H. McKitterick, who was in charge of the ground school, told me many years later that he didn't know what he was supposed to do. It had never been done before, and he didn't know what kind of instruction and courses that we would have; but he got quite a bit of help from the staff at MIT in laying out the curriculum.

I think maybe the only reason I got through that was that my name started with "W." McKitterick told me, from his experience at the Naval Academy, that they generally wash out about one-third of the class. So as he was going down the list and washing out one-third, "W" was down at the end, and he had already accomplished his budget so I survived.

So after going through all that, we had to be able to read and send fifteen words a minute in Morse code. We all had these little gadgets that would da-da-da, and we were supposed to send a message. We were all at about the same speed, and we finally got to the fifteen words a minute. We didn't have any particular trouble with that. Of course, we had a certain amount of navigation, very limited; we took a few engines apart and put them back together again; we studied the theory of flight, things of that nature.

After two months of training there, I got my orders to Pensacola, Florida, and arrived there sometime around the middle of September. Since we had gotten our ground school work completed, we could concentrate on trying to learn to fly. The most disappointing flight I ever had was my first flight down at Pensacola. The instructor took me up in a Curtiss N-9 to get the feel of the air and the plane, and after getting off the water, we just seemed to stand still. There was a lot of wind blowing in my face and a lot of noise and vibration, with no sensation of speed or anything of the sort—no glamour whatsoever. We just sat there and in fact did nothing while we could see the water passing by.

We had dual instruction, and I think after about six hours of dual instruction, we could solo. That was kind of fun, being up there all by yourself. We had orders to fly a certain prescribed course around Pensacola Bay so that the rescue sea sled could follow us around the course. The sea sled was rectangular in shape, and it was called the "solo coffin." You could look down and see this thing following you all around the bay.

To qualify on your solo you just had to fly around two or three times and make a landing up in front of the beach where the instructors could see you. If you made a satisfactory landing they would wave you on to do it again. After about three landings, they waved me in, said I was all right, that I had soloed, that I would be able to continue to solo for another twenty hours. At the end of twenty hours you could take the plane up for a qualification flight to qualify as a naval aviator.

To do that, we had to go up to 6,000 feet, spiral down to 3,000 feet, and then cut the switch and land with a dead engine, or a dead stick as we called it, within 50 feet of a boat that had a big red flag on it out in Pensacola Bay. If you could do that with a dead stick, then you were a naval aviator—after twenty hours of solo.

My instructor in Pensacola was "Shorty" Enos, George Enos—a small man, weighed maybe 110 or 115 pounds. He had more time in the air than the other instructors because he was so light that he could get the plane up in the air when the others who weighed more couldn't do it. Being small was an advantage because you couldn't get those Curtiss N-9s off the water unless there was a breeze, and the strength of the breeze determined how fast you could get the plane off the water.

We tried everything, including rocking the plane back and forth to get it up on the step of the pontoon; then there was less friction on the pontoon and sometimes we could get going. We would also circle on the water and develop a little wake, and then come around and hit that wake and use waves to help us out. If that didn't work, we would take two planes, one behind the other, give the gun to both planes, and the following plane got enough breeze from the wash of the propeller of the first plane to be able to get up on the step and take off. Then we would try to go around the plane still on the water and get in front of him and give him prop wash in hopes that he could get up, but you were going so much faster than he was it was just lucky if he was able to get off. He'd have to wait until someone else came out and gave him a little breeze.

After we had qualified as naval aviators, there had been strict orders that there would be no stunting in planes in any way whatsoever. We all wanted to do it, but nobody had, so Pensacola finally set aside one N-9 airplane for stunting duty. It had an air speed meter on it, which the other planes didn't have. Then we went to our instructors to see what was necessary to do a loop; of course, they had never looped themselves! The theory was that you had to nose over in a little dive in order to get up enough speed to carry it up over the top—and trust that it held together.

Eventually, I got that plane one day. I had previously gone down the bay and pulled a few whip stalls to get the feel of the plane. So on that day I was going out to loop, I took the plane way down the bay where nobody could see me and pulled a few whip stalls to try to get my courage up. Our instructions were to come over in front of the station for our loops, so that if anything happened they could get to us quicker.

Eventually I was up to about 5,300 feet; I nosed the ship over and thought I had enough flying speed. I could see the needle on the air-speed meter was up to 100 miles an hour and banging up against the pin, so I didn't know how fast I really was going. I pulled back easily—not too quickly—to get the proper curve. All we had was this little safety belt that went across our waist, just as automobiles use today. I could envision the possibility that when you were upside down you might slip through that belt. There were longerons on the sides of the cockpit, and I locked my elbows underneath the longerons and then pulled the control back so I was able to hold myself into the seat when upside down. But I found I hadn't had enough speed and the plane turned a little bit up there in the air and finally fell off on the nose because of the weight of the engine. We knew the plane would eventually go into a dive and from that you could pull it out and fly it.

Then I went upstairs again to get a little more altitude and tried it again. The second one worked out a little bit better. Then I thought that instead of wasting time climbing up and then making a dive to make a loop, why not use the dive at the end of a loop to start another loop? So that worked, and I pulled three loops in succession. I don't know just what the records were, but some of the other fellows told me that as far as they knew I was the first one to ever make three loops in succession.

That was the beginning of my interest in stunt flying, as far as I was concerned. All the other fellows, as they were coming along, some would go for the stunts, and some wouldn't. That was up to them and their choice. This was a case of whetting my appetite, and I wanted to do more stunt flying. The instructors said if you once got into a spin, you were done, you would never be able to get out. So we didn't know when we went into a loop whether we were going to come out in a spin or whether we were going to come out level or not. But the instructors didn't know what the devil they were talking about, because later I found that you could throw the darned thing into a spin, and you could get it out with no trouble whatsoever.

They were trying to qualify other fellows, so we didn't have too much opportunity to fly after we had our qualification flight. To keep us busy, they'd send us out in a long boat to row around Pensacola Harbor, and we would have duty on the rescue boat, two of us at one time along with the coxswain and one other crew member assigned to the boat. One time a young fellow by the name of Herman Bose was taking his qualification flight, and he tried to hold the plane up—he was landing too short—so consequently he stalled and flopped into the bay and the plane turned over on him.

This other fellow and I hopped into the sea sled and went right out there. That sea sled would travel about 50 miles an hour, so it didn't take us long to get there. We told the coxswain to keep going as we passed the plane, and this other fellow, Francis Allen, and I dove over the side of the speed boat as it was passing through there at about 50 miles an hour. We wanted to save every second we could. We had to dive down and try to reach up underneath the airplane to try to reach the snap on the safety belt and get him out. Bose was wearing some heavy sweaters at the time, which were floating around in the water so that we couldn't find the doggone safety belt. We had no breathing apparatus and could only stay down maybe about a minute, or something like that, at the most. So we had to wait for the old *Mary Ann* to come out and lift up the tail and get him out. Of course, that was too late to save Bose.

In those days, parachutes were only used by some of the balloonists, not heavier-than-air pilots. They were so new, and they hadn't been developed; they had no technique for properly folding the parachute in order to make a seat pack out of it so that you could get into the cockpit of the plane. The cockpits were very, very small. It just wasn't practical at that time. You simply crashed with the machine; the theory was that the best thing to do was to stay with the ship and try to bring it down as best you could because there might be some way that you might be able to control the crash so that it wouldn't be fatal. Maybe you could come down and bring it into a stall just before it hit and drop down. Another thing that we always said we would do if we had no place to land, whatsoever, would be to look around for some trees, as the next best thing, and land in the trees because the branches would break your fall.

The pilots knew enough about the mechanics of the construction of the plane, what all the various control centers were supposed to do, where the control wires were, and also had enough instruction on the engines so we knew what to do in case we got in trouble. One time I had a dead engine out over Pensacola Bay. I was the only man in the plane, and it was a question of how to get the doggone motor started again. I had to take my handkerchief out of my pocket, soak the handkerchief in the gasoline tank, and squeeze the gasoline into a petcock on the sides of the cylinders. There was a hand crank you could work while you were standing on the wing. I got the thing to go that way and came home so I didn't have to wait to be towed in.

I flew both in the Curtiss N-9 and the Curtiss R-6, which was a little bigger twin-pontoon plane. I eventually got a total of about thirty-three hours before I got leave to go home for Christmas 1917, where I was sent to await orders. Finally the orders came for me to report to the naval air station at San Diego, California. This was a disappointment because we were all hoping for duty overseas. However, we had our orders, and we had to go, but in the back of our minds we figured we would go out there for two or three months and then have an opportunity to go overseas.

We got to San Diego about 1 January 1918, and we had one hell of a bawling out from our new commanding officer, E. W. Spencer, Jr., who had his offices in Balboa Park in San Diego. There were two other fellows with me, and the three of us got an awful bawling out because we were so stupid that we didn't properly report. We should have been wearing white gloves and carrying a sword, which none of us had. We were just a bunch of young boys who wanted to try and win the war. I hadn't been to Annapolis, and we didn't have that indoctrination.

There was no established base out there then. The navy had been able to wangle a small strip of beach on the bay side of North Island. There were three Burgess U-2s, and three little wooden hangars that Glenn Curtiss had built about 1911, when he was experimenting with the seaplanes. Only one of the three aircraft could fly because we had to cannibalize the other two planes for parts to keep one going.

Here I was, a twenty-year-old kid with a single stripe on my shoulder, and one of my jobs was to confirm some chief petty officers who had temporary appointments in their rating. These chiefs had maybe fifteen, twenty years of service in the navy, and here I had maybe six months and knew practically nothing at all about it. So I got ahold of the *Bluejacket's Manual* and read questions from it, flipping from page to page. Every single one of these chief petty officers gave the answer verbatim, as it was given in the *Bluejacket's Manual*, so there was nothing I could do except confirm them in their rating.

The petty officers never expressed their opinions of us young officers because we were commissioned officers and they were enlisted men, but I think the general attitude was that they were willing to accept us, primarily because we knew how to fly. I bought an automobile down there, a used car, and one of the mechanics came up and said he would be very happy to go over that car and fix up anything that might need fixing up. I think I bought the car for four hundred dollars; when it came time to sell the car, we took it back to the same dealer, and he gave us four hundred dollars for it, after using it for a number of months. He knew that navy mechanics were keeping the car in shape, and it would be in better shape when he got it back than when he sold it to us.

Our commanding officer, Spencer, would take us over to North Island so we could get our pay hops in. We were paid an extra 50 percent in pay and had to fly each month to qualify. Spencer would take each one of us up for four or five minutes in the one plane that would operate. We would just take off, fly around in a circle, land, and that was it. He did that in

January and February until we began to get a few more flight operations going there on North Island. Then we were able to get our own pay hops in.

Earl Winfield Spencer was quite a strict disciplinarian of the old navy, Annapolis background. He wasn't particularly popular with the other officers at the station. He had a rather difficult personality to understand—that's about the kindest thing I can say about that. His wife, Wallis Warfield, was a delightful girl, one or two years older than some of us and an extremely good hostess. Three or four of us junior officers would have dinner with the Spencers, and Wally would be able to keep the conversation going around the table even though each of us came from a different section of the country and had different interests. I thought it was kind of an art, to be able to do that.

Wally had come from a very good, but at that time, quite an impoverished Baltimore family. We really quite enjoyed seeing her and going to some of the dinner dances on Saturday nights at the Hotel Del Coronado. We would share tables and dance with her and the other girls around the place. There were some fellows there that had considerable social position in New England and New York, and also considerable means, much more so than the rest of us, and you could see that Wally Warfield would give a little bit more attention to those fellows than to the rest of us. This indicated to us that she was trying to do a little social climbing, to better her position. In fact she told the wife of one of the junior officers that she would never have any children because she was afraid it would affect her figure and make her less attractive. As we know from history she never had any children.

Two years later, in April 1920, the British warship HMS *Renown*, which was taking the Prince of Wales on a goodwill trip around the world, stopped in San Diego Harbor. It was the duty of Commander Spencer to act as host for the prince. A friend of mine said that that was the first time that Wallis Warfield met the prince, and the speculation was that there was an understanding reached at that particular time. I think that some of the other moves that she made later were to get in a position where she could see and do more things. After she divorced Spencer, she married an Englishman named Earnest Simpson, who took her over to England, where she had more of an opportunity to see the prince, who, of course, later became King Edward VIII. In December 1936, Edward renounced the throne and married Wallis Warfield Simpson.

* * *

The time came when they needed a commissioned officer over at North Island. They started to get a few mechanics over there on the island, and they had to have a mess and a galley and someone to take care of them. They needed a commissioned officer over there to sign receipts for things coming aboard the island—maybe a bushel of potatoes, a gallon of milk, a few sides of beef or something like that—so I was designated as sort of assistant supply officer and had to go over there from time to time to talk with the cook in the galley. Then we began to get a few more planes in and get set up, and it was about March 1918 when we started fairly regular flight operations there.

The objective of the station was a primary flight school to give the boys their first primary flight instruction and then send them off to Pensacola to polish them up. In the beginning, we didn't have any students to train so we were doing a little flying around on our own. We had no particular operational function at that particular time. We had established what they called flight school, and there was a two-striper, Frank Simpson, a naval militia man from California, who was set up as the head of the flight school. Another fellow, Bert Ames, and myself were the first two flight instructors. There were three other naval aviators there, but they were given certain ground operations—one would be disciplinary officer, another would be the gunnery officer, another would be something else, so they didn't have any active flight duties. About once a month they would come down to the beach and take the plane up for four or five minutes in order to get their pay hop in.

So there were only two of us that were really doing any flying at North Island. Spencer would come down once a month for the pay hops, and Frank Simpson of the flight school didn't do much flying either except for his pay hop. We weren't supervised too much, and we'd go down the bay pretty much out of sight of the tower and pull some things that nobody ever knew anything about. It was at that time I practiced up on barrel rolls and things of that nature. I was getting ready for barnstorming.

It was about April 1918 when we began getting a few students on North Island. We had pretty regular flight operations and eventually received more planes. We got rid of the Burgesses that we were flying at that time and began to get the N-9s. The amount of dual instruction we gave each student depended on the fellow and the feel he had for flying. We were very, very careful. The instructor was never allowed to let the fellow go out for solo. He had to be checked by another instructor, and if the second instructor felt the fellow was flying properly, making his landings properly, then we'd give the boy a chance to try his solo. We didn't use the solo coffin with them at North Island because we kept them within a rather short circle from where we were at the station on the beach watching him. We had him just fly around, make a landing; if it looked all right we'd wave him on for another one and after he had three landings, then we would wave him in.

We did have one fellow, Danny O'Connell, who was quite a character. He went up for his solo flight, and he made his circle but he didn't turn around and make his landing; he just went down the bay. We finally saw him coming back up the bay, and he was a little higher than he was the first time. You wouldn't have time on a regular solo flight to go up more than maybe 300, 400, or 500 feet. Well, he must have been about 2,000 feet when he came back, and we thought he would come in for a landing. No, not a bit of it. He turned around and went down the bay again. We were afraid he was going to run out of gas and land with a dead stick. Eventually he did come down and made his landing and of course, immediately, we waved him in. As I had charge of the division at that time, it was up to me to bawl him out for not following orders and find out why.

He said to me, "Mr. Warren, you know I got up there, and I looked at that throttle and that was the only friend I had left. I didn't dare touch it!"

We had no casualties at San Diego, we were proud to say. We had a few broken landing struts or something like that, but we didn't have any serious accidents. We tried to be very careful that the fellows were competent enough to handle the plane, take it out, make the landing, and came back in safely. Also, every morning before we sent the students out soloing, one of the regular instructors would go up and make an air test to see how rough the air was, and the roughness of the air determined which group of students we let out. Those that had more solo time would go out when the air was rough; we looked for smooth air for the young or inexperienced solo pilots.

I know as far as I was concerned, making an air test fairly early in the morning, about six o'clock, could be a little fun. A couple of times I went up making an air test, and we had a certain amount of cloud cover around

1,500 or 2,000 feet in the air, and I'd try to go up through the clouds. It was one of the most beautiful sights I've ever seen, to be up there above the clouds at sunrise. The colors of the clouds were much more beautiful to watch than a sunset. One time I tried to go up through a cloud at about 1,500 feet. Of course, we had no instruments to guide us; we didn't even have a compass to tell us whether we were going straight or not. People had said that once you get into a cloud you lose all references, you could fall off your wing, or anything could happen. Well, that was not exactly true because you could tell from the seat of your pants whether your plane was in the proper attitude.

So I kept climbing, climbing through this cloud, and I didn't break through, so I decided I had better turn around and come back and come down through the clouds. I made my turn and of course, I didn't know if I was going in the same direction when I entered the cloud as when I returned. I had no idea where I was. But I came down and I watched the altimeter, got down to a 1,000 feet, still clouds, 500 feet, still clouds. I was getting a little concerned. I went down to 400 feet, still clouds, 300 feet, still having a difficult time. Eventually I broke out of the clouds a little under 200 feet and down below me I could see houses and streets and everything else. Being in a seaplane, I needed water to land on, so I had to circle there for a moment or two to get my bearings and try to determine which highway or road was leading down to the water or leading away from it. I finally chose a road that led me down to San Diego Bay, and when I got down there I found that over the bay the clouds were still at 1,500 feet, but over land they were really down low. About six o'clock that morning I woke a few people up who wondered what the devil was going on upstairs!

Our means of communications out there were pigeons. A little later on when we got some Curtiss HS-2L flying boats and went flying out over the Pacific Ocean to give some of our students some aerial navigation, we would take a crate of three homing pigeons along with us. I had the great responsibility of having command of all of the homing pigeons, and I was the so-called "pigeon officer." We would take these three pigeons out in this crate, and if anything happened we would write a message and put it in a cylinder attached to the pigeon's leg and toss the bird over the side and hope he would get back in.

It was a pretty effective system. I only know of one or two birds that did not get back. But we had a very fortunate experience as far as any accidents or emergencies were concerned, so usually there was no particular reason to release the bird. We would bring them back with us, although there was one time when two or three congressmen were going to inspect the naval air station, and we had occasion to use the pigeons. The day before the congressmen were due, Spencer, the commanding officer, called us all in his office, and he said, "Haskell, you have a scarf ring and machine guns ready. Shay, you go to the ammunition dump and have two Mark IV bombs in a carrier all ready to run down to the beach, and Warren, you select an HS-2L that you have confidence in, that you know is going to start and get going. Every fifteen minutes get that engine warmed up and started, because as I escort these representatives around the station, I will tell them that this is a primary flight station, but we are prepared and equipped for action if necessary. We'd like to have them see how quickly we could convert a plane for action. So I'll have the bugler sound the alarm, and the sirens will begin to blow. When the sirens go, Haskell, you bring down the machine gun and the scarf ring. Shay, you bring the bombs. Warren, you get the motor turning over and the boys to assemble all the gear on the plane."

Well, with all this prior preparation, as I recall, I was out on the bay taxiing for a takeoff in something less than two minutes. We also had the pigeons brought down, too. So we flew out over the Pacific Ocean, and I'd be damned if I was going to land with two Mark IV bombs beneath the wings, not trusting the gear holding the bombs. If it should break and the bombs go down, we'd go up. So I dropped one of the bombs out off of Point Loma somewhere, and we saw it splash in the water, and it didn't go off. I thought that was occasion to release one of the birds with a message that we had dropped a bomb, approximate location and so on, and it didn't go off.

So we flew on a little farther and decided to drop the second bomb. Well, that did go off. There again, we released a pigeon reporting that the bomb had been released and had gone off. But we had not tried the machine gun—nothing to practice on. But the Coronados Islands, which belong to Mexico, had a lot of seals and things swimming around the shore and rocks, and we thought that a little target practice on a seal or two might be a little fun. So this fellow Haskell was sitting up in the observer's cockpit, where the machine gun was mounted, and I had to bring it down to about 100- or 150-foot altitude. I put her in a glide, cut back on the throttle, and came down to about 150 feet and leveled off and gave it the gun—but the motor quit!

There we were, flying with the wind, crossway to the swells, no altitude left to turn around or to quarter the wind to land along the top of the swells. We just had to sit there and take it. We hit a wave so hard that the mechanic sitting alongside of me disappeared from sight. I didn't know where the hell he went. I was busy trying to handle those controls to get us down safely. It was something to see—this big wall of water coming up in front of me and headed right like that for it. Eventually we were able to get it down. Well, then we only had one pigeon left, so it was a question of whether we released the pigeon then or whether we would wait a little bit to see whether or not we drifted down onto the Coronados Islands. We decided to wait. Then I looked for the mechanic and here he was down on the bottom of the boat. We had hit so hard that his seat had carried away—went right straight through his seat. I often thought how lucky it was that his seat was carried away and not mine. Then the poor mechanic got seasick. He was no help whatsoever. Haskell and I had to hang our toes over the edges of the gunwale on both sides and crank up this motor to see if we could get it going again, which we eventually did. Wouldn't you know, when we were taking off, there was a fairly high swell running. We finally managed to get the plane into the air, and then we decided maybe we'd better go back. We saw some navigational beacons; Haskell fired a few bursts at this beacon, and with the splash in the water, we could tell how close we came to it.

We got over the bay and there was another beacon, and he fired a burst of three shots. One hit on one side, and the other hit on the far side, so the middle one must have been a hit. As we got closer to the beacon, we saw it was a rowboat with two men fishing. When we saw that, Haskell turned around to me, put his hands to his lips, and shook his head. I shook my head, and we snuck back to the station as quickly as we could and got in, waiting for a phone call to come about these goddamn fools shooting at fishermen out there in the bay, which could have been quite disastrous for us. But we never heard a word. That third shot must have missed them or put a hole in the bottom of the boat!

One morning, we were called out about three o'clock in the morning. There were no quarters for us aboard the station, so we all had to live ashore. This other fellow and I were living at the University Club in San

Diego. Spencer sent a motorcycle sidecar around to route us out with orders to get down to the naval air station right away. But we had to wait for sunrise before we could start any operation. We were advised when we got to North Island what the trouble was. A German submarine had been sighted a little bit off San Diego. It was our job to fly out there and seek out and destroy this submarine. So when daylight came, here we were in the N-9, which was a two-passenger ship—wasn't equipped to carry any bombs, wasn't equipped to carry any machine guns—but the pilot, a commissioned officer, was permitted to strap on a .45 on his waist; the mechanic was not allowed to because he wasn't a commissioned officer!

So we were loaded for bear, with a .45 to destroy this German submarine, if we found it. Eventually it turned out to be a dead whale, not a submarine at all. But we had the experience of seeing how quickly we could get organized and get out there!

While we were there in San Diego, this fellow, Bert Ames, and I were sent up to Santa Barbara, where the Loughead [pronounced Lockheed] brothers, Allen and Malcolm, were building a flying boat that they hoped to sell to the navy. We went up there and took a look at this plane, and it looked as though they were doing a pretty good job—although we didn't particularly like the construction of their hull or their flotation gear. They were building the plane in a garage across the road from Santa Barbara Harbor. They finally flew the boat down to San Diego where we were going to give it further evaluation. We believed at that particular time that the Loughead brothers established a world's record. Here was a two-engine flying boat that *flew all the way* from Santa Barbara down to San Diego, a distance of about 250 miles, with five men aboard, *nonstop*. That nonstop was the most important thing. But we didn't feel that the hull was quite seaworthy. It didn't have the conformations and the shapes that would be safe to land out in the rough water, on swells in the ocean.

In September of that year, Mr. Boeing also brought down a little seaplane that the Boeing Company had built up in Seattle. It was quite a nice little plane, the first plane that Boeing had ever built to show the navy. He had his pilot come along with him, and he also had his factory superintendent, man by the name of Berlin. I remember Berlin particularly because when he was down here, I took him up in one of the N-9s, with a Hispano-Suiza motor, and I took him down the bay and put him through a loop. He never had looped before.

That was a nice little craft that Boeing had, but it had quite a bit of inherent stability built into the plane. I know that I had a little difficulty controlling it one time when I was trying it out because it had more inherent stability than the old N-9, our regular training ship. When we began to hit some bumps and what have you, I was correcting for them when I shouldn't have. With this inherent stability I was fighting the design of the ship. The thing to do was to let the darn thing alone, and it would handle itself. We caught up with that pretty quick. I don't recall Boeing ever getting the contract for the navy with that particular plane.

I left San Diego just about Thanksgiving time in 1918 when the war was over, and we were looking to get out of the service. We knew that Pensacola had some advanced training that they had thought up since we had gone through the year before, and we wanted to have that experience before getting out of the service. So eventually I got back to Pensacola and began to take some of the courses they had—aerial gunnery, bombing, navigation, things of that nature. However, I had a problem in that I had been flight instructor for almost a year, with hundreds of hours in the air, compared to many of the instructors at Pensacola at that time. But the regulations were that a new pilot coming to Pensacola, no matter how much time he had, had to have what they called a safety pilot fly with him when he was on gunnery practice or his bombing runs.

It could have been based on some sad experience they had, but I think they were just trying to be safe. I'm not trying to brag about my flying ability or anything of the sort, but I had two experiences that gave me an idea that those safety pilots were not quite as safe as they might have been. I was flying an HS-2L, where the bomber sat in a little cockpit up in the bow of the boat, and the pilot and the safety pilot sat side by side in an aft cockpit. The safety pilot took the plane up, and then he turned the controls over to me when it was time for me to do bombing runs. The bombing was controlled by the so-called observer up in the forward cockpit, who would direct the airplane toward the target. We would go over the target, and then we'd have to circle around to come back to make another run. Every time we started to make another circle this safety pilot pulled back on the wheel to pull the nose up. I didn't like that too much because the way he was pulling it up we could have been thrown into a spin. I didn't want anything like that happening. So after doing it two or three times, I finally cut the gun, and I told him to keep his goddamn hands off of that wheel when I was flying. He did after that, and we came back all right.

Another time when we were going on a flight, the safety pilot made several runs trying to get the boat off the water without success, so he finally said, "I guess we had better go in and get another boat. This engine doesn't have enough power to get us out."

I said, "Let's try it once more." So we did. He gave her the gun, and I put my hands on the wheel just so he could not pull back on the wheel. He was trying to get the plane off the water before it had flying speed. As soon as he got flying speed, I began to ease up on the control, and we took off and had a successful flight.

In this period of time, they had quite a serious crash, and four or five fellows were killed. I don't know whether they had a safety pilot with them or not, but my guess was they had a safety pilot that wasn't safe. So I talked to a fellow on the beach there, Hamilton Gardner, and he said, "Well you'd better report this to the commanding officer of the flight school. Write him a letter." I said, "Oh no. Not me. I'm trying to get out of this service, not being hooked to stay for any length of time." So I kind of talked him into making my report to the commanding officer of the flight school.

Many years later I ran across this guy and talked about when we had gotten out of the service and so on, and the fellow said he had written that letter and because of his writing the letter, he was given the job of checking out safety pilots, which had kept him in the service several months more. That was just what I was afraid of if I had done it myself. But I was glad that he did that because you never know how many boys he might have saved.

By the time the war was over, the thrill and the glamour of the whole thing was no longer quite as gripping as it had been because we had had our experiences in flying. I said to myself that with the amount of flying I had, I would never spend any money to go up in a plane, or hire one somewhere, because I thought I knew all about it. And the war was over. We had gone into the service to try to help win a war, and it was over and people were getting out of the service and getting established in business and going on with their lives. Another thing was my girlfriend and I were kind of thinking of getting married as soon as we could.

I never did go back and finish my education. I was foolish in that regard and often wished I had. But there I was, a naval aviator. Finally I had gotten my half stripe, my lieutenant (jg), and I had a grand total of 423 flight hours. I had held my own with all those other boys who were college graduates and everything else, and I mistakenly thought that maybe, intellectually, I was as good, if not better, than they. If I were to go back to school it would be another three or four years out of my life before getting married and doing other things. So I never did go on. I eventually got a job with the General Electric Company, and had I gone to college I might have ended up as the president of the company instead of the manager of one of the districts!

1. The navy's first aeronautic station was established at Pensacola, Florida, on 20 January 1914, under the command of Lt. Comdr. Henry C. Mustin.

2. Early naval aviators pose in Pensacola, c. 1914–15. Standing (*left to right*) are: R. R. Paunack, E. W. Spencer, Jr., H. T. Bartlett, Edwards, C. K. Bronson, W. M. Corry, J. P. Norfleet, E. O. McDonnell, and H. W. Scofield. Sitting (*left to right*) are: R. C. Saufley, P. N. L. Bellinger, K. Whiting, H. C. Mustin, A. C. Read, E. F. Johnson, A. A. Cunningham, F. T. Evans, and Haas.

3. Powered by a Hispano-Suiza engine, the Burgess N-9H was an improved model of the Curtiss-designed N-9, the standard navy primary and advanced seaplane trainer of World War I. N-9Hs remained in use until 1926.

4. The Curtiss HS-2L was flown by navy pilots on antisubmarine patrols from naval air stations in France during World War I and remained in service as a patrol and training flying boat in the postwar years.

5. Joseph Cline (*center*) poses with other enlisted members of the First Aeronautic Detachment in front of a French Caudron G-3 at the *Ecole d'Aviation Militaire de Tours*, 1917. *(Courtesy National Air and Space Museum)*

6. Student pilots of the First Aeronautic Detachment assemble at Tours, France, with U.S. Navy and French officers, June 1917. *(Courtesy National Air and Space Museum)*

7. Joseph Cline (*standing, far left*), with other enlisted pilots and observers of the First Aeronautic Detachment, flew patrol missions in French-built Tellier flying boats at Le Croisic Air Station, beginning in November 1917. *(Courtesy National Air and Space Museum)*

8. The U.S. Navy–operated FBA (Franco-British Aviation) flying boats were stationed at NAS Moutchic, a training base at the mouth of the Loire River. *(Courtesy National Air and Space Museum)*

9. The Navy/Curtiss NC-4 flying boat, under the command of Lt. Comdr. A. C. Read, landed at Lisbon, Portugal, on 27 May 1919, having completed the first crossing of the Atlantic Ocean by air. *(Courtesy National Air and Space Museum)*

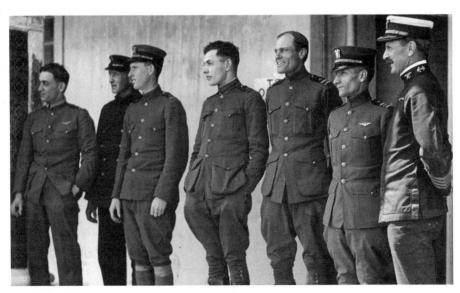

10. The six members of the NC-4 crew stand with Capt. R. H. Jackson *(far right)*. They were *(left to right)*: Lt. E. F. Stone, USCG, CMM E. C. Rhoads, Lt. (jg) Walter Hinton, Ens. H. C. Rodd, Lt. J. L. Breese, and Lt. Comdr. A. C. Read.

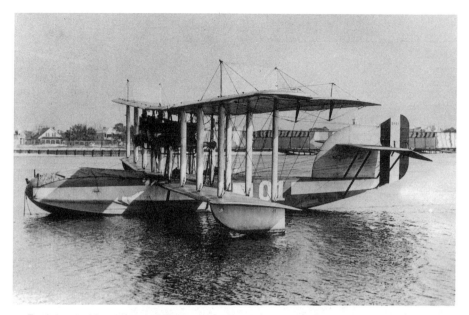

11. Built by the Naval Aircraft Factory, this F-5L was used for training purposes at NAS Pensacola, Florida, after World War I. The wooden-hulled F-5L remained the standard patrol boat for the navy until the late 1920s.

PART TWO

THE ROARING TWENTIES

THROUGHOUT THE DECADE known as the "Roaring Twenties," long-distance flights dramatized in spectacular fashion just how far we had come, and where we were heading in our ability to span the continent and the oceans of the world. The impetus came in 1919, when Rear Adm. David W. Taylor, chief of the Bureau of Construction and Repair, ordered Comdrs. Jerome C. Hunsaker, George C. Westervelt, and Holden C. Richardson to team with Glenn H. Curtiss (pioneer aviator and flying boat designer) to design a flying boat that could fly across the Atlantic. The Navy-Curtiss NC boats evolved, three of which attempted the crossing in May 1919. Only the NC-4, commanded by Lt. Comdr. A. C. Read, completed the flight to become the "first across the pond." In addition to Read, future flag officers on the flight were Comdr. John H. Towers, commander of the formation of "NC Seaplane Division 1," Lt. Comdr. Patrick N. L. Bellinger, commanding the NC-1, and Marc A. Mitscher, pilot of the NC-1.

The flights by the NC-4 and others that would soon follow by no means demonstrated that the dawn of safe commercial air travel across the Atlantic had arrived. Unsuccessful attempts to cross the ocean outnumbered the successful ones by a factor of about two to one for the next ten years. Some sixteen successful crossings were documented, however, including the first nonstop South Atlantic crossing by the Frenchmen Costes and Le Brix in 1927, the first nonstop east-to-west crossing by the Junkers *Bremen* in 1928, and Amelia Earhart's crossing in 1928 as a passenger in the Fokker *Friendship*, making her the first woman to cross the Atlantic by air. For sheer drama and public appeal, however, Charles Lindbergh's nonstop solo flight from New York to Paris in May 1927 was unsurpassed. That single, heroic flight caught and held the world's imagination more than any other of the era and proved beyond a doubt that America and Europe could be linked by aviation. Almost as a postscript less than a month later, Americans Clarence Chamberlain and Charles Levine flew nonstop from New York to Eisleben, Germany, breaking Lindbergh's distance mark by three hundred miles. By 1930 the North and the South Atlantic had been crossed in both directions, nonstop, by airship and airplane.

As the competition for "firsts" in Atlantic crossings waged on in the 1920s, the army and the navy focused on the Pacific Ocean as an arena for their continuing struggle for honors and recognition for their emerging air arms. The army had thrown down the gauntlet in the challenge for long-distance honors when army aviators made the first nonstop flight across the United States in a Fokker T-2 on 2 May 1923. A spectacular six-month around-the-world trip by a flight of army Douglas World Cruisers followed in 1924. The navy then decided to balance the scales with a nonstop flight from mainland United States to Hawaii. The ensuing 1925 flight of the PN-9, commanded by Comdr. John Rodgers, established a nonstop distance record but landed short of its intended destination, and Rodgers was forced to sail the flying boat to the nearest land. Not to be outdone, two years later army pilots Albert F. Hegenberger and Lester J. Maitland flew the 2,400 miles to Hawaii in the Fokker trimotor *Bird of Paradise*, landing at Wheeler Field, Oahu, with fuel to spare. Encouraged by the success of the *Bird of Paradise*, many others attempted the very demanding Pacific crossing. As in the case of the Atlantic crossings, these attempts often resulted in unnecessary crashes and loss of life, frequently because of lack of proper preparations and inadequate equipment.

Public and military interest in air racing in the United States centered on two prestigious events: the Pulitzer Trophy Race and the Schneider Trophy Race for seaplanes, the latter established in 1913 as an international "hydro-aeroplane" race. These races inspired intense competition between the navy and the Army Air Service, while such companies as Curtiss, Thomas-Morse, Wright, Sperry, and Boeing also contended for honors in the field of aircraft design and manufacture. As engine and airframe design improved dramatically, new speed records became routine. The 140 mph of World War I had doubled to 280 mph by 1924, and not long thereafter the record would creep up to 300 mph.

Naval aviators and their Curtiss racers were frequent and successful participants in these races. By far the best-known aviator was Lt. Alford J. Williams, a frequent competitor during his thirteen-year navy hitch. Navy pilots took top honors in 1923, winning both the Pulitzer and the Schneider trophy races. Williams won the Pulitzer with a speed of 243.67 mph in a Navy Curtiss R2C-1 racer. He was followed by navy Lt. H. J. Brow, Lt. L. H. "Sandy" Sanderson, USMC, and navy Lt. S. W. Calloway. Lt. Dave Rittenhouse won the Schneider Trophy Race for seaplanes, with Lt. Rutledge Irvin placing second. The last Pulitzer race took place in 1925, but for several years thereafter, other events in the annual National Air Races provided the opportunity for dozens of navy carrier pilots to fly stock airplanes in head-to-head competition against opposing Army Air Corps pursuit pilots.

Bernt Balchen, Comdr. Richard E. Byrd's pilot on his 1929 flight to the South Pole, once wondered, "What driving force causes a man to leave comfort and security, and risk hunger and privation and even death in search of something he cannot keep even when he finds it?" Some went for adventure, or curiosity, some sought new lands and opportunity, some went for conquest—and some wanted to make history. The aerial explorations of the 1920s reflected a combination of personal, economic, military, and scientific motives. Norwegian Roald Amundsen, the Italian Umberto Nobile, and Americans Lincoln Ellsworth, Hubert Wilkins, and Ben Eielson were polar explorers who often made headlines. Few exploration flights, military or otherwise, caught the public eye as did those of Comdr. Richard E. Byrd's flights over the North and South Poles. On 9 May 1926 Commander Byrd and his pilot Floyd Bennett returned to their base at Spitzbergen, Norway, reporting that they had become the first persons ever to fly over the North Pole. Their round-trip flight in the Fokker trimotor *Josephine Ford* took fifteen and a half hours.

Byrd's next goal was to make the first flight over the South Pole. He equipped a large expedition to the Antarctic continent and established his base at "Little America." On 28 November 1929 Byrd, Bernt Balchen, copilot Harold June, and aerial mapping expert Ashley McKinley took off in their Ford 4-AT *Floyd Bennett,* named for Byrd's Arctic pilot who had died of pneumonia the year before. By Byrd's calculation, they crossed the South Pole at 1:14 A.M. on 29 November.

Other naval aviators made significant exploration flights with lasting commercial as well as military implications. Typical of these were the U.S. Navy Alaskan Aerial Survey Expeditions in 1926 and 1929. Lt. Ben H. Wyatt led the 1926 flight of three Loening amphibians on the world's first serious survey of the Alaskan territory near the Arctic. In four months, the team mapped more than eleven thousand square miles of territory, taking about forty thousand aerial photographs. The 1929 Alaskan Aerial Survey Detachment, commanded by Lt. Comdr. Arthur W. Radford, a future chairman of the Joint Chiefs of Staff, produced valuable photographs of heretofore inaccessible glaciers such as the great Mendenhall Glacier region.

Against the backdrop of spectacular long-distance flights, air races, and exploration, there were drastically needed and lasting changes in the management and direction of naval aviation. The size and strength of the operating forces improved tremendously, and a wide range of technological improvements contributed immeasurably to the operational effectiveness of naval aviation in the fleet. On 12 July 1921, after a decade of administrative neglect, naval aviation took a giant step forward toward adequate representation and recognition in the bureaucracy of the Navy Department with the creation of a separate Bureau of Aeronautics. A month later, Rear Adm. William A. Moffett became the first chief of the bureau, a post he would hold until his tragic death in the crash of the airship *Akron* in 1933. During his tenure, Moffett, whose leadership earned him the title "architect of naval aviation," integrated aircraft into fleet operations, managed the introduction of new technology, and fought aggressively to remedy glaring deficiencies in procurement and personnel. A smooth, articulate master of public relations and politics, he successfully defended naval aviation against the ultraconservatives within the navy, and those from without who sought to destroy naval aviation. The controversial and flamboyant Brig. Gen. William "Billy" Mitchell and

Admiral Moffett became the protagonists in the acrimonious public debate between the navy and the Army Air Service over the pros and cons of a separate air force.

Of all the advances in technology in the twenties—flight and navigational instruments, propellers, metal aircraft structures, weapons, arresting gear, catapults, bomb sights, radios—perhaps none was as significant to the navy, and to civil aviation, as the development of the air-cooled radial engine. As the radial engine became more fully developed, it offered considerable advantages over the widely used liquid-cooled engines of the times—high fuel economy, long service life, ease and economy of maintenance, and low weight-to-horsepower ratio. In 1922 the navy decided to switch from water-cooled engines to the air-cooled Lawrence radial engine. As a result of the navy's interest, such air-cooled engines as the Wright "Whirlwind" and "Cyclone" and the Pratt & Whitney "Wasp" and "Hornet" had been developed by the mid-to-late twenties. These types of engines became the standards for use on naval aircraft, and their advantages also appealed to designers of commercial air transports. With few exceptions, commercial air transports relied on air-cooled radial engines until the advent of jet engines.

By the end of the decade, it was evident that the navy had made measurable progress in taking aviation to sea. Squadrons of fighters, scout-bombers, and torpedo planes were operating from three aircraft carriers, scout and observations squadrons were assigned to cruisers and battleships of the fleet, and patrol squadrons were operating from naval air stations in Panama and Pearl Harbor. To a considerable degree, bureaucratic inertia had been overcome and replaced with a real sense of purpose and a concept of what the aviation navy might become. A host of problems had been identified, many had been solved, even more remained. A never-ending process had begun.

Few naval officers performed as magnificently across so wide a spectrum of naval aviation assignments as Alfred Melville Pride. In a day when naval aviation consisted only of seaplanes, Pride learned to fly land planes with the army to qualify for operations off battleship turret platforms, a one-way mission not very conducive to longevity. To add insult to injury, battleship captains did not look favorably on any kind of contraption that interfered with firing their big guns. Pride soon transferred from battleships to carriers and applied his engineering talent to developing and flight-testing arresting gear for the USS *Langley*. It was a time when ingenuity, innovation, and improvisation—as well as superb flying skills—were at a premium. Each launch and recovery was a new experience; crashes were routine and a part of the learning process. Admiral Pride continued to apply his unusual blend of engineering expertise and superb airmanship to the development of all manner of systems and equipment for the aircraft carriers *Lexington* and *Saratoga*. In later years, he recalled his experiences with a becoming sense of modesty, belying the considerable skill, courage, and imagination that were the hallmarks of his innumerable accomplishments in the field of naval aviation.

Woven through Rear Adm. Jackson R. Tate's account of his experiences on the USS *Langley* are such names as Whiting, Pride, Chevalier, and Griffin—pioneer aviators who laid their service reputations and their lives on the line in the face of great adversity and uncertainty. It is clear from Admiral Tate's memories of the early *Langley* days that the impressive advances in carrier aviation were because of the cumulative efforts of these and many other very talented officers. No handbooks of standard operating procedures existed, no years of experience upon which to rely for instant answers. Still, from the fertile minds of these marvelously inventive officers sprang ideas and solutions, procedures and doctrine that endured through the years, well into the jet age.

Bored with his life as a destroyer engineering officer, George Van Deurs left a world where "boilers glared like arc lights and a slight mistake meant catastrophe" for another life where the slightest mistake could also be injurious to one's health—flight training at Pensacola in the 1920s. Van Deurs was an accomplished raconteur who spun a thoroughly delightful, humorous yarn of sun, sand, and seaplanes in south Florida. There were daily adventures in open cockpit floatplanes and flying boats ("angel makers"), droning along at 60 knots in front of a pusher engine, without parachute, disdaining the use of a safety belt. Despite the hazards and distractions of his newly chosen profession, Admiral Van Deurs soon fell in love with flying (sort of) and moved on to a series of challenging aviation duties, including an unusual tour of duty on a seaplane tender in the Asiatic—but that's another story.

Capt. "Tommy" Tomlinson was the personification of the popular image of the 1920s aviator—daredevil stunt pilot, barnstormer, "free spirit."

Irrepressible, an independent thinker whose opinions on flying (and other subjects) were often out of sync with those of his superiors, he was also a superb performer who skillfully used naval aviation as his personal stage. Whether leading his Three Sea Hawks stunt team through their dazzling aerobatic routine, flying inverted through downtown San Francisco, or demonstrating his own way of landing on an aircraft carrier, Capt. Daniel Webb Tomlinson was an aviator—first, last, and always. His devotion to aviation is the essence of a story that provides rare insights into the carrier aircraft of the day, and the evolution of combat tactics that were used so successfully during World War II.

The nation's first recognized glider pilot, and a leading authority on gliders, Capt. Ralph Barnaby spent most of his naval career trying to convince his superiors of the potential of the glider in naval aviation—with mixed results. Although Barnaby did persuade Rear Adm. Ernest J. King to institute a glider training course at Pensacola in 1933, it was a short-lived experiment that lasted about a year. Aside from some World War II experimentation on adapting the glider to combat use in the navy, much of Barnaby's efforts was to no avail. Barnaby's stories of his experimental glider flight from the USS *Los Angeles* and later duties at Pensacola as a glider instructor are glimpses of a little-known or appreciated phase of naval aviation history. His memories of earlier duties as a civilian aeronautical engineer before World War I provide a fascinating insight into the aviation industry in its infancy.

3

SEA LEGS

Adm. Alfred Melville Pride

BORN IN SOMERVILLE, *Massachusetts, on 10 September 1897, Alfred Melville Pride served as a machinist's mate and was later commissioned an ensign in the Naval Reserve Flying Corps in England and France during World War I. He subsequently transferred to the U.S. Navy and, as an aviator, was attached to various naval air stations, the aircraft carriers USS* Langley *(CV-1) and USS* Lexington *(CV-2), and for two years commanded Fighting Squadron 3 (VF-3) on board the* Langley. *Prior to World War II, he served in the Navy Department's Bureau of Aeronautics, as air officer of the seaplane tender* Wright *(AV-1), and on the staff of commander Patrol Wing 1, based at San Diego.*

At the outbreak of war, Pride was at sea as executive officer of the carrier USS Saratoga *(CV-3). After brief duty in 1942 in the Bureau of Aeronautics, he assumed command of the USS* Belleau Wood *(CVL-24) on 31 March 1943, later participating in numerous operations in the Pacific in 1943–44. Subsequent wartime duties included command of the Naval Air Center, Pearl Harbor, and of naval air bases of the 14th Naval District, and commander Air Support Control Unit, Amphibious Forces, Pacific Fleet.*

After World War II, Admiral Pride commanded Carrier Divisions 4 and 6, was chief of the Bureau of Aeronautics, commander, Carrier Division 2, and commander, Naval Air Test Center, Patuxent River, Maryland. From December 1953 until December 1955, he served as commander, Seventh Fleet, and on 1 February 1956, he assumed command of the Naval Air Force, U.S. Pacific Fleet. Admiral Pride was transferred to the retired list of the U.S. Navy on 1 October 1959.

Admiral Pride's decorations include the Distinguished Service Medal with Gold Star, the Legion of Merit with Combat "V," Letter of Commendation with Ribbon and Combat "V," and Presidential Unit Citation with Combat "V" (USS Belleau Wood).

I only got in one or two antisubmarine patrols off the French coast before World War I ended. By that time, I loved aviation. It was pretty hard to be in at all without being very enthusiastic about it. Being a youngster, it was a whole new environment, and there was a lot of satisfaction in just flying an aircraft. You felt rather egotistical about it, as if you were one of the privileged.

When the war was over, I was still a reserve, and we were ordered to the stations nearest our homes in the United States until it was determined what should be done with us. The navy had a coastal air station at Chatham, Massachusetts, so that was the one that I was ordered to. While there, I learned that the navy was about to fly aircraft off of battleships for spotting gunfire. Chevalier, Whiting, and others who were influential in naval aviation had watched the British experiments in flying off ships to scout for the ships and spot their gunfire. Chevalier went over to Britain and observed the tests that they were making. Our Navy Department thought this was a pretty good idea because our aerial observation from battleships was confined to the use of kite balloons. They obviously couldn't leave the ship to go out on scouting trips since they were moored to the ship.

So the Navy Department made some tests on the USS *Texas* (BB-35) on which they built a platform on the guns of the number two turret, the high turret. The platforms were made of the wooden painting stages, which all the battleships carried. The framework could be assembled very quickly on top of the guns. In March 1919, Lt. Comdr. E. O. McDonnell, flying a Sopwith Camel, made the first successful flight from the number two turret of the *Texas,* lying at anchor at Guantánamo.

So I thought I'd like to try flying from battleships, and I wrote a letter via channels and asked to be assigned to this duty, which I was. I went to Carlstrom Field in Florida, where I joined what was to become the Atlantic Fleet Ship Plane Division. This group at Carlstrom Field, an Army Air Service field, was under the command of Lt. Comdr. Godfrey de Courcelles Chevalier (naval aviator no. 7). I think there were eighteen of us that were assigned to this duty for the air service to teach us to fly land planes, because we were to fly them off the battleships. We had no land planes in the navy, except for the few we had used in the Northern Bombing Group in France and a few here and there on special projects.

They started us right in through the air service's elementary training, as though we had never seen an airplane before. This was rather hard on our egos because very few of the instructors had been on duty in Europe during the war, and most all of us had been. They put us right through their elementary and advanced training. We got into their single-engine fighters, then were turned loose to go to our battleships. I was ordered to the USS *Arizona* (BB-39). I joined the ship in her home yard, the Brooklyn Navy Yard. Then we left for Guantánamo within a week or two, where we did most of the work.

On the forward turrets of the *Arizona* we were to use an aircraft called a Sopwith-Strutter, which was a two-seater British airplane. On the after turrets, we had French Nieuport 28s. The runway was fifty-two feet long, as I remember, which meant that you had to have a pretty good breeze blowing down the line of the runway to be sure to get you in the air before you struck the water. In fact, we had two or three airplanes go in the water. Then we arrived through experience at the notion that you had to have at least 22 knots of wind down the runway. That meant that with the number three turret—the battleship had a speed of about 20 to 22 knots—you had to get a fairly good breeze blowing. Then the ship would be steaming almost across the wind to make the apparent wind come down the deck.

I flew off number three turret because that was a single-seater, and I was the senior of the two aviators. The other pilot on the *Arizona* was Lt. (jg) Jacob F. Wolfer, who unfortunately was killed the following year when he spun in down in Guantánamo Bay. The single-seaters were always thought to be more desirable probably because they were more lively, more maneuverable. We put the tail up on a wooden horse and restrained the plane with a pelican hook, a quick-release device shaped somewhat like a pelican's beak. Then you revved the engine up full, nodded your head, and somebody released the pelican hook. Down the platform you went, hoping to God that you'd get flying speed before you got to the water. You always barely made it, if you made it at all. I never went in the water that way. I've been in the water several times, but I never failed to take off from the turret.

Both types of airplanes had rotary engines, which sometimes were rather unreliable. The nonaviators didn't think much of all this. I caught hell because the rotary engine used castor oil, which would spew out, and drops of it would go down on the beautiful teak on the quarterdeck of the *Arizona*. When I reported in, the skipper, Capt. John H. Dayton—who was a very fine man—told me that he didn't believe in airplanes on ships, and that the only future for aviation in the fleet that he could see was small dirigibles towed by the battleships. They could cast them loose and go out and scout and come back to another ship. I think that they appreciated our spotting for long-range firing very much, but they regretted these damn dirty airplanes on their ships.

When we operated from the battleship, we landed on the beach, wherever we could find a field, and towed the airplane with anything we could since these planes weren't very heavy. I used an ox team in Cuba to tow the airplane down to the shore. We got them onto a fifty-foot motor launch and brought them back out and hoisted them back on the ship with a boat crane. Most of the time that we were around Guantánamo, we'd keep the airplanes flying to keep our hands in. We operated from Hicacal Beach over on the west side of Guantánamo Bay, where we established a camp.

There were other battleships with us: the *Nevada* (BB-36), the *Oklahoma* (BB-37), and the *Pennsylvania* (BB-38), all of which had their turrets rigged for aircraft. The pilots would gather together a great deal in port, and every day we were over at Hicacal Beach flying. In fact, we had to assemble our aircraft there. We didn't take any planes south with us in the battleships on the first cruise. We got down there and were met by a collier, which had our aircraft aboard in crates. We took those ashore, up over Conde Bluff and down onto the flats, and assembled them ourselves. Even though we had a ground crew with us, everybody had to work on the aircraft, despite the fact that most of us had never seen any of these aircraft before.

When the ship came back to the navy yard after the cruise to Guantánamo, we assembled out at Mitchel Field at Mineola, Long Island, New York, where we borrowed facilities from the air service. We spent that summer of 1921 flying around there to keep our hands in, then we went back to battleships in the autumn, at which time I was shifted to the *Nevada* for the same type of duty. After another cruise in the winter in the *Nevada* to Guantánamo Bay, we came back and assembled again at Norfolk Naval Air Station.

Just prior to that, the people who were interested in this business, Chevalier and Whiting particularly, had figured out that we'd better get a carrier in the navy. The collier *Jupiter* (AC-3) was sent to the navy yard at Norfolk to be converted into a carrier and named the *Langley*. Chevalier told me that I was to stay ashore at Norfolk the summer of 1921 and devise an arresting gear to stop the aircraft on the *Langley* deck. There was no provision for arresting in her original plans—in fact, nobody had figured what to do about that. So I stayed at Norfolk and worked on the arresting gear, designed it, and saw it installed. When the *Langley* went into commission in '22, I was in their commissioning detail.

There had been some previous work done on arresting gear. Eugene Ely had made a landing on 18 January 1911 on the stern of the USS *Pennsylvania* (ACR-4) in San Francisco with an old pusher aircraft. They had built a long platform from her mainmast out over the stern. To stop the airplane, they hung some hooks on it and put lines across the deck with a sandbag on each end of each line. There were quite a lot of them, so that when Ely came down and landed, the hooks snagged the lines and dragged more and more of the sandbags, bringing him to rest. It seemed such an obvious way to stop anything that I started out to try and see how this thing was going to work out. I just put sandbags on wires across the roadway down there, to find out how I should design the hook for the planes that we then had.

In the meantime, the Navy Department had built a turntable on the field at Hampton Roads, about a hundred feet in diameter, flush with the ground. They mounted some gear on it that the British were then using. The British type of gear simply used some cables stretched real taut about nine inches apart and a little over a foot off the deck, running fore-and-aft on the flight deck. Our version of it had them fifteen inches off the deck. On the axle of the landing gear were hooks, like anchors, that went down between the longitudinal cables. Just the friction of the cables was supposed to stop the airplane.

It never did; the plane went up on its nose at the end of the run. The British called it a Harp or a B-gear. In their version, the wires were high enough so the plane actually rested on them and coasted along on the wires. The friction was much greater. It tore up the plane and busted the propeller in almost every landing. It was disastrous. They never put it into other than experimental use.

On the same turntable I mounted some crosswires that were going to drag along weights suspended in towers. Then it became much more of an engineering operation; you knew what the plane weighed, you knew about how fast it was coming in, so you knew its kinetic energy. You knew how much weight you had and how high the weights could go, so you knew how much potential energy they were going to have. You could balance those out and come up with a rational prediction of where the airplane was going to stop, how far it was going to run out. Actually, there was such a great loss of friction in the system that the potential energy of the weights at the end of a run was usually only a part of the kinetic energy of the aircraft as it landed. But at least you had a rational approach to the thing, whereas you never knew what you were going to get dragging the sandbags along.

I tested the designs that I came up with. I was not confident that it was going to work; every test was a question of whether it would work. We were shortsighted. We should have discarded the fore-and-aft cables at the very beginning, but we didn't, and they even put them into the *Lexington* and *Saratoga*. It was there that a naval constructor named Leslie C. Stevens said, "Let's do away with those fore-and-aft cables." They were breaking up more aircraft than they were saving, but there was a great fear of going over the side. The British had used these because they had had some very disastrous experiences in early experiments. Because they were going to have to take off from the ship, they built the platform forward. They used very small, light airplanes, Sopwith Pups and Camels. They would come in, have to make a very sharp turn in by the foremast and down onto the platform. There was one of the cruises when they lost some overboard. It was a bad place to go overboard, because the ship ran over you.

So the British were very strongly orientated toward the fore-and-aft wires, and we were too, but it began to dawn on us that these things were causing more breakups than they were worth. If you were low enough so that your axle hooks engaged the fore-and-aft wires, and your trailing hook did not engage a crosswire, then you came to the end of the fore-and-aft wires, and you went up on your nose.

There were usually two or three other people involved in my experiments at Norfolk, but I was pretty much on my own. It didn't take very long to come up with a good design, probably not more than five or six months. I had to because I understood the ship was going into commission in April 1922, and this was the start of the summer of '21. As I would get ideas, I would have to go to Norfolk to tell the draftsmen over there what we'd better put in the ship. I had to work pretty fast.

The weights that were designed for the system obviously were heavy and cumbersome. They had a great advantage in that the system was self-contained. If the ship would lose its power, you could still fly airplanes after the wire had been pulled out. You had to get the wire back into battery, and the weights took care of that. I had a come-along arrangement. The wire would play out, but then you could control its coming back. The first weights were just blocks of cast iron on the towers that supported the flight deck. Later, much better-designed weights were put down in one of the holds of the ship. However, it was still a bulky and an awkward system.

The landing area was about 265 feet long. On the earliest design we graduated the weights; the top weight was the lightest, and the bottom was the heaviest. A light airplane would drag the arresting wire out aways. When the top weight had moved up a little bit, it picked up another weight, and so forth. So there was no adjustment when a different type of airplane landed on the deck. As planes became faster and larger and more diverse in their types, this became necessary.

Not the least of the problems on the *Langley* was the matter of power. She was, I guess, the first electric drive ship in the navy, and it wasn't too reliable. I remember when we left the navy yard at Norfolk, we went at about 6 knots out the channel. The maximum speed was about 13 knots, and we were lucky if we got that. But she was a very useful ship and taught us an awful lot about carrier technique.

We spent the summer, autumn, and part of the winter of 1922 shaking down, which was a very eventful, and rewarding, time since almost everything we were doing was a first-time experience. As an example, the business of using arm signals to show whether the pilot was high or low or fast or slow came about in an interesting way. We were at anchor in the York River when the *Langley* was being shaken down. The executive officer, Comdr. Kenneth Whiting—who had been largely responsible for our having a carrier—was in the netting, just below the flight deck level where the personnel go while aircraft are landing. He used to stand in the netting all the way aft on the port side. That was a good place to see what was going on.

We had one pilot who had not landed on the deck before but had had a lot of training and practice ashore. Up to that moment, it never occurred to any of us that anybody could know any more about handling the airplane than the fellow that was flying in it. It was a very parochial point of view, but it was one that all pilots had at that time. This chap came in, and apparently he was very reluctant to actually set his plane down. He kept coming in high, and then he'd give her the gun before he quite got to the deck and go around again. This had happened several times.

Whiting jumped up on the deck and grabbed the white hats from two bluejackets who were there. He held them up to indicate that this character was too high, then he put them down. He coached the fellow in, and that seemed like a good idea. So from then on, an officer was stationed aft there with flags to signal whether the plane was high or low or coming in too fast or too slow. It was a stroke of genius by Whiting, and out of that has grown the present, very sophisticated electrical signaling system.

Up to the time the *Langley* was commissioned, every naval air station had carrier pigeons that we used to take on flights. Before you started on your flight, you went over to the pigeon loft and got your little box with four pigeons in it. If you had a forced landing, of which we had quite a number, you wrote your message on the piece of paper, stuck it in the capsule that was fastened to the pigeon's leg, and let it go. It flew back to the air station, and the people there knew where you were, presumably. This had been going on for a long while in the very early days of aviation.

On the fantail of the *Langley* was a room that was the pigeon loft. The pigeon quartermaster—there was such a fellow—would let his pigeons out, one or two at a time, for exercise. They'd leave the ship and fly around, and they usually stayed in sight. Pretty soon they'd come back and land on a little platform outside the coop, the little alarm bell would ring, and the pigeon quartermaster opened the door, and in they'd go. While we were in the navy yard, after we were commissioned and before we went to shake down, the pigeon quartermaster would put the pigeons in a cage and put them on railway express and send them to Richmond or somewhere where the expressman would let them go, and they'd all come back to Norfolk.

We went into the Chesapeake Bay and anchored off Tangier Island during the shakedown. It was a beautiful morning; I remember it well. The assistant flight officer, Lieutenant Commander Griffin, said to the pigeon quartermaster, "Let them all go." The pigeon quartermaster demurred a little, but the commander said, "Go ahead, let them all go." So the pigeon quartermaster opened the coop and let all the pigeons out at once. They took off just like that, heading for Norfolk. They had been trained while the ship was in the Norfolk Navy Yard. They go back to a locality—they don't go back to a coop. So all at once, we had no pigeons on the *Langley*.

Pretty soon we got a dispatch from the Norfolk Navy Yard. I don't know how they knew they were ours. They said, "Your pigeons are all back here. We haven't got any appropriation for pigeon feed." So we put the pigeon quartermaster in a plane and flew him down to Norfolk. They were all roosting in the crane where we'd been fitting out. After dark, he climbed up in the crane and picked them up and took them over to the Naval Air Station Norfolk. That's the last we ever saw of pigeons on the *Langley*. So they made the pigeon coop into the executive officer's cabin, a very nice one. Later on, we got the pigeon lofts deleted from the plans of the *Lexington* and *Saratoga* and made them into berthing compartments!

After the shakedown, in the late spring–early summer of '23, we started a cruise to publicize the navy's carrier. There were about six of us who were qualified to land and take off and fly from the ship—Boatswain Walter J. Daly, Boatswain Anthony Feher, Lt. (jg) Delbert L. Conley, Lt. Comdr. Virgil C. Griffin, who made the first takeoff from the *Langley*, myself, and one or two more.

We started at Bar Harbor, Maine, and came down to Portland, Portsmouth, Gloucester, Boston, and New York. At each of those places we would anchor out and make landings and takeoffs for the entertainment of the people on the beach. The navy advertised that we had a carrier, published the times when we would be making takeoffs and landings, and then we went ahead and made them. The timing coincided with some 150-year celebrations they were having in some of the New England towns.

In fact, by the time we got to Washington, there was a Shriners' convention, which was most fortunate.

The reaction of the public was very enthusiastic. It was rather spectacular to see an airplane come to rest and to take off in such a short distance. The takeoffs at anchor, with little or no wind, were usually spectacular because the plane frequently would not quite have flying speed when it got to the end of the deck, and it would sink a little. People would wonder how far it was going to go down. We had done it enough so that we were confident. We had a fifty-two-foot drop from the deck to the water, and we would always get flying speed in that height.

We had made our original test landings and takeoffs with Aeromarine 39-Bs, which were light aircraft. You could land and take off at very low speed in a very short distance. During the cruise we were using Vought VE-7s, which were two-seated airplanes of considerably higher performance. We had no aircraft that were built especially for carriers at that time, although we were thinking at that time about possibly designing aircraft for carriers. What was done was that perfectly conventional aircraft—aircraft that had been designed without the carriers in mind particularly—were modified by having trailing hooks and axle hooks put in, practically all of it by ourselves in the shops at Hampton Roads.

Our arresting gear worked all right, although the weight system was cumbersome; it was heavy in the ship, and I wasn't at all satisfied with it. Also, I didn't feel it was as flexible as it needed to be to take care of aircraft that probably would be coming along in the future. At that time, the rate at which aircraft performance was increasing and the rate at which aircraft weight was going up were following a pretty predictable curve. So we knew in a very short time we were going to have aircraft probably weighing twice as much and landing at appreciably higher speeds. The energy to be absorbed was going up proportionately. In fact, it was going to go up as the square of the landing speed and directly as the weight, so that the weight system of arresting gear was going to reach its limit in a very short time.

After I went on this cruise on the Eastern Seaboard, I was detached from the ship and sent ashore to Norfolk to work on arresting gear for the *Lexington* and the *Saratoga*. I stayed there until the spring of 1924, still working on weights and trying to refine that system. But in the back of my mind I began to have notions; we had quite a number of notions. I worked very closely with opposite numbers in the Bureau of Aeronautics because I had to get my money from them and made all my reports to them. A whole lot of my work was improvisation with material and equipment that I could get out of the navy stock catalog over at the Norfolk Naval Yard or the air station.

There was never any lack of support, but I had had only about a year of college. I wanted more engineering education very badly, so I had asked to go to the postgraduate school in 1923. Capt. Emory S. Land was then the head of the Material Division of the Bureau of Aeronautics. He told me that he would like to have me stay at Norfolk for another year, and then he would try to see that I went to the postgraduate school, and he did. I went to the postgraduate school in 1924 in Annapolis, and then the following year I went to the Massachusetts Institute of Technology to do postgraduate work in aeronautical engineering.

After I finished MIT in the summer of 1926, I was ordered to the fitting-out detail of the *Saratoga* at New York Shipbuilding Company, Camden, New Jersey. I had been there but a few months when I was transferred to the fitting-out detail of the *Lexington* at Quincy, Massachusetts. Both ships were fitted out with arresting gear that had been devised by Carl Norden, the inventor of the Norden bombsight. Norden started with an entirely different concept from mine. He designed some very ingenious winches, in which the above-deck equipment still employed wires across the deck that the trailing hooks could engage. Each end of the athwartship wire led to a winch. As the wire unreeled from the winch, the winch operated a Waterbury speed gear, which was a pump that applied pressure to the brake on the winch. That stopped the aircraft.

Then there had to be an electric motor to rewind the winch, to bring the cable back into battery. I didn't like this idea very much because it seemed to me that if you lost power in the ship, you could no longer land the aircraft. If you had your aircraft all in the air, you were going to lose them all at sea. I'd been in battleships and in the *Langley,* and I'd seen the ships lose their power; the ship just stopped. It would be very embarrassing if you had all of your aircraft in the air at that time.

So I wanted to get back to a self-contained system, one that would keep on landing airplanes whether the ship had any power or not. That's why I dreamed up the hydraulic system that went into the *Lexington* and the *Saratoga* to replace the Norden gear. The hydraulic system uses the energy of the plane in landing to retrieve the system and get it back in battery. As it drags the wire out, it builds up pressure in the hydraulic system, which is used to pull the wire back into battery after the airplane has been unhooked from the wire. There are only a few seconds until the next airplane's coming in, so it has to be done quickly. There were many lessons that I learned in the *Langley* that could be applied to the *Lexington* and *Saratoga* when we commissioned them. We had learned a considerable amount about what sort of repair work you would do on a ship. We rearranged the shops and their equipment accordingly. We had found out what spares you needed to carry. For instance, you were going to have a fairly high incidence of landing gear failures, much more so than in landing aircraft ashore. We were able to readjust our supply list and the supply storage in the ship. We had some very firm ideas about the handling of the aviation gasoline, the handling of the aircraft on deck, and the securing of the aircraft when they were on the ship. We stowed aircraft below or kept them on deck, according to the next operation. We liked to get as many of them below as possible, of course, to get them out of the weather.

The *Lexington* went into commission at Quincy on 14 December 1927. The USS *Saratoga* had already been commissioned a month earlier, on 16 November. We did some taking on of stores and fitting out and so forth in Boston and went in dry dock there. We were keen rivals with the *Saratoga*. Then there was much rivalry as to who should have the first landing aboard. The *Lexington* was to go right from the shipyard at Quincy into dry dock in Boston. The *Saratoga*, a day or two after that, was to go down the Delaware River and have her trials. I suspected that the *Saratoga* figured they'd beat us out by having a landing on board while they were going down the Delaware River.

Our skipper, Capt. Albert W. Marshall, instead of going straight to South Boston, detoured out into Massachusetts Bay just long enough for me to land aboard in a Vought UO-1 on 5 January 1928. Then he went up into the dry dock in South Boston, figuring we'd done pretty well. It turned out that Comdr. Marc A. Mitscher made the first takeoff and landing on the *Saratoga* in a UO-1 on 11 January 1928, so we made our landing before the *Saratoga*. It was very childish, but those things, of course, are part of life. Until the *Lexington* was sunk in World War II, we were always in keen rivalry. That's human as can be, and it's very fortunate it's that way. For one thing in the carrier development, it sped up our operations because we were always trying to land aircraft or take them off more rapidly than the other ship. It was a powerful incentive.

After that, we went down to Norfolk and took some squadrons aboard and then went around to the West Coast through the Panama Canal, which was disastrous for the Panama Canal. The ships had huge overhangs, and the canal pilots had never handled ships like that before. As we went into the Gatun Locks, the overhang struck those huge concrete lampposts they had, and over they'd go. The first one everyone regarded as quite a disaster and, of course, it was regretted. But as the second and each succeeding one went down, the crew all had a great interest, which provoked a certain amount of irritation as far as the canal people were concerned.

We went around in company with the *Saratoga*. The Navy Department had decided to have both ships on the West Coast; the major threat was felt to be in the Pacific at that time. When we got to the West Coast, we went in for posttrial repairs in San Francisco, then the *Lexington* was selected to make a high-speed run to Hawaii. On 12 June 1928, the *Lexington* anchored in Lahaina Roads, Honolulu, Hawaii, having broken all existing records for the distance. Our elapsed time was seventy-two hours and thirty-four minutes.

During my tour of duty on the *Lexington*, I had been thinking about the Norden gear and another technical disadvantage. If an aircraft hooked a wire, and it was off center, the gear—just through physics—had to steer the aircraft toward the side of the ship, and it would go overboard, which I knew because I'd seen planes go over. So I felt that the design had to be changed to obviate that difficulty. So I was ordered back to Hampton Roads when I left the *Lexington* in '29.

I didn't ask for that duty, but I was pretty well identified with this business by that time. The navy wasn't very big, and individuals were identified with particular interests. I was a little worried, though, because I was a line officer, and I felt that I was getting somewhat overspecialized in engineering. The aeronautical engineering duty designation didn't come in until I left the *Lexington*, when it was suggested that I join that group. I declined because I wanted to retain the prerogative of command.

I was ordered back to Norfolk, and once I got back there, I really got down to work on it and developed the hydraulic gear and some other deck fittings. In the experimental division there, we were not only working on arresting gear but other miscellaneous tasks and experiments. The Norfolk station was large, but my own group was small. I usually had only a civilian engineer and probably three or four pilots in a little machine shop. A warrant machinist, a couple of chief machinist's mates—probably in the whole crew there were fifty or sixty people.

The aeronautical experiments were very diversified. For one thing, because the water was there, we got all the seaplanes for their rough-water trials. I ran all of those. We'd get experiments like a radio ranging system that some Frenchman sold to the navy. It looked much like the omnirange of modern times. It was way ahead of its time; it didn't work at all. We had ordnance trials occasionally, the ones that were of interest to the Bureau of Aeronautics. All of those that were of interest to the Bureau of Ordnance went on at Dahlgren, Virginia. Sometimes there'd be overlap, and we'd get the aeronautics part of it.

One of the experiments we spent quite a bit of time in developing was a deck lighting system. The original lights in the ships' decks for landing were simply deadlights with electric light shining up, which gave a very poor sense of depth. A pilot didn't have very much of an idea how far away they were; there was a certain glare around them. We went back through the literature and found that the French, in World War I, had to establish little emergency landing fields for their planes returning at night. They found that if they just put lanterns out, and the pilots looked directly at the source of light, they didn't do very well. But if they shaded the lantern so that the light was reflected from a board painted white, they had pretty good depth perception.

So we made the deck lights that involved reflection, and it turned out that was the only thing that I got a patent for. I didn't want a patent for it. Being a deck fixture, it came under the Bureau of Ships, but to my astonishment, one day, I got an imposing-looking document saying that I had been awarded patent number so-and-so for a deck light that was being assigned to the navy, for which I was receiving one dollar—which I never received. I thought that if I got that check, I'd frame it.

There was urgent need for a deck fitting, to tie the aircraft down. Simple as it sounds, it isn't quite that simple, because it has to be flush with the deck, obviously, and there had to be an awful lot of them. They shouldn't form pockets that could retain fuel that could burn. So we developed the cross-deck channels with the hold-down fittings in the covers of these channels.

I loved that kind of work because I had a free hand. We had projects assigned to us, but we would also dream them up ourselves. There was a desk in the Bureau of Aeronautics, of course, to which I made my weekly reports, or special reports on projects. They sent various ones, simple things like shock absorbers—and wheel brakes; in the olden days, there were no brakes on the wheels.

We had one project that was quite peculiar that somebody thought we might be able to use on carrier decks. Instead of a wheel, it was a little caterpillar tread about five feet long that went right on where the wheels go on an aircraft. Of course, it was pretty silly engineering-wise, landing on a belt at 65 to 70 mph, and here was a tread that had to get up to that speed right now. A wheel would scuff a little—you'd hear them squeak when you'd land. That's quite different than having a mechanical tread that leads over a couple of pulleys—one fore and one aft and some others in between. They'd have to start that whole mechanism going from nothing up to 60 or 70 mph, right now. It didn't last long.

They sent us down a set of skis, saying, "Instead of landing on wheels on the ship's deck, if you land on skis you'll have enough drag. So try them out." This was to get rid of all the cables. I tried those out because it was easier to try them out and show their fallacies than to go into an argument about it. It was very evident right away that you never knew precisely, within some fairly large range, where an airplane would touch the deck, for one thing. It might touch at the stern, or it might touch halfway up through the arresting gear. When you wanted to land, where it was going to stop, you had no idea. Furthermore, with all that drag without the axle, you went right over on your nose. Then, of course, if you did stop, you had to handle the thing and push it out of the way. They had a lot of notions like that.

We didn't have an aircraft carrier at our disposal, so we started on a turntable that was only a hundred feet in diameter. By the time I got back there in '29, there had been built a dummy wooden deck, which you could not rotate into the wind as you could the turntable, but it was built into the prevailing wind. It was several hundred feet long and a very good replica of the ship's deck, flush with the ground. It had the galleries underneath, on which you could mount the arresting gear and all that stuff. When you wanted to try out anything, it was easy to cut up the deck and put in the fixtures.

At that time, the Pitcairn XOP-1 autogiro was under development, and someone—it might have been me—suggested that we ought to test it aboard ship. The autogiro differed from a helicopter in that in a helicopter, you've got power to the rotor, which wasn't true in the autogiro. Sometimes when the main engine goes out in a helicopter, it will autogiro to the ground. The autogiro could make a vertical landing onto a carrier's deck, but it took off like a conventional plane.

So one fine day in September 1931, when the *Langley* was off Hampton Roads, I flew out to the ship and landed. You had to be careful because the deck was so narrow, and there was also a problem when landing into a breeze. Unless you turned left immediately, the rotor would fly up and break a blade. So, as soon as it landed, I swung hard left and had to stop before going over the side. Nothing came of this development because it became obvious that a helicopter would be much more capable.

During this experimental work we had a great deal of contact with companies that were developing aircraft. I knew all the head people on a personal, first-name basis. We usually ferried a new airplane down to Norfolk ourselves, while others would arrive in crates. According to the contract, the demonstration flight had to be made by a company pilot. The pilot demonstrated that the thing could be recovered from certain attitudes. He dived and was required to pull a certain amount of "gees" to see if it was structurally sound. That usually took only one or two flights, if it was satisfactory.

Then a navy pilot took it over and did lots of things—fired the guns, bombing, and everything. He felt the controls to see if the thing was a good flying machine. Inevitably, there would be bugs in the first demonstration. The company people would be right there as you came down and would say, "What do you think of it?" And you told them what you thought was wrong or what you thought was right. They would always have a crew there to try and fix it up right away.

We had reached the point where we were asking for aircraft designed for aircraft carriers. As the planes grew heavier and faster, it was no longer a question of just hanging a hook on the tail somewhere. The loads in the tailhook were getting very high. They were running about three "gees"; for a twelve thousand–pound plane, there would be a thirty-six thousand–pound load in the trailing hook with peaks that would run sometimes as high as six "gees." So you had to absorb these loads into the structure of the airplane. These loads began to have to be worked into the design of the aircraft. Also the landing gear loads—the wheels and axles—had to be beefed up and stresses carried up through into the airplane structure. So we couldn't just take the same aircraft that the air corps, for instance, was using and hang a hook on it and land it on the aircraft carrier. If we did, it wasn't going to work. The plane had to be designed for this work.

Even when I attended postgraduate school in 1924, my intention had been to remain as a line officer. Generally, those who specialized in aeronautical engineering and design work became members of the Construction Corps. The Construction Corps no longer exists; aircraft design is now done by aeronautical engineering duty officers (AEDOs). I felt deeply interested in engineering and mechanical design. I knew there would always be room for people with such qualifications in the line. And it worked out that way because that training, although it eventually became very old, still stood me in good stead when I was chief of the Bureau of Aeronautics many years later, where much of my consideration had to be based on engineering judgment. My decision to combine my engineering interests and training with a career as a line officer was certainly one I never regretted.

4

WE RODE THE COVERED WAGON

Rear Adm. Jackson R. Tate

JACKSON R. TATE *enlisted in the Naval Reserve in April 1917, after the United States entered World War I. He was subsequently commissioned as an officer in the Naval Reserve and later in the U.S. Navy. He spent most of his thirty-three-year active naval career in aviation, particularly with fighter planes. He served in the USS* Langley *(CV-1),* Saratoga *(CV-3),* Lexington *(CV-2), and* Ranger *(CV-4), and commanded the USS* Altamaha *(CVE-18) and USS* Randolph *(CV-15). He served in Fighter Squadrons 1, 2, and 5 (VF-1, 2, and 5), commanding the last and an earlier enlisted-pilot torpedo squadron. Admiral Tate served ashore as a test pilot, an envoy with the special military mission to the U.S.S.R., and a commanding officer of advanced training, night flying, and fighters at Pensacola. After retiring from active duty in 1950, he worked for several different companies. Admiral Tate died on 19 July 1978.*

The *Langley* was unpopular, unlovely, unusual, and ugly—to say the least. Her unpopularity stemmed from her first mission as a collier, when she was named the USS *Jupiter* (AC-3). In 1917, something happened that was a precursor of things to come. The *Jupiter* was suddenly pulled away from her coaling duties, loaded with aviation supplies and a contingent of aviation personnel headed by Lt. Kenneth Whiting (naval aviator no. 16), and sailed for France. This was the first U.S. aviation unit to arrive overseas. The 7 officers and 122 enlisted men of the First Aeronautic Detachment were welcomed by a personal note written in longhand by King George V of Great Britain to Lieutenant Whiting.

At the Washington Naval Conference in the early 1920s, the great naval powers haggled over what they would have in the way of ships and tonnages. The big item was the battleship, then the queen of the fleet, and after that came the cruiser, and on down the list. The high-ranking officers in the front seats fought for battleship and cruiser power; in the back sat a junior commander named Kenneth Whiting who kept insisting on being heard for something called the airplane carrier. No one cared much, but he finally got authority for an experimental carrier, and when the United States agreed to scrap her new battle cruisers, he held out to get the first two, the *Lexington* and the *Saratoga,* converted to airplane carriers. Whiting was asking for ships that would replace the battleship as the backbone of the fleet and would thus change the whole concept of naval warfare.

The director of naval aviation at that time was a nonaviator, Capt. T. T. "Terrible Tom" Craven. Whiting went to him with his ideas for the authorized experimental carrier. During World War I, the navy had taken over two high-speed passenger liners to use as transports. These ships were built to beat train time between San Diego and Seattle, and they did it. Whiting wanted one for his experimental carrier. His request was refused, and Craven and the navy's General Board, which had the final say, recommended that the collier *Jupiter* be converted. Congress appropriated the money, and the collier, first commissioned in 1913, was on her way to becoming the USS *Langley.*

Men build ships, and the reincarnation of the *Jupiter* into the USS *Langley* was mainly the effort of four men. In addition to Whiting, those men were Lt. Comdr. Godfrey de Courcelles "Chevvy" Chevalier, Lt. A. Melville Pride, and Lt. Fred William Pennoyer. While in England during World War I, Chevalier had observed the British attempts to operate land planes from ships and was very impressed with the efforts. He and Whiting had long discussions on the subject of airplane carriers and arranged visits to various ships to observe operations. They determined to establish an operation of this sort when they returned to the States. Whiting was a man far ahead of his time in the very conservative navy of the 1920s. He had little use for battleships. His junior years—spent mostly in armored cruisers and in the navy's earliest submarines—built up his lack of awe for the so-called backbone of the fleet.

Whiting and Theodore G. "Spuds" Ellyson (naval aviator no. 1) had been roommates at the Naval Academy and were the first to apply for assignment to the new flying service. Ellyson had trained with Glenn Curtiss at San Diego and Whiting with the Wright Brothers at Dayton, Ohio. While at Pensacola, Whiting and Chevalier flew together a great deal and developed a great friendship and admiration for each other. Lt. Mel Pride was a reserve officer who came into naval aviation from the Massachusetts Institute of Technology at the beginning of World War I. He was a brilliant officer with an engineering mind and one of the most expert pilots of his time. Lt. "Horse" Pennoyer was a construction engineer. A dedicated officer to whom fell all the details of designing the gear to handling planes, he worked on the arresting gear of both the *Langley* and her planes. Like the others, he was a naval aviator.

The *Langley*'s conversion to an aircraft carrier took place at the Norfolk Navy Yard in Portsmouth, Virginia. As Whiting looked at her while the coal handling gear was being stripped off, he remarked, "Well, they will certainly get their money's worth out of her." Actually, there was not a lot of conversion to be done. The hull and engines remained intact, as did the two 5-inch guns on the fantail. The navy yard was not particularly interested in rebuilding the ship because too many new ideas were involved. No one was sure what the aviators wanted, except that there was to be a deck that planes could land on. The flight deck was to consist of several sections because a solid deck was deemed unable to withstand the ship's hogging and sagging in a seaway. There would be a catapult on the forward end of the flight deck, and some sort of arresting gear to stop the planes. Small items came up from time to time, such as side booms for radio antennas, a net aft to catch any planes that might fly into the stern, and extensions on the bridge under the flight deck to obtain some additional visibility.

Finding pilots for this carrier-to-be was something of a problem. Navy pilots were not trained in land planes until class no. 10 at Pensacola, so the original *Langley* pilots were sent to Carlstrom Field at Arcadia, Florida, for land plane training. The war was over, and the reservists were going home in droves. In 1922, there were only 314 pilots in the navy, and few of them were trained to fly land planes. On the *Langley* detail, they were here one day and gone or killed the next.

Those of us who were attached to the navy's first carrier were not treated to a life of luxury. The flight officers' quarters were built of wood on top of the wardroom and the old ship's staterooms. They competed with the uptakes from the boilers for space under the flight deck and constituted one of the best fire hazards the navy ever built. Whiting and Chevalier were involved in almost continuous daily conferences with the navy yard officials. Whiting insisted on a large and complete photo lab because he proposed to take both still and motion pictures of every landing. On the stern, an elaborate pigeon house was built with food storage, nesting, training, and trapping areas. It was later to be rebuilt into the executive officer's quarters. The radios of those days were very rudimentary, and most cross-country flights carried crates of homing pigeons in case of emergency. The attempt to train pigeons to return to a ship was a great failure, but provided an excellent supply of squab for the mess.

To bring the ship to the desired draft, a ten-foot-deep layer of cement was poured into the holds that once had been filled with coal. The building of the flight deck progressed slowly. There arose new problems daily, such as where to establish stations for control of the flight deck and arresting gear. To provide refuge for the deck crew during landings, outriggers were installed about three feet below the flight deck level. Wire netting was installed for the crew to jump into in order to observe and control the gear.

The actual arresting gear had to be designed as well. The British had used fore-and-aft wires strung about a foot apart, ten inches off the deck and covering the aft two hundred feet. These wires converged at the forward end. Friction on the hooks on the landing gear axles provided the retarding element. It had not been very satisfactory, and Whiting and Chevalier felt there should be a positive and controlled arresting moment. In a previous experiment on a special deck built on the armored cruiser *Pennsylvania* (ACR-4), Eugene Ely had successfully used cross-deck pendants with sand bags at each end and a hook on the landing gear of the plane. Lieutenant Pride, aided by "Horse" Pennoyer, did most of the work in designing the *Langley's* arresting gear.

The new carrier's planes were stationed at the Norfolk Naval Air Station, twenty-five miles from the navy yard. For the crew, this involved a trolley ride in Portsmouth, the ferry to Norfolk, a long trolley ride to Hampton Roads, and a bus ride to the air station. Pride did most of the testing with a circular platform that could be turned into the wind then set up on the northeast corner of Chambers Field. Various methods were tried out for both plane gear and deck gear. Some of these methods would be considered ridiculous today, but we had to learn the hard way.

The pilots practiced "precision landings" daily. A sixty-foot-long cloth strip, representing the stern of the flight deck, was put on the field at the air station. The pilots landed over it and attempted to drop on as soon as possible after passing it. An observer sat by and kept a log on each pilot's performance. There was no landing signal officer, and each pilot had his own technique. This went on in all types of planes, but the emphasis was on the Aeromarine 39-B, a seaplane with the floats removed and wheels installed. Pennoyer and Pride worked closely together on the design and manufacture of the gear to go in the plane.

An early member of the *Langley* detail was Lt. W. B. Haviland, who had been a member of the original Lafayette Escadrille. The squadron insignia of the Escadrille had been a red, white, and blue slanted *cocarde* painted on each side of a plane's fuselage. This was adopted for the *Langley* planes and for the ship. It is interesting to note that at that time it was common practice for aviators to request leave and a plane to fly home and back. Whiting called all pilots in one day and announced, "Pilots taking planes cross-country will not take up passengers for hire." A sign had been found in one plane: "Ride with me and see the town, $5.00."

Meanwhile, work on the ship was going very slowly. The *Jupiter* had the lowest priority in the yard, and Whiting felt too much of the conversion money was going to the navy yard overhead and not into the ship. Finally, the decision was reached to commission the ex-*Jupiter* into the USS *Langley* on 20 March 1922. Her acting commanding officer was Commander Whiting, the ship's prospective executive officer. Her future commanding officer was to be Capt. Stafford H. R. "Stiffy" Doyle, a nonaviator who had no idea what the ship was all about, what her mission was, or any of the ideas Whiting and Chevalier were working toward.

Though stationed only twenty-five miles away at Hampton Roads, Doyle did not see fit to attend the commissioning. The ceremony was held on the just-completed flight deck. Whiting ordered Lt. Comdr. Hugh Victor McCabe, the navigator, to set the colors and break the commission pennant on signal at the commissioning. Unfortunately, the hoisting gear had not been installed to raise the masts, so there was no place to break the commission pennant. Whiting said it was McCabe's problem. At the end of the ceremony, Whiting turned to McCabe and said, "Set the watches, hoist the colors, and break the commission pennant." McCabe had found a way: when the bugle sounded "colors," the chief quartermaster and an assistant jumped off the bridge with a commission pennant secured on the end of a swab handle, and nailed it to the edge of the flight deck.

Even after the commissioning, work progressed very slowly. It was almost six months until the *Langley* was able to leave the yard. Late in the summer, the new carrier was finally ready to go out for her postconversion trials; Capt. Doyle took over, and the ship proceeded down to the Hampton Roads Naval Base, where she was assigned dockage at the merchant ship end of the terminal. The masts were in the up position, and a commission pennant now flew proudly from the main, but no one at the base was yet willing to admit that this unusual and ugly apparition was a warship. Planes of various types were brought down from the air station and hoisted aboard for the training of the crew in plane handling. After loading supplies, the *Langley* finally got under way and proceeded up the Chesapeake Bay to Tangier Sound for tests of the new installations.

Whiting had developed a routine of daily conferences in the wardroom to settle all problems, both major and minor. He had listed a series of tests with smoke pots to examine the flow of air over the flight deck under various conditions of speed and at headings up to 10 degrees off the direction of the wind. Another minor problem was the choice of a bugle call to use for "flight quarters." Some argument arose when he selected "Boots and Saddles," the old cavalry call to mount horses. The pigeon quartermaster appeared once to protest vociferously against the test firing of the 5-inch, 51-caliber guns situated on either side of the stern; the pigeon house was a wooden structure built between the guns and not more than twenty feet away. The gun firing was deferred more or less permanently.

While in Tangier Sound, drills were the order of the day, but first it had to be decided what and how things were to be done before the crew could drill. Planes in those days had no brakes or tail wheels; shock absorbers for the main gear and tail skid consisted of rubber bungees. Engines were started by swinging the prop by hand and using a magneto booster. These proved to be problems on a crowded deck. Plane handling crews were established, with one man on each wing and a man on the tail dolly. The plane captain was the director, and signals had to be devised to direct the crew and pilot. There were no radios, so we had to figure out how to tell the planes to land. The solution was to fly a white flag at the aft end of the flight deck as a signal to land, and a red flag as a signal not to land. It was suggested that a steam jet be placed in the bow to assist the officer of the deck in keeping the ship headed into the wind. The chief engineer objected to this waste of steam, and so the jet was operated, when desired, from the bridge. All of this shows that the problems and growing pains on board the *Langley* were many, but somehow solutions were found.

In September 1922, the *Langley* established an anchorage in the York River adjacent to the mine depot at Yorktown. A circle of buoyed anchors was positioned so that the ship could be pulled into the wind using the after winches to the proper anchor. A landing field was established in a convenient pasture at the mine depot, and the planes were flown up from the Norfolk Naval Air Station. Daily, the ship would be hauled into the wind, and the pilots would make practice approaches. The strict orders were to make only approaches and no touchdowns. On one occasion, Pride barely kissed the deck with his wheels. Whiting hit the roof. Another day, an army bomber came by and started to make approaches. Again, Whiting blew his top and sent Lt. Carlton Palmer over to Langley Field to protest. He was too late. The bomber had crashed in an attempt to land on its home field, and the pilot was killed.

Finally, on 17 October, Lt. Comdr. Virgil C. "Squash" Griffin was designated by Whiting to make the first carrier takeoff. This was not so simple as it sounds or as it is today. Since planes had no brakes, it was necessary to develop a device consisting of a bomb release attached to a wire about five feet long to allow a plane to turn up to full power and start its deck run. The bomb release was hooked to a ring on the landing gear and the end of the wire to a hold-down fitting on deck. A cord led from the bomb-release trigger to an operator on deck, who could release the plane on signal.

Planes at rest sat nose high, and it was necessary to raise the tail three to four feet at the start of the roll. A trough about four feet long was built and mounted on sawhorses, and the tail skid was placed in the trough to keep the plane in flight position. The ship was hauled into the wind laboriously by the winches to the stern anchors, and a plane's propeller was started by hand. After all tests were completed, Griffin turned the Hispano-Suiza engine in the Vought VE-7SF up to its full 150 horsepower and gave the signal to pull the trigger on the bomb-release gadget, which had been given the name "tension gun." The released plane rolled down the deck and lifted off easily before it reached the elevator. Griffin flew back to Norfolk.

More days were devoted to practice approaches, especially using the Aeromarine 39-B. Finally, a week later, the *Langley* got under way and proceeded out into the Chesapeake Bay for the first landing. It was a cool Monday morning, 26 October 1922, when the ship turned into the northeast wind off the "Tail of the Shoe" shoal inside Cape Henry. Chevalier flew out from the beach in an Aeromarine 39-B and passed along the deck. The arresting gear was all set, and the white flag was flying at the stern.

The idea of having a landing signal officer was not to be thought of until six months later, so Chevalier was entirely on his own. His right wing dropped slightly at the end, but he corrected and made a landing catching the second wire. The fiddle bridges crashed down and were showered down on the deck along with the pies. The axle hooks held the plane down, and the tail hook stopped her in a very short run; but a high tail rise let the propeller nick the deck. Overall, it was a good landing, and the crew went wild with joy.

The following Saturday night, there was a celebration at the Norfolk Yacht and Country Club, and the pilots presented Chevalier with a silver cup to commemorate the first landing. No one at the celebration could predict that in less than two weeks "Chevvy" would be killed in a plane crash.

The *Langley*'s next air operation was the launching of a Naval Aircraft Factory PT-2 seaplane piloted by Commander Whiting by catapult from the flight deck. This twin-float seaplane was set on a remarkable carriage mounted on castors, a device designed by Pennoyer and built by the ship's force. The carriage was set on deck and attached to the catapult traveler. The pontoons were locked to the carriage by hooks that were released at the end of the catapult run, when they were hit by a trigger sticking up from the deck. Whiting turned the Liberty engine up to its full 2,000 rpm and gave the signal to fire. The PT-2 went rolling down the deck, but both plane and carriage became airborne just before they arrived at the release triggers. The trigger on the port side hit and released that pontoon, but the other side had lifted off the deck high enough to miss the trigger. The plane went off the deck with one pontoon still attached to the car. Whiting righted the plane and flew off with only one pontoon. It was a beautiful flying job. He finally landed in the river alongside the crash boat, which towed the wreck to the ship's crane to be salvaged. It was a somewhat unusual start for air operations.

Most of the pilots lived in Norfolk and flew down there from York-town for weekends. Ironically, it was on one of these homeward flights that Chevalier was killed. He was flying a VE-7, which had two gas tanks. The forward tank held ten gallons and the after one, on which the pilot sat, held twelve. The tanks were separate, with a complicated system of air valves and gas valves. In order to shift tanks, the valves needed to be operated in exact sequence. Each tank had its own filler, and there was no gauge for either.

Chevalier came down from Yorktown on a Saturday on the aft tank and used up most of the gas in it. On Monday morning before the flight to return to the ship, the station line crewman, who was unfamiliar with VE-7s, lifted the cap on the still-full forward tank and incorrectly reported that the plane was fully gassed. While still at low altitude shortly after takeoff, the plane ran out of gas on the after tank. Chevalier put it down for a forced landing in what looked like a meadow. The land turned out to be swampy, and the plane went over on its back. Two days later, "Chevvy" died. His loss was a terrific setback to the infant carrier avia-tion, and the load was heavy on Ken Whiting's shoulders.

"Squash" Griffin moved up into Chevalier's job, and the *Langley* returned to the shipyard for the posttrial rework. Two important decisions were made. The first was that the Chesapeake Bay area was too inclement and cold in the winter to do the intensive flying contemplated, so the ship would go to Pensacola. The second decision was that all pilots would qualify in the Aeromarine 39-B at anchor before moving on to the more dangerous work under way and before landing the more advanced service types.

In January 1923, the *Langley* went to Pensacola. The air station there had just inaugurated the first land plane classes and had a small field alongside the hangar for lighter-than-air craft. The trolley line to town passed alongside one side of the field and the approach over the trolley wire was a mental hazard. The *Langley* transferred most of her planes ashore. Operations commenced with groups of three Aeromarine 39-Bs in the landing circle. With the new gear, deck time averaged about two minutes, and on several occasions the three planes were landed in eight minutes. One factor that slowed operations was the elevator. When it was necessary to strike a plane below, the slow speed of the elevator and the difficulty of getting the plane off at the bottom meant the operation took about fifteen minutes.

Whiting's notebook rapidly became filled with new ideas, for he was thinking not only of the *Langley* but also of those two magnificent battle cruiser conversions he had fought so hard for and that Congress had finally approved. Though "Horse" Pennoyer was continuously redesigning the arresting gear, both on the planes and on the ship, Whiting was in communication with civilian design engineer Carl L. Norden concerning a new type of gear to be used on board the *Lexington* and the *Saratoga*. There were long discussions about the needs for these ships. Whiting suggested a ready room for assembly of pilots prior to flight. Doyle said the pilots were already pampered enough and saw no use for it. It was also pointed out that a table and radio key could be installed so that the pilot could practice maintaining his proficiency in code transmission and reception of the twenty words per minute then required of all aviators.

Each landing was photographed in both slow motion and normal movies, and after each crash or malfunction these movies were carefully studied, frame by frame. Crashes were not infrequent, and soon a reel of crash movies was developed. Whiting was very cost-conscious and finally ordered that, to save film, only landings that appeared to be potential crashes were to be photographed. The movie cameras were cranked by hand and the sight of the chief photographer cranking away was usually followed by the crash siren!

Most planes were designed to be flown from the back seat, so when the nose came up in a stall it was very difficult to keep sight of the deck. This was solved by putting additional cushions under the pilot. Depending on a pilot's height, he was rated as a two-, three-, or even four-cushion man. A recommendation went in for adjustable seats.

Up until this time, each pilot was strictly on his own, and various types of landing approaches were employed. Mel Pride, the man who made the most and the best landings, used a slow-turning, flat approach with the nose high and using power. This was finally accepted by all pilots and became standard. After the Aeromarine phase was completed, we then

started on the service types—the Vought VE-7SFs and the Naval Aircraft
Factory TS-2 first, then the Vought UO-1s. This required much more work
because these planes were much faster and the landing speed much higher.

During the Aeromarine phase, Whiting made his first landing. Mrs.
Whiting and their eight-year-old daughter, Eddie, came out to watch the
landing from the deck-edge nets. The three planes took off and started
the landing circle. Each of the first two landed with some minor damage and taxied forward. Whiting came in last and made a perfect landing.
When he wasn't flying, the executive officer watched every landing from
the after port corner of the flight deck and mentally made each landing
himself. He talked each plane in: "He's too low . . . now OK . . . too high,"
etc., with appropriate motions of his hands. Whiting was surprised when
informed that all the pilots had noted his anxiety and actions. They did
agree that it was a good idea to place an experienced pilot aft on the port
side, so at a later conference the job of landing signal officer was set up.
The "cut" and other signals were added later and from then on the pilot
was no longer just "on his own."

It is almost impossible to believe but, for the first four years, we worked
without a barrier. This happened because most planes that did not engage
an athwartship wire rode fore-and-aft wires and usually wiped out the
landing gear at the forward end of the arresting gear.

In 1926, Lt. Dorris Gurley went through the arresting gear and almost
wiped out all twelve planes of VF-2 on the forward deck. Capt. E. S. Jackson, the skipper, ordered the bosun to rig a section of ten-inch hawser
across the deck on sawhorses and the barrier was born. Also, in 1929, the
fore-and-aft wires were removed from the carriers, and the planes no
longer needed axle hooks, thus simplifying undercarriage design.

Amidst the roar of the engines and the crashing down of the fiddle
bridges, a new series of orders evolved: "Rig the deck," "Pilots, man your
planes," "White flag," "Stand by to start engines," and others that were all
new to navy jargon. A new movie reel was put together to show perfect
landings with each type of plane, and all pilots competed to star in it. But
when the crash reel developed into multiple reels, though there was no
deliberate competition, all pilots' names appeared there. Another reel
showed material failures. Pennoyer and Pride worked endlessly, redesigning
and revamping to correct these deficiencies. In addition, Pennoyer took
the flight course at the Pensacola Naval Air Station and became the only

Construction Corps pilot in the navy. He soon joined the circle of landing pilots in addition to doing his other work.

The winter drew to a close, and the *Langley* headed north again to Norfolk for modifications of the ship found necessary by the six months of experience. Before entering the yard, she made a publicity cruise up the coast—much against Whiting's wishes. Landings were made at anchor in New York and Boston and were a sensation for the press. Captain Doyle went ashore and attended a few Chamber of Commerce meetings. Some of his speeches revealed his utter ignorance of the aims of what was being done and so infuriated Whiting that he went to Washington and convinced a few influential political figures to pass a law requiring that all ships directly connected with aviation be commanded by aviators. Few people then realized how far into the future he was looking. It was not until well into World War II that the correctness of his judgment was understood; President Roosevelt issued an order that also required that all carrier task forces be commanded by aviators.

In the summer of 1923, while the ship was undergoing a considerable modification, the flight section at the Norfolk Naval Air Station received new planes, including three new Douglas DT-2 torpedo planes, a Martin MS-1, and Cox-Klemin XS-I submarine planes. With the last two, "Squash" Griffin carried on a series of experiments with the submarine S-1. DT-2s had to have arresting hooks designed for them and installed. This was the only type still not qualified. As soon as this was accomplished, the *Langley* would then have proved that she could operate all types of current fighter, observation, and torpedo planes. After modification was completed and all the new gear was aboard, the carrier proceeded to Pensacola for tests of the new gear.

In January 1924, the Battle Fleet in the Pacific and the Scouting Fleet from the Atlantic proceeded to Panama to engage in Fleet Problem II, which was to consist of an attack on the Panama Canal. Although not attached to either fleet, the *Langley* also proceeded to Panama to observe and determine how she might be used. She sailed directly from Pensacola to Chiriqui Lagoon in Panama and anchored about one hundred miles north of the canal just prior to the start of the problem. The Battle Fleet was in the Pacific approaching Panama. To demonstrate that carrier planes could bomb in the Caribbean, Whiting sent two DT-2 planes across the isthmus with cameras and photographers.

After the Scouting Fleet entered Colón-Cristobal, the *Langley* demonstrated how a fleet might be attacked when in port by a carrier at sea. The two DT-2 seaplanes were dropped with a forty-foot motor launch as a tender with gas in Porto Bello harbor and directed to make torpedo attacks on the battleships and bombing runs on a spillway at dawn and dusk. The *Langley* stood out to sea and launched similar attacks with the Vought VE-7SF, UO-1s, and the TS-2 from the flight deck. She fought a good war, and Whiting submitted a paper on the use of aircraft in the problem. At the critique later, no mention was made of the *Langley*'s effort except to express annoyance at low "stunting" airplanes, and that it was impossible to drop torpedoes from a plane in shallow water harbors. The carrier plodded back to Pensacola for more landings. Now that the DT-2s were qualified, the *Langley* could land all current types of land planes. Landing gear failures were reduced drastically.

When spring approached, the ship went back to Norfolk and to operations in the Chesapeake. Whiting, Pride, and Pennoyer made frequent trips to Washington with ideas for the slow development of the battle cruiser hulls *Saratoga* and *Lexington*. They had notebooks full of many controversial ideas, advocating such things as heavier arresting gear, land plane catapults, space available on board for aircraft overhaul, and so forth. The major item in Whiting's mind was the tactical use of aircraft. But that was an idea whose time was still a few years away.

Landings, landings, landings—landings under way, landings at anchor. Then suddenly, Whiting, Griffin, Pride, and Pennoyer were detached to Washington and finally to the prospective crew of the *Saratoga*. Comdr. Warren G. Child took over as executive officer. He was naval aviator no. 29, and a nice person but not much of a pilot; he possessed none of Whiting's fire, vision, or ideas about carriers. Lt. Comdr. Charles Perry Mason took over as air officer from "Squash" Griffin. Mason, whose career had been with F-5L patrol flying boats, was transferred to land planes and carriers. As fall approached, the *Langley* headed for the West Coast and on 17 November 1924 joined the Battle Fleet. She abandoned her status as "experimental" and became the first operational carrier in the U.S. Navy. She was also assigned as flagship of commander Aircraft Squadrons, Battle Fleet for Capt. Stanford E. Moses.

Even before the commissioning of the *Langley*, Whiting, Chevalier, and Griffin had discussed with the pilots of the prospective crew the idea of night flying and how it could be adapted to carrier operation. Whiting was insistent that it was extremely pertinent, even though field operations at that time were sketchy, to say the least. The pictures Whiting drew up of whole squadrons taking off, going on missions of a hundred miles, and returning to the carrier were almost inconceivable to us. He did concede most missions would terminate before sundown but insisted all pilots be qualified in night landings in case of emergency.

With this directive, viewed with some skepticism by quite a few pilots, a program of night flying was scheduled. The first problem was landing lights. At this time, there were no night landing lights of any sort, even for field use. Night flying was scheduled for full moon periods at NAS Hampton Roads. Two rows of buckets, spaced fifty feet apart and the width of *Langley*'s deck, were put on the field and filled with rags doused in oil and a little gasoline. This was supposed to represent the flight deck.

For the first few months, night flying consisted of two or three hours of circling the field and making landings. An officer sat to the side recording each landing and estimating which wire would have been engaged. "Horse" Pennoyer designed a series of boxes with various types of deck lights and louvers to be used as deck edge lights. These were put on the field in place of the buckets of burning rags. The best of these designs was selected for the ship's deck lights. Whiting also investigated the use of various types of floodlights and asked Professor Meggars of the Bureau of Standards down to discuss the use of ultraviolet lighting on the decks. No further work was done on night operations until *Langley* arrived in San Diego in November 1924.

It then became a prime project. All pilots were required to do extensive night flying at North Island in all types of aircraft—VE-7, TS-2, and DT-2. Flare buckets were used on the field, but deck lights were fitted on the mock deck, built on the field alongside the balloon hangar. Practice approaches were made on this field. All pilots made at least one night cross-country to San Pedro and returned following the coastline. Fortunately, *Langley*'s deck was almost into the prevailing wind when port-side-to, and plans were made for actual landings on a flight deck at night.

Some new difficulties immediately appeared. During the day, landing approaches were made in a left-hand turn. To do this required most of the approach to be over North Island and Coronado. The night approach was modified to a run up San Diego Bay with a slight left turn into the groove to landing. Lt. "Gotch" Dillon came in very nicely in a VE-9 and landed with no difficulty but complained about all the miscellaneous lights in the dock area and suggested they be turned out.

Soon all pilots qualified in the VE and TS fighters. Then all qualified in the UO-1 and finally in the Douglas torpedo plane, DT-2. There were several casualties, with one TS ending up still hooked to a wire on the deck while hanging over the side. Most casualties, however, were caused by the tail hook riding a fore-and-aft wire. Pilots were directed, if they went over the side, to try to make it to starboard, as a water landing was considered better than going off onto the dock. The ship's only truck was badly damaged on the dock by a TS! (Trucks were not replaceable in those days.) Finally, landings were made at sea, under way, successfully, and it was considered that all carrier pilots should be qualified for both day and night operations.

The *Langley* was a proud old/new gal. She and those of her kind to follow would show those battleships. From the wrong side of the tracks, and built for a menial job, she was now a flagship in the Battle Fleet. Perhaps she was flagship of a small and—to most of the senior officers— inconsequential force, but the "Covered Wagon" had pioneered one of the greatest innovations in naval warfare.

5

AVIATORS ARE A CRAZY BUNCH OF PEOPLE

Rear Adm. George Van Deurs

G EORGE VAN DEURS *was born in Portland, Oregon, on 25 July 1901, the son of Henry Martin Van Deurs and Sallie Forester Nice Van Deurs. After attending Jefferson High School in Portland, he entered the U.S. Naval Academy with the class of 1921 but was graduated ahead of schedule (because of World War I) and commissioned ensign in June 1920. He subsequently advanced to the grade of commodore, then reverted back to captain in 1946. He transferred to the retired list of the U.S. Navy on 30 June 1951 and was advanced to rear admiral on the basis of combat decorations.*

After graduation, Admiral Van Deurs served in various sea duty assignments before reporting to flight training at Pensacola in the summer of 1923. Designated a naval aviator in January 1924, he subsequently flew with Torpedo Squadron 1 (VT-1), Observation Squadron 3 (VO-3), based on the USS Memphis *(CL-13), Observation Squadron 1 (VO-1), on board the USS* West Virginia *(BB-48), Naval Air Station, Pensacola, and Scouting Squadron 8 (VS-8), based on the tender USS* Jason *(AV-2) on the Asiatic Station. Returning from the Far East in 1932, Admiral Van Deurs served in various aviation billets ashore and afloat, and his wartime duties included the staff of commander,*

Aircraft, South Pacific Force, commanding officer of the escort carrier USS
Chenango *(CVE-28) during the seizure of Morotai, Leyte, and Okinawa,*
and chief of staff to commander, Battleship Squadron 1.

After World War II, Admiral Van Deurs attended the Naval War College,
commanded the carrier USS Philippine Sea *(CV-47), and served on the plan-*
ning staffs of the chief of naval operations and the commander, Eastern Atlantic
and Mediterranean.

Admiral Van Deurs's decorations include the Legion of Merit with two Gold
Stars with Combat "V" and the Navy Unit Commendation ribbon with Bronze
Star. He was made an honorary commander of the Order of the British Empire
by the New Zealand government.

In June 1923, after almost two years as chief engineer on the destroyer
Coghlan (DD-326), I got tired of going down to Philadelphia, Guantánamo Bay, Cuba, and return—and I didn't like either Guantánamo or
Philadelphia. I put in a request for every ship I heard of that was going
somewhere else—surveys, ships in Central America, destroyers going to
China, anything. They all came back the same way: they weren't trans-
ferring engineers as long as their plants were running. I was too proud to
sabotage mine. Besides, I got a tremendous kick out of running it. Nothing ever gave us a bigger thrill, or feeling of power, than standing in the
Coghlan's fire rooms at full power. The blowers drowned speech. Orders
went by sign language. The boilers glared like arc lights, and a slight mistake meant catastrophe.

So I griped about that in Philadelphia one night at a drinking party.
Somebody—I never knew who—said, "I'll tell you how to get out of this
if you want to. Write out a request for aviation. They're hard up for pilots,
and the casualty rate's pretty bad. They're not getting many, and it's got
an overriding priority down in Washington. Anybody that asks for it and
can pass the physical can go to flying."

I said, "I don't know anything about flying machines, never saw any.
I'm an engineer, and I like it, but I don't like this."

"Well, that's easy. You put in for flying, and if you pass the physical they
send you some place in Florida, I can't remember the name of it, to go to
school down there somewhere. You go to ground school for a month.
Then you ride around with some Joe for another month before you have
to try to run the thing yourself. It's all voluntary. You can quit any time

you want to. You just say you don't like it, and they'll send you back to sea—but that's far enough away so there's a fifty-fifty chance they might send you to the West Coast."

So I went back to the ship and wrote out a request for aviation. A fifty-fifty chance was good enough. I hoped to get out to San Diego again. The commanding officer at the time was Lt. Comdr. F. A. LaRoche—"Cocky" LaRoche. I put the request on Cocky's desk, and later LaRoche got me in there and talked to me like a Dutch uncle. "Don't put this thing in, you're ruining your career, you've got a good future ahead of you. You're a good engineer and a good officer. This will ruin you. Aviators are a crazy bunch of people. They haven't got any future at all."

Cocky talked to me for an hour trying to talk me out of it. I didn't want to tell him that I was just putting it in to get off his ship. He was too nice a fellow. I never did tell him that. He finally let it go, but he felt awfully bad about it.

I got down to Pensacola on the 30th of June 1923, and it was hotter'n a firecracker. The whole station was powdery white sand with little narrow concrete roads around it, and you had to hoof it all over the place with a check-in list, and somewhere they loaded you down with a big stack of textbooks that you had to carry back. You checked in here and there, and you got a psychological re-exam in the sick bay. They had a bunch of doctors down there who were "makeylearn" flight surgeons and looking for practice. Then, the last thing on a hot afternoon, they surprised me by saying, "All right, you're checked in. Now go down to the beach and get your pay hop."

Well, going down to the beach was about a mile walk in the heat down there, which I didn't like, and the idea of flying was out. This was the first day, and you're not officially a student till you've been up once. Your flight pay started then. So I hoofed it down to the beach, and they loaded about a dozen of us into a flying boat; Bill Peterson took off and flew us around the bay once. Well, I sat jammed into the bow cockpit with two other people and wondering if it would scare the daylights out of me. But it didn't seem too bad. Finally, after we got up in the air we squeezed up high enough to look out of the plane, and it was fun.

That was my first look at a plane, and it was also love at first sight—sort of—with everybody, I think. We went to ground school for a month, then we went down to the beach half the day and to ground school the other half. The ground school was mostly aeronautical stuff—air navigation, engines, structure of planes, both of which had some shop work connected, a lot of practical work, and a bit of air gunnery and bombing theory and radio code practice, which almost made a nonaviator out of me. I never could read that buzz-buzz worth a hoot.

There was an order at the time that every aviator had to be able to receive twenty words of radio code a minute. At the Naval Academy they tried to teach it to me; every time we went into an electrical engineering class a buzzer started in. It ran for two minutes, and if you copied the message you got a +.3 on your grade for the day. You got .1 off for every mistake to −.3. Well, I took the −.3 every day I was there. I'd been building radio sets since I was ten years old trying to read them, but I never could.

When you got the twenty words of Morse code you could check out of that department. I never did get it, but at Christmas time, I was the last student they'd been working on for a couple of months, and I think everybody in the radio place wanted to get some Christmas leave, so they said I took twenty words a minute. I'm not sure I ever did, but they let me loose. I'd been taking extra instruction for months over there.

In the flight syllabus, I started out in a Curtiss N-9, a single-float seaplane with a fuselage very much like a Jenny, the old land plane trainer. The wings were a little bigger, and it had a float under it. It wasn't too bad with the engines they had in them then. The original engine they had during World War I was a 100-horsepower Curtiss OXX-6 that was very much underpowered. By the time I got there they had a Hispano-Suiza A engine that gave it about 150 horses, and they still had a margin of about 5 knots between full speed and stalling. You had to hold the speed just right.

The instructor rode the front seat, and the student rode the back seat where he had no instruments except a tachometer and an oil pressure gauge. Anybody that needed instruments to fly by in those days was considered unsafe. As a matter of fact, "instrument flier" was a term of contempt, you just didn't ride with one. Night flying you did when there was enough starlight or moonlight to see something, but you didn't fly in a fog. You had to learn the feel of the things. The plane was unstable. If a wing went down, you had to pick it up. Same with the nose. There was no inherent stability in the plane. You had to keep within that 5-knot speed and keep it from slipping or skidding.

The instructor took you out and rode you around the bay and said, "Now you try it, fly straight down the bay." You had a crash helmet on that had speaking tubes in the ears and a flexible tube that went up to the instructor, and he had a canvas mouthpiece so he could yell into your ears, but it was purely one way. You couldn't tell him anything. We went around the bay, with him saying, "Your left wing is low, pick up your right wing, don't dive, your nose is too high." That went on for three-quarters of an hour, and by that time you were pretty well pooped. Actually, that was about all you could take to start out with. You had to get enough to solo after about ten hours of instruction. When your instructor thought you were ready, he'd put you up for a solo check. If you didn't pass the solo check in ten hours, you might by grace of the academic board get an extra three. If you didn't make it on that, you were out, back to sea.

One of the first things your instructor did was to put the plane in a spin and bring it out, to show you what it felt like, because if you stalled the thing, it spun right now. If you lost that 5 knots with the nose up, why the wing would whip down and you were in a spin, and if you didn't know how to come out, it could be fatal. So that was practically the first instruction you got. The instructor talking through this mouthpiece would put the plane in and bring it out, "See, this is the way it is, just pull the nose up, it's stalling, the wing'll fall off in a minute—there she goes, now, let it go 'round once, let it go round twice, now put the controls forward, kick the opposite rudder—it straightens out. Now it's in a dive. Pull it out, and we're flying."

That was easy. One classmate there named Hanson, an ex-bluejacket, kind of an anemic looking little bird, had a great big instructor named Joe Finch, built like a barrel-chested bull, a big husky guy. Well, after a couple of hours of instruction, Hanson let this thing get into a spin on him, and he froze at the controls; he yanked the wheel back to his chest and hung onto it just scared to death. Finch had been sitting with his arms crossed on his chest, and the wheel came back in the front cockpit where there wasn't much room and jammed his arm so he couldn't get loose. He whooped and yelled at Hanson and struggled to get loose and push the wheel forward. He couldn't do it. They spun in. Everybody kidded Joe Finch for letting a little bit of a guy like that spin him in, but it was just the extra strength of stark terror.

They landed in the water of Pensacola Bay, and when they hit, the wheel just cushioned Finch. He didn't get hurt at all. He just rode the wheel forward. The little guy in the back seat was still hanging onto the wheel, and he went right through into the forward cockpit. Those planes were made of wood and fabric, and the fuselage was braced with cross-wires like piano wire. Those crosswires carved Hanson's shins all to pieces. He was in the hospital for months before they got his legs back in shape. But he never got another chance to fly. After freezing on the controls, he was finished.

When your instructor thought you'd learned enough to stagger around the bay and land and take off, he'd put you up for a solo check, which meant the chief inspector took you up, and you flew him around, and if it seemed like you were safe he'd send you out alone. That was really the big test. The rumor was that nobody who'd ever soloed had busted out afterward. It was pretty close to true. If you soloed, in time you'd be an aviator. You were pretty ragged and so on, but . . . .

It was a very tense deal, so of course, I guess everybody did worse on the solo check than they ever did with their own instructor. Before I got that far, about the middle of the ten hours, I got a finger caught in an engine over in the ground school and clipped about a quarter of an inch off one finger. I walked down to sick bay, walked in holding this thing up, "Hey, doc, I cut the end off my finger, do something about it."

Dr. Defony happened to be there. Through the years we got to be great pals. We served together a lot of times after that. But at that time Defony had never been sick a day in his life, and to him sailor men were tough characters, could take anything. The doctor hunted around the little surgery they had there, and he couldn't find sutures, and he couldn't find needles. He messed around until all the shock wore off and then without any kind of anesthesia at all, he started sewing it up—nearly killed me. He took two or three stitches, put a bandage on it, and said, "Go back to school."

Well, for a couple of days I tried to fly with this thing, but every time I'd reach for the throttle or the bandage touched anything, I pretty nearly jumped out of the plane. I was using up my ten hours without getting anywhere, so I went on the sick list and waited till I got a little bit better. I got a bit behind the class that way, but I still did alright on the solo thing.

After that there was maybe thirty more hours of instruction and practice. You flew for five hours practicing something they told you to, then you'd go up for the five-hour check. Then the instructor would show you the stuff you were supposed to practice for the next five hours. That ended up with a stunt check. You had to loop, spin, do wingovers and the falling leaf, maybe two or three other things. Then you had to shoot the boat.

They had a boat or marker anchored out in the bay, and you climbed up, got about 1,000 feet over it, and then cut the switch. With a dead engine, you had to spiral down and make a landing so that the plane stopped within fifty feet of the boat—and it wasn't fair to hit the boat. If you saw you were going to overshoot and hit the boat to keep from overshooting, that was a foul. One bird landed in the boat, and that didn't go either. There was one more catch to it. After you landed close to the boat, you had to get out and crank the engine and start it and fly it back to the beach. If you couldn't get the engine started, you flunked. People used to line up on the beach watching somebody take a boat shot, and if he didn't get the engine going that was a big joke. You'd sit there and laugh while he cranked and cranked. If you didn't get it going by sundown they'd send a boat out to tow you in—and you were busted, although you'd probably get another shot at it.

In the N-9, there was a gas tank in front of the forward cockpit, between the cockpit and the engine. In the middle of the gas tank was a tube, and there was a long crank that went through that tube and catch on the back of the engine. If you had to crank the thing, you stood on a wing and leaned down into the cockpit and cranked. It was a backbreaking sort of a show. If you were wise you took an oil tank full of gasoline with you. Before you tried to start the engine, you opened little priming cocks on top of the engine, squirted a little gas in each cylinder, closed the cocks, then cranked it and made it go. One marine pal of mine got caught without his gas can. He finally got wise. He had his necktie in his pocket—took the top off the gas tank, dangled the necktie down there, soaked up some gas so then he could squeeze that into the petcocks.

After we finished up the N-9, we moved over to the little Curtiss HS-2 flying boat—a three-place biplane, with a Liberty engine behind your neck, two pilots with a man on the bow. They called them "angel makers." When they crashed it was always fatal. This was the smallest flying boat they had, and plenty were left over from World War I. The reason they were unsafe was that they were built like no other plane I ever flew. Ordinarily, on the tail surface of a plane, a modern plane, the force is down on the tail when you're flying so if the engines quit, or you lose power, the plane goes into a glide. When the air pressure on the tail is released, the tail tends to rise.

The HS-2 was built the other way. The tail was contributing to the lift, so if the engine quit, the tail dropped, the nose went up, and the plane stalled, and there wasn't enough control surface to lift the stalled tail. If you ever got in that position there was nothing you could do to get that nose down again and get it into a glide. You'd just spin and keep on spinning; you couldn't take it out, unless you had power. You had to use full power to come out of a spin, so they never spun them.

It was a nice boat; the engine was behind you, and there was a pusher propeller back of the wings. You were sitting out front. You flew it about 60 knots, and you didn't have to wear goggles if you didn't want to. None of us wore safety belts in flying boats in those days. They were there, but nobody bothered wearing them. You didn't have a parachute. You were just sitting there like driving a car—nice, sunny day, it was fun riding around in the things. But if the engine so much as coughed, you slammed the controls right to the dashboard to get the nose down and into a glide, and then you looked around to see what went wrong. You didn't hesitate. If the oil pressure started to get down or the water temperature started to go up or the engine just missed once, why you slammed it into a glide quick!

We soloed those things for about ten hours and then started in gunnery. They put two students in an H-boat. One of them would fly it, the other would be up on the bow with a machine gun shooting at a target or bombing with little miniature bombs. You were supposed to do your stuff and then land and swap places, and the other man would do his turn. But that was sissy. If you stood up in the bow cockpit of one of these things, you were out of the cockpit about to your waist or more, and you'd flop down on the rounded hull top; you could just get your fingers on the pilot's cockpit. So the man on the bow would secure his gun after he'd done the shooting, stand up, flop down, then pull himself over the top of the plane into the pilot's cockpit and sit down in the other seat. Then if you weren't a sissy, you stood up in the pilot's cockpit and dove for the forward cockpit and pulled yourself in.

Some of the people used to shoot ducks from the H-boats. There wasn't any law against it then, and it was fun to take her out and put one man in the bow with a shotgun. If you came up behind a herd of ducks flying along, cruising nice and easy, you could get one blast at them with the shotgun, and then the ducks would cut in another boiler, put on the speed, and go right off and leave you. You never got two shots. They could go a lot faster than an H-boat. They just didn't do it unless you shot at them once. And if you hit anything, then you circled around and landed and picked it up.

If you didn't get killed in the H-boats—none of my class did—then you went to twin-engine boats, the Curtiss F-5Ls, which were probably the finest wooden flying boats that were ever built. They were really quite a machine. They had two Liberty engines, about 104-foot wing span, two pilots, and a bow cockpit like an H-boat, with the gas tanks in the hull behind the pilots. But behind them there was another compartment with a place for a radio man, and three machine guns, one on top and one on each side.

You got some instruction, a solo check, then practiced in those a bit, and did some more gunnery, bombing, and navigational work. For navigation training, they put three students in an F-5L—one of them back in the tail working the radio, one flying, and one up in the bow doing the navigating. You'd have a problem to go twenty, thirty miles down the coast, then cut out into the gulf to intercept a tug that was supposed to be out there somewhere, then go back in and make a landfall on the lighthouse at Pensacola.

I was teamed up with a little marine who had been thrown out three times for being undersized, and he finally had enough political pull the fourth time to come down there to stay in the class. Well, none of the seats or controls on any of these planes was adjustable; it was quite a distance from the seat of an F-5L to the rudder bars that you kept your feet on. During World War I, and for quite a while afterward, they always picked the biggest men to fly the flying boats because you needed a very long reach and long legs to really handle them. For certain maneuvers in a flying boat you had to be able to get the controls all the way back or all the way forward. If you didn't have a long reach, you couldn't get that wheel forward enough. The distance during normal operations was about average for anybody, perfectly comfortable; but with the full throw you had to have pretty long arms.

To reach the rudder bars, and to be able to get adequate forward movement on the controls, little Jack the marine had a sawed off apple box that he'd put behind him, so that he was just sitting on about an inch of the seat. It was kind of scary to be up in the bow as the navigator and look back and see Jack flying along, and all of a sudden, if the air got a little rough, he'd fall off the seat, just disappear. The plane would be going this way or that while he climbed back up into his seat and grabbed the controls. Then we'd be all right.

They had a crash alarm system, and when a plane crashed anywhere bells rang all over the station, and a siren went off. There was a big tower down at the waterfront, three, four hundred feet high, with watchstanders on top of the tower who could survey the whole seaplane course. They controlled the crash bell from up there. At the base of the tower was a wet basin for crash boats, ready all the time, and two or three of them were big high-powered sea sleds that could do about 40 or 50 knots. One of them was tied with the stern up against the seawall headed out, with the engine warmed up.

When the crash bell rang, a couple of doctors would come sprinting out of sick bay, about a block away, racing like hell, and when the first one of them jumped from the seawall into the boat, the coxswain threw off the line and away they went. Little Dr. Poppin—kind of roly-poly with a red moustache and red hair—always won the race, was always the first guy in the crash boat. He was quite a bird. He was too kindhearted to be a good doctor. It hurt him to do anything to anybody. But he was a wonderful research man, and he had some things that seemed like far out theories at the time, but some of them proved out.

The crash bell went off while we were still in ground school; a formation of marines had had a collision. They were in land planes flying back to the station. One plane went across and cut the tail off another one. The crew didn't have any parachutes. The plane that lost the tail had two people in it, and it flipped over on its back and spun in. The other plane was chopped up, flopped over on its back, and spun down. Just before it hit, it flopped right side up and landed right in the middle of the main road up to the station—right behind a team of mules that an old black man was driving in a wagon. He used to drive the mules through the swamps with a barrel of kerosene, putting it in ponds to kill the mosquitoes.

When we got there the mules had left horseshoe marks in the concrete, and wagon, mules, and driver were missing. It took about three days to find him out in the woods. He really took off. The marine who was in that one wasn't hurt badly, but he was in the hospital for shock for quite some time, and he never flew again. Just the sight of an airplane did things to him. He went down to Haiti and lost an eye down there in some mess with the guerrillas. Under the law you couldn't retire a man for injury in battle, so he was around as a one-eyed marine for years after that.

I had a couple of crashes down there. Little Dr. Poppin found me in both of them. I told him years later I felt safer when he wasn't around; he'd pulled me out of every crash I ever had—I liked him but I thought I was better off when he was somewhere else.

We got by the seaplane training all right without anybody getting killed. There were some funny crashes—and a lot of near misses. We got our wings when we finished the flying boat business, in January 1924. I was in class no. 19, naval aviator no. 3109. The attrition for my class after we completed training and went on to the fleet was pretty high. I think there were only about half of us still flying about three years later. Some were killed; some of them were crippled; some of them were retired; some of them got the wind up and quit. One of them was lost in the Dole race to Honolulu. He was navigating one of the planes and was never heard of again. One of them retired with a bad back. One got married, and his wife talked him out of the navy. Jack Clausing, the little marine that used to fly with me, died in a fire in Shanghai. They weren't all aviation accidents, but funny things happened, they just got cleaned out. After that most of us lasted till the Second World War.

Up to that time all naval aviators had been seaplane pilots, but the *Langley* (CV-1) was coming along, and we knew we were going to have land planes on carriers, so we started to do land plane training. You got your wings, were designated a naval aviator, then stuck around a little while to learn land planes. We got into flying Jennies, the old JN Curtiss plane used by the navy from 1916 into the early 1920s, and they were more fun than an N-9. You had to go through the same kind of training routine— five hours and a check, finally ending up with a stunt hop and so on.

We also had to do cross-country flying, which was new and kind of fun, maybe a hundred miles. They put two students in a plane, and they would fly to Pascagoula, Mississippi, get some gas, take off, and come back. They usually sent two planes together because we didn't have any radio. We navigated by land marks. We'd have a Rand McNally state map, and we looked at that, picking out railroads and rivers and other land- marks. The fellow who did the flying going over would do the navigating coming back and vice versa.

After we got through with the Jennies they split the class up; some people took fighter training in some little land planes we had—they weren't much in the way of fighters—and about six people took spotting training, to go spotting for ships. They used de Havilland DH-4B land planes, a big heavy army type with a Liberty engine in them. There was a big space, about ten feet maybe, between the front cockpit and the rear cockpit. They took the controls out of the rear cockpit and put a radio set in there, so one student would be back there with the radio. The other student up front was flying the DH. The DH was kind of heavy, and they were flying formation and practicing spotting all the time with these radio sets.

On a Monday morning—17 March 1924—the spotters took off, including Henry Mullinnix, one of the senior people in the class. He died years later at Tarawa during World War II when the Japanese blew up the USS *Liscome Bay* (CVE-56). Henry graduated at the top of his class at the Academy; he was sort of a stolid type, a serious student, but he didn't catch onto ideas quick. He thought kind of slow but very certain. Henry was leading the formation, and his backseat man was a chap named "Bubbles" Fisher, who later pulled the wings off a plane practicing dive-bombing at San Diego.

To form up the formation, Mullinnix flew in a very careful circle while the other people came in and joined up. Henry was very intent, looking only ahead and keeping his plane at a constant speed. Finally the plane that was supposed to be on his starboard side came in too fast and overshot. Charlie Porter was flying it, with Olin R. Minor in the backseat, and Charlie tried to pull up and check his speed, but he'd already closed his throttle when he saw he was coming in fast. Well, if you pulled the DH up without power on, it settled, and poor Bubbles Fisher was sitting in the backseat watching this thing come right at him, and it squatted on top of him. It just missed Bubbles, but hit the top wing. The two wings locked, and the landing gear of the top plane cut about a foot off each end of the propeller on Mullinnix's plane, so the engine began racing like crazy. Porter's propeller also punched holes in Henry's wing and cut the control wire for the ailerons. Porter's wing collapsed, then fell off. His plane flopped over on its back and spun in the middle of the field, killing them both right there.

Mullinnix, this stolid Dutchman, kept his engine wide open, made one big sweep around the air station, just got over the fence and managed to get that wing up some way and landed all right—rolled out in the middle of the field and started to open the throttle and taxi into the flight line! By that time the cylinders were all ready to come off the over-speeding engine, and everything was loose on the plane. Fisher jumped up in the backseat with a fire extinguisher, hit Henry over the head, and said, "I've had enough, I'm walking from here!" Henry thought it over and decided he'd walk too, so they cut the switch and walked in. Porter and Olin Minor were the only two casualties in my class of about thirty-six before we got out of there. There were more later.

This incident happened on a day they didn't have parachutes. That made Christians out of us because people stood there on the field watching this plane slowly spin around upside down, and the two people in it, all they had to do was release their belt and fall out if they'd had a 'chute—but they didn't. As soon as we got parachutes we all wore them. But a lot of people didn't think they were worthwhile, and for a long time we didn't wear them in the flying boats because there was no way to get out of a flying boat. The propellers on the twin-engine flying boat were right behind the pilot. If you went out of the cockpit the prop would chew you up. You couldn't possibly miss it.

I was assigned to torpedo plane training at Pensacola, which lasted about a month. While Mullinnix and the others were flying DHs, we were flying twin-float seaplanes. It was the first twin-float stuff we had— a wartime plane, the Curtiss R-6L, sort of a hermaphrodite that had been built as a training plane and somebody finally put a Liberty V-12 engine in the front end of it and added an extra panel on the wings. It would just stagger off the water with a pint of gas and a little tiny torpedo that was about twelve inches in diameter and maybe six or eight feet long. It had been built for the first submarines we ever had, the A-class submarines. If you didn't drop it higher than about three or four feet, it might run maybe about two thousand yards.

After you got used to the planes, they'd put a dummy on one, just a log that was shaped like a torpedo, with some fins on it. You tried to get down within six feet of the water and aim at the target and let it go. After practicing with the dummy, I think you had three live drops. I was out for my first live drop, and I suddenly realized the water was very glassy. When the water is absolutely smooth, you can't tell how high you are above it at all. It's just like looking at a mirror. You can't tell where that mirror is.

I came down thinking I was six feet high and headed for a target boat right in Pensacola Bay in front of the air station. I suddenly thought, "Gee whiz, I don't know where I am, this is too low, I'd better pull up"—and just at that time I hit. I just kissed the water. It was perfectly flat, but with the extra weight of the torpedo, the plane couldn't take it—the pontoons spread out, and the plane went in nose down. All I could think of was, "Crashed again!" I didn't get wet more than up to my knees. The crash boat came out, and my friend Dr. Poppin fished me out.

There was a plane following me; one of the H-boats used to follow planes on the range and chase torpedoes down the range. When I crashed my torpedo broke loose and kept going. I wondered why the hell the chase plane didn't land and fish me out, but he disappeared down range, chasing the torpedo. Believe it or not, the torpedo made a hit down at the other end of the range. I had to argue like hell to get that hit counted. I said, "If it was wartime you wouldn't care whether the plane crashed or not if it got a hit—it's a hit." I finally got the school talked into counting that as a hit, one of my live drops, regardless of the fact that I ruined one airplane.

In May of that year I was assigned duty with Torpedo Squadron 1 attached to the tender USS *Wright* at Norfolk. I was kind of chagrined when I reported in to VT-1 and on the bulletin board was a clipping from some newspaper that Lt. (jg) G. Van Deurs had made the first submerged launching of a torpedo from an airplane!

6

THE THREE SEA HAWKS

Capt. Daniel Webb Tomlinson IV

DANIEL WEBB TOMLINSON IV, *born in Batavia, New York, 28 April 1897, was appointed to the U.S. Naval Academy in 1914 and was commissioned ensign in June 1917 with the class of 1918. Subsequent sea-duty stations included the minelayer USS* Dubuque *(PG-17), the battleship USS* Georgia *(BB-15), and the destroyer USS* Breese *(DD-122), before he reported to Pensacola for flight training.*

Tomlinson's assignments following his designation as a naval aviator on 11 August 1921 included Naval Air Station, San Diego, the battleship USS Oklahoma *(BB-37), and the Department of Marine Engineering and Naval Construction at the Naval Academy. In October 1925 Tomlinson reported to Fighting Squadron 2B (VF-2B), which over the next three years became VF-6B and then VB-2B in July 1928. Tomlinson served as flight officer, executive officer, and was commanding officer when he led the squadron's aerobatic group, the Three Sea Hawks, at the National Air Races at Mines Field, California, in 1928.*

After duty with the Test Section, Naval Air Station, Anacostia, D.C., Tomlinson resigned from the navy on 28 February 1929 to enter commercial aviation. During the period between his resignation and his return to active duty with the U.S. Naval Reserve in 1941, he was a recognized figure in commercial aviation, serving in administrative, management, and engineering positions with Trans World Airlines (TWA), and as a pilot flying the night mail across the Alleghenies. He set new speed and endurance records for transport planes in the Douglas DC-1 while conducting engineering and flight research for TWA. Later Tomlinson flew test flights for North American Aviation and the Curtiss Wright Company; he flew for TWA between Kansas City and New York; and, in June 1939, he became chief engineer for TWA.

Following a year as vice president in charge of engineering for TWA, Tomlinson returned to active duty in the rank of commander, U.S. Naval Reserve. Subsequent assignments included commanding officer of the Naval Reserve Aviation Base, Kansas City, Kansas, commander of the Naval Reserve Aviation Base Gardner, Kansas, and chief of staff to the commander, Naval Air Primary Training Command. In September 1943 he reported as commander, Air Transport Squadron, Pacific, and in March 1945 he was designated commander, Naval Air Transport Service, Pacific Wing.

Captain Tomlinson left active service in 1946 and then was recalled to active duty in 1948 to serve as deputy commander of the Berlin Airlift. He closed his service career as deputy commander, Continental Division, Military Air Transport Service, and retired officially on 1 August 1951.

It's significant in respect to my development that I was taken to see the first hot-air balloon ascension in my hometown of Batavia, New York. It was one of those early hot-air balloons where they built a big bonfire, filled the bag through a conduit, and launched the balloon into the air, with the balloonist hanging onto a trapeze. When the bag was filled full of hot air and smoke, it would go up maybe 1,000 or 1,500 feet. When he sensed the time was right, the balloonist just cut loose and came down with a parachute. Then the balloon turned over, belched smoke out into the sky, and fell!

I became enamored of kite flying—anything that went up in the air. There was an older boy who lived across the street who was really good at building and flying kites, and he taught me how to build all kinds of kites. I built one big enough so that I had to use a clothesline to hold it. I rigged a little trapeze on the line, and I was going to send a little kid, about five years old, up with it. I said, "I'll give you a ride. Here, you sit on this bar." Fortunately, when the kid was only about six or seven feet in the air, my stepmother came out and stopped that monkey business.

The next thing that impressed me greatly was the Curtiss exhibition flier who was paid to come and put on a flight from the half-mile track west of town while I was in high school. I skipped school and went to the fairgrounds and was out on the racetrack. The pilot was going to take off in front of the grandstands toward the north. Airplanes had no brakes in those days, so he had to have people hold the plane as he ran up the engine. I was there hanging on when he nodded his head, and everybody let go. He got off the ground, and when he was just about at the end of the grandstand, he suddenly hit a down draft and crashed into a fence at the edge of the track. I was the first one to reach the wrecked plane. He had one leg broken, tangled up in the wires. He was smoking a cigar and cursing a blue streak. I decided then, "I'm going to be an aviator!"

The next airplane pilot I saw was Calbraith P. Rodgers, a civilian, who made the first coast-to-coast airplane flight in 1911. Cal Rodgers wanted $500 to fly over towns on his route. The Batavia tightwads wouldn't pay the $500, but we figured he'd circle close enough so we could see him. They were just finishing the new Episcopal church steeple at that time. My grandfather and uncle took me up in this tower to watch the plane. We could see him coming from Buffalo. He was flying 200 or 300 feet over the New York Central tracks, which went right through the center of town. When he came to the west edge of the town, he turned and went around the south side. I'll never forget my very dignified old grandfather; as the plane went by, he started jabbing his walking stick on the floor and said, "Damn fool! Damn fool!" I have often wished that the old gentleman had lived long enough to see what happened to the grandson at his side. He died in 1917, just before I graduated from the Naval Academy.

I had a great-uncle by marriage, Charles Jackson Train, who married my great-aunt Grace Tomlinson. He became a rear admiral and was commander, U.S. Asiatic Fleet, from March 1905 to his death in August 1906. He visited my grandfather a number of times, and there was a lot of talk about Europe and Russia. At the appropriate time, I was taken by my father down to the Brooklyn Navy Yard and taken through some ships to excite my interest.

I took my entrance examinations at the post office in Rochester, New York, in April 1914 and entered the Naval Academy in June. After I got in there, I discovered I was being paid $60 a month and getting my education. It was kind of rigorous, but I decided, "This is all right."

I had no serious trouble at the Naval Academy. I could have probably stood better scholastically than I did, but, again, I was deeply interested in aviation. I spent a lot of time building model airplanes, flying them with rubber bands in the armory. I knew a lot about models, how they flew, basic aerodynamics. In 1916, on leave from the Naval Academy, I bought a motorcycle. My father said, "Young man, you had better learn how to take care of the engine and the whole machine. I will show you, and then you will take care of it yourself." Of course, it was only a one-cylinder Indian engine, but the principles of the internal-combustion engine were all there. Later at the Naval Academy, when the time came for me to study internal-combustion engines, I knew more about them than the lieutenant who was trying to instruct. I would take over and explain them. I obviously inherited my father's mechanical bent.

In 1915 I went to the West Coast on cruise as a midshipman and watched Art Smith fly at the San Francisco Exposition. Art Smith was good; he was my hero. He did loops and spins and everything with his pusher. I thought, "That's for me." Then 1916 came along, and Glenn Curtiss set up a school in Buffalo to train people to go to England as instructors. No fee—he'd train you, but then you had to go to England as an instructor. I applied, without consulting my family. I was accepted, but to get out of the Naval Academy honorably—I discovered to my horror—I'd have to have my father's permission. Of course, he wouldn't give it. I was brokenhearted, because I didn't care about anything except flying. I stuck it out, hoping that when I graduated I'd be able to get into the aviation branch of the navy.

In 1917 the war was on, and we were graduated a year ahead of time because there was a shortage of junior officers. I applied for aviation—period! However, all my class had to go to sea because we'd studied steam engineering, navigation, regulations, etc. So it was not until I had completed several different sea duty assignments that I was able to go to flight training. Upon completion of flight training, I served a year at the Naval Air Station, San Diego, and then received orders to the battleship *Oklahoma*, and I bought my first Curtiss JN from the army. During weekends ashore, or whenever I could, I barnstormed the Pacific Northwest.

Between 1923 and 1925, I was an instructor in the Department of Marine Engineering and Naval Construction at the Naval Academy. During this period I completely overhauled my second Jenny in the pattern shop of the department. The interest engendered in the midshipmen while I was rebuilding this airplane resulted in the incorporation of a course in aeronautics in the Academy curriculum. In September 1925, when I left the Academy, I obtained thirty days leave and flew my rebuilt Jenny across the continent to my new duty station in San Diego. This type of plane had never been flown across the continental divide, and there was considerable doubt that it could be done, but I managed to fly from my home, Batavia, New York, to San Diego without too much trouble.

I joined Fighting Squadron 2B (VF-2B) at North Island in October 1925 and began one of the most exciting and rewarding squadron tours of my career. After I joined the squadron, Lt. Comdr. F. W. "Spig" Wead conceived the idea of glide bombing. We had Vought VE-7s, which were nice airplanes—180-horsepower, Hispano engines built under a license by Wright—a good-flying airplane. We fixed up the original experimental bomb racks under the wings to drop little marker bombs that had smoke shells in them. We started trying this style of attack at Ream Field, a little Army Air Corps practice landing field that had been abandoned. But the field was available as a place where we could place a marker, so we started trying the idea.

We found that we could come somewhere within a couple of hundred feet of the target. We couldn't dive the VE-7s steep enough to give accuracy. In late September 1926, we got the first Curtiss F6C Hawks, which had a top speed of 155 mph at sea level. That was a horse of a different color. We soon found out that with this one airplane, which could really dive, we could start hitting the target. We'd approach in echelon at about 20,000 feet—the leader choosing the approach altitude—and fly over the target. We liked to make the dive into the wind if possible. We would come downwind and look over the side until you figured you were above the target. Then you'd do a half roll, and down you'd come. We were making maybe 60- to 70-degree dives, at least. If you did it right, you'd be near vertical over that target at about 1,500 feet. We tried to release somewhere around 1,000 to 1,500 feet or under. We had to be careful because sometimes we'd get too near terminal velocity as we got the newer airplanes and learned how to fly them. In the average pullout, we'd probably get seven or eight "gees."

Before long, we got an F6C-4 with a Wasp engine. It had a special landing gear for landing aboard the carrier. It had hooks on the axle to pick up the fore-and-aft wires; that was the only difference between the standard army version, Curtiss PW-8, that we first received. Then, in a very short time, less than a month, we got two Boeing FB-2s. They were what the army called the PW-9; it was the Boeing answer to the Hawk. It had the same 12-cylinder Curtiss engine, known as the D-12. Their flight characteristics were very close to the Curtiss Hawk. It wasn't quite as nice handling or as maneuverable a plane as the Hawk was, but it was okay.

Soon we transferred our practice dive-bombing operations from Ream Field to the old parade ground at Camp Kearny, which today is NAS Miramar. Then Spig put in official reports on what we were doing. We'd been doing this at first strictly off the cuff to find out if it was feasible. The Bureau of Ordnance set up annual dive-bombing exercises to be carried out and official records to be kept of each pilot's accuracy. It has always irritated me that Spig Wead never received any credit for it. He got credit for a lot of things, but that was the greatest contribution that he made. After all, it was dive-bombing that won the Battle of Midway and other major battles; it was what sank the Jap carriers and major ships.

After I had landed on North Island in October 1925, I wondered what I was going to do with my Jenny. I looked around. VF-2B had two hangars, the operations hangar and the engineering hangar. One side of the engineering hangar might have one VE-7 in it. There was a lot of available space. We got permission from Capt. Joseph M. Reeves, who was commander, Aircraft Squadrons Battle Fleet, to keep my airplane in the engineering hangar. There I was, flight officer of the squadron, with my own private airplane and special permission to keep it in the engineering hangar. Very handy. When the navy hauled down the "balls"—signals on the mast on the balloon annex—it meant the weather was unfit to fly. I could then pull the Jenny out and would fly it to Long Beach to have a chat with Earl Daugherty or drop in and see Eddie Martin at Santa Ana. I flew at night, too, just to make people aware that night flying was no real problem.

I used it a lot for hunting in the fall. I'd come over before daylight and take off. I had a number of fields picked in the back country. I'd always drive over these in my Ford car before I landed there because of the gopher holes and ditches not easily seen from the air. I'd come back with my limit of dove or quail in time for quarters for muster at nine o'clock in the morning. That was a great life I had with that plane at my disposal any time. I don't know of anybody else in naval aviation who enjoyed that prerogative.

In January 1926, we were to make a cruise on the *Langley* (CV-1), so we started training in December 1925. A practice landing field was set up on the area of North Island that was Rockwell Field. Everybody was supposed to make a hundred practice landings on this crazy training deck. I laughed. I went down and looked at the *Langley* and said to the flight deck officer, "This is easy. For three years I have been flying passengers off fields smaller than this. What's the mystery?"

Of course, they didn't like that at all because the *Langley* was a real sacred cow, the first navy carrier. Landing on it was supposed to be very difficult. Actually, the established landing procedure was what made the landing difficult. The approaching pilot was to fly his airplane searching for signals from a signal officer on a platform on the stern, just off the port side of the landing area; he had a flag in each hand. The pilot was *not* to use the landing deck in any way as a point of reference. The results—and there are ample movies to confirm my estimate of the picture—were from ludicrous to sad.

After I made two or three landings, then I started coming in doing a loop to a landing. I'd just come down, practically roll my wheels up and over, and land on the spot. Lt. Comdr. Frank D. "Honus" Wagner, who was now the squadron commander, got a little irritated about that and said, "I don't think you need to make any more landings."

Lt. Adolphus W. "Jake" Gorton and a couple of other guys were signalmen. The idea was that you were supposed to come in and watch the signalman. You were supposed to watch him and fly your airplane from what he was telling you with these flags. Then, when he ran the flag across his throat, you were supposed to cut your throttle and fall on the deck. The number one signal officer, Jake Gorton, was a friend of mine. I told Jake what he could do with his flags when he knew I was coming in.

The regulation procedure was supposed to terminate in a full-stall landing, minimum speed. They frequently did it with the result that the plane crashed into the barrier or on the deck with broken wheels or broken landing gear. I simply watched the rise and fall of the stern and kept a safe 5 mph above stall speed. That gave me adequate control, and I made a wheel landing under control between the ramp and the first wire. True, I pulled the first wire out maybe ten feet farther than if my landing speed was full stall. As my hook caught, I would ease forward slightly on the stick—always a gentle, smooth landing. I made sixty-one landings and missed the first wire once. I got bawled out several times, but they finally gave up. It was impossible for certain senior people, real old-timers, to admit they were wrong.

I could lay the plane on the deck where I wanted it to go. The tail would probably be about six inches off the deck. These other people were coming in there falling onto the deck—a damn good landing if they didn't fall over two feet. Some of them would fall three or four feet, break the wheels, catch the third or fourth wire. Some of them would float over the gear; they'd wait too long. They would watch the signal man and fly into the barrier. It was a laugh. They got a little irate at me, but I just said, "Sorry, boys. *I'm* flying that airplane." Of course, that's what they're doing today. They're flying into the gear. There have been changes.

We checked out on board ship with the VE-7s, and then I checked out on the Curtiss Hawks and the FB-2s. No problem; I used my procedure. I went six or seven miles an hour faster because it was a little heavier airplane and more tender near stall.

Old "Whiskers" Reeves, as we called him, wanted to put on a demonstration of an attack on the flagship in the Pacific Fleet. So in October 1926, we went out from San Diego with F6C Hawks and made this dive-bombing attack, and it really shook them up. When we got back from the exercise, we were laughing. We could look down and see people ducking and lying down on the bridge. We came down a little bit low. Those things made the damnedest roar you ever heard. They were something.

Coming to the end of 1926, the admiral figured that's what we'd take on the cruise to the Caribbean in 1927. The *Langley* was going to go through the canal to the Caribbean that year. By the end of January 1927, we had been designated VF-6B, and we had Boeing FB-5s, which had one bad characteristic that I didn't like. It had this big, heavy Packard motor. When you were coming in the way these signal flag people were bringing people in, practically on the edge of a stall, it was very critical. You could just give it a little power to increase speed. The FB-5 fully stalled if you gave it too much power. The sudden torque of this 500-horsepower motor meant you were on your back in a flash. I could see pilots getting low on *Langley* approaches goosing that Packard a mite too much, then on their backs 100 to 200 feet off the water. It took the FB-5 a good 500 feet to recover from an inverted stall position—deadly at low altitude. I did a lot of practice at altitude. I used to practice marginal conditions, get at top cloud level and fall into cloud layers. I didn't like that

FB-5 characteristic a bit. In that squadron, I could practically put my finger on certain pilots and say that they were sure to go in.

Boeing had used excess World War I wheels on the FB-5s. These wheels used to collapse with the plane parked in the hangar! Only a few pilots qualified with them on the *Langley*. I had no trouble, but others attempting the standard stall landing broke many wheels. I always wrote my father newsy letters about what was going on and what I thought about things. I never pulled any punches. I wrote a letter to him when we got the FB-5s. The admiral was joyous about what they did as dive-bombers, and he was all gung ho to take them on the cruise on the *Langley* in early 1927. I said, "I'm afraid if we take those airplanes, we're going to lose two or three people in the squadron for sure." What I didn't know was that my father played baseball on the Cornell team with Jim Wadsworth, who at that time was a senator and chairman of the Military Affairs Committee. Without consulting me, he sent my letter to Senator Wadsworth, and Wadsworth took it up to the Navy Department.

I heard about that right quick. It happened pretty fast, just before these planes were supposed to go on the *Langley*. That scared old Reeves, and, boy, he didn't dare take them. But he wrote me a letter, grounding me from flying fast airplanes because of my expressed fear of them. I was left behind to have the FB-5 all ready when the *Langley* returned. So I laughed. When the *Langley* finally took off with the VE-7s on the cruise, I took off in my JN as a good-bye gesture. They were out probably ten to fifteen miles off the shore. I dived right down alongside the bridge with the Jenny, did a loop, and thumbed my nose at them as I went by. Not a word was ever said about it.

By the time they came back from the cruise, I had the FB-5s all ready for big squadron operations for the summer of 1927. We were afraid—and the admiral was too—of what would happen if we had to land one of the FB-5s in the water. With that big, heavy motor up in the nose, it would go down like a rock. So we got engineers from Boeing down, and they conceived the idea of putting inflatable balloons in the V of the shock struts on each side. If you went in, you could trip them, and then they would be flotation gear. We said we would have to test them coming out of terminal-velocity dives.

I was selected to go up to the Boeing factory to run these tests. I was up there about six weeks, and it was a circus. I'd take the plane and go into a terminal-velocity dive. These balloons would come out and inflate; for a minute or so, the balloons would just go crazy. Of course, the balloons would tear off. Boeing finally made an installation that would stay put. I climbed to 20,000 feet on full throttle, then dived until the airspeed stabilized at terminal velocity.

By that time, I had learned that they were going to hold the 1927 National Air Races at Spokane. It just worked out perfectly. I wrote Captain Reeves requesting permission to return the FB-5 via Spokane, so I could observe the National Air Races. This came back approved. Without my knowledge, Captain Reeves had designated three pilots to participate in the air show. The one from our squadron had an F2B. Another one from an observation squadron had a UO used as an observation plane on a battleship. Then I think there was one torpedo plane. These three different types of planes were sent up to represent the navy at the National Air Races. I flew the FB-5 over there. Jim Doolittle was there, as were the army's "Three Musketeers," flying Curtiss Hawks. They had their carburetors fixed so they could fly at full power inverted. They did perfectly beautiful formation acrobatics, slow rolls off the ground, and they didn't have to worry about losing power inverted. They put on a beautiful show.

The marines had a squadron, flying the same airplanes, except they didn't have their carburetors fixed. Tex Rogers was their leader; he was a Naval Academy man. He had one pilot with him who misjudged. They came down at an angle to the spectator stands at about 45 degrees. Each one came down to about 10 feet, and then each did a climbing slow roll on the pullout. This pilot rolled upside down, and his motor conked out. Instead of trying to complete the slow roll, he tried a half loop out. When he came down out of that half loop, he was turned at 45 degrees back toward the stand. He didn't quite make it. His wheels hit the ground. The wheels came up and broke the two front spars in each lower wing, and the wheels flew off. One wheel went into the stands but didn't hurt anybody too seriously. His propeller tips were curled back. You've never heard anything howl like that engine.

Here was this half-wrecked airplane; he just cleared the stands and went over some wires, and he used his head. He had enough speed coming down out of this half loop, so he turned and made a belly landing out in the field. I never saw a pilot so scared in my life. That broke up the marines' act.

I had known Jim Doolittle before, and finally at a party I got Jim over to one side and said, "Goddamn you. What did you do to those carburetors to make them run upside down?"

He said, "Tommy, that's simple. Disconnect your gas line to your carburetor and fill it full of solder. Then drill the right size hole through that solder so that you've got one master jet. When you turn upside down, that master jet, regardless of the nonoperation of your float, meters enough fuel for the engine to run at full throttle."

Of course there was one other little joker. You had a reserve pipe in the bottom of your gas tank that stuck up about six inches. So when you were going to do that act, you wanted to take off with a full tank and be using the reserve fuel valve. When you turned upside down, the stand pipe would be sticking up into the fuel, and you wouldn't lose suction. It worked. You can run at full power for forty-five seconds inverted. You could do outside loops and all kinds of things that you couldn't do without that continuity of power in the inverted position. I figured I had forty-five seconds that I could run without losing oil pressure. That was the critical thing.

During my shows, I always came in downwind. I'd roll inverted as I crossed the border of the field, and in thirty to forty-five seconds I was past the main grandstands. I could roll out climbing with no problem. That's how I got started on the formation acrobatics. These three pilots from the navy with three different airplanes tried to fly formation, and it was absolutely ludicrous! It was silly to even try. Right then I decided that the navy would have a topnotch team at the 1928 races.

When we got the Boeing F2Bs, starting in 1928, I began selecting my wingmen. I picked out Lt. (jg) William V. Davis Jr. and Lt. (jg) Aaron P. Storrs III, both excellent acrobatic pilots. I selected them by simply watching the pilots in day-to-day operations, then taking them up to try them out. I said, "You're going to fly ten feet apart, and we'll do a loop in formation. All you've got to do is watch me. Just look at my airplane. Don't look at another thing. Just watch me for signals, look at my airplane, and fly close. There's nothing to it." LIKE "THE BLUE ANGLES"

I made my selection and began training them. The ticklish part of it was that it was all contrary to flight regulations. Nothing like that had ever been done before. I had to train them to do this stuff off the ground so it would be impressive. When I first started training them, I'd get them on top of an overcast with a markedly level top. That was after we had been doing flipper turns and wingovers and easy maneuvers. You can do that and be seen with no kickback. Then we started doing loops up on top. Looping, I just touched my wheels on top of the clouds, and I'd come out at least a hundred feet higher. Then I started going back and doing it alongside of a mountain, and then finally level with the ground in the back country, around Ramona and Escondido, where we hoped not to be seen. I started doing it right off the ground. Bill Davis and Putt Storrs learned fast. Then we graduated into slow rolls, squirrel-cage loops, and inverted flight.

There wasn't any approval to do this. It was all on the "QT." Our necks were out—but good. In 1928 I had them pretty well trained after a couple of months. They were doing well. You can't keep a thing like that absolutely quiet, but nobody had even seen anything and couldn't pin anything on us. But then we got up to San Francisco on the old *Langley*, on the cruise to Hawaii in the spring of 1928. The fleet air was to put on a big parade over San Francisco. I was told by the chief of staff—not by the admiral, but by Gene Wilson, chief of staff—"At the end of the parade, Tommy, I want you and your section to put on a show." I said, "Okay."

We did put on a show! For a finale, I flew inverted halfway down Market Street—below the tops of the buildings. I didn't trust Bill and Putt to be inverted under such conditions, so they flew cocked up on each side. I was upside down, going right down the middle of Market Street. After that, the fog moved in. I sneaked out—not to the Golden Gate, but I went out another little pass I knew just south of the city. I knew about where the *Langley* was going to be, and I flew a couple of hundred feet underneath the fog back to land aboard the *Langley*. We were the only ones who got back; the rest of them all landed at Crissy Field and waited till the next day. We never heard a word of comment. It was significant that, Reeves, now Admiral Reeves, included the three of us to attend a very fancy luncheon for the "brass."

On a previous *Langley* cruise to Hawaii, the fighter squadrons had flown Curtiss-built TSs, biplanes that had Wright J-4 engines, with the fuselage sort of halfway between the upper and lower wings. It was not a good fighter. At that time the army had MB-3As, a Boeing-built monoplane fighter—fast but tricky control-wise, with a 300-horsepower Hisso engine. It wasn't a popular airplane. I knew several pilots were killed in this plane. It wasn't a good-flying airplane, but it was fast, much faster than the ones the navy had. So when the TSs flew to Ford Island at Pearl Harbor, the army pilots just crucified them. They scared the navy squadron commander so badly he got right down on the water, and he finally flew into the water. It didn't kill him, but it hurt his pride to no end! We all knew about this and were prepared to have revenge.

By now I was the squadron commanding officer, having taken over from Lt. Comdr. J. E. "Ossie" Ostrander just before we sailed for Hawaii. We reached the island of Oahu on 29 April 1928. I had coached my people, "We're going to take those crummy army pilots to town." With the F2B we had enough superior performance—speed, controllability, and an altitude edge—to outmaneuver their PW-9s. I saw to it that our pilots had plenty of practice dogfighting. I said, "When you get on a PW-9's tail, you stay on his tail until he lands at Wheeler Field. Don't you let him go."

That was exactly what we did the first time we were in the air. We had twelve planes in the air, and we ran twelve of them right back to Wheeler Field before we let go of them. We had fun. The tables were turned. That irritated the army pilots to no end. It was only about a week after this, a Saturday morning inspection, when our planes were all lined up out in front of the hangar on Ford Island. Here came this PW-9, diving down out of the clouds, right across our line of F2Bs, missing the airplanes by five or ten feet, the pilot thumbing his nose as he went by. So I called to Putt and Bill, "Wind up our airplanes."

It was a day when there were broken cumulus clouds. Some of them went up to 10,000, 12,000 feet or more, with spaces in between them. I just had a hunch that the pilot who buzzed our line did it as a decoy to get us to take off and chase him. They had other people hiding in the clouds, waiting to jump us from a superior altitude. They'd get the edge on us. We'd get away in time probably, but at least they'd get at us for a while. But they failed.

I took off in a hurry, and Putt joined later. I spiraled up through the clouds and came out on top, around 14,000 to 15,000 feet. I started looking for the sneaks, and, sure enough, there were two more. The first pilot was climbing back up to join the two people who were waiting to pounce on us. Putt and I just clobbered them; in a flash we were on their tails, and we ran them back to Wheeler Field.

But we still had fun with the air corps. At a cocktail party some of the air corps pilots started yapping about how dangerous it was to fly through the Pali, which was a gap in the mountains on Oahu. Quite a stream of air goes through it. There is a cliff that drops off about 3,000 feet straight down—vertical. I'd flown through the Pali before; it wasn't *that* bad. Putt and Bill were standing there, the air corps group around, so I said, "Okay, let's see if it is really that bad. At nine o'clock tomorrow morning, we will fly through the Pali in formation, inverted." And we did.

The army had an ON observation plane at that time, built by Douglas. The pilot's cockpit was just forward of the wing, right in back of the Liberty engine. The ON was circling up above the Pali when we went through inverted. We had fun and got away with it. After our demonstration, navy air was respected. They knew we were not to be fooled with.

We returned from Hawaii on the *Lexington* (CV-2), which had made a high-speed run from San Francisco to Oahu in a record-setting seventy-two hours. After she arrived at Pearl Harbor, Admiral Reeves shifted all the *Langley*'s planes over to the *Lexington* for the trip back. After our return we were redesignated Light Bombing Squadron 2 (VB-2B) and spent the summer of 1928 in intensive gunnery and bombing training. However, the highlight of the summer was the dedication of Lindbergh Field in San Diego. For the dedication, Admiral Reeves again decided to have a grand aircraft parade because a lot of bigwigs—navy and army brass besides civilians—were going to be there for this dedication. There were elaborate plans for this parade. The first flights to go through were the fighters, two squadrons that made up the Fighter Wing, and I was to follow with VB-2B, followed by the rest of the squadrons.

In the morning there was fog—not a dense fog. We had 1,000 feet of vertical visibility, very little horizontal visibility. Above 1,000 feet, it was approaching dense fog. So we took off as planned. My section was leading the Light Bombing Wing. I said, "We will fly down to the lower bay and keep underneath this fog. I will circle at about 500 feet," which I did. All the other planes took off and disappeared. When the time came, according to schedule, I was on time with VB-2B. I think there was some part of the observation wing. The other fighting squadrons never did tell where they went; they never did show up. We went by on schedule.

Then it was time for our show. We had been told by Gene Wilson, "Put on your show in front of the grandstand."

I said, "This is make or break. Either we go to the air races, or we get general courts-martial."

In our introductory thing we came in not over five to ten feet apart. I always figured to raise dust with my wheels when I pulled up. Right in front of the grandstand, we did three successive loops and then our inverted stuff. Because of the buildings and obstructions, I didn't fly quite as low as I did later at the National Air Races, but I made an inverted pass across at maybe 50 feet or so. The admiral made no comment. Gene Wilson congratulated us, and we were selected to go to the National Air Races to represent the navy. It was very gratifying after the clandestine beginnings. We could have been court-martialed offhand for any number of reasons if the brass wished because nothing of that kind had ever been thought of or done in the navy.

To cap it off, I trained the entire squadron. To have a little fun, I had fifteen planes in V formation. We came in over North Island at about 1,500 feet and looped the whole squadron in formation. People still remember that. We had five three-plane sections, the lead section and two on each side. It made a beautiful show. There was a lot of talk, but nobody ever said "Boo!" officially.

I kept the team training during the summer of 1928 for the air races. There were some names people were trying to call us. One day, sitting out in front of the squadron office in the grass, Putt and Bill and I were talking about it. Putt Storrs said, "How about the Three Sea Hawks?" It took. We decided that was a good name. We simply became known as the Three Sea Hawks, and that was it! And we were billed as such at the air races. The whole squadron went up, and, on Saturday, 8 September 1928, VB-2B put on its show in the morning and the Three Sea Hawks flew in the afternoon.

I can't remember the exact order in which we did things, but we did a series of four loops, then a squirrel-cage loop, chasing each other's tails. We did inverted flying, climbing slow rolls, wingovers, flipper turns, and then we did a special simulated dive-bombing attack, a little on the hairy side. We'd climb up and peel off to dive three ways. I would always come in on the dive over, but away from the stands. Putt and Bill would dive parallel to the stands in opposite directions. We had a target on the runway for bombing attacks. We had a time with it because it required close timing. I'd come down and go by Bill; Putt then whizzed by. That was a good act, coordinated to a split second. Putt and Bill were dependable. We practiced it, so we never had any what I could dangerous close calls.

The final act was when I would do this inverted flight at low altitude the length of Mines Field, the Los Angeles municipal airport. I never trusted Putt and Bill to fly so low in close formation inverted. At that time, we were at least wearing parachutes, which were of no value at 50 feet. At 50 feet, they'd just be cocked up at angles from me on each side. I'd be upside down. It was fun.

I got to meet a lot of people. One was Jack Maddux, who was president of Maddux Air Lines. He had started Maddux Air Lines with Ford trimotors in 1927. I knew most of the commercial people in the area around Los Angeles as a result of flying the Jenny, particularly all the ones who went to the air meets. I got cups and won cash awards in the various events. The events at the air meets always included a Jenny scramble and a stunting contest. There were balloon-busting contests and dead-stick landings to a mark. They'd release a balloon and time it until you broke the balloon. It wasn't that easy to dive down and hit that balloon; those balloons could be elusive.

Somebody always had a fast airplane. There were free-for-all races. Owners would ask me to fly their airplanes for them, especially in the free-for-all. I could beat the others turning at the pylons marking the course. I'd talk to everybody about this or that, find a nugget now and then; it all added up. I flew every plane that was available. There were a couple of them that I flew for five minutes—no more! I took them off and flew around and back to the field. I could have done without that; I was lucky to land in one piece. On one of them, the next pilot who flew it washed it out and was bent himself. They were curiosities—but I considered it all experience.

Rear Adm. William A. Moffett, chief of the Bureau of Aeronautics, was at the national races, and afterward he congratulated the squadron and had the three of us at a big formal affair. He asked what duty I wanted next. I was supposed to have been detached in June of 1928, but Admiral Reeves had requested that I be held over for the races. I told him I wanted to go to the NAS Anacostia test section. Steve Callaway was the head of the test section and was due to be relieved, and I was senior to Steve.

To this day, I don't know what happened, but when I landed at El Paso, flying back home in New York with the Jenny, I was handed a telegram dispatch. It was to the effect that my orders had been changed, and I was to report to NAS Pensacola to be the chief of pilot training. That didn't interest me; instructing was too routine and monotonous. I knew that I would get into endless arguments with people. Many of my ideas about flying were quite contrary to the accepted navy standards at that time. Knowing the attitude in the high ranks, people who knew nothing of what I was talking about and trying to do, I wouldn't get anywhere.

So I just went on to western New York. When I got up there, I called the Navy Department and said, "Now, look!" My orders were changed back to the test section at Anacostia.

I flew into Buffalo, New York—no problem across the country. Beyond Buffalo I flew under an overcast, about 300 feet, to Batavia, New York, my old hometown, about 30 miles down the New York Central Railroad tracks. I was going to land in LeRoy, ten miles farther east, since Batavia had no landing field at that time. My father and mother and other people were going to meet me out there, and I had the Jenny all loaded up with my personal gear. I had thirty days' leave, and then I planned to fly to Anacostia.

I flew over Batavia and on to Woodward Field at LeRoy. I'd never been there before, so I took a look at it. It was a peculiar field on a slope, east to west, with the wind sock indicating a ground-level wind a little from the west. I was flying right at the base of this overcast. I decided to land downwind and uphill to save taxiing distance—just dive into the wind and do a wingover to a landing uphill. What I didn't take into account was that where I was, at the base of that overcast, the wind was probably going 20 to 25 mph. But right on the ground the wind sock indicated maybe just 5 mph, nothing to worry about.

I pulled up and went into the overcast at the top of my wingover. As I dropped down out of the overcast, I could see I was in trouble. The stronger wind in the cloud layer had drifted the plane closer to the rising landing strip than I had expected. I was simply too low to get my right wingtip up. That wingtip guard dragged on the ground, and the plane cartwheeled. That JN really splintered; the ash longeron in front of the cockpit shattered. I went forward, and my face hit the compass on the cowling and knocked out four front teeth.

For several days I stayed in Batavia to get false teeth put in before I reported to Anacostia. I went out to look at the wreckage, and it had been hauled off into a hangar. I salvaged the motor and a few items; the rest of it was hopeless. There was an old cabinetmaker there who did woodwork on the airplanes on the field. He came up and introduced himself to my father. He told my father, "I'd like to point something out to your son."

He went over to the old Jenny. It had old ash longerons about 1-¾ inches square, which began in back of the pilot's cockpit. They were tapered, glued, and wrapped to the spruce longerons forming the tail structure. Those ash longerons were the main structural members up to the fire wall, where the engine mounts were attached. The lower wings attached to the bottom longerons at the front cockpit. Short struts came down from the upper center wing section on each side of the front cockpit and attached to the upper ash longerons. They had shattered. Where there was a bolt hole through these longerons, they looked as though they had been cut through with a knife.

This old cabinetmaker told me, "Live ash does not shatter. Do you realize those longerons were all spruce?"

I don't think it had anything to do with the cause of the accident, but I wrote up my accident and sent it to Clarence Young, director of aeronautics with the Department of Commerce, whom I knew, and said that the cause of the accident was "cockpit trouble." A year or two later, when I again met Clarence, he said, "Tommy, you submitted the first honest accident report we received."

Sometimes I've wondered; I flew that JN over eight hundred hours in all kinds of weather. I had no idea as to the condition of the longerons. I might have flown into some severe turbulence, and it would have come apart in the air with fatal results. That particular accident was pure cockpit trouble but possibly a blessing in disguise.

The first project that I was assigned to at Anacostia was an observation-type Vought Corsair, which was a beautiful biplane with a Wasp engine. It was a lovely airplane to fly; there was talk of using it for dive-bombing. I had relieved Steve Callaway as head of the section, and I decided that any dive-bomber had better be tested at 10-G pullouts at terminal velocity. That was whatever registered when you were in a vertical dive at full power, and the airspeed had ceased to increase.

The Corsair was a nice airplane to fly, a wonderful cross-country airplane with perfect control at low speed and slow landing speed. In this vertical, terminal-velocity dive pullout, the structure was subjected to maximum stress. On the pullout, I got elevator flutter. I cut the power off and got the flutter manageable. I had enough elevator control for a safe landing. The left rear stabilizer spar had broken, so the left side of the stabilizer at the flipper hinge point was flopping.

At that time we knew we were about to receive an airplane built by Curtiss, the XF8C-2 prototype of the famed Helldiver series. I insisted that the factory pilot demonstrate the plane in a terminal-velocity dive with a 10-G pullout. There was some huffing and puffing in the bureau, but my recommendation was approved. When that plane was brought down by the Curtiss pilot, he did it. Sure enough, the wings came off. I was standing there with some of these people who had questioned my recommendation, and I said, "Admiral, there's your airplane."

The pilot jumped, and the parachute opened okay. He and the plane ended up somewhere east along the river and didn't do any damage. After that it became standard procedure for company test pilots to demonstrate terminal-velocity pullouts at ten "gees."

Then the PN-11 came along, built at the Naval Aircraft Factory. It was a nice biplane, twin-engine flying boat. I was flying it over the speed course. Navy regulations required them before other performance tests were made, and it had to be in full-combat readiness. The plane had machine guns, ammunition, everything in it. I never gave it a thought. You'd level off on a steady flight over the speed course, time the run, check your airspeed, and then you could calibrate your airspeed instrument error on the basis of the actual speed. That's the way you calibrated the instrument for location error as there was a variation due to the position of the pitot tube. You'd fly it at several different speeds, correcting for air density.

This course was up and down the Potomac River. I was flying upriver toward Anacostia. We'd pass the mark at the ends of the course, start or stop our watches, and I'd pull up to reverse course. It wasn't exactly a wingover but combined with a tight, climbing turn and then back down and level off for another run down the river. Right at the top of this turn, I looked out to the left, and the engine was on fire. I put the plane into a side slip to keep the flame away from the tail surface. I got the plane on the water quickly. The wind was so that I could taxi on the water with full throttle on the right engine toward the beach. It began to get hot in the left cockpit seat once I got on the water; the fire was roaring. They didn't have flexible gas lines in those days; they just ran the line from the hull to the engine mount. The difference in vibration period between the engine mount and the hull structure caused the line to break, and the exhaust ignited the gasoline.

I headed for the beach, and it was cold. This was in December. The crew climbed up the nose in front and took off their winter gear and piled it over between me and the fire. I headed for the beach hell-bent. The plane had gas tanks in the hull on each side. I could see that when the motor and wing fell the blades were going to rupture those gas tanks, and hell would break loose. As long as I could keep moving, the fire was back. I just made it to the beach. As we got out, the whole left side collapsed, the tanks went up, and we were all lying on our bellies on the far side of the dike. Then the machine-gun ammunition started to go off like firecrackers.

After the air races, during my thirty days' leave, I had taken two weeks and flown for Jack Maddux. He wanted me then to resign from the navy and take over operations of Maddux Air Lines, which was strictly a barnstorming outfit. They picked the best pilots available, who were all fine people, but in those days they never had any plans or any discipline or organization. It horrified me, and I told him so. I told Jack I'd think about it.

Then my good friend Earl Daugherty killed himself. He had a J-5 Laird, which was a beautiful little airplane. I'd gotten Earl a commission as lieutenant (jg), U.S. Naval Reserve. He and his wife would come down and spend two weeks active duty with me in VF-2B at North Island. He'd fly our fighters, fit in, liked by all. Everybody appreciated Earl, and he was liked by all hands. He took his place in squadron flying, and he loved to perform acrobatics. He had a particular Jenny, and he'd snap roll that Jenny to the point where he'd stretched the wires so that the turnbuckles wouldn't take them up any tighter. Then he tied knots in the wires. I was horrified. I knew too much about structures and safety factors; I knew what Earl was doing was deadly, and I tried to warn him.

Then he got this Laird, a nice airplane. It had performance; it would do these acrobatics that he was doing with our fighters, but it didn't have the strength. One of his favorite tricks was a nice one, something that I used to do with the F2Bs. You'd go across a field doing a precise slow roll. Then when you were on top of the roll, you hauled the elevators full up, kicked the rudder, and did a quick snap roll in the opposite direction to that of the slow roll. It was a very pretty but tricky maneuver. He was doing these things with his J-5 Laird. I told him, and other people did, too, "Earl, don't do that. That airplane isn't built for it."

What finally got him was that he liked to practice. He was out practicing a show, quit, came in, and filled the tank full of gas. In times past he had promised a stunt ride to two newspapermen, and they came along and put the arm on him. I guess Earl said, "Oh, hell," and took the airplane out of the hangar after he had put it away full of gas. Now, he put these two men in the front seat, and away he went. He did this trick of a slow roll, then the reverse snap roll. The wings came off. The "gees" that you put on an airplane when you do a snap roll with a lot of speed are way high.

Well, that was the end of Earl. He'd been my mentor, introducing me into commercial aviation, barnstorming, and stunt flying. He was one of the closest friends I had in my life. The only way I could get out for the funeral was to fly out. Anacostia had several DHs sitting around there that weren't doing anything, and I tried to get permission to get a DH to fly out to Long Beach. Earl had done a lot publicity-wise for the navy, too. There were times when the spotter squadrons had camped on his field to operate off San Pedro with the fleet, and I thought the navy owed him something.

I finally wound up going to old Adm. Charles F. Hughes, who was chief of naval operations. When he finally turned me down, I said, "Thank you, Admiral. I will resign from the navy immediately."

And I did. I wired Jack Maddux and accepted his offer to be vice president of operations for Maddux Air Lines. Jack said, "Meet me in Detroit in two days." I had decided that if they'd let me fly out for the funeral, I'd probably have stayed in the navy; I'm not sure. I knew it was a risk; I had a family, two kids. By that time, with the Sea Hawk background and my barnstorming, I felt that I was pretty well established in aviation and had a reputation that would stand. When the navy let me down, I said, "To hell with you."

7

RIDING THE WAVES

Capt. Ralph Stanton Barnaby

RALPH STANTON BARNABY *was born in Meadville, Pennsylvania, on 21 January 1893, the son of Charles Weaver Barnaby and Jenny Christy Barnaby. He attended private school in New York City before entering Columbia University, where he received the degree of bachelor of mechanical engineering in 1915. He was assistant chief engineer and head of the engineering department of Standard Aeronautical Corporation, Plainfield, New Jersey, until he enlisted in the U.S. Navy in December 1917. He was commissioned ensign in the U.S. Naval Reserve Force, to date from 26 March 1918. Later in his naval career, he was designated for aeronautical engineering duty only. He attained the rank of captain on 11 November 1942.*

During World War I, Barnaby became inspector of naval aircraft in the plant of the L.W.F. Engineering Corporation, and he subsequently studied European aircraft developments in England and France. In February 1919 he assisted in the preparation of the NC flying boats for the transatlantic flights of that year. After three years at the Naval Aircraft Factory, Philadelphia, he reported in November 1922 to the Bureau of Aeronautics as head of the Specifications Section, where he served a total of nine years. He had detached duty for one year, 1928–29, at Wright Field, Dayton, Ohio, as assistant general inspector and material liaison officer with the Engineering Division of the Army Air Corps. In January 1930 he achieved international recognition by making a glider flight from the rigid airship Los Angeles *(ZR-3). Later assignments included inspector of naval aircraft, Baltimore, Maryland; duty at the Naval Air Station, Pensacola, Florida; the Fleet Air Base, Coco Solo, Canal Zone; chief engineer at the Naval Aircraft Factory, Philadelphia; and commanding officer of the Naval Aircraft Modification Unit, Johnsville, Pennsylvania. Captain Barnaby was transferred to the retired list on 1 January 1947.*

Ralph Stanton Barnaby was recognized as a leading authority on gliders, holder of the National Aeronautical Association Number One Soaring Certificate, a founder-member and fellow of the Institute of Aeronautical Sciences, and charter member, director, and president of the Soaring Society of America. In 1945 Columbia University awarded him its Medal of Excellence for his many achievements in aeronautics, and he was awarded the Air Medal and Legion of Merit for his period of naval service. Captain Barnaby died on 14 May 1986.

My interest in aviation began in 1908 with the newspaper accounts of Orville Wright's flights at Fort Myer, Virginia, for the army, which resulted in the crash in which Lt. Tom Selfridge of the army was killed. That got me enthused about aviation. I had thought about it, and I'd done a little kite-flying, but reading of the stories of the Wright brothers actually changed the course of my life because I had been set on an art career. I dropped back a year in order to get more math in high school and took an engineering course instead because I wanted to go into aviation.

Of course, I'd never seen anything except some of the old hot-air balloon ascensions and parachutes at country fairs out in Meadville, Pennsylvania, where I was born. My father was a mechanical engineer, and I don't think he thought that aviation was anything really to go into. But he raised no opposition. He was very pleased to see me go into mechanical engineering, although he would have liked to steer me toward architectural engineering, so I could combine art and engineering.

In 1909 I designed, built, and flew my first glider, which was before I had ever seen any other heavier-than-air craft fly. I had built flying models, mostly gliders because it wasn't until along in 1909 that the rubber band–powered idea for driving model airplanes became generally known.

But most of my models were gliders. I had read about Lilienthal's experiments, and actually my first glider was patterned more on Lilienthal's gliders than, for instance, on the Wright gliders. I don't think it was until somewhat later that the whole story of the Wright brothers and the wonderful soaring and gliding work they did down at Kitty Hawk got the publicity that it rated.

I did consult my father somewhat on structural design problems, and he would advise me on how to put things together. I think his only enthusiasm was to see that I didn't build something I was going to break my neck in, to see that it was at least strong enough to do what it was supposed to do. But I don't think he took it seriously at all for a long time.

At that time, in 1909, my father was superintendent of a quartz grinding mill at Roxbury Falls, Connecticut, which is up the Shepaug River, up toward Litchfield. I went up and spent the summer with my father on a farm near the mill, which was where I built this huge glider. There was a large pasture with sufficient slope and sufficient length so that I could make glides down the hillside. I didn't do any soaring there. They were just coasting downhill flights that I could do in still air, although the more wind you had, the less your ground speed and the safer it was in that respect. But it was sufficient for me to get short glides. I don't think I ever made any longer than perhaps three hundred feet, getting maybe ten or fifteen feet in the air at the highest part. My season terminated the same way the Wrights' did with their first powered flight in 1903. I'd finished my gliding and was sitting there thinking it over and talking with my father about it. Then a gust of wind came along and picked the glider up. Before we could rescue it, it had rolled it up in a ball, the same way the Wrights' experiment ended in 1903.

It was a very discouraging thing for me, but, on the other hand, I had built it, and I had flown it, and I was already thinking about what the next one would look like. So that's how I got started into it, and then I got associated with some of the model-flying boys in New York City. In 1909 we organized what I believe was the first model aero club in the United States, called the New York Model Aero Club.

One of the best of our group was a high school and college classmate of mine, Jean Roche, who was one of the original team that Col. Virginius E. Clark, U.S.A., got together in 1917 to form the original engineering division, which became Wright-Patterson Air Force Base and that whole system. Jean was with the air force as one of their highest paid civilian engineers. He also was the designer and original president of the Aeronca Company and designed the early Aeroncas, which were very popular. I did some of his test flying for him back in 1928 and 1929, during the time that I was stationed out of Wright Field as liaison officer.

Then I began getting with other people interested in flying, and we built and flew a number of man-carrying gliders. That's how I knew Oakwood Heights down in Staten Island because we used to keep our glider in Captain Baldwin's hangar, and we'd go down weekends and fly. That was Captain Tom Baldwin, the old balloonist and designer of the army's first airship. He loved young people—witness the fact that he let us store our glider in his hangar down there and would always be ready with, "Are you sure you have enough carfare to get home?" and things like that. He looked after the boys. He was a wonderful man and I was very fond of him.

It was during my senior year at Columbia University that I was in some classes with Eugene E. Wilson, Naval Academy class of 1908. There were a number of naval officers there, but Gene is the one that I knew best because we were later together in the Bureau of Aeronautics for a number of years when he was heading up the power plant section. Actually, my first job when I graduated from college was with the Elco Motor Boat Works in Bayonne, New Jersey. Engineering graduates had a pretty rough time back in those days. I went around applying for jobs, and I finally took the best offer I got, which was as a stockroom helper at the Elco company for $11.00 a week. This was in 1915, and we were in the neutrality kick at that time with William Jennings Bryan as secretary of state in the Wilson administration. We were neutral, and there wasn't going to be any war. But it was while I was with the Elco company that I met a naval aviator whom I got to know very well much later. That was George D. Murray, USNA class of 1911, who died in 1956 as a retired vice admiral.

The Elco company was a subsidiary of the Electric Boat Company, which became part of General Dynamics. Knowing that I had some knowledge in aviation, they sent me up to Connecticut to the Gallaudet Engineering Company to witness some flight tests of the Gallaudet D-1 seaplane. Gallaudet had been at Electric Boat seeking financing, and they wanted someone to tell them what Gallaudet thought of the job and whether they should put money into it. So they sent me up there, and among the witnesses of these flight tests was Lt. (jg) George D. Murray, and he really was the first naval aviator I ever met. Also among those present was Dusenberg because two of his engines were in this Gallaudet seaplane.

I had one of my early flights because I flew as observer on the first flights of this plane in December 1916, flown by a Swedish test pilot by the name of Bjorkland. It was a very far-out design, with twin engines, mounted side-by-side amidships, driving one propeller mounted on a ring encircling the fuselage behind the wings. It was a pusher. It looked like the fuselage was cut in half. I was in the front cockpit, and the pilot was behind me in the second cockpit. It was famous locally and in this country as being the first seaplane to cruise at over 100 mph, so the navy was very interested in it.

Because of structural and other problems, we nearly crashed because the rudder pedals collapsed during the flight. We had a pretty rough time, but we managed to get down and stay right side up. There were a number of design features that I didn't like about the plane. I didn't recommend that Electric Boat put any money into the Gallaudet Company, fond as I was of Edison Gallaudet, president of the company and a fine gentleman. I just didn't feel that he had the engineering staff that he needed at the time.

Just a footnote, but Edison was from the same Gallaudet family that established Gallaudet College for the deaf in Washington, D.C., named in honor of Thomas H. Gallaudet (1787–1851). There were two brothers. Edison I knew best. When I first met them in 1909, they were operating out of the old Mineola flying field on Long Island. There was a very early aviation center there at Mineola, Long Island, and then later it became famous as the takeoff site for the early transatlantic flights, including the Lindbergh flight.

I left Elco in December of 1916 because my college classmate, Jean Roche, was assistant chief engineer of the old Standard Aero Corporation in Plainfield, New Jersey. It was built around one Charles H. Day, who was one of the early airplane builders, and whose Day tractor was one of the early tractor biplanes. By July 1917 aviation was starting to pick up because the war feeling was building up, so I left the Elco Motor Boat Works and went over to Standard.

I stayed with Standard until the fall of 1917. Roche had left to go with the army, with Colonel Clark setting up the engineering division; that division started in the galvanized iron Quonset Hut building, which used to be part of the Smithsonian Institution. That was the Colonel Clark who left his name in aviation as an airfoil designer. The Clark Y wing section was the most popular wing used, not only in this country but by the British. After the war, Colonel Clark left the army, and he and Reuben H. Fleet went together and formed Consolidated Aircraft in Buffalo.

Along in the spring of 1917, Standard Aero got an order for training planes. In April war was declared, the Aircraft Production Board got going, and they standardized on training planes. There were to be two American training planes built—the famous Curtiss JN Jenny and the Standard J-1 training plane, which was to utilize the Hall-Scott A-7a, four-cylinder, water-cooled engine. We at Standard went into production on the J-1s.

At that time I was assistant chief engineer, having taken Roche's job when he left. So I had to build up an engineering group and a group of designers and draftsmen to turn out production plans for this thing. The plans were then furnished to companies all over the country to build J-1 training planes. One of the big jobs that we had to do was to design and build the jigs and fixtures so that a wing built by the Lincoln Company would fit on a fuselage built by some other company. The components were all interchangeable, regardless of where they were built. At least, that was the intent.

The company began growing and bringing in management on top and on top. Finally, I decided I was going to get out and get into something a little closer to the war. I went to the post office and got an application for the Naval Reserve Flying Corps and also the aviation branch of the Army Signal Corps. I filled them out and sent them in, then sat back and waited to see which would answer first. The navy answered first, and I was partway through ground school at the Massachusetts Institute of Technology before I got an acknowledgment from the army. I told them they were too late; I was already in the navy, happily so, although I think I would have been happy either way. So long as it concerned flying, I'd have been happy either way.

Having started in gliders, I was always interested in them. As a sport I liked to fly the gliders. In those days, if you had a few seconds of glider time, you were an expert. In 1920, we began hearing about the German gliding schools and the things they were doing. It was in 1920 when Dr. Otto Klemperer acquired the first soaring certificate over in Germany by making a flight of over an hour in his glider. Of course, that intrigued all of us who had been interested in gliding from the start.

From then on, gliding grew over there, and in 1928 some American industrialists, one of them being James C. Penney, brought over some German glider pilots with their gliders, and they did some flying around the country. A school was established on Cape Cod, at South Wellfleet, by an outfit called the American Motorless Aviation Corporation—AMAC. The president of AMAC was Gen. John F. O'Ryan, who was a well-known businessman in New York, a general in World War I. One of the directors was Sumner Sewall, who later served as Republican governor of Maine from 1941 to 1945.

In 1928 I had tried to get a month's leave from the navy to go over to Germany to take a course in one of their glider schools, but I was turned down. So when I read in the spring of 1929 that there was this school up in Cape Cod, I decided to pool my leave and go up and take the course at Cape Cod, which I did. I was fortunate enough with my background and gliding experience to be the first one to fulfill the requirements and get what was the first American soaring certificate. My *Federation Aeronautique International* (FAI) soaring certificate issued by the National Aeronautics Association was number one, authenticated and signed by Orville Wright.

Now, the first chief of the Bureau of Aeronautics, Rear Adm. William A. Moffett, was a great believer in the power of publicity, and he felt that in order for the service to get anywhere—the part of the service he was interested in—you had to have the people on your side, particularly as represented in Congress. He went in for things that would get favorable publicity for what he was doing and for what he thought the navy should be doing, particularly in aviation.

So, along in the fall of 1929, shortly after I had received my soaring certificate, Admiral Moffett sent for me, and I thought, "What have I done wrong now?" But when I got in his office he said, "Sit down, Barnaby. Barnaby, do you think it would be possible to launch a glider from the rigid airship USS *Los Angeles?*"

That sort of staggered me. Then he said, "I don't want an answer now. You think it over and come in and see me tomorrow. Think it over carefully because if your answer is 'yes,' you're going to do it."

Well, I didn't sleep much that night, but the next day I went up to see him and told him I thought it was possible, and I would do it under certain conditions. One was that the navy acquire for me the glider that I had used in making my soaring flights on Cape Cod. The other condition was that I go to the Naval Air Station Lakehurst, New Jersey, the navy's East Coast site for lighter-than-air operations, and supervise putting the launching gear in the airship.

He said, "OK."

The gliding school had folded up by then, and I made arrangements with them for the navy to buy this German glider. They hadn't disposed of them. As a matter of fact, they still were in a state of flux. They didn't know what they were going to do, and I think they were glad to get the money. I wanted this particular glider because I'd got more time in that one than any other glider I'd ever flown. The soaring flight, in which I'd gotten my soaring certificate, had lasted for fifteen minutes and six seconds. That was an American record at that time because it exceeded the flight that Orville Wright had made in 1911 of nine minutes and forty-five seconds. Then I had made several flights in it after that. Actually, I had become quite an expert because by then I had nearly twenty minutes of gliding time in that glider, which was probably three-quarters of my total gliding time.

So we got the glider down to Lakehurst. I went up about the first of January 1930 to Lakehurst and stayed there to supervise the installation of the release gear. They already had the trapeze and gear for attaching and launching the Curtiss F9C aircraft that the airship carried. I used the basic equipment structure that they had under the *Los Angeles* to make a mounting to hold the glider.

I knew what the normal gliding speed of a glider was, and I wanted to have that much airspeed showing on my airspeed indicator before they released me. The first lieutenant of the airship was Lt. Calvin M. Bolster, Construction Corps, who was later, as a rear admiral, chief of the Office of Naval Research. Cal and I designed the gear to hold the glider, and he actually operated the lanyard that released the glider.

We had brought the glider to Lakehurst in the fall of 1929, so it was six months since I had flown it, and I wondered whether, maybe, I should make some test flights. The only way we could do it there at Lakehurst was by automobile tow because there were no hills. I was afraid that maybe we would wreck it, so I decided that the best way to do it was to set it up and leave it alone. We would release at a high enough altitude so that I had plenty of time to learn to fly it again on the way down. So we picked 3,000 feet as being high enough, and that was what the release height was set at.

We picked the 31st of January as being the day. The weather reports were good, and I slept there at the air station at Lakehurst. I'll never forget that morning. I was up at five o'clock because at six o'clock they were going to walk the airship out of the hangar. It was 16 degrees above zero at that time—a clear, crisp, beautiful day but bitter cold. The first hitch was they couldn't get the hangar doors open. The ice had frozen in around them, so actually it was a couple of hours later before they brought the airship out.

Admiral Moffett was unable to be there at that time because he was attending the disarmament conference in London that led to the London Naval Treaty of April 1930. Comdr. John H. Towers was assistant chief at the time and acting in his absence. There were a lot of newspaper people about. As a matter of fact, they had three blimps that accompanied us and flew along with us with newspaper reporters and movie cameras. Two of them were blimps that Goodyear had built for the navy. The third one was the old ZMC-2, designed by Ralph Upson of the Aircraft Development Corporation of Detroit. It was a nonrigid but had a thin aluminum skin instead of the usual fabric skin. That ship was quite an historic experiment.

After they'd finally walked the airship out and had it balanced and everything, we attached the glider. For the takeoff, I rode in the control car of the *Los Angeles*. We cruised around, went down over Atlantic City, climbing gradually until we got up to 3,000 feet. Then, as the dirigible headed back toward the air station, I went back amidships where there was a ladder that I climbed down to get into the cockpit. They stopped the engines while I was climbing down to make it a little easier for me.

When I was down in the cockpit, I could talk to Bolster, who was in the hatch above me. After I was all set, I asked him to tell the crew to go ahead with the ship. I wanted them to speed up the engines, and I would let him know when I was reading 40 knots on my airspeed indicator. So it proceeded that way, and when I got my airspeed up to 40 knots, I told Cal to tell them to hold that speed till we got to where they wanted to launch me. We were headed west toward the station, into the wind, and I told Cal when to release me. I told him, "Okay, go ahead." He gave me a ten count and pulled the lanyard.

I sat there thinking, "How the hell did I ever let myself get maneuvered into this situation!?"

Actually, the instant I was released, I felt perfectly happy. I stuck the nose down and got away from under the ship because there were two big eighteen-foot propellers out in front of me and two behind me that seemed kind of close. Actually, I had no worry because she dropped away fast. I leveled off possibly a hundred feet below the ship, and then it was just a nice ride down but awfully cold. I couldn't wear too much clothing because there wasn't room enough in the cockpit for too much. I had on a summer flight suit and a leather jacket over that.

It was about thirteen minutes coming down, which added over 50 percent to my total flying time. I could have stayed up longer if I hadn't been so cold. I just flew at a comfortable gliding speed, making no attempt to hunt out up-currents and try to soar. I was asked why the flight was conducted in the middle of the winter rather than on a nice, balmy summer day. Admiral Moffett had the idea in December and said, "Let's get to it and do it." That was the only reason.

The navy seemed happy with the success of the flight. I had the whole cover sheet of the rotogravure section of the *New York Times* on 1 February 1930, so I think the navy people were very pleased at the publicity they got from it. The experiment was repeated only once again, on the 4th of July down over Anacostia in Washington, again with the *Los Angeles.* Lt. Thomas G. "Tex" Settle, who was later Vice Admiral Settle, was the pilot on that launching.

The question arises as to why the navy was interested in gliders in the first place? Was it only because of the publicity or what? There was an idea—also Admiral Moffett's—that it could be put to a practical use. They carried on these large rigid airships a landing officer in case a landing was to be made at a place other than a navy lighter-than-air base. I think that was true of all the rigid airships; even the German rigid airships carried a landing officer. They'd fly over the field, and this officer would parachute down. It was his job to organize and direct a landing crew. By prearrangement, I guess they would get the fire department, the police department, the Boy Scouts, the Rotary Club, and whatnot. They would gather people, and it was his job to explain what the functions were because handling one of these big rigid airships was a tremendous job, particularly if there was any wind running.

It was the thought that possibly they could release the glider for this purpose. Say they'd be cruising along at 6,000 or 8,000 feet. The glider pilot could release and proceed on and land at the field in his glider without the airship having to make a pass over the field first. The airship could lay off until he would go down and land where he wanted, which wasn't always true with the parachutes in those days.

That *Los Angeles* experiment was really the first of the navy involvement with the glider as a military aircraft. The navy never went on to actually attach them to the lighter-than-air craft, and that was the end of that experiment. The airships didn't last very long, and, of course, the later airships, the *Akron* (ZRS-4) and the *Macon* (ZRS-5), carried aircraft aboard, which could do the same thing and much better. You could send an airplane fifty miles or a hundred miles ahead of the airship to a field, and it could get there half a day in advance to make preparations. So there was no need for the glider.

A glider is just an airplane with no power, and any time you have an engine failure you're in a glider. I started back in 1930 trying to sell that to the navy. I tried to sell them into instituting a glider course at Pensacola for two reasons. First of all, I felt that every pilot should know how to handle his aircraft if the engine went out and that a basic course in gliding would give him more confidence in his ability to try to handle an aircraft than anything else. Actually, that feeling has always existed in Europe where practically all commercial pilots were required to be glider pilots first. They felt that it was part of the basic training. I had many arguments back in the very early thirties down in the Bureau of Aeronautics on that subject, particularly with Comdr. Marc A. Mitscher, who was chief of the Flight Division of BuAer at the time. But I never was able to sell him. He could see no use, no reason, for gliders.

I said, "Commander, at Annapolis I see they have a big fleet of sailboats down there, that every midshipman has to learn to sail. Why is that?"

He said, "Well, any man who goes to sea should know how to sail a boat because sometime he may have to sail. You may be damaged or your ship may be sunk and may be in a lifeboat, he's going to have to know how to sail."

I said, "That's the same thing that happens any time an engine quits in an airplane."

He couldn't see the analogy. Rear Adm. Ernest J. King did, and it was Admiral King, when he was chief of the Bureau of Aeronautics, who finally decided that we should institute a glider training course at Pensacola on an experimental basis. I had given up trying to sell it as a means of improving the aviator's skill and so forth. I then tried to sell it as a quick means of evaluating the prospective student's adaptability to learning to fly. I worked out a two week glider training course. I said I could tell in two weeks whether a man was going to make an aviator or wasn't going to make an aviator. Before you went to the expense of shipping a student down to Pensacola, starting him through, using up all the flying time, and then determining he wasn't flight material, you could give him a two weeks' course of glider training and determine whether he was going to make an aviator. There was considerable interest also expressed in it by the medical department at Pensacola because they were picking prospective pilots on the basis of psychological tests, and we were very interested in comparing notes.

On that basis, the navy ordered six gliders purchased and sent to Pensacola. At that time, a very fine glider had been developed in this country by Prof. R. E. Franklin of the University of Michigan. It had become practically a standard glider used for training all around the country for glider clubs and so forth. We bought six of those PS-2 gliders, and the first two of them were to be delivered in June of 1933. I was ordered down on temporary duty to instruct some instructors at Pensacola as glider instructors, to start an experiment on a glider training course there.

The instruction from BuAer was that four, I believe, of their regular naval aviator instructors were to be taught to be glider instructors by me. The instruction also said they were to be volunteers. We ran into a snag. When I arrived there in June, the commandant, Capt. Rufus S. Zogbaum, said, "Barnaby, I don't know what we're going to do. We put the notice on the bulletin board. It's been on the board now ever since we got it a couple of weeks ago, and we have received no volunteers."

I said, "Captain, don't you do anything about it, except I would like to have it posted and also announced at weekly inspection and so forth, that on next Saturday at Corry Field there will be an exhibition of glider flying. Then let's see what happens."

Well, two gliders came down over the road on trailers from Michigan, arriving on 6 June 1933, and the two fellows that brought them down were both glider pilots. They were University of Michigan students who had teamed to fly on the Franklin gliders up there, and, of course, I'd done a fair amount of flying with them at Elmira. We had these gliders set up, and the Franklin man who actually made the first flight was Wally Franklin, Dr. Franklin's younger brother.

They were auto-towed with a 500-foot manila towline, ⅜-inch diameter line. You can get up to 300 feet altitude on a 500-foot line. He was cut loose, did some figure eights, came back, and landed in front of the crowd. There was quite a decent crowd out there because I think they were looking for blood. Then I got in, and I was towed off and made a few flights. Then after I came down to land, I said, "Well, anyone else like to try it?" and with that they started lining up. We had no trouble with volunteers after that.

I think while I was down there during that first month, I trained two instructors. Then I went back to my job as inspector of naval aircraft at Glenn Martin's plant in Baltimore. Those first two trained four more men to be instructors. Then, the following June 1934, I was ordered to Pensacola to be the assembly and repair officer, with the additional duty of supervising the glider course. Beginning with the student class that was due to arrive on the first of July, it was arranged that the first half of that class, which I believe was about twenty students, was to come two weeks early. They would get the glider training course, then proceed on with the rest of their class.

After these men had finished their two-weeks' glider training course—if they finished because some of them were grounded for their own safety—the instructor's job was to rate each student. He had ratings of superior, above average, average, below average, inferior, and "He'll kill himself" when they didn't even want him to finish the glider course. These records were kept confidential. They did not go on to the flight instructors.

The whole class of forty students went to the regular flight school and then proceeded on through the flight course. Then at the end we tried to compare their flight records through the flight school, which at that time lasted pretty close to a year. They started in primary seaplanes and got trained in everything, right up through big flying boats to carrier fighters, the whole works. Later on, when the wartime speedup started, they started splitting them off. There were carrier pilots and the big-boat pilots, but in those days you got the full treatment.

The results, I think, confirmed my feeling that we could predict flying aptitude. The project lasted about a year. The war came on, and they didn't have time to waste with it. I saw the final report from Pensacola that went to BuAer giving the results and telling how they compared with the flight course. I forget what the total number of students that went through the glider course was, maybe around fifty. Of those who did average and above on the glider course, only two failed to pass the flight course. Of those rated inferior and impossible, about the same proportion, about two of them passed the flight test. And in comparing them with the psychological tests they were pretty good, too, although I think the glider training hit it a little closer than they did, which I would have expected.

There were no fatalities, although there were a number of casualties. We had a number of crashes. Of course, the casualties to gliders were considerable; we'd bust them up now and then. That was my headache because I had the overhaul shops. We started with six gliders, and we finished with six gliders, but some of them that were flying had an awful lot of parts that weren't in the original gliders. I was practically manufacturing them to keep them going. We wrecked a lot of gliders.

On the report that got to BuAer, one of the endorsements to it was Admiral King's note, "Something should be done about this. EJK." His intent was that it be continued, and on top of that was a note, "File this."

It went in the files, and that was the end of it. There was no more gliding in the navy after that until, just before Pearl Harbor, the navy again started an interest in gliders for military purposes.

12. Rear Adm. William A. Moffett, chief of the navy's Bureau of Aeronautics from 1921 until his death in 1933, played a pivotal role in shaping naval aviation in the 1920s and early '30s. *(Courtesy Special Collections, Nimitz Library, U.S. Naval Academy)*

13. Civilian pilot Bert Acosta poses with his winning Navy/Curtiss racer and the 1921 Pulitzer Trophy, taken on the lawn of the Curtiss factory on Long Island. Acosta's winning performance started a chain of victories for Curtiss aircraft that was to give the United States air-racing superiority for several years to come. *(Courtesy National Air and Space Museum)*

14. The USS *Arizona* (BB-39) was photographed with a Nieuport 28 aircraft on the flying-off platform on the no. 3 turret at Guantánamo Bay, Cuba, c. spring 1921.

15. During the summer of 1921, flying an Aeromarine 39-B, Lt. Alfred M. Pride tested various types of arresting gear on a turntable at Hampton Roads, Virginia.

16. A Vought VE-7 lands on the USS *Langley* (CV-1), for five years (1922–27) the navy's only aircraft carrier.

17. Lt. Comdr. Godfrey de Courcelles Chevalier made the first landing aboard the *Langley* (CV-1) on 26 October 1922, while the carrier was under way off Cape Henry. Chevalier died on 14 November from injuries received in a plane crash.

18. Flying a Navy/Curtiss racer, the CR-3, Lt. David Rittenhouse (*center*) won the 1923 Schneider Trophy race for seaplanes at an average speed of 177.4 mph. Other members of the navy team were Lt. Rutledge Irvin, Lt. Frank Wead, and Lt. A. W. Gorton.

19. Winner of the 1923 Pulitzer Trophy, world speed-record holder, renowned test and aerobatic pilot, and rugged individualist Lt. Alford "Al" Williams devoted his life to the advancement of U.S. aviation.

20. In July 1927, Lt. C. C. Champion, flying a Wright F3W Apache fighter powered with a 420-horsepower Pratt & Whitney Wasp engine, established world altitude records for seaplanes (37,995 feet) and land planes (38,419 feet).

21. Flying a Vought UO-1, the USS *Saratoga's* (CV-3) air officer, Lt. Comdr. Marc Mitscher, with Lt. Selden Spangler as passenger, made the first takeoff and landing on 11 January 1928, while the ship was steaming in Delaware Bay.

22. Flying their Boeing F2Bs in spectacular performances of formation and aerobatic flying, the "Three Sea Hawks" made headlines at the 1928 National Air Races at Mines Field, Los Angeles. *(Courtesy National Air and Space Museum)*

23. "The Three Sea Hawks" (*left to right*): Lts. W. V. "Bill" Davis Jr., D. W. "Tommy" Tomlinson IV (leader), and A. P. "Putt" Storrs III. *(Courtesy National Air and Space Museum)*

24. Lts. Tommy Tomlinson (*left*) and G. W. D. Covell, flying in Tomlinson's personal "Jenny," were the first to arrive at the Second California Aviation Conference, Mills Field, San Francisco, on 5 May 1927. *(Courtesy National Air and Space Museum)*

25. One of many record-breaking naval aviators of the 1920s, Lt. Apollo Soucek set a new world altitude record for seaplanes on 4 June 1929, reaching 38,560 feet in a Wright Apache.

26. Aircraft from the carriers *Langley* (CV-1), *Lexington* (CV-2), and *Saratoga* (CV-3) line up at the Naval Air Station North Island, San Diego, in February 1930, prior to embarkation for the 1930 Fleet Problem.

27. Lt. Ralph Barnaby's glider is attached to the USS *Los Angeles* (ZR-3), from which Barnaby made a successful flight on 31 January 1930.

28. Lt. Ralph Barnaby readies himself for takeoff in a Washington Glider Club training glider on 27 April 1930. *(Courtesy National Soaring Museum)*

PART THREE

EXPANSION AND APPROACH TO WAR

In the early 1930s, few Americans anticipated that by the end of the decade much of the world would be in the throes of another war. People had a far greater concern at the time—the Great Depression, brought on by the catastrophic collapse of the stock market in October 1929. The failure of almost half the banks in the United States, combined with a nationwide loss of confidence in the economy, led to much-reduced levels of spending and demand, making matters even worse. After becoming president in 1932, Franklin D. Roosevelt introduced a number of changes in the structure of the economy, using increased government regulation and massive public works projects to promote a recovery. Naval aviation benefited immensely from allocations of funds from the government agencies created in the wake of the depression.

Aviation began the decade in spectacular fashion, with more than a score of record-breaking flights in 1930. The Atlantic was crossed five times, transcontinental speed records were broken, and world altitude and refueling duration marks were raised. The German rigid airship *Graf Zeppelin* braved equatorial storms on a four-continent flight, the first nonstop flight from Paris to New York occurred, and Comdr. Richard E. Byrd returned from the South Pole to receive a hero's welcome. The spectacular flights, many of them measures of engineering progress, served an important purpose in sustaining public interest in aviation during a year when the world was plunging deep into the depression.

Following the five successful crossings in 1930, the "Atlantic follies" that had begun in the 1920s continued unabated. The motivations to fly across the ocean were as diverse as the hundreds of amateurs and professionals who tried it. Prize money, a desire to be the first to fly home to one's mother country, and the usual thirst for adventure were all prime motivators. Whatever the reason, the sad fact was that many of the intrepid aviators who tried to conquer the North Atlantic were ill-prepared to do so—and the results were predictable.

By 1933, however, the Commerce Department had begun to enforce new restrictions on transatlantic flight, and the "going home" flights decreased in frequency. In their place came the first transatlantic passenger service in May 1936 by the German airship *Hindenburg*, followed in 1937 by the first commercial survey flights by flying boats. In June 1939 the graceful, elegant Boeing 314 clippers of Pan American Airways began weekly service to France and England, ending three years of competition among Germany, France, Great Britain, and the United States for commercial conquest of the Atlantic.

The Atlantic crossings of the 1930s were a microcosm of hundreds of long-distance flights throughout the world. Among these history-making odysseys were Kingsford-Smith's "'round-the-world flight" in the *Southern Cross* in 1930; Wiley Post's and Harold Gatty's trip around the world in 1931 in a little more than eight days; Italo Balbo's trip in 1933 to America with his fleet of Savoia-Marchetti flying boats; Wiley Post's solo flight around the world in the *Winnie May* that same year; and in July 1938, Howard Hughes and his four-man crew cut Wiley Post's around-the-world record in half with their Lockheed 14 airliner.

Pioneering the Arctic great circle route between continents was a particular challenge for American, German, and Russian aviators who were convinced that the great circle route was the most logical way to fly between Europe, North America, and Asia. One of the more noteworthy efforts was the ten thousand–mile 1931 flight by Charles and Anne Lindbergh across the Arctic to the Orient in a Lockheed Sirius floatplane, the first time anyone had accomplished such a feat. Not to be outdone, in 1937 Russian airmen twice flew gliderlike, single-engine Tupolev ANT-25s nonstop across the North Pole from the Soviet Union to the West Coast of the United States in sixty-two hours.

The U.S. Navy continued to demonstrate the mobility afforded by improvements in engine and airframe design. Patrol squadrons began to fly nonstop over much greater distances, routinely deploying entire squadrons to such remote locations as the Panama Canal, the Aleutians, and Hawaii. Mass formation flights of more than twenty-four hours' duration were not uncommon. Typical of these were the 1933 nonstop formation flight of Consolidated P2Y-1s from Norfolk, Virginia, to Coco Solo, Panama Canal Zone, followed in 1934 by Lt. Comdr. K. McGinnis's Pacific crossing with six P2Y-1s from San Francisco to Pearl Harbor in slightly more than twenty-four hours.

The pattern of aerial exploration flights established throughout the world in the 1920s continued. Antarctica attracted such explorers as Byrd, Wilkins, and Ellsworth, while Americans Martin and Osa Johnson conducted aerial safaris over the back country of Kenya and Tanganyika. By the close of the decade, polar ice fields, jungles, desert wastelands, and the world's highest mountains had been photographed and explored from the air for the first time.

By 1932 the National Air Races had become one of the nation's leading sporting events. Each September, all eyes turned toward Cleveland, Ohio, where enormous crowds of more than a hundred thousand put aside the gloom of the depression to enjoy the aerobatics, wing walking, and precision formation flying by army, navy, and marine squadrons. But what they really came to see were the races, particularly the Thompson Trophy classic, an unlimited free-for-all that was the fastest event of the meet. Since the mid-1920s, development of special racing planes by the military had declined to the point where "homemade," one-off designs with increasingly powerful engines dominated the course. The Granville brothers, Jimmy Wedell, Ben Howard, and Steve Wittman produced innovative designs for the races; Roscoe Turner proved to be not only colorful but also the best of the racing pilots, while Jimmie Doolittle continued to distinguish himself as one of the finest pilots of all time.

Manufacturer Vincent Bendix created the other speed classic of the age in 1931 when he offered a trophy for cross-country flying. Open to both men and women, the Bendix race was an annual cross-country, high-speed race flown between two cities on opposite sides of the continent. Passenger cabin planes as well as modified pylon racers competed, and new transcontinental records became an annual occurrence. On the international racing scene, England won permanent possession of the Schneider Trophy in 1931. Without representation by any of the European countries or the United States, England won by default, thus retiring the trophy.

A postscript to the 1931 Schneider Trophy event was a successful attempt on the world's straightaway speed record by the Supermarine S-6B, designed by Britain's brilliant R. J. Mitchell. With a specially built Rolls-Royce V-12 developing more than 2,600 horsepower, the S-6B broke the 400 mph barrier with an average speed of 407 mph! In 1934 Italy raised the speed record to 440 mph with a Macchi MC-72 seaplane that had been developed for the 1931 Schneider Trophy race. In the United States, as engine and airframe designs improved over time, new aircraft performance records were set daily. The transcontinental speed record held the center of public attention, but shorter speed flights linking major cities demonstrated the possibilities for faster commercial air transportation. No single individual set up more inter-city records than did Frank Monroe Hawks, the premier record setter of the decade. U.S. Navy pilots also had their share of records, including Lt. Apollo Soucek's altitude records in 1929–30, which earned him the billing "America's premier altitude flier."

The best measure of progress in all phases of naval aviation was the effectiveness of aircraft carriers and patrol aviation in the annual Fleet Problems. Good use of the *Langley* had been made in the 1927 and 1928 exercises, but in these, and earlier exercises, much of the air activity had been "constructive" in nature, with single aircraft simulating entire squadrons of different types, and battleships acting as carriers. With the 1929 exercises, the new carriers *Lexington* and *Saratoga* entered the picture and immediately proved beyond any doubt that air power could be the determining factor in a war at sea. The 1930 Fleet Problem reemphasized the importance of command of the air and brought up the particular study of the "carrier group," consisting of a complete tactical unit of one carrier and supporting cruisers and destroyers. As new carriers and aircraft joined the fleet during the prewar years, the annual Fleet Problems—as well as numerous smaller-scale training exercises conducted throughout the year—continued to be invaluable proving grounds for people and their machines.

During his twelve years as chief of the Bureau of Aeronautics, Rear Admiral Moffett established high standards for the naval aviation establishment. The navy was most fortunate at the time of Moffett's death to have Rear Adm. Ernest J. King available to take over the helm as his successor. A fighter, hard driver, and martinet with the courage of his convictions, King would keep the aviation navy on the proper course for many years to come, first as the chief of the Bureau of Aeronautics, and later as chief of naval operations and commander in chief of the U.S. Fleet during the war. In June 1936 Admiral King was relieved by another extremely able, energetic administrator, Rear Adm. Arthur B. Cook, and in 1939, Rear Adm. John Towers became the head of the bureau. Both of these officers continued to provide naval aviation with the same degree of competent leadership to which it had become accustomed for many years. And, of no little importance, President Roosevelt's enthusiastic interest in the navy and high personal regard for Admiral King added to the U.S. Navy's continued success.

The problems facing King and his successors were magnified by events abroad: Japanese aggression in the Far East, the emergence of Hitler in Europe, Mussolini's invasion of Ethiopia, and the Spanish revolution. At home, the depression imposed limits on any grandiose plans for expansion. Yet, liberal allocations from such New Deal agencies as the National Recovery Administration (NRA) and the Public Works Administration (PWA) kept naval aviation solvent and, with congressional support, permitted expansion and improvements in operating forces, bases, manpower, and technology. On the eve of the U.S. entry into World War II, seven fleet carriers and one escort carrier were in commission; five patrol wings and two marine aircraft wings were in operation. There were 5,260 aircraft of all types, with 6,750 Coast Guard, navy, and marine pilots to fly them and 21,678 enlisted men to keep them flying. Naval aviation was hardly ready to fight the global war that was coming.

Rear Adm. George Van Deurs brings his own personal charm, wit, and knack for spinning a good yarn to his account of life on a decrepit, rusting seaplane tender on the Asiatic Station. Flying was fun, though useless, as far as any military value was concerned; relationships with the Japanese were uneasy and sensitive during the early days of Japanese aggression in the Pacific; and in the absence of timely direction or guidance from Washington, San Diego, or Pearl Harbor, ingenuity, self-reliance, and resourcefulness were often the keys to solving operational problems.

Rare indeed was the navy pilot of the 1930s who did not have operational experience across a wide spectrum of aviation duties: flying floatplanes off battleships and cruisers, fighters or dive-bombers off aircraft carriers, and patrol planes on long-range missions to faraway places. Rear Adm. Harold B. Miller experienced all that—and more. He was one of a relative handful of officers who flew the tiny F9C Sparrowhawk fighters from the airships *Akron* and *Macon*. By a stroke of luck he was not on the *Akron* the night of its fateful crash off the Atlantic coast, and he miraculously survived the *Macon* disaster in the Pacific. His is one of the few firsthand accounts of the role of the Sparrowhawks in lighter-than-air operations and of the events leading up to the end of the navy's involvement with the rigid airship.

In one's career, as in most things in life, timing is everything. As a midshipman, Herbert D. Riley shoveled coal on coal-burning battleships, and as a vice admiral, flew his flag on the nuclear-powered carrier *Enterprise*. His first solo flight was in a wood-and-fabric biplane, which took off from a cow pasture; his first carrier landing was on the converted collier *Langley*, and his last carrier landing was in a supersonic fighter on the *Enterprise*. Admiral Riley makes a case that the Naval Academy class of 1927 was a "vintage class," an exceptionally good group of people who got the breaks as far as timing was concerned. As a young naval aviator, Riley became intrigued with the challenges of long-distance flying, and seemed to spend a considerable amount of his flight time flying from here to there. Like Columbus, Riley always seemed to be exploring new horizons, not waiting for new techniques, but modifying what he had, making the best of it—and being lucky. He relied on his flying skill, ingenuity, and stamina to pick his way through rugged mountains and wilderness, to lead others over uncharted waters, or to explore the Pacific "looking for places [we] didn't know much about."

Lt. Comdr. Robert E. Carl relives his days on the carrier *Saratoga* during the depression years, an era when carrier sailors slept in hammocks, heated their wash water with steam jets, and lived on a monthly take-home pay of $19.50, $10 of which was sent home. Carl learned early on that carrying a typewriter from one duty station to another signified a special talent that would at least keep him out of the deck force or the engine room. From a yeoman's perspective, Carl viewed a carrier aviator's life with awe and great admiration, and he offers a critical appraisal of some of the customs and traditions of the naval service that, fortunately or unfortunately, depending on one's point of view, have not withstood the test of time.

From Rear Adm. Francis D. Foley's descriptions of squadron operations on the navy's first true aircraft carrier, the *Ranger,* one can begin to appreciate how the carrier navy matured into the potent offensive force of World War II. Dive-bombing, coordinated attacks, competitions between squadrons, integration of the carrier into fleet dispositions, battle tactics that worked (and didn't work), evolution of the air group concept—all contributed mightily to the maturation of the carrier navy during the decade. Admiral Foley's routine on the *Ranger* was interrupted briefly in 1937 by a short cruise on the *Lexington* to search for Amelia Earhart, and he provides an interesting firsthand account of this inconclusive chapter in U.S. aeronautical history that to this day evokes much controversy and speculation.

Adm. John S. "Jimmie" Thach is perhaps best known for his exploits during World War II. His heroics at the Battle of Midway, where he put to good use the "Thach weave"—the defensive aerial maneuver that he developed before the war—earned Thach a memorable chapter in naval aviation history. Like so many of his contemporaries, Thach was equally at home in seaplanes or land planes. In the 1930s, flying-boat pilots seemed to have more adventures, more challenges, and more excitement. Horrible weather in the Aleutians, ferocious insects in the tropics, and St. Elmo's fire were typical of the hazards encountered by Thach and his compatriots as they explored some of the more godforsaken corners of the globe in their P2Y and PBY flying boats.

CWO Cecil King fell in love with the navy early on and developed a lasting devotion and respect for the service that shines through his reminiscences like a beacon. With great enthusiasm, King shares his fond memories of boot camp: old, fatherly chief petty officers who commanded abiding respect; the challenge of sleeping in hammocks, but "you just didn't dare to fall out"; drill, discipline, and strict attention to uniform regulations that bothered some—but not him; the unquestioning obedience that was expected—and given. The navy was a no-nonsense organization and "people better get along in it." King fondly remembers his duty on the cruiser *Portland,* meeting President Franklin D. Roosevelt during Roosevelt's 1935 fishing trip on the cruiser *Houston.* King also vividly recalls his tour at the Fleet Air Base, Coco Solo, where he established a tenuous relationship with then-captain John S. McCain, a man who King thought was a "hell of a skipper," and a legend in his time. One of the proudest moments of King's life was when he filled in his occupation on his reenlistment papers as "mariner."

Admiral Foley's experiences flying PBY Catalinas on aerial surveys to Central America and on neutrality patrols prior to World War II taught him that it helped to be a good seaman in handling the big patrol boats on the water. Anchoring, making beach approaches, going to buoys, forced landings at sea—all challenged the abilities of an airman to judge wind, waves, and current. While Admiral Foley was flying neutrality patrols in the Atlantic and the Caribbean, Adm. Thomas H. Moorer was flying PBYs in the Pacific, initially on long-range survey flights and later, as war approached, eighteen-hour patrols from Hawaii and scouting flights from Midway and Wake Islands. On the night of 7 December 1941, in the aftermath of the Japanese attack, then-lieutenant Moorer was airborne from Pearl Harbor in one of the two serviceable aircraft left in his squadron, flying out to sea in a vain attempt to find the retreating Japanese carrier task force.

For Admiral Moorer, and all the other officers and men of naval aviation, the golden age would soon be but a memory.

8

On the Far China Station

Rear Adm. George Van Deurs

In the old days, if an officer had orders for a tour of duty in the Western Pacific, he wasn't ordered to his ship or squadron—he was ordered to the Asiatic Station, period. The commander-in-chief out there was the whole Navy Department himself. My wife and I were on a ship destined for the Asiatic Station in the summer of 1929, when the ship made Kobe, Japan. A courier came aboard and any naval officers on board were given orders there as to where they were going. My orders were to the aircraft ship, the old USS *Jason* (AV-2), down in Manila. It was what we had expected. There was one other aviator on board, and we were both going out to be part of a new squadron. There was one six-plane torpedo plane squadron out there, and they were going to form a six-plane scouting squadron, Scouting Squadron 8A (VS-8A), equipped with Vought O2U-3s, and we were going to be part of that.

We got to Shanghai, and I left my wife, Ann, on the ship nursing the children while I went ashore with one of the other passengers, took in a few bars and things to see in the sink hole of the Orient. Late in the evening, when we were in the Astor Bar, a classmate with another set of orders for me found me. He had gone to the ship after I got ashore and had been hunting for me all afternoon. The new orders said to get off the liner at Shanghai and go up to Tsingtao and join the *Jason* there.

So I went back to the ship and put what I needed into the suitcases, which took most of the family suitcases. Our money was in traveler's checks with my name on them, so they were no good to Ann. We had a few hundred bucks in the bank in Annapolis, so I wrote her a check for $300 and said, "Here, when you get to Manila cash this and find a place to live, and I'll be back in a month or so." The next morning I got on a little Japanese steamer and went up to Tsingtao, and, of course, the *Jason* wasn't there.

Ann went on to Manila. When she got there, she had to get the car off the dock. The Filipino workers weren't used to seeing blondes, and she got jolly-well pinched going and coming. When she got to a navy club, she tried to cash the check, and nobody would cash a check for $300. They said if it was a low one they could cash it but, gee, for $300! You can get out of the islands for that. He wouldn't think of that. She had to borrow some suitcases from the other passengers to get some of her stuff ashore. She couldn't pack it all in the ones I had left her. She was pretty bitter.

She was sitting in the club wondering what to do and got to talking to Mrs. Clyde Smith, who had gotten there a week or so before. Her husband was to join the same squadron. Eddie Smith had opened a banking account about a week before. When she endorsed Ann's check they took that right away. That cleared up her money trouble, but she was alone with two babies and a car in a strange land! She made out, but she had things to say to me when I got there!

In the meantime the *Jason* was not in Tsingtao, so I went to the senior officer present on the submarine tender there and was on her for about a week or so during which I spent three or four days in one of the old S-boats. A classmate skipper invited me to go for a ride while he went out and shot some torpedoes. That cured me of ever wanting to be a submariner. It was a very dull three or four days. Eventually the *Jason* came in about a week late. She had just finished being overhauled in the Cavite yard, and this was about September when she got up there. She was only there two or three weeks and went back to Manila.

An old friend of mine, Mike Avery, showed up on the next steamer coming out to be the exec of the new squadron. The three of us needed flight time. You could make up flight time for pay for three months. If you went over three months you were just out of luck. I had been traveling and on leave, so it was getting close to the end of the three months when the *Jason* came in. The only planes the *Jason* had were Martin T3M-2 torpedo planes with Packard engines in them. They had a pretty poor squadron commander, and the plane maintenance was terrible. They were about as crummy-looking planes as I ever saw, but we needed time, so we borrowed them.

Mike and I got one going and took off and flew around Kiaochow Wan Bay for a while. After fifteen minutes by the clock the engine quit cold. We landed, looked it over, couldn't find anything wrong with it, tried to start it, but no dice. We sat there for a while and in about fifteen minutes we tried it again, and it started off right normal. So we took off and flew around until fifteen minutes later it cut out cold again. After we got it cooled down and started it, we took it back to the ship and got another plane. It did the same thing.

The torpedo squadron commander said they didn't know why but they always did that. They didn't know what was the trouble. We got the twelve hours or more that we needed in fifteen minute chunks, with cranking in between. Those things would fly for exactly fifteen minutes and quit. It wasn't really a happy experience. Some months later I found what was the matter with them. The magneto coils were condemned. The department had found out about it a long time before, but word never got to China. The Scintilla magneto people had made a batch of coils that had bad insulation. They would test perfectly cold on a test bench. However, in the air, the engine got warm, the insulation got hot and broke down, and you had no spark. It was a wax composition of some kind, and when the wax cooled off it was a perfectly good insulator again, and you could start it. There were certain serial numbers that had to be thrown out. It just happened that the only ones on the China station were in that batch of serial numbers, and they had never gotten the word. It was a pretty hard thing to show up on a test bench. About a year later those torpedo planes were taken out of service, and that squadron got new planes with radial engines. The Packard engine wasn't too good anyway.

The ship's routine was to spend about six months in the wintertime in the Philippines, mostly in Manila, some of it in Subic Bay. One summer we operated in Tsingtao and the other summer in Chefoo. When the ship was under way we were all standing watch, acting as ship's watch officers, flying as squadron pilots, and doing our squadron jobs. I happened to be engineer of the scouting squadron, and also because of the experience I had picked up earlier in my career I ended up as the repair officer of the whole outfit.

It was a strange arrangement. Under the Washington Naval Treaty of 1922 we couldn't put any aviation on the beach. So we worked a shenanigan. There was a boat shed in the Cavite Navy Yard where two warrant officers taught native workmen to overhaul airplanes. We couldn't put a seaplane ramp there because then we'd make it an air station. We had an old hand-crank crane that we'd pick the plane up with and haul it into the shop. They couldn't test engines over there or overhaul them because the commandant didn't like the noise. He wouldn't let them run an airplane engine in the navy yard. So we got a coal barge, a flat lighter, and put the engine in a plane and tied the plane down on the lighter. Then we towed the lighter out into the middle of Manila Bay, and somebody would sit there in the sun all day testing the engine or breaking it in after overhaul. I spent a lot of hours with a pith helmet and what-have-you sitting on that darned barge running two or three engines where they were far enough away that we wouldn't annoy the commandant with the noise!

About a week after I got aboard the *Jason* at Tsingtao that first time, the fleet flagship came in, the USS *Pittsburgh* (CA-4)—old Adm. Charlie Butler McVay Jr. Our skipper was a really wonderful guy, A. L. Bristol, who had just finished Pensacola as a commander. Bristol put on his shiny clean uniform and sword and gloves and went over to make an official call. McVay had just come out and taken command of the China station. It was a very powerful job in those days. He was Jesus Christ and the Navy Department all the way from the international date line to the Suez Canal. He ran everything. He didn't have to ask the Navy Department for anything. He had the rank of ambassador to China and three or four other different countries out there as a diplomatic status.

Bristol went aboard the *Pittsburgh*, reported, and said he had command of the Asiatic Fleet Air Force. "Oh yes," McVay says, "the air force." He pulled out a desk drawer and said, "You've got a couple of young officers over there I want to talk about." He pulled out a Dollar Line passenger list. "Oh yes. Van Deurs and Berner." Well, Bristol came back and sent for us and said, "What the hell did you guys do?"

We said, "Nothing. Why?"

He said, "I went over there, and McVay never asked me any questions about air, what we had, or anything else; he talked the whole time about you guys. He was on the Dollar boat with you from San Francisco to Honolulu. He got off there to see his son. And he said you had insulted him and paid no attention to him."

We had seen his name on the passenger list. As a matter of fact Warren Berner and I had talked it over and said, "We don't know what to do, a couple of young lieutenants. If we were wearing four stars and traveling in civilian clothes, we wouldn't want to be bothered with us. The best thing we can do is pay no attention."

We told Bristol we didn't know what to do, and that's the way we figured it. If we were wearing four stars we wouldn't want to be bothered with a couple of young squirts. He said, "I see what you mean. It's perfectly logical, but if you ever get caught that way again send a card around. But in the meantime get shined up, get in a boat, and go over and apologize to him. That's all we can do now."

So we went over there, and this old bastard stood us up like plebes. We explained what had happened. We were very sorry we had offended him. He never said, "Yes, no, boo," or anything except, "All right, gentlemen, that is all."

That was that. But that was the way aviation rated in those days. We found out later that the only things that interested McVay were the proper personal honors and his golf score. The only way aviation got things out there from there on was that Bristol, being quite a diplomat, would play golf with the old man, let him beat him, and get something we needed out of him. But we weren't something to even speak to. Nobody that ran the navy, or very few of them, ever thought that aviation could count for anything, and we were tolerated I guess for publicity value more than anything else.

The *Jason* was an old collier, with all the coaling gear and everything. We used to use the coaling booms to hoist the planes, and we nested them on cradles on the hatches between the towers that held the coaling booms. The planes, six torpedo planes and six scouts, rode with one wing sticking over the side and the other sticking in between the towers. Kelly Turner, who was the skipper just before Bristol came out, tried to improve things, and he had gotten a lot of alterations approved, including an extra deck house above the poop with enough rooms to house the second squadron pilots. He cleaned out one of the coal holds—number ten hold—and put in some decks to make a bomb storage, engine shop, and an armory that we needed for the planes. The rest of the ship was still carrying coal. We had a lot of coal in the other holds for ballast. We put spare planes and spare wings down in a hold on top of the coal. We'd drop the crates down there and let them sit—no place else to put them.

Throughout the year we ran the prescribed practices of gunnery and bombing and so on. In Manila we had to fly out beyond Corregidor to use live bombs or fire machine guns. I don't remember how far our planes could fly at that time, but Clyde Smith and I had spent a lot of time trying to figure how to get more mileage out of them—how far we could stretch them doing the best we could. We wanted to figure how we could get from the northern part of Luzon over to the mainland of China, and we never could figure any closer than about fifty miles no matter what we did. We tried all kinds of tricks on those engines and tried all kinds of tests, but they couldn't fly far enough to get across.

During the time that we were out there, in the summer of '31, we operated at Chefoo, and it was in September that the Japanese invaded Manchuria. For a while everybody out there was nervous, and thought it might mean the Japanese war that everybody said was coming some day. We started flying navigation problems. The only navigation we could do on those planes was dead reckoning. But we started running some triangular courses from the *Jason* anchored off Chefoo into the Gulf of Chihli, down the gulf out of sight of land and back to see how accurately we could make a landfall. Some of them we ran in pretty hazy weather, where the visibility wasn't very good. Apparently we flew over some Japanese fishing boats somewhere when our course was aimed in the general direction of Port Arthur.

Right away quick the skipper was called over to the American consulate to explain why American planes were flying over Port Arthur. The State Department wanted to know; the Japanese had kicked to Washington that we were flying over Port Arthur. Well, the answer was we weren't, but apparently they didn't believe it.

There was a little Japanese jeweler named Nosy Dragon who had letters of recommendation from everybody from Admiral Dewey on down. We gave him permission to come aboard, spread out some jewelry on the poop deck there, and sell it. He had a little shop over in Chefoo where he made the stuff. A couple of days after the alleged flight over Port Arthur, little Nosey Dragon came out to the ship, and he was whiter than a sheet. He wanted to see the exec right away, quick. He explained that so-and-so of the Japanese embassy over there, the military guy, was going to kill him if he didn't find out what the Americans were doing over Port Arthur. He said all his life he had been doing business with American ships, and he liked them; he didn't want to make any trouble with the Americans, they were his friends. But this guy was going to kill him if he didn't get an answer. Please could he have some story he could tell to satisfy the Jap consulate. Two or three people put their heads together, and they worked up a yarn and told Nosey Dragon to go back and tell it. It worked apparently because Nosey was back in business the next week.

The Japanese had a very big consulate in Chefoo that was mostly involved in keeping track of the Americans. The American destroyers had been using that as a summer base for years. Down the coast a few miles the British from Hong Kong used Wei Hai Wei for a summer base. They had a carrier out there at the time that used to work out of Wei Hai Wei. We had some drinking connections with them at various times. So the Japs were worried about both of us, but we never saw any of their ships or any of their actions at all. We had orders to stay away from them, so we did. But they were very touchy about it.

At that time we had no naval air attaché in Japan, so each year one officer from the *Jason* would go up there for three months temporary duty in our embassy as the naval aviation attaché. They tried to pick somebody that could go two years in a row so that they would get a chance to double-check everything without being snowed under. Before I got out there John J. Ballentine, who later made admiral, did that job one year, and he reported the Japanese were just as good at aviation as we were. Their planes were number one, and from what he had been able to observe they were doing all right. We'd better watch them, that they really were not the inferior pilots that the world said they were. We had at that time said, "Oh, they all wear glasses, their eyes are no good, they're just a bunch of monkeys, and they can't fly at all." They maybe were good acrobats but not aviators. Well, Ballentine in his report denied all this.

The next two years a classmate of mine, Malcolm E. Selby, went there. Selby was an awful nice guy. He was a heavyweight boxer at the Naval

Academy, and he probably took a couple too many on the chin. He had his wings taken off twice for foolish stunts that had fatal results, and the last time they stayed off. But Selby went to Japan and the Japanese navy was as nice as hell to him. They showed him everything he asked about. He said, "The poor guys are way behind. They are years behind us with that stuff they've got." There was a rumor that they were building a plane somewhere. He didn't see it, but they were building a plane something like the ones we were flying—but he didn't believe it. He thought that was just boasting. They really had nothing; there was nothing to it. We could lick them with one hand behind our back. And that was the kind of report that everybody believed.

The last two years Clyde Smith went up there. Clyde was a red-headed, thoughtful chap, and he said he thought Selby had had the wrong dope. He said Japanese naval aviators aren't dopes at all; they were darned good. The only place he could see anything new at all, it was just as good as we had. They were doing all right. And for two years his report said that, but his reports and Ballentine's were just filed in the department until after the Zero began knocking down our people.

One day after that Manchurian thing some of us were sitting around in the wardroom arguing about what we were supposed to do in case the Japanese did start toward the Philippines. Nobody could really think what the dozen airplanes we had could accomplish against the Japanese fleet. Our planes had machine guns, they could carry one hundred–pound bombs, and they could go four hundred miles. The other squadron had six planes that could carry one torpedo each. We finally got arguing, and Clyde Smith went up to the skipper and got him to open the safe and give him the war plans for the Orange War. We took it back to the wardroom, and we began reading through it to see what we were supposed to do. Finally, we all got laughing so hard that it was hard to keep reading. Various people were taking turns reading out of this thing, and it was just like reading the funny papers. It was completely ridiculous.

The Dewey Drydock, a big, wooden floating drydock, was in Subic Bay because Subic Bay was deep enough to operate it. There was no place in Manila Bay where the water was deep enough to sink the thing to get a ship in, therefore it was kept at Subic. These war plans had pages and pages of detailed instructions on how to get the Dewey Drydock under way. It told where each anchor was to be picked up, and exactly where it was to be placed on the dock, and what they were to use to pick it up with, and which boats would take the thing in tow, and what size tow line they would use, what course they'd steer to get it down to Manila Bay, and when they got to Corregidor—it stopped. By that time the decisions would have been reached as to where to put it!

Our planes were supposed to tell the U.S. Army whether the Japanese were going to invade on the east coast or the west coast of Luzon—and they were to be based at Manila Bay. The only trouble was that it was possible to see farther from the north end of Luzon than we could fly from Manila Bay! It was pretty silly. They were worrying about a landing at Lingayen, where the Japs actually did land, and there was one place on the other side of Luzon where it seemed possible to make a landing.

We knew we didn't have enough gas to get away so some of us figured that if this war comes along and going gets tough, we will fly as far north as long as the gas holds out, then bail out in the Bontoc country where the Igorotes live and turn guerrilla with them. They were the most loyal natives in the islands at the time, the non-Christian tribes in the north. The Spaniards had never conquered them, and we thought maybe the Japs would have a tough time too. That was purely a personal decision. There was nothing in the plans.

The flying was fun though it was completely useless as far as military value was concerned. The scouts were the newest things the navy had when they sent them out there, there just weren't enough of them to do any good. The twelve planes of the *Jason* were the only naval air that side of Guam, and they had no power at all. They didn't have the range to do any scouting. It was a silly gesture. Mainly I believe it was there because under the 1922 treaty we couldn't increase the defenses of the Philippines, so they wanted to be able to say that there was an air force there, to keep something there, so you could expand it and say, "Those aren't shore defenses." It was an ace in the hole.

But by January of '32 they ordered the *Jason* home for decommissioning. She was getting pretty old and in pretty terrible shape, so we got all ready to come home. Some of us were disappointed. We'd expected to come home commercially and our tours were up, two and a half years. We were held over to act as ship's officers bringing her home.

Then the Japanese moved into Shanghai and right quick every fighting ship in Manila was ordered to Shanghai. The *Jason* was told to fill up with provisions and follow along to provision the fleet since the fighting in Shanghai might mean a shortage of provisions. Well, we couldn't find enough provisions in Manila to cover the bottom of one hold because every destroyer and gunboat and everything else had filled up before sailing, and the ship chandlers and provision merchants in Manila were cleaned out. It was several weeks before ships from the States brought in more supplies. By that time things had calmed down in Shanghai. Our people were just watching and they were doing all right, so we were held there on standby until April. Then the new replacement pilots that had come out took our scouting planes and put them ashore over in Cavite, to wait for the *Langley* to arrive. The rest of us were to sail for the States in the *Jason* with the old torpedo planes.

We put the *Jason* in drydock and started chipping the water line. The first thing that happened, one of the kids lost his chipping hammer right through the side of the ship, so they stopped chipping, put a scab patch on that, and let it go. Then they got the ship's bunkers emptied. The first lieutenant was in there looking around and suddenly realized that all the girders that held the ship together had rusted away, and there was nothing holding the stern of the ship to the rest of it except the skin plating. These colliers were built with big I-beams about three feet thick, like multiple keels. They were all gone.

We had planned to go to Shanghai and Japan and across to Seattle, but the weather was apt to be bad up there. They sent us way south hoping we'd make it without breaking in two—which is probably what happened to the *Cyclops* and other sister ships of the *Jason*—the *Proteus* (ex-AC-9) and *Nereus* (ex-AC-10). They were sold to Canada in 1941 and put to hauling bauxite from the Virgin Islands to Canada in the summertime and Portland, Maine, in the winter. Just about the time of Pearl Harbor, about a week apart, they sailed from St. Thomas with a heavy load of ore, and each disappeared, just as the *Cyclops* had disappeared between Barbados and Norfolk years before.

According to weather bureau records they'd all run into a fast-moving front where the wave structure ran ahead of the wind. In other words, the ship was steaming in perfectly smooth water with a light southerly wind on their tails, and all of a sudden she hit big waves, and after the waves had arrived the wind shifted into the north. The weather bureau has assured me that on the dates that all of those ships would have been somewhere off the Carolina coast they would have hit that kind of weather.

The *Cyclops,* while she was newer, had been weakened by pounding along all the way from Brazil with one engine cylinder out—unbalanced in other words, so her stern was shaking. When I was on the *Jason* under way at any speed the back end of her flopped up and down like a springboard that somebody was bouncing on. We never understood it until we got into that coal bunker, and there was just the skin holding the ship together.

The sulphur in the coal had rusted the I-beams out. The bunker completely surrounded the fire room. It was on both sides and on top, with the boilers right inside. If the ship split there, the water would immediately rush into the fire room and probably cause a boiler explosion or at least stop everything right there. I believe the *Jason* was on the verge of a catastrophe, with her rusted hull. The two ships that were lost under Canadian colors had rusted ten years longer and were probably in worse shape, and the *Cyclops* had been running for a long period with her unbalanced engine. I believe all three broke right in the fire room; neither end would have floated for more than seconds.

Before we started on our trip back we got a new executive officer named Burke, a lieutenant commander mustang who had been the skipper of the naval station up at Olongapo in the Philippines. Olongapo was a funny place. Essentially it was abandoned, although they had the drydock there. When the ship was in it they'd take a lot of workmen from Cavite up there to work on it. There was a marine barracks that policed a big naval reservation that had a lot of native towns on it and a radio station.

The station executive officer was a chief bosun, and there was also a doctor on board. The bosun and the doctor put their heads together and decided that the old man, Burke, was crazy. They didn't play it very smart. The only way to get to Olongapo at that time was by sea, a little boat once a week from Cavite. There were no roads over the mountains, no connection with the rest of Luzon. The bosun and the doctor relieved the skipper of command and sent him down to Cavite, practically as a prisoner, to the hospital for observation.

Burke was crazy like a fox. He sat in the hospital at Sangley Point, took all their tests, behaved himself, and read a lot of books. After a month or so the doctor said, "He's perfectly sane," and turned him loose. Immediately, Burke broke out the books he had been reading and prepared charges for a general court against the chief bosun and the doctor, for mutiny. They went on trial, and they were convicted of unwarranted assumption of authority. They should have fired up the radio and communicated with Cavite instead of taking action on it themselves. But the fact is that radio station never transmitted in those days, wasn't allowed to.

Burke was restored to duty and the other two got some sort of punishment. Then Burke came to the *Jason* as the chief engineer. He was an old engineer, and he seemed a very pleasant guy with an attractive wife and small child. She was quite a bit younger than he was. We all felt sort of sorry for the guy. Maybe he did get a raw deal. He seemed pretty nice. Just before we started home, Norman Scott, the executive officer, was detached and went to some other station out there. Burke was the next senior man so he stayed as chief engineer and exec.

So, we left Manila on the 2nd of April 1932, and it took about two months to get back. She was only making about eight knots most of the time. The engineers cut down on the pressure on her boilers because they were old. She was so slow that in the glassy tropic sea an officer about to relieve the deck would spit over the side and watch it, to prove that the ship was still moving! We were aware at that time that there was nothing holding the ship together. I knew about the *Cyclops*, but nobody knew how she'd been lost, and the other two ships hadn't been lost at that time. They were lost in '41, and we brought her home in 1932.

After we got to sea, we began getting all sorts of strange orders through Burke. At first they just seemed a little odd. The skipper, Capt. Ernest D. McWhorter, had a cabin up under the bridge with a little pantry, so he messed up there. He was an aviator, and we all knew him pretty well, but some of these things we were getting from Burke— "The captain says we gotta do this, the captain says we gotta do that"—didn't sound quite like McWhorter. We began to wonder.

Then at Guam we took aboard coal. Normally the *Jason* coaled herself. For years two men had done the job; one stood at the rail signaling up and down, while the other ran the winches that yanked a clam-shell bucket up and down. It grabbed a ton at a time out of a lighter and dropped it into the bunker hatch. However, at Guam Burke said that according to the navy regulations coaling was an all-hands evolution. He sent a lot of officers and men with shovels onto the lighter. We sat there all day in the sun and dust with nothing to do while the clam shell went up and down.

Things began to get weirder and weirder. We found out long afterward that this bird Burke was going up forward and telling the skipper that he had a mutiny back in the wardroom. The officers were all doing thus and so, saying thus and so. He picked his yarns right out of the air. Then he came aft and said the captain ordered this and that. He was telling different stories at each end of the ship. Things got pretty thick and complicated.

We stopped again for coal in Honolulu and finally made San Diego the end of May. We put the planes on the beach, did a little flying, and then I had to finish the trip to Bremerton and put her out of commission. At that point I lost track of Burke until three or four years later when I saw him on the dock in San Pedro, selling life insurance. He had been retired physically at Mare Island for being psycho!

And so that was the end of the China story—or so I thought, until, years later, after the war, I was skipper of the carrier *Philippine Sea* (CV-47), and we were in the Brooklyn Navy Yard. I was driving down East River Drive one morning when I saw a ship coming up the river with *Jason* on the bow. I looked at the lines and said, "By golly, that *is* the *Jason!*" Her hull shape had not changed. The last I had heard of her somebody had bought her, towed her out of Bremerton, and ran her onto a reef in the Caribbean. I'd thought that was the end of her.

I got hold of the navy yard pilot, who said she'd been hauling coal from Norfolk to the powerhouse at Hellgate for years. They had put some trick unloading gear into her and ran her up and down the coast all during the war. It wasn't until some time in 1950 or '51 when they finally scrapped her—and finally ended a most unusual and interesting chapter in naval aviation history.

9

ON THE FLYING TRAPEZE

Rear Adm. Harold Blaine Miller

HAROLD BLAINE MILLER *was born in Newton, Iowa, on 4 January 1903, son of Abraham K. Miller and Nora Belle Vanscoy Miller. On 10 June 1920 he entered the U.S. Naval Academy, was commissioned ensign on 5 June 1924, and served as a junior officer on the USS* California *(BB-44) before reporting for flight training at Pensacola. He was designated a naval aviator on 17 November 1926. He subsequently served in Observation Squadron 1 (VO-1); with the aviation unit of the USS* West Virginia *(BB-48); in Fighting Squadron 2 (VF-2); as an instructor at Pensacola; and on the heavier-than-air units of the airships* Akron *(ZRS-4) and* Macon *(ZRS-5). He also served with Scouting Squadron 9 (VS-9); with aviation units of the heavy cruisers USS* Northampton *(CA-26) and USS* Salt Lake City *(CA-25); with Patrol Squadron 16 (VP-16); and with Patrol Squadron 5 (VP-5, later VP-33) as commanding officer.*

During World War II, Admiral Miller's assignments included the staff of commander, Support Force, U.S. Atlantic Fleet; the Training Division, Bureau of Aeronautics; naval attaché and naval attaché for air, American Embassy, London, England; and public relations officer on the staff of the commander in chief, U.S. Pacific Fleet. On 23 April 1945, Rear Admiral Miller served as director of the Office of Public Relations (later changed to director of Public Information), Navy Department, and he was transferred to the retired list on 1 December 1946. Admiral Miller's decorations include the Legion of Merit with Gold Star and a special Letter of Commendation from the Secretary of the Navy.

After retirement Admiral Miller became vice president of Trans World Airlines, and later director of information, American Petroleum Institute, and director of public relations, Pan American World Airways.

Perhaps one of the most exciting periods I had in my life in the navy began in June 1932 when I was transferred to the heavier-than-air unit of the USS *Akron*, a rigid airship commissioned on 27 October 1931. The odd thing was that when I was a student at Pensacola in 1926 they brought an officer by the name of Lt. Comdr. Charles E. Rosendahl to give a talk to the students with the view, I presume, of doing a little proselytizing. Rosendahl, who later became a flag officer, was for many years one of the navy's leading exponents of lighter-than-air craft. He became the first commanding officer when the *Akron* was commissioned. It was a very, very interesting discussion, of course. In 1926, Rosendahl had just the year before been on the *Shenandoah* (ZR-1), which cracked up and fell apart in Ohio.

So I went back to Pensacola as an instructor in 1929, and at that time the *Akron* and the *Macon* had already been approved, so I knew they were under construction. I had always been interested in anything that was a little out of the normal course of events, so I became intrigued when I heard that they were going to have a heavier-than-air unit attached to the airships. I began writing letters at that particular point applying for this duty. I guess I became a bit of a pest, too, but it turned out that I got that assignment, which I was very excited about.

Two people had preceded me up there. One was Lt. Daniel W. Harrigan, class of 1922, and the other was Lt. (jg) Howard L. "Brig" Young from the class of 1923. I guess they reported probably in 1931 before either of the ships had been built or delivered. The USS *Los Angeles* (ZR-3) was still in commission at that time, and she had already had a certain amount of experimental work done on her. For example, Ralph Barnaby, flying a glider, demonstrated that an airship could carry a heavier-than-air craft and could release it from the trapeze. That part of the experiment was certainly

My CO 1939- VF6
Bonnie God father

successful. As a matter of fact, there was nothing new about that. There had been releases made by the British many years before.

About that time they were trying to bring along an airplane that would fit the specifications of the airships. The airships each would have a hangar, and there would be a trapeze gear that the pilot flew onto and was hoisted into the hangar. But the dimensions were so tight that it had to be a particular airplane. In an effort to get more fighters aboard an aircraft carrier, the navy had already dealt with several companies: one was Curtiss, one was General, and one was Berliner Joyce in Baltimore. Those three had the specifications, and the idea was to get a small fighting plane for the carriers to get more planes aboard the ship itself.

None of the prototypes were acceptable for carrier operations, except one little fighter that would just exactly fit into an airship. It wasn't designed for the airship at all; it just happened that its dimensions permitted that. It weighed about 2,800 pounds and had a 25-foot, 6-inch wingspan. It was the Curtiss F9C-2, called the Sparrowhawk. The contract called for six of those, but there were two X jobs—one XF9C-1 and one XF9C-2, plus six production F9C-2s. In effect, before we got through we had eight airplanes that were capable of being fitted into the airship program.

Here now was an airship that had a range of eight thousand miles, and, by golly, that just sounded like the answer to any scouting operation that the navy could ever require. There were a lot of minuses to this problem, too, which the lighter-than-air crowd often tended to overlook. There weren't many places where you could land an airship. There was Lakehurst, there was a mast at San Diego, they were building Sunnyvale, and there was still a mast at Fort Lewis in Washington. The ex–oil tanker USS *Patoka* (AV-6) had a mast at the stern that took the USS *Los Angeles* on one or two occasions. In Germany, of course, there were facilities. But basically, where were you going to put that ship if you were in trouble? It took a tremendous ground crew with some knowledge to operate those ships.

The Germans were considered the answer to all airship operations. The fact was that simply wasn't the case. The Germans lucked out just about as much as anybody in the world, but you never knew about it. So we considered them the master builders, the master operators. Part of the 1919 Treaty of Versailles, which came after World War I, permitted us to have two naval officers on every flight of the German airship *Graf Zeppelin* going around the world or wherever she went. We always had two observers aboard. They told stories that would curl your hair about the problems that the Germans had, which no one ever knew about.

For example, the airship was coming in from Brazil, going into Friedrichshafen, Germany. She went, of course, through the Strait of Gibraltar. Up the Rhone Valley she developed some sort of a problem, a vibration of her engines. They lost one engine; the crankshaft carried away. They lost the second engine and finally got into Friedrichshafen on one engine. Those things weren't known particularly.

They had another case when they were landing in Pernambuco down in South America, where it was a wild day. The Germans would parachute about four or five supervisors from the ship and then have a native ground crew there to haul the ship down and put it on the mast. This particular time, the ship was bucking like a bronco. It came down on a cabin that had a tall roof, a chimney, and a fire in the fireplace down below. Here was a hydrogen ship that actually came down on this chimney—but they got away with that. Finally they got it off, and it didn't burn. The Germans weren't the answer to this thing, and lighter-than-air hadn't proven itself.

The ZR-2 was the British R-38. We had an American crew in England doing a test job on her. She crashed on 24 August 1922, during a trial flight. One of the tests required was a complete full-rudder turn over the Humber River. That turn just simply broke the ship up, and down she went. Among the forty-four people killed were Lt. Comdr. Lewis H. Maxfield and fifteen other U.S. Navy personnel. Then, in October 1924, the German-built ZR-3, later to be named the *Los Angeles,* was flown from Friedrichshafen to Lakehurst. The fourth and the fifth came later— the *Akron* and the *Macon,* both American built. So the enthusiasm was there, and I must say there was no one more enthusiastic than I was.

It was around the first of July 1932 when I got to Lakehurst, New Jersey. The *Los Angeles* was still in the hangar, and she never flew again. They took the gas out of her and disassembled her finally because they had to get her out of there and get room for the big ships. Along about spring, just before I got there, the *Akron* had been delivered. I had kept in touch with Harrigan and Young. What we had to work with then were the XF9C-1 and the XF9C-2. We also had about two or three Consolidated N2Ys, the old navy training planes with hooks on them. Altogether the navy purchased six N2Y-1s to serve as familiarization trainers for pilots attached to the *Akron* and *Macon.* So we had about five hook-on airplanes at the time.

Harrigan and Young were the two experts, of course, by that time. Yet it was still experimental, even as far as they were concerned. I'll never forget when the time came, Ward said, "Come on, let's go up." So I climbed up in the front seat of one of the N2Ys, and away we went. He made about ten landings, and there were certainly no problems connected with them at all. We went on back down again, and when he got out of the airplane, I went up and played around with this. The first one, of course, is always a little touchy, but as time went on, it was just an everyday occurrence, as though you were landing on a field.

In my three years with lighter-than-air, we never took off the ground in an airship with our airplanes on board, because the airship itself needed every pound that it could carry in fuel. Each plane weighed about twenty-eight hundred to three thousand pounds. If we had four planes aboard, the twelve thousand pounds was better carried in fuel than in airplanes. But once you are in the air, she could carry us dynamically by dropping her tail, and she could carry up to four thousand pounds heavy. So we would always fly aboard after she had taken off.

"Four thousand pounds heavy" means that if they lost all their power, she would no longer be a lighter-than-air machine. You would have to balance out by dropping ballast in order to become zero, to have buoyancy. People seem to think that you just go up and fly an airship. That isn't so; it's a very technical job that you fly with a slide rule. It's a matter of pounds and weight and air pressure. For example, if the ship goes up with her bags pretty well inflated, say, 80 percent, as she goes higher that 80 percent becomes 85 percent and then 90 percent as the gas expands. The first thing you know, the ship has a full bag. At that point, a pressure valve in the ballonets would open and, if she went any higher, the gas would be lost. Then when the ship came down again, if the gas in there was compressed, there was no longer 80 percent to work with anymore—perhaps only 70 percent, and now you had landing problems. So they were very tricky things.

The weather controlled everything we did. There was a slight feeling among heavier-than-air people, "My God, all the airship people do is wait for good weather." If they got the ship out and got it back, that was a great successful flight. The only thing that was accomplished was that, and it didn't seem to make that much difference. But the fact was that the lighter-than-air people were still, after all, learning how to fly the airships.

I must say, we were probably very harsh in our judgment on that score because we were used to working off of carriers.

We became very good friends with all of these people. They, of course, looked at us somewhat askance, too. They thought, "Are these guys going to come and pull a boo-boo and fly into the ship, or how are they going to make out? Are they any good at all?" Well, we had to prove ourselves, which was no particular problem because flying the airplane on and off was so simple. It was the easiest thing in the world. I suppose you'd say that anything you can do well is easy.

As we would fly alongside the airship, the ship would lower a red flag or a green flag. The green flag told us to come aboard when we were ready. The ship had to be up to speed. In those earlier days, we thought we were landing pretty fast; we had a landing speed of 68 or 70 knots, somewhere along in there. If the ship wasn't up to that speed, theoretically we would stall before we could get aboard and spin out. Frequently, we'd get a flag to come aboard when the ship hadn't gotten up to speed. We would get up there and nibble and just couldn't make it. We just lost speed and fell away, which had a bearing on what altitude we should be at to hook on.

Where was the danger in that? We reached the point where we were hooking on at 800-feet altitude with no problem at all on the thing. If the ship was up to speed, we got the green flag, and by this time we all knew each other and our capabilities and what we could do, and they knew us, too. We would fly alongside that number one engine, which was about where the trapeze was, about twenty-five feet below the ship and maybe twenty-five feet aside from there. Then with our rudder, we would just skid under the ship slowly.

Now, you're under the ship and behind the trapeze about twenty-five or fifty feet. At this point, the pilot has to change from normal horizon flight by looking up, so he is now flying on something that's up above him. You get in some queer situations there because occasionally the ship would turn while you were looking at the ship. You didn't know what she was doing; all you knew was you had to hold your relative position on this thing. You'd find yourself skidding on one side or the other, which was very annoying. Of course, we had voice radio, but by this time you were pretty busy, and you didn't have time to talk. It didn't make any difference. It wasn't even a problem; it was just one of the annoying things of going aboard.

So now you were underneath and behind it. It was so simple because you had only one task to do, and that was to decrease the distance between the trapeze and your hook. All you had to do was to pull it up there. You didn't care about anything else. I had gone on many times with the throttle completely closed and the ship coming down. It made no difference; the relative speed and closing the distance were all I was interested in.

Two-thirds of the way back on the ship, we had what we called a perch, a trapeze about six feet from the ship. It was right up against the skin of the ship, where we could transfer pilots if we had to, or we could refuel the airplane back there. I don't think we ever did refuel there, though. It was just an emergency sort of thing. We couldn't take the airplane aboard. The idea of that was that if you thought you had some problems and you wanted both planes in action fast, you would have one on each hook and get up and go. That was the point of the perch. It had no other value. The perch at that area was a much smoother approach than farther forward because the forward trapeze was astern of the control car, so it did develop some bumps that didn't amount to a damn thing.

The hook was spring-loaded, so at that point when you hit it reasonably hard, it would lock you on. The idea was to get on the center of the trapeze. But if the ship really turned, as often happened, you'd end up way out on the side of the trapeze. There was no problem getting back to center; you'd just kick your rudder, and it would slide back down again. The reason for being in the center was that you only had about a four-inch clearance on each wing tip as you went through the hangar door.

The tripod carrying the hook had an extension bar out over the propeller. Nobody knew quite how easy it would be to hook on, so they put that out there so that the pilot wouldn't knock the propeller off on the trapeze. They also thought the pilot could put that bar on the trapeze and then slide the trapeze in through the hook. But after we got reasonably familiar, we never did anything but put the hook around the trapeze. We never used that sliding technique at all because we had no need for it. We just simply hooked on. At that point, you were locked on, and you knew you're locked on, although there were a couple of times when I thought I was locked on, and I'd sit back fat, dumb, and happy and just fall off. That was no problem either; all I had to do was drop the nose a little bit and pick up a little flying speed and come back and go on again. But we learned to insure that we were on by giving a little burst of power.

The hangar door, which would slide open at this point, now looked like a "T." The plane had to be lined up exactly straight or the wings were going to hit the hangar. So Lt. (jg) Frederick M. Trapnell, who in later years was noted for his work in running the navy's test pilot operation, devised what we called a "saddle," which would lower down on the fuselage and keep the airplane from wiggling. So they'd just lower that down on a pivot from the ship, and you were, in effect, locked into place, and they'd hoist you aboard. Of course, you cut your engine at that point.

There were six of us assigned to the *Akron*, including Ward Harrigan and Brig Young, who had come up earlier; Trapnell of '23, Lt. (jg) Robert W. "Swede" Larson from my class, Lt. (jg) Frederick N. "Knappy" Kivette of '25, and me. During almost a year that I was assigned to the *Akron*, the ship didn't do very much. She'd go up and down the coast, and we took her down to Miami once and worked with the fleet down there. But she pretty well stayed close to home, which was the attitude of those lighter-than-air boys at that time—get her out and get her back and have a very successful flight on the thing.

Then the *Akron* went down on 4 April 1933. That was one of those twists of fate that take place. The airship never took us aboard before takeoff, and it was a foggy night, although it wasn't very thick fog. The big ship took off with no problem at all, and it just went on up through the stuff. It was a little too much for those of us in the airplanes that night, so we thought we'd join them in the morning. That was a Godsend to us because a storm came up, and the *Akron* crashed into the sea off Barnegat Light, New Jersey. Of the seventy-six men on board, seventy-three were killed, including Rear Adm. William A. Moffett, chief of the Bureau of Aeronautics.

As a result of that accident with the *Akron*, I suppose there was more concern about the vulnerability of these ships, certainly among the people like Rear Adm. Ernest J. King, who became chief of the Bureau of Aeronautics following Admiral Moffett's death. The whole point was that if lighter-than-air was as good as people thought it was, we needed to go out and serve with the fleet and see what it could do. But the old-timers there in lighter-than-air were very loath to get out there and kick around with the fleet. For example, the *Akron* was down in the Caribbean, and there was a matter of fuel; she could always find a reason to get the hell back fast even before the exercises were over. It always annoyed us, the air group that we had there. We always felt they ought to stretch us somewhat and show what could be done.

But we had all kinds of episodes at that time. While the *Akron* was at Lakehurst, I had a lot of classmates around. Lakehurst had the navy parachute school where they'd train these young packers from the fleet. Their graduation exercise was a jump with a chute that they themselves had packed. That kind of proved that they could pack a chute. They would take them up in a blimp with an open cockpit that had handrails along the side.

One day they had a graduation exercise coming on, and I asked Charlie, a classmate, "How about going out with you? I'd like to see the graduation." We had taken sort of a lighter-than-air course while we were there. We had lots of time on our hands, and we went through most of it. We had more than a smattering of what it was all about. We certainly didn't qualify for lighter-than-air wings or anything, but Charlie said, "Sure, come on up." So I went as his number two pilot, and we went up.

We were over the field at about 1,500 feet or something of that sort. One of these kids would climb out facing the interior of the ship, standing on the handrail. He was holding on, and an old chief, sort of a jump master, would come pat him on the back, and he would fall off spread eagle on his back and pull his chute and have no problem. We got to the last chap, a little runt, eighteen years old perhaps, and he got out, and the chief tapped him, and he let go—and grabbed back again. That guy got him by the pants and pulled him aboard.

He wasn't keen on jumping at all. My classmate who was flying the ship just ate him up. I was ashamed of him as an officer talking to a little "scared-rabbit" boy the way he did. It was just terrible. I've never seen such an exhibition of temper. He said, "We went to all the trouble of flying up here, and you haven't got the guts to jump," and all this kind of stuff. It was awful.

I was sore by that time. This was the period when lighter-than-air and heavier-than-air weren't entirely simpatico. I told the gang down below— there were six of us—"By God, we ought to show these guys a thing or two." At that time, you could make a parachute jump with the authority of the commanding officer. Well, we were all attached to the *Akron* and were all upset by this time about it, so in our anger we said, "By God, we'll show them a thing or two." We typed out a little letter saying, "I hereby request permission to make a parachute jump, blah, blah, blah." So I carried them all in to Lt. Comdr. Herbert V. "Doc" Wiley, the skipper, and asked him to sign them. He looked at them and looked at me and signed all of them.

Now we were locked up. We had to make a parachute jump just to show them up. Well, we got an old Ford airplane up from Anacostia one day and took the door off and all of us went up and made our jump just to prove something, but I don't know what we proved.

The loss of the *Akron* was a blow to the prospects of lighter-than-air; it was terrible, but the enthusiasm was still there. It didn't stop us at all; we just went right on about our business, except we had to do gunnery and things of that sort. We had no airship to work with at all. We'd fly back and forth to Akron, Ohio, to Goodyear, quite often just to see how things were coming along out there because we had the *Macon* coming along very fast at this point. It was basically almost a German company that did it. They brought all their German talent over there to work on that thing.

We sort of fiddled around there for a little while until the *Macon* was commissioned on 23 June 1933. Comdr. Alger H. Dresel brought her over from Akron to Lakehurst, and the first thing you know, the time had come to go west to the naval air station at Sunnyvale, California. Brig Young hadn't left yet, and he ended up in Sunnyvale with us for a few months before he left. Trapnell followed him shortly. Ward Harrigan had gone earlier. Ward was a fascinating person and very ingenious. While he was there, he designed this parachute-raft business that saved so many lives in the Pacific during the war. He blended together a parachute and a raft. He was always working on the theory of things.

One of the big arguments at that point was, "What is an airship for? What's it supposed to do?" Finally, there was only one thing that you could conclude—that there had to be a long-range scout. You could also conclude that those things sure needed a lot of defenses built around to keep them from getting shot down. So, what were these planes for then? They were designed as fighters. But could four planes—even if there were four on board—do anything to defend themselves against a squadron? And, of course, this was long before the *kamikaze*, which would break the back of a ship one-on-one and bring her down so fast it wouldn't be funny.

So the theory became that the airship had to be used as a scout and had to be kept back; it couldn't go forward. Out of that then evolved a job for the planes. We were going to be the scouts. The ship would be the base sitting back three or four hundred miles, and we would go up in our planes and tell what we saw. That is really what finally evolved as the mission for these airplanes. As a fighter, its performance was obviously noncompetitive with any carrier fighter that was in operation in those days. So that became the accepted mission of the airplane—to go on out and find out what was going on and keep the ship out of trouble.

In maneuvers, every time the ship started moseying around and nosing into problems, boy, she got shot down so goddamn fast that it wasn't even funny. It became intolerable. Al Dresel was a real gentleman, but he was not an aggressive commander of an airship. Later on, when Doc Wiley came along, he took a very aggressive attitude on the whole thing. We got out to the West Coast, and things began to perk up. Doc Wiley had gone to sea as a navigator of some ship or other, and finally he came along and relieved Al Dresel. Doc now had been pretty well indoctrinated with the fleet itself. An interesting thing about lighter-than-air people— they had to have alleged sea duty on a lighter-than-air craft, and they'd have shore duty at Lakehurst, followed by sea duty also at Lakehurst, so they never left. They never really had a feel or a touch of what the hell the fleet was doing. It was sort of a closed corporation—not very promising for advancement. The notion developed to get the ship out and get it back and so on because if we didn't have the ship, we didn't have anything to work with.

A couple of months after the *Macon* got to Sunnyvale, I got command of the airplane unit. So I had "Knappy" Kivette and picked up two new pilots—Lt. (jg) Leroy C. Simpler and Lt. (jg) Gerald L. Huff. I started writing memos to Doc Wiley about things that ought to be done and things we were going to do and make. I was trying to promote the airship through the airplanes. I was an avid lighter-than-air man. I thought that these things had the answers to so much, despite knowing their weaknesses. We had previously done some landings on the carrier *Lexington* (CV-2). We had a tailhook on the airplanes, so we had checked out our little fighters on the carriers as well. We were pretty well rounded out, as we could do most anything.

There were two things we had talked about somewhat but had never done. I put these two things in a memo to Doc Wiley—pull the landing gear and fly singly. There was no place else to land. We would go out two or three hundred miles from the ship, and I might say that when you saw the ship coming back at the end of a four-hour flight, it was a damn welcome sight—to see that blob up in the sky and have a place to go to. But we always went out in pairs. Well, what were we doing? We were burning all the gas the ship carried, and we were tiring our pilots going out. Really, what could the second plane do if the first one went down, anyway? We couldn't afford to fly twin operations out there.

Old Doc Wiley was for everything. He was just an old go-getter; he was great. He approved of everything I wanted. So the next time out, we took the landing gear off of my airplane. We'd practiced that in the hangar and could do it all right. Now I had a plane with no landing gear. I couldn't land on the beach. It would be better to land in the water anyway. So I got hoisted out, with an extra thirty gallons of fuel in the back, which was an hour and a half of flight time. I'd rather have that than landing gear. We were so far at sea that we couldn't go back to land anyway. So I had the engine going, and I pulled and dropped off, and she performed just like a dream. You wouldn't know the difference except for an hour-and-a-half extra gas.

So now we had about four and a half hours of fuel, which was great. The next thing, as the problem developed that day, was to have one plane on each side of the ship, rather than two on each side. The planes would come back and be relieved by other pilots going out. So we did that, and a lot of it was sort of confidence in ourselves, being alone out there. It was a hell of a lonely feeling.

The first thing you know, the tactical officer on the *Macon* developed a plan. The ship would hold whatever the course was, at a speed of 50 knots. We would double the speed and search on a 60-degree angle to the airship's track. Any time we wanted to go back to the ship, no matter what side we were on, we would do a 120-degree turn that converged with the airship's track at 60 degrees. On the homeward leg, we would return to the airship in the same amount of time flown on the outbound leg. We'd go out, and after about four hours it was a really good feeling to see that airship up ahead when you finally came back.

We weren't operating in conjunction with the fleet at that point; primarily we were doing this stuff all on the side, and it revealed the weaknesses they had. The next step came from Lt. Donald M. Mackey, who was a great guy. The idea then was to have the ship control the airplanes because the plane obviously couldn't have enough communications to figure out where to do this or do that. The ship then would direct us. If the ship were to turn and go 180 degrees, we might lose her and have no idea where she was. So while theoretically it was nice to have a 400-mile front moving ahead, it failed if the ship turned at all—60 degrees, 20 degrees, or whatever it was—because we'd be out of position, and we wouldn't know where the hell we were, and that would be fatal for us.

So then the next step in that was to have Don Mackey tell us what to do, and he would plot our position relative to the airship throughout the mission. That began to work very well. That's really where we were headed—when we ran out of airships. We were headed for a real good scouting operation at that point and, of course, the fleet was screaming bloody murder—Admiral King and so on—"For Christ's sake, show us what you can do." Old Doc Wiley was headed right in that direction, I'll tell you. But we hadn't been given that period of grace to work out our techniques before joining the fleet.

About that time, we read in the paper that President Franklin D. Roosevelt was going to go through the Panama Canal on the cruiser USS *Houston* (CA-30) to Pearl Harbor. He had a second cruiser with him, the *New Orleans* (CA-32), that had all the reporters aboard. From the press accounts, we knew that they were going to come close to Clipperton Island. I was a promoter type, so I got together with Doc Wiley and said, "Gee, this is our chance. Let's go out and intercept the president. We'll drop all this news stuff on him the newspaper published the morning before, and we'll just really let the world know he met an airship around here." He thought that was great.

By this time we always operated without wheels and never thought to keep our wheels on. That was just routine stuff. So "Knappy Kivette" and I went out from Sunnyvale, and each of us practiced. We had a line about two hundred feet long with a waterproof rubber bag on the end. We could drop it just about where we wanted it.

So the ship shoved off, and Doc did not report to anybody; we were just going to sea for local exercises. He didn't tell anybody what we were going to do. About eighteen hours later, on 19 July 1934, the *Macon* was on the line somewhere between Pearl and Clipperton, and "Knappy" and I were launched in our planes. In each of our bags was a San Francisco *Chronicle* of the day we had left; there was the latest issue of *Time;* I knew the president was a stamp collector, so in the bag there were also about twenty letters addressed to people: one to Min Miller, one to the president, one to Eleanor, and one to Wiley.

We both shoved off from the ship, and now we were trailing these bags. We had planned just a light, little bag, but by this time, the bags had gotten rather bulky. I had mine wrapped around my hand on the throttle, trying to keep the throttle open, and the load was just about to tear me out of that airplane. It was awful.

The weather was pretty stinky at that point, cloudy with squalls. So we went ahead to about where we thought we might find something and sure as hell, out of that mess were two cruisers steaming along at about 15 or 18 knots. When these two little planes dove down on them from these cloudy skies, they should have shot us down. They had the president aboard.

At this time, the *Macon* had asked permission to drop something, so I made a pass over the *Houston*'s forecastle and overshot. "Knappy" came along behind me, and he overshot. Well, both cruisers stopped dead in the water and put whaleboats over the side and rescued these things. At that point, of course, the radios were going back and forth, and the president said, "Well done, *Macon*." Oh, he gave us a great big boost, which is what we were looking for.

The *Macon* wasn't visible yet, but she finally came up in another half hour. She caught up with us, and we went back to the ship and went back aboard. Within fifteen minutes of our drop, the sky was filled with messages from the chief of naval operations and the commander in chief, U.S. Fleet, saying, "What the hell are you doing out there? What was in the bags?"

Old Doc Wiley thought, "Oh, Christ"—that he was fired from the navy now. It was not a very happy trip back to Sunnyvale. We had accomplished what we had started to do, but it wasn't really very successful after all. About ten days or two weeks later, these letters started coming back in the U.S. mail. I don't know who opened the bags; I suppose it was the captain of the ship or the exec or maybe Roosevelt. At any rate, the mail clerk of the *Houston*—or whoever he was—was a very ingenious young man. He cut out aluminum airship figures and pasted them on each of the letters. The president signed each of the letters, and they came back through the U.S. mail. I got Doc Wiley to sign these and I signed them, and they turned out to be quite a plus.

About forty-five years later, an old friend of mine in New York said, "Say, you were in aviation. I saw a letter in some stamp shop in New York

City that had your name on it. Could that be you?" He described it, and I said that was one of my letters. I didn't pursue it by going up there, but about a year later, I had a phone call from Chicago. It was from a lad by the name of Bill Boss, and he said, "Are you Admiral Miller? Did you fly off the *Macon?*"

I said "Yes," and he asked, "Could I describe an envelope to you?" It turned out it was the same letter that had been in the stamp shop window in New York City.

He said, "Would you mind identifying it?"

I went down and got mine out.

We became good pen pals, and I finally said, "Would you mind telling me what you paid for this?"

He said, "No. I paid 2,400 dollars for it."

I called Mrs. Kivette, since "Knappy" had died in the meantime, and asked if "Knappy" had one of those letters in his file. She looked and said he had one. I told her this story. The envelopes are now listed in all of the stamp books. There are only something like twenty of them.

Well, we went back to Sunnyvale and did all kinds of experiments. We always wondered what would happen if we did have a plane down at sea. We carried a four thousand–foot reel of quarter-inch cable on board the airship. Its function was to carry the spy basket. During World War I, the Germans eventually used spy baskets but weren't very successful at it. They'd lower somebody below the cloud level, and he would tell the airship's crew where they were and how to bomb and navigate. So we played around with our spy basket, which was a small airplane fuselage, really, with no wings. It had an empennage, and you could use a half an inch of rudder and that's all. It had kind of a tripod wire connection to the fuselage. We wanted a telephone from the observer to the ship, but we couldn't make a one-wire telephone system work, so we put in a little key radio set.

Lt. Comdr. Jesse L. Kenworthy Jr., executive officer of the *Macon*, was the first passenger in the *Macon*'s sky basket, on 27 September 1934. In early experiments, this thing was really hazardous when it started oscillating. We finally got it stabilized in some way. Jess did this first one, and I don't know whether anymore lighter-than-air people did. I said I wanted to do that. Of course, it was felt that the spy basket would be heavier-than-air's job. So I went down, and it was really weird. As it lowered away, it would begin to trail the ship and develop a catenary back there. I would be 1,000 or 1,500 feet below and about 200 feet behind the ship with no sound at all—absolutely no sound. It was just quiet and I was sitting there—just me and nobody else. I had a parachute, but what the hell I'd do with a parachute, I don't know. They'd never know if I was below a cloud, and they lost me. At any rate, that experiment didn't last very long either, but it was sort of interesting to try. The whole thing was a little cockeyed.

Now, what were we going to do if an airplane was down in the water? We rigged up a circular insulated life raft with webbing inside a safety belt. The idea was to lower that onto the water with this four thousand–foot cable, and a downed pilot would get in the raft and get hoisted aboard. Doc Wiley lowered that thing in San Francisco Bay and would tow it from this big airship down there alongside of a buoy—he could do any damn thing he wanted with this thing. The only regret that I have in that three-year experience was that I missed out on one thing I wanted to do: I wanted to climb into the raft and then get hoisted aboard, just to show it could be done.

Now, when the ship would come back from an eighty-hour flight or something like that, she would have burned maybe sixty thousand pounds of fuel. Then we couldn't get her on the ground because she was too light. Somehow, we had to compensate for the sixty thousand pounds. The navy did it by water recovery gear. Above each of the eight engines was an apparatus about six feet in width that extended halfway up the ship. That was water recovery gear through which the exhaust gas from the engine would be allowed to filter. The cool air would condense the moisture out of the gases, and that water would then run down into our ballast tanks so that we were recovering weight. Theoretically, we could get back about 115 pounds of water for every 100 pounds of fuel we'd burn. We never did because they leaked, but if we got 80 percent back, 80 percent of sixty thousand pounds means we're only short about twelve thousand pounds to get down to the ground.

By this time, we also had picked up a couple of Waco XJW-1s, the old commercial Waco biplane with two seats forward and the pilot aft. We put hooks on those so that we had a taxi airplane that could carry people back and forth to the airship. So when the ship would get back to the area of San Francisco Bay, we would take one of the fighters and go down, and maybe we had a pilot on the ground or something. We would get one of our little Wacos, and all the lighter-than-air boys who weren't able to make the flight for various reasons, we'd taxi them up and put them on the airship so they'd get flight time. The ship might be hanging around the bay there for six or eight hours. It would add weight to the ship, and they'd get their flight time. So now we had a ship that was reasonably close to equilibrium but still light. When we finally decided to come down to the ground and everybody was ready down there, we'd make our approach into the wind and stick that nose down and with our eight engines, eight propellers—just drive her down to the ground at probably about a 45-degree angle.

The first object was to marry the cable of the airship to the cable on the ground so we had the ship's nose locked up. They pulled it down fast and got the nose in the cone there and put together the water line, which ran from the bow of the ship all the way back aft. Now we started pumping water fast to get the weight of the water back aft. That brought the tail down, and it would rest on a car that was on a circular track. With the tail locked down on the railroad car and the nose locked up, we now had a big wind sock. The ship was free to swing and, depending on how much wind we had, we swung her so that she was parallel to the hangar and then started just pulling her into the hangar. Then she was put to bed— and we didn't have many places in the world where we could do that.

The idea of all that mechanism was to eliminate manpower. In the old days, we had to mule-haul every one of them. Of course, there was that sad case that occurred on 11 May 1932 at Camp Kearny, California, near San Diego. The *Akron* was in there, and they did have a mast, but three of the kids didn't get the word to let go in time; the first thing they knew, they were a hundred feet in the air. They finally pulled one of them aboard, and I think two of them fell to their deaths. So everything was mechanized where it could be.

We then had these two Waco taxi planes, and we'd do all sorts of things. If the ship was going to go to Miami to work with the fleet in the Caribbean, we'd all fly independently. There were four of us now— "Knappy" Kivette, Simpler, Huff, and myself. I'd usually go by way of Iowa to visit my grandmother, and somebody was heading someplace in Tennessee he wanted to visit. We'd all leave together and arrive at the same time someplace, all traveling four different routes. We were very independent, and really it was a great duty. Doc Wiley had great confidence in us to do most anything.

This was the challenge for Doc Wiley and the *Macon:* to go out and show the fleet what we could do. The fleet exercises were rather extensive— all up and down the West Coast. By then we had reached the point where, with wheels off and extra gas, we could go out for four and a half hours. We were in pretty good shape. We worked in an exercise with the fleet, and the ship received excellent comments. The job we had been doing just looked like things were going to come to fruition here—Doc Wiley's hard work and the planes' progress. Things were going along very well.

On 12 February 1935, we had been engaged for two days in maneuvers with the fleet, which was in passage en route to San Francisco from the southern operating bases. Our mission consisted mainly of scouting, and we had made every endeavor to escape detection. To this end we had sent the planes far ahead while the ship kept well out of sight in back of the Channel Islands. We found everything we were looking for in the enemy fleet, except for a cruiser. The *Macon* by now was somewhere off of San Luis Obispo. It was the cruisers we wanted, so Gerry Huff and I launched and started out trying to find them. We did find them, way up toward Monterey and well offshore. When we reported them, we were out about two and a half hours, I would say. At that time we received word that the exercises were over. The ship turned for everybody to go home. I wasn't with Gerry now; I was alone and so was Gerry. We both returned to the ship, where I met Gerry and he went aboard. It was a very lonely feeling being outside the ship in an airplane with no place to go if you had any problems. So I made it a point to always be the last aboard and get my guys on. So I went aboard after Gerry.

Little did I know at that time that it was the last landing ever made on the airship.

I reported to the officer of the deck, Lt. (jg) George W. Campbell, and to Captain Wiley that there was quite a tough weather front up ahead in the vicinity of Monterey and Carmel. We had gone through tougher ones down in the Caribbean than this one, so we kept on going north, and every- one was getting ready. We'd be back in Sunnyvale in another eight hours. Finally, as we were coming up to Point Sur, we were in the weather, and suddenly the ship went through some maneuvers: the nose kicked and pulled over to the right, and it went up and down and so on and on and on.

I don't know if there was any thunder or lightning connected with the storm, but there were violent air currents. I was in the control car because, after all, the heavier-than-air people had nothing to do after flying except to sit there and play acey-deucy or read a book. It was obvious in a very short time that we had a real problem on our hands. The word then came back that the ship was beginning to break up back aft, that some of the girders had carried away. An effort was made to lighten the ship because we were flying heavy at that particular time. We had to get some weight off the ship, so they dropped a lot of ballast.

It was obvious that things were really not going right. The first thing we knew, we were up around 5,000 feet instead of around 1,800 feet where we had been, or perhaps even lower. We simply went up like a free balloon at this point, and the nose of the ship was up. An effort was made to get the engine started, but we couldn't because, with the angle of the ship, the fuel wasn't getting into the carburetor. Until we could get the bow down, we couldn't get the engines started. Then they called for all hands together in the nose, way up there in the cone to try to get some weight up there. Finally that was done, the nose came down, and a couple of engines got started.

By this time it was obvious that disintegration was taking place back in the tail. As one ring would collapse, the broken aluminum parts would make holes in the next bag, and we'd lose all that lift. So the ship was getting awfully heavy back in the tail, and the nose was still trying to get light. It became apparent that the crew wasn't going to save the ship. They simply couldn't fly the ship. The only thing to do was to get down in the water. The concern was that maybe we were drifting back in over the mountains behind Point Sur. With a couple of engines going, we got the ship headed back to sea and began to let down by valving. Of course, we were probably heavy at that time anyway. We started down, and then the point was whether we would come down over land or water.

It turned out to be over water, about twelve or fifteen miles off of Point Sur. I think at about 500 feet we could begin to see the water and realize we were coming down. We landed on the water in a horizontal position, just as gently and as softly as you please. People had broken out life rafts and dropped lines from the ship, and the order was given to abandon ship. Those with any sense lowered themselves into the life rafts, and some didn't even get wet. We had about eighty-three people aboard. Out of that we lost two men, as opposed to the *Akron*, which saved three men and lost seventy-three. One of the three survivors from the *Akron* was Doc Wiley, who also survived the loss of the *Macon*.

Some of us stayed on board. I was among those, and I thought, "My God, this ship is afloat. This ship will never sink. We'll just sit this out until the fleet shows up. We won't even get wet." Well, at this point those people in the boats pulled away from the ship. It must have been around 4:00 P.M., and this was February, and the days were short. It was cold and beginning to rain. It was not a very encouraging picture at all.

Those in boats pulled off a quarter or half a mile away and huddled in a group out there. Here we were high and dry on the ship, thinking how stupid they were. Then, the first thing we knew, instead of being horizontal in the water, the ship suddenly assumed a very slow upward movement to a vertical position. Instead of being fifty feet from the water, we were four hundred feet up in the air. We were sitting there on top of a cone in this beautiful airship, the lower part of it being in the water. That didn't look as good as it did a few moments before.

Those of us in the ship had gathered in the bow and were all up there around the nose cone. We heard a rumble, and we didn't know what it was. Finally, there was a whoosh of some currents of air or gases or something coming up from the ship, escaping through the top of it. I had always heard that helium had the unique characteristic of making your vocal cords inactive—you lose your voice if you were surrounded by helium and inhaled it. I think that is true because I practically lost my voice at that time. I realized what was happening; the gas cells were breaking down below, and here was a natural cone bringing the gas up to us.

I said to come on and get outside. We all scrambled out and broke out all the lines, and we had a maypole up there, each person outside the ship hanging onto a line. Of course, the ship was so big that it was still practically like a haystack up there. It wasn't sharp, and you weren't in danger of slipping off or anything. It was raining, it was cold, and we'd hear another blast and the ship would settle deeper and deeper. Every time we heard a blast, we knew another cell had carried away, another ring. Now it was getting dark; it was about five o'clock. We knew we had gotten out an SOS to the fleet, but nothing had happened as yet.

We were now down to the size of a two-story house. I guess I was probably the senior one there and said, "Well, boys, the time has come. We have to get out of here." Most of us had on a life jacket of sorts. I think two or three didn't have any at all. So we said, "Let's get in the water and get out of here before this whole thing goes down." So we started letting go of the line and sliding over the haystack into the water, and it was cold as hell. We didn't know quite what to do. I took off my shoes and threw them away. To get rid of weight, I attempted to get my class ring off and throw it away. All kinds of silly ideas came to my mind.

Just about the time we were going in the water, there were searchlights way in the distance; the cruisers were looking for us. We turned around, and there was one little bluejacket still on this haystack. He didn't want to come in the water at all, and we shouted and screamed. Finally, he let go and got in the water. He no more had gotten in there than we pulled him up; we were all swimming over to the boats by this time.

The navigation flares ignited gasoline that had also blown up inside the envelope. On the outside of the envelope was the red, white, and blue star of the national insignia, and the inside was all aflame. The silhouette of the star was the most beautiful sight I had ever seen.

She finally just lay down, sort of like an old dog. Away she went and disappeared.

We finally worked our way over to the boats, and people just held on. Actually, we were warmer in the water than we were in the air. Oh, it was terrible. We were there for forty-five minutes or an hour—some in the boat but most in the water. Everybody had something to cling to. Then in the darkness the motor launches began to show up. I'll never forget, a classmate of mine had the boat that I got into and was passing around a bottle and saying, "Be careful now; that's just alcohol." Well, everybody was swigging this stuff. I never heard teeth chatter so much in my life. You'd just simply think they'd shake apart.

We got over to three of the cruisers, the ten thousand–tonners. I think it was the *Richmond* (CL-9) that picked me up. They wouldn't let us aboard until we had given our service number and name and everything else. Then they rushed us down to sick bay and looked us over and turned us in with blankets. The first thing we knew, we were warm. We ended up in San Francisco the next morning, and so it worked out quite well.

I looked back on my three years with the airships with some fond memories. It was a colorful episode, and I got something out of it myself, personally. But there were too many things working against the airship. Weather was a big factor. In the crash of the *Macon,* an airplane could have gotten through but not an airship. I was no longer a convert by that time. I realized that the disadvantages of the lighter-than-air were too great. I think even the lighter-than-air people began to think so. It was the Consolidated PBY Catalina flying boat that also helped kill the airship. For the price of four million dollars for each of those airships you could get twelve PBYs. You put them on a search, and they could cover twice as much as the airship could, get back, and not be shot down. I think what the navy proved was that the airships weren't here to stay.

WHERE NEXT, COLUMBUS?

Vice Adm. Herbert D. Riley

H ERBERT DOUGLAS RILEY *was a ninth-generation Marylander, born on 24 December 1904 to Mr. and Mrs. Marion H. Riley. In 1923 he was appointed to the U.S. Naval Academy and was graduated on 2 June 1927. Following graduation and two years at sea in the USS* New Mexico *(BB-40), he received flight training at Pensacola and was designated a naval aviator on 1 July 1930. Thereafter, he had duty in all types of naval aviation squadrons, from carrier-based fighters and scouting planes to patrol and transport aircraft. Duty as a VIP transport and test pilot was followed by serving as aide to President Franklin D. Roosevelt, then aide and flag lieutenant to commander, Carrier Division 1. Still later, Riley became aide and flag secretary to Rear Adm. John S. McCain, commander, Patrol Wings, U.S. Fleet.*

During World War II Riley served as operations officer, commander, Fleet Air West Coast; participated in air operations at Guadalcanal while on temporary duty in the South Pacific; served in the Aviation Plans Division in the office of the deputy chief of naval operations (air), then–Vice Admiral McCain; and commanded the USS Makassar Strait *(CVE-91) during the Iwo Jima and Okinawa operations.*

Admiral Riley's many staff and operational assignments after World War II included command of the USS Coral Sea *(CVA-43); chief of staff, Carrier Division 2; assistant director, Politico-Military Policy, Office of the Chief of Naval Operations; commander, Carrier Division 1; chief of staff of the Pacific Command; deputy chief of naval operations (fleet operations and readiness), Navy Department; and in February 1962, director of the Joint Staff, Joint Chiefs of Staff. On 1 April 1964, he was transferred to the retired list of the U.S. Navy.*

Vice Admiral Riley's decorations include the Distinguished Service Medal, Distinguished Flying Cross, the Bronze Star Medal with Combat "V," the Navy Commendation Medal, and the Army Commendation Ribbon with Oak Leaf Cluster. Foreign decorations include the Rank of Commander, Distinguished Order of the British Empire, and the Peruvian Air Cross (First Class).

When I went through training in 1929–30, there were five squadrons that one went through en route to wings. We started out in Consolidated NY-1 seaplanes in Squadron 1, then a land plane course also with NYs on wheels in Squadron 2. Squadron 3 was in Vought O2U-1s—a communication and spotting course. Spotting was the big thing in those days. Squadron 4 was a very primitive, rudimentary type of blind-flying training that nobody knew anything about, including the instructors. Squadron 5 was the fighter training.

It was a period of great strain, particularly for people like me whose hearts had been set on it for so long. A great number of people busted out of my class and were heartbroken when they didn't make it. The attrition was pretty high, but fortunately I managed to survive, and I was designated a naval aviator on 1 July 1930. My classmates at Pensacola included some names that became quite famous during the war and in subsequent years for other reasons. Included were Tom Hamilton, who was our class president; George Anderson, who became chief of naval operations and then later U.S. Ambassador to Portugal; Jimmy Thach of Thach weave fame; Don Griffin, who wound up his career as the NATO commander, CinCSouth at Naples; Paul Ramsey, one of our most distinguished combat pilots; Bob Dixon, another in the same category. We also had a number of marines who went on to distinguished careers during the war and subsequently. The significant fact to me is that of all of those who were students at Pensacola during the time I was there, a rather startling number became very well known in the navy in later years.

There is a lot of argument in favor of calling my class a "vintage class." They were an exceptionally good group of people, and they were people who got the breaks as far as timing was concerned. Shortly after the war broke out, members of my class were squadron commanders, air group commanders, then air officers of carriers right on up to skippers of carriers by the end of the war. My initial actual combat flying in the war was as a lieutenant commander at Guadalcanal in an F4F fighter. Before the war was over, I was a captain—four stripes—command of a combat carrier, although it was a jeep carrier. That, to me, is quite a jump, from sitting in the cockpit of a fighter to command of a carrier. Again, our timing was just right. My case wasn't distinctive. We were just a group who were very fortunate in that respect.

During our time frame of active duty, we covered quite an era, entirely apart from our combat experience in war, either declared or undeclared war. For example, all three of our midshipmen cruises were made in coal-burning battleships, whereas the last ship to fly my flag before I retired was the nuclear-powered carrier USS *Enterprise* (CVAN-65). My first solo flight was made on 15 April 1929 from Ream Field near San Diego, which was at that time literally a cow pasture. We often had to buzz the cows to chase them to the side of the field so that we could land our airplanes. Ream Field went on to become a tremendous training field with runways and all sorts of installations. I made my first carrier landing on the original *Langley* (CV-1); my last carrier landing was made on the nuclear-powered carrier *Enterprise*. When one examines comparisons like that closely, I think that the term "vintage class" of 1927 is a rather apt term.

Looking back on the flight training course at Pensacola at the time when I received my training, I can only sit back and admire the value of that training and the dedication of the people who gave it. On the negative side, I can think of only one area of flight training in which they were deficient. That is the area of cross-country flight training. It was virtually nil. It appeared in the curriculum, and I think something like five hours was devoted to the instruction and check of cross-country capability. Actually, the training given called for the student pilot to go out with his instructor in an NY-1, and the instructor would emphasize some of the student's weak points in his flying capability while proceeding to an area removed from the normal training area.

At some stage while the student pilot was trying to correct the errors that were being pointed to his attention, the instructor would say, "Look down there on the right, and you will see Montgomery," or, "You will see Mobile," or some other city in the vicinity of Pensacola, and then he would wheel the plane around and say, "Let's go back to the barn," and we would head in the general direction of Pensacola. Naturally, when we got into that area, we would recognize a number of things and be able to find our way back. All we needed was the general direction. Then for a check on our capability in cross-country flying, instructors were sent to several very small towns in the vicinity of Pensacola. I recall Bruton, Alabama, another was Flomaton, Alabama, and Pascagoula, Mississippi.

Instructors were sent to little cow pastures that served those towns as flying fields, and then students were sent off at about fifteen- or twenty-minute intervals, solo, with instructions to fly a loop course to Flomaton, Bruton, Pascagoula, and towns of about that size, and then to return to the field at Pensacola. If the pilot got back before he ran out of gas, he qualified. That was about the limit of cross-country training. I distinctly remember on my cross-country flight check I never even so much as saw any of the check points I was supposed to have logged in. Whether the instructors on the ground ever saw me and identified me will always remain a moot question. I did get back to Pensacola before I ran out of gasoline, and therefore I qualified. After leaving Pensacola and being designated as a naval aviator, I would have been unsafe for any flight from A to B, regardless of the distance of terrain. I literally knew how to fly, but establishing my position was not one of my accomplishments at that time.

Following my completion of the course at Pensacola in 1930, I spent three years in scouting squadrons, one year of it in Scouting 6 (VS-6) and two years in Scouting 5 (VS-5), a companion squadron attached to the *Richmond* (CL-9) unit. There was nothing very significant about my duty in either squadron, other than one incident in my period of time in Scouting 5, which was rather interesting.

In early 1931, a brushfire war, or "musical comedy revolution," whichever you want to call it, broke out in Honduras, where the United Fruit Company had vast interests. So that their business might continue without interruption by the revolutionaries, it was decided to send a U.S. cruiser to Honduras and have it appear in the various Honduran ports along the Atlantic seaboard; there were four of them: Puerto Cortes, La Ceiba, Tela, and Puerto Castilla. It was only necessary for the ship to be in any one of those four ports to exert a calming influence on any interruption of the work of the United Fruit Company. The rebels stayed in the hills and harassed the back country but kept clear of the ports in which the important installations of the fruit company's operations were located.

We would spend usually three or four days in one port, proceed leisurely to the next one, spend three or four days there, and make the circuit of the four ports, so that we would make the whole loop in about two weeks. We were in Honduras for several months altogether. The ships going into those ports, banana boats primarily, and a few tankers would come directly from the deep water of the Atlantic into the marked channels to each of the four ports. However, there was no commercial traffic by sea in between the ports, so that to go from Tela to La Ceiba it was necessary to go out to deep water, then parallel the coast, then come back in through a tortuous channel to the harbor of the other port. This took an inordinate amount of time, much more time than it would have taken had we been able to follow close to the coastline.

Examination of the charts showed that water depths would make it practical to follow the coastline, although the obstructions, largely coral reefs, were completely unmarked. It would be necessary to find them and sort of thread the needle to make the passage up the coast. Our skipper was a rather adventuresome sort, and he decided that he would do this. He had airplanes that could help him do it, and he would use them.

So immediately upon getting under way from La Ceiba one morning, the two airplanes, Curtiss SOCs, were catapulted. I was flying the lead plane, and I had a continuous wave (CW) key radio with an operator in the back seat to send Morse code; there was no voice radio in those days. One of the other pilots was flying the second plane, similarly equipped, in case I should have any difficulty with my radio. Radios in those days were notoriously unreliable; the second plane was merely a standby for me in case my radio didn't work. My instructions were to fly ahead of the ship, and when the ship made its turn to parallel the coast to make continuous passes past the bridge of the ship over the bow and in the direction the ship would head. They would then take whichever direction I gave them to evade the various coral pinnacles and reefs. Some of these were above water, but the vast majority were below the surface.

My problem was that the water is so clear down there and the reefs stood out so clearly, it was impossible for me to tell how much water there was over the reef—whether the ship could clear safely by going straight ahead, or whether it would be better to dodge and be sure to get into water that was much deeper. All they could do on board ship, since they had no reliable depth-finding equipment in those days, was to depend upon the hand lead line. Imagine using a hand lead line approaching a reef that was coming straight up like a wall in front of you. It would have been no good at all. I decided to take the better part of valor and have them avoid everything, no matter how many turns they had to make.

We started out, and there was a question of whether I would have enough gas to thread the ship all the way through from La Ceiba to Tela without having to land and refuel. My instructions in that event were to land somewhere off Tela and wait for the ship, and my number two plane would take over. Of course, he was in the air the same length of time I was, but he could conserve fuel by not diving and zooming as much as I did; this burned my fuel up rather rapidly. We started out from La Ceiba and everything went well for about three-quarters of the way. As a matter of fact, Tela was in sight, but there was a pinnacle that I could tell was almost to the surface of the water directly ahead of the path I'd given the ship in order to evade a previous pinnacle. I tried to turn the ship around the pinnacle; then from there on would have been a clear shot into Tela. There was nothing further in the way.

About that time, the people on the bridge of the ship sighted Tela and thought they had it made. They sent me a message telling me to secure my operations, proceed to Tela, and await their arrival to be hoisted back aboard—that they could dispense with my services from then on because they had Tela in sight. What they didn't know was that directly ahead of them, about a mile, was a huge pinnacle, probably the largest that we had seen on the whole trip.

So I had my key radio operator send them a message telling them to take two more course changes from me before they secured me—one to evade the pinnacle, then one to put them on the course that would clear all the obstacles, which I was confident I could do. They never received the message, and in retrospect, I can only guess that when they sent the message to me to secure my operations, they then secured their radio operator at the same time. So I was totally out of communication with the ship. They put on extra speed to head in, and they were closing in on the pinnacle.

I didn't know quite what I could do. I made about six passes low over the bridge and headed in the direction I wanted them to go; they simply ignored me and continued their course toward the coral reef. They were getting closer and closer, and I was getting more and more frustrated. Finally, I decided there was only one way to do it, and that was to get well up ahead of the ship and come down low on the water right at the bow of the ship, and at the last minute pull up over the bridge to indicate that they should stop. I thought perhaps at the least they would man their radio again to see what was driving me so crazy. They didn't catch on as far as the radio was concerned, but they did get my meaning to stop.

As soon as I got them stopped—and they were then within a quarter mile of this reef, if not closer—I flew by and indicated the course to them. They got under way and took the course I gave them; when they were clear of the pinnacle, I gave them another course that would take them into Tela, then rocked my wings to say good-bye to them and went off to Tela—and they knew that I was all finished. So we got the ship into Tela without hitting a reef. I am quite sure that up until that time in early 1931 there had been no air piloting for ships to point out channels and coral reefs.

It so happened that in 1930 and 1931, world tensions were building up in the Pacific area to a much greater extent than they were in the Atlantic, aside from the minor brushfire wars among the alleged American republics of Central America and places that required the presence of U.S. forces to protect the interests of our business empire. But so far as general world tensions were concerned, the trend was toward the Pacific. For that reason, there were numerous transfers of naval forces effected from the Atlantic to the Pacific Fleet. The effect of these transfers did not become significant to a great extent until they began to affect aviation units.

That may sound peculiar, but it was because the maintenance of our aviation units was keyed particularly to the overhaul shops at San Diego for the Pacific forces and Norfolk for the Atlantic forces. When they transferred ships from the Atlantic to the Pacific, their aircraft units went with them, and so when it became time to overhaul airplanes, we found ourselves in the position where most of our airplanes were in the Pacific Ocean, and we had a mammoth overhaul shop at Norfolk that was starving to death and was practically out of business. So the solution was to ferry aircraft that were in need of overhaul from California to Norfolk and then fly the overhauled planes back to the Pacific. This really showed up the weaknesses in the cross-country training that had been given heretofore.

I had developed an interest in cross-country flying, which I was not able to do much about except to make flights on weekends when I was attached to squadrons based at Norfolk. This was something we had to do on our own time. It was not included in our training program to any significant extent. I did do this, and I liked cross-country flying. So, about mid-1931, when VS-5 was transferred to the West Coast, there was a call sent out to aviators in all units on the West Coast for volunteers to ferry aircraft back to Norfolk for overhaul.

After volunteering, we were ordered from wherever we were to the Naval Air Station, San Diego, Operations Division, and given our instructions for the cross-country flight to Norfolk. They made an effort to have each flight led by a pilot who had made a flight all the way across the country previously, but there weren't enough of them. They couldn't find that many people to lead the flights. So then they compromised by having pilots who claimed to have cross-country experience lead the flights, although their seniority had something to do with it.

I found that I was assigned to a flight of three planes to leave San Diego for Norfolk. The planes had gone long past their proper period for overhaul and were not in very good shape. They were convertible planes in that they had been on floats and were converted to land planes by having landing gear attached in lieu of the floats. Hence, the brake system was not too reliable. I found that I was assigned to a flight led by a marine captain with a marine first lieutenant as the number two officer in seniority; I brought up the rear as a lieutenant (jg) in the navy.

We were given aviation charts from San Diego to Yuma. We were told we would be able to get charts at Yuma that would take us to El Paso and, by following similar procedures at each stop and getting the charts that were needed for the next flight, we would have charts all of the way across the country. The naval air station at San Diego only had aviation charts from San Diego to Yuma and to San Francisco. That was the limit of their stock. There were no allowances for aviation charts. As a matter of fact, there were not then in existence aviation charts covering all of the United States. Now, there was such a thing as commercial aviation in those days. It wasn't very far advanced, but you would certainly think that the whole country would have been mapped by the government. It had not been. The airline companies had their own route maps for their pilots. They didn't trust what they could get from the government. It was that bad.

The three of us started from San Diego with our first stop at El Centro because we didn't know just how fit these airplanes were, and we only had a five-minute check flight before taking off. We went to El Centro without difficulty and landed there but found that we had excessive oil consumption and that therefore our oil consumption would dictate the length of the legs that we would fly, rather than our fuel consumption. We refueled and departed for Tucson and made it without difficulty; there we decided to call it a night. We serviced the airplanes and were out on the field early the next morning to go to El Paso and on east.

The direct line between Tucson and El Paso comes quite close to the border of Mexico, and our route went from Tucson to El Paso. We commented on the fact that our route paralleled the border very closely. U.S. relations with Mexico were tender, as they usually were in those days. It was essential that we not cross the border. We were not able to get the maps that we had been told would be available. Furthermore, the people at the airport said that there were no aviation maps for that area of the country, and that the only maps we could find would be at filling stations where we could get automobile maps put out by the oil companies. We did this. As a matter of fact, I went from Tucson to Norfolk on nothing but automobile maps I picked up at filling stations. I never did find the aviation maps that I was told about in San Diego.

Shortly after we took off from Tucson, it seemed to me that my flight leader was easing a trifle too close to the Mexican border. I pulled up alongside of him and pointed to the northeast and wheeled away from him in that direction to try to indicate that I thought we were too close to the border and should get comfortably into the United States. He shook his head and indicated by hand that he was on the right course; his wingman, the marine lieutenant, stayed with him. I went back to my position and stuck it out as long as I could.

Then I knew I was getting off what little map help I had, and that we were definitely going into Mexico. I made one more attempt to get my leader to turn, and he wouldn't. So I just waved him good-bye and headed off in the direction I thought I should go to get to El Paso. It was insubordinate; there's no question about it because he was in charge of the flight. But, on the other hand, he had a plane of the same speed and power that I did, and he could catch me if he wanted to. I was going in the direction I wanted to go, so I let it go at that. I headed right for where I thought El Paso would be, and, sure enough, in a short time found a landfall that I could identify and felt comfortable as to where I was for the first time since leaving Tucson.

From time to time I looked over my shoulder in the direction where the two marines had disappeared. They gradually disappeared from view, going, I was sure, into Mexico. Without difficulty I came to the field at El Paso and landed and was quite worried about my flying companions. I gassed my plane and waited for about two hours. I waited until I knew they had to be down somewhere because they would be out of gas by that time. Then I made a long-distance collect telephone call to the operations officer at the air station at San Diego. This was something that was far from authorized. People just didn't make collect telephone calls in those days, but I thought that I should do something, and that was all I could think of to do.

So I called the operations officer and reported what had transpired and asked him for instructions. This was about noon. He said to stay where I was overnight and inform him if the marines showed up. In the meantime, he would try to get messages out on the teletype. This had already been started in El Paso, to get any possible lead as to where those two might be. He said if they did not arrive by the next morning, I was to proceed alone to Norfolk.

I stayed at the airport until about 6:00 or 7:00 that evening and heard nothing of the marines; there was nothing on the teletype about their being located. I went into town to a hotel and spent the night. When I came out to the field the next morning, they still had no word from the marines, so, carrying out the orders I had been given, I took off. In very easy stages and by finding my way by automobile road maps, I flew across country to Norfolk. I completed the flight without further incident, although I had one forced landing due to low oil pressure. I had stretched my oil too far for the consumption, which was so exorbitant, and had to land in a small cow pasture and buy some oil at a gasoline filling station, put it in the plane, crank it up, and take off from the cow pasture and continue to Norfolk. That was the only incident of the remainder of that flight.

Not until I arrived at Norfolk did I learn what happened to the marines. As I feared, they had gone deep into Mexico, became thoroughly lost, and landed in the desert—both planes suffered severe damage. The pilots were not hurt, but there was quite an international incident precipitated by their landing in Mexico without authority. The Mexicans simply would not believe that they were lost, or that they were not snooping. It wound up that they would not let the planes be repaired and flown out of there. They had to be disassembled, boxed and crated, and shipped out by rail, and the two marines were sent back from Mexico by train.

There is some justification, but very little, for this lack of appreciation for cross-country flights and training for them, due to the nature of the planes then existing. Their short-legged characteristics in themselves impaired the development of the concept of their use for transcontinental flight. But I think in retrospect, at least, that it was extremely short-sighted for the people laying out curricula to overlook the tremendous possibilities for distance flying that were inherent in aviation. I don't think that they gave it any significant thought, particularly in the navy, where they would be flying from ships at sea and doing navigation by methods heretofore used in ships, and not by "contact flying" by identification of landmarks. This added to the early tendency to overlook what normally became known as cross-country flying.

I think that the transfer of so many planes to the West Coast from the East Coast and the overhaul facilities being divided between Norfolk and San Diego had more to do with the development of cross-country flying capabilities in naval aviation than any other one thing. We had to do it. We had to keep both shops going. Without cross-country ferrying, we could not keep the shop going at Norfolk, and we also could not afford to overload the San Diego installation. It was an economic fact, and they had to do something about it.

When I got to Norfolk after that first transcontinental flight, I found that I was qualified for the elite crowd who had completed a flight across the country; I was a veteran. Going back to San Diego, I was designated to lead a flight, although all of the pilots in the flight were senior to me. However, we got along all right and made the flight back to San Diego, the six of us, without difficulty. I was having a ball. I never enjoyed any flying as much in my life as I did this. I was fascinated by cross-country flying, so upon arrival at San Diego I immediately signed up in the operations office as a permanent volunteer for any cross-country flying that might come up. They told me that they would use me as much as my superior would permit. So I bugged my superior to let me off to make cross-country flights; I made about six of them during that period, each time leading a flight of planes.

I had some varying experiences, some really wild ones. One was with an old Loening OL-8 amphibian, built by Grover Loening's company. I had eight forced landings with that plane between San Diego and Norfolk, involving everything up to and including changing cylinders. That's how bad the condition of the plane was before it was sent out on a flight across the country. It was inexcusable. The navy just had not learned enough about that sort of thing at that time. But, with the impact of ferrying, the necessity for cross-country flying grew, and more and more people attained some degree of proficiency in it. By means of these flights between the overhaul establishments we gradually built up a reservoir of people who knew something about it, and many people, such as myself, became quite interested in cross-country flying. We forced it into training courses to make it count a little more. It was, to me, one of the most fascinating types of flying that could be done.

In 1937, by a stroke of luck, I was assigned to the naval air station at Anacostia for my first tour of shore duty, flying commercial-type transports. The navy had no instrument course of any sort; they had no real organization for cross-country flying; the only official unit for VIP transport was the unit based at Anacostia. We built up a stable of a rather elite group of cross-country experts. We only had six or seven pilots, but they all flew VIP transports all the time. Every one of us qualified for Department of Commerce certification. That department was then running commercial aviation, issuing licenses to fly commercial transports, awarding Department of Commerce ratings in every type and every weight class of aircraft, both land planes and seaplanes. That was as qualified a group of cross-country pilots as you could find anywhere. Naval aviators used to get into very fierce competition to get assigned to a group as elite as that and to do this sort of flying; it was a fascinating experience. So, long before the war, at least some of us were pretty well cross-country oriented.

In January of 1934 I was transferred from Patrol Squadron 1 (VP-1) to Patrol Squadron 10 (VP-10) flying Consolidated P2Y-1s, the forerunners of the Catalina. So I had two years of flying boats, of which a year and a half was in VP-10 and was very interesting flying. We went over just about all of the Central Pacific. The objective was to find out how to navigate and operate over long distances because we finally had planes that had the endurance. We had to take extra gas with us in those huge extra tanks that they had. We had the range, and we used it. The idea was to do the exploratory work that was necessary to go by air over the Pacific. There were a lot of places around there in Hawaii that they didn't know much about, and they wanted to get all the information that they could on the various islands. We went on advance base operations regularly. We'd fly to these places, land by them, live in tents on the beach while we did the exploratory work. Sometimes an aviation tender would anchor offshore, and we would live aboard when not flying.

Pan American Airways sponsored a book about blazing the trail across the Pacific. They blazed a trail across the Pacific using aviation stores that were laid down by VP-10 when we'd been there previously and established facilities! We had aviation gasoline and oil cached away in all those places for our future use. All of their information on these places came from VP-10. So when they put out their book about their trailblazing across the Pacific, we all got quite a chuckle out of it. It was all a friendly thing, but, of course, they were commercial, and this meant dollars in the bank to them if they got the credit for doing a lot of things that they didn't do, actually.

We were interested in some of the mandated islands but we didn't get into them for political reasons; at least during my time, from 1933 to 1935, I know we never got there. We did quite a bit of long-distance flying to various islands, but not into the mandated area. That was out of bounds for us. We were at that point beginning to be concerned about the Japanese threat, and all of our fleet problems were keyed to war with Japan. Everything we did was set up on that basis.

I think everybody in those days had some pretty interesting experiences while flying the patrol planes. The engines weren't reliable, and we didn't have the benefit of the electronic aids to navigation and things like that. The worst time I had in the boats was when Capt. Charles T. P. Ulm of the Australian Air Service and his fellow pilots took off from Oakland on 3 December 1934 trying to make a record flight down to Australia and were forced down at sea near Hawaii on 4 December. He took off from the West Coast, and that was the last anybody ever saw of him. A search line went out from Hawaii, and all the patrol boats that were there were sent out on it. VP-10 had the planes with the longest range, so we got the longest searches—twelve-, fifteen-, eighteen-hour flights.

For five days after this plane obviously had gone down, they ran those search flights. Finally, they gave VP-10 the most unlikely and distant sectors since they'd combed all the others without any evidence. We were sent out to the northwest of the islands in case Ulm had missed the islands in that direction. Shortly after we got into that area, we ran into a terrific weather front. We were spending all of our time flying our airplanes and very little time looking. We couldn't see anything anyhow because of the torrential rain. The length of the flight was such and the wind changes were so great that all six aircraft when they came back missed the landfalls that they were planning on. They all came up someplace else, but they all happened to hit someplace that they could identify—that is, all but me.

I had the longest sector, and when I was due back in Hawaii, I looked down, and it wasn't there. So I did all the rechecking of navigation I could. Of course, our greatest problem was getting an accurate fix on the force and direction of the wind. You determined the direction by your magnetic compass, flying into the wind streaks on the water, and then reading it and the force with a drift sight that was not very efficient. That's where you would be most likely to go off in your navigation, and I did. I went off in my estimates of the force of the wind quite badly.

When I got to where I should have made my landfall, the western end of Molokai, I couldn't see it, so I "reviewed the bidding" by key radio with our base. We had no beacons or beams of any sort, nothing to home in on, and no direction finder, at least in the airplane. There was one radio direction finder in the islands. It was an experimental thing out there. I requested that they take bearings on me.

In the meantime, I got a message from another pilot, who had just gotten back to base and knew I was still out and probably off in my navigation. He sent a message saying that he came out ninety miles to the east of where he expected to make his landfall. He had reworked his navigation and figured what the wind had to be in order to put him where he came out; he suggested that I rework my navigation on that basis and see what that might indicate.

Well, I did rework the navigation on the basis of that average force and direction of the wind that he gave me on the radio. That put me at a place one hundred miles north of Molokai. So, on that basis, I changed my course for Molokai. Later on, the radio direction finder picked up my signal and cut me in, then checked out my position. They couldn't tell you how far you were out but could give you the direction. It checked with my navigation rework, so I kept on slugging it out on my new course.

It got dark, and we went through all sorts of horrible weather. We weren't searching; we were just flying the airplane. Finally, I picked up a light and was delighted because it had to be on something, so I followed it in. It turned out to be the lighthouse on the point on the north side of Molokai. I consulted my light list and identified the characteristics of its flashing signal. It was Kalaupapa Light, which is located at about the midpoint of the north side of the island of Molokai, right at the site of the leper colony. I had missed my landfall by approximately forty miles; I was supposed to have it at Makapuu Point, Oahu. That was on the night of the 6th of December 1934, a night I am unlikely to forget.

By that time, the Honolulu evening paper had an extra on the streets with a banner headline: "Pearl Harbor Flight Crew Lost in Search for Ulm." They had written me off in the newspapers as being lost. That was probably the closest one that I had in flying boats. However, I still had lots of gas left, enough for about four more hours. In those days, we were able to fly farther than we ever had before, and since we didn't have things like automatic pilots and radio direction finders, etc., it was more difficult then. Our navigation was celestial navigation and dead reckoning. That was all. That was adequate for the shorter-range planes, but when we got planes that had a range of over two thousand miles, dead reckoning and celestial navigation were rather inadequate. Other help was needed, which we didn't have. The greatest advances in over-the-water flying were made because we needed the things that would make it possible to make flights safely and accurately. Those things were forced into invention because we had to have something better. We did an awful lot of long-distance flying without more than rudimentary equipment.

The accuracy of the bombsight in use in the early thirties was so poor that the scoring system, particularly for night bombing, was very, very generous. Otherwise, everyone would have gotten a complete zero every year. This, in itself, was ridiculous; we were kidding ourselves. If anybody got a hit in the target area on a night bombing practice, believe me, it was an unusual thing. I'm talking about the target that's on a float out there in the water. Of course, there are plenty of near misses all around the target, but the navy didn't give credit for near misses at all. They were thrown out.

So about the winter of 1934–35, out of the blue we received a message from the Bureau of Ordnance and the Bureau of Aeronautics saying that they had just shipped to VP-10 six of the new Norden bombsights, which had been tested out at Dahlgren but had never been used in an operating squadron. Lt. Comdr. John J. Ballentine, who eventually retired as a four-star admiral and was then serving in the Bureau of Aeronautics, was active in the testing of the Norden sight.

Now they felt that the Norden bombsight was ready to go operational, and they sent it to VP-10—the patrol squadron with the newest planes— to run the tests. They said that the sights would arrive with full instructions, as far as all the manuals were concerned, but unfortunately they had not been able to train any bombsight mechanics other than those that were urgently needed at Dahlgren. We would have to depend on the bombsight people we had, the officers that we had, and the manuals, to start the shakedown test. They wanted us to put every possible minute on it, to get these sights into operation and make an operational report to them.

I was the gunnery officer of the squadron, so this became my baby. Lt. Comdr. Harold M. Martin, who retired as a four-star admiral in 1956 after commanding the U.S. Seventh Fleet during the Korean War, was the skipper. His nickname was "Beauty" because he was not very beautiful— but a great guy. He said, "Okay, there's your baby. You're relieved of all responsibilities except getting that bombsight working; get it going."

There were six large crates sitting out there. We opened all six crates, but there was no manual of any sort. We whistled off a message to the bureau about it. The bureau came back and said unfortunately, they'd found so many errors in the draft of the manual they'd put out that they thought it would probably do us more harm than good. But they told us that the thing wasn't so complex, for us to go ahead with it anyhow and get them assembled.

So we started the assembly. I was in charge of it, together with my ordnance crew from the squadron. I spent every waking minute and a lot of times when I should have been asleep trying to get the first one put together so it would work. I finally got it to the point where I thought it would, still without manuals; but having gone over it from the inside out, I knew the principle of how it operated, and I got it installed in my airplane and went out to make bomb runs with it.

Well, phenomenally, from my point of view, the thing started making hits right from the start. It really worked. We must have done it right because the results were better than anything I'd ever been able to accomplish with the old sight. The first day I was out there, I made better drops than I'd ever made in my life. I couldn't believe it. So I had my copilot get up there, and he started doing the same thing, hitting beautifully. I flew back, thoroughly elated, and reported to Beauty Martin that I thought we had a bombsight in commission, that it worked, and that this thing was really fine. I said that the squadron had better get really humping on it, but first I'd like to take him out and show him what it would do.

I took Beauty out. We had an anchored target way over by the western end of Oahu, about ten miles out to sea. We got out there and made some test drops. Beauty was an enthusiastic sort of person anyhow, and he was very excited. He thought this was great. I got up there with him at the bombsight while the copilot took over running the plane and showed him how to do it and let him make a few runs himself. He started making hits. He really got enthusiastic and told me to go ahead, do anything I wanted, get all the help I wanted, to get these bombsights in all the other planes of the squadron, so they could be used on our annual bombing competition.

After we got them all assembled and gave just a modicum of training to the pilots, we ran off our individual bombing practice and made more hits than we'd ever made before. Of course, the other squadrons that didn't have the Norden sight wanted to outlaw our squadron from the competition because we had better equipment. They had a good point, but the bureau decided not to do that, that it wouldn't make too much difference; they would consider that we had this better equipment, and if we did so much better than anybody else, it wouldn't deprive them of honors for doing the best they could with the old sight.

So we kept going, and then the time came for this night bombing practice. Night bombing had been so bad before that except for an occasional wild shot, par for the course was no hits in squadron formation night bombing. Sometimes individuals on night bombing would get a hit, but nobody had any confidence we'd ever be able to hit consistently at night until we got a better sight.

I did quite a bit of night bombing with my plane, and I was getting hits with it at night just as well as I had in the daytime, so I told Beauty. He said, "Well, this is the way we're going to work it on the formation bombing. We're going to have the squadron in the air, and we're going to have somebody else fly your airplane for you, and you're going to be the bombardier for the whole formation."

I didn't like that much. I'd always liked to fly my own plane. But from then on I was wiped out of using my own plane for bombing entirely, went out on all practice runs with Beauty Martin's crew, and was the bombardier for the formation. The pilot of each plane was responsible for the bombsight when it was in his plane. We didn't have bombardiers in the navy. The pilots did their own bombing, and we had pilots who operated the bombsight in each plane when on individual bombing practices. When we were formation bombing, the sight was handled by the bombing pilot in the leading plane. He'd make his run, and the rest of the formation would close into tight formation on him. He would give the drop signal at the time he pulled his drop, and the other planes would drop their bombs too. They tracked the bombing run on their bombsights, but they didn't control the drop. I controlled the drop in the number one plane.

The time came for the actual practice. On the first drop of six bombs, four of them hit the target. On the second drop of six bombs, five hit the target. Well, that was something unheard of. That was more hits than all the five squadrons based there normally would have made in one practice. This was observed, for scoring purposes, by another squadron. They had other observers out there too because of the new sight. And, of course, there's the target to be examined, so there's no question about hits.

And so the question arose of working up our score, under the rules of the old *Orders for Gunnery Exercises (OGE)*. It was so liberal for night bombing, when they didn't expect anything, that if you hit within half a mile of the target, you got some credit. Only for this reason did anyone get something other than a zero score every year. I think a satisfactory score then was about 40 percent of bombs within a great circle around the target, not the target itself. We had put a total of nine bombs right on the target.

Under the *OGE* rules we had a score of I don't know how many thousand percent. Nothing had ever been made like that before. So this report went back to Washington, then they had to rewrite the *OGE*. But we got all sorts of kudos for the bombing we did—which was not to our credit at all but entirely to the credit of the Norden bombsight, which then became *the* bombsight that carried the navy and the Army Air Forces through the war. That bombsight was virtually unchanged at the end of the war. It was the same as it was when we saw it for the first time.

While this was going on, it was inevitable that the word would spread like wildfire among all military aviators that the navy had really come up with a bombsight. Other squadrons even had their gunnery officers take rides with us to watch us. There was great interest, even on the other side of Ford Island, where we were based. The other side of the island was the Army Air Corps base, where they had the old Keystone bombers. They were on the west side, we were on the east side, and "the word" got over to the west side of the island.

They had nothing like our Norden sight, yet they were called "bombardment squadrons." They couldn't hit the side of a barn. This was not their fault; they didn't have the equipment. They heard about our bombsight, which was purely a navy development with Norden; they wanted to get in on it. I knew these fellows, knew them pretty well and liked them, so I took a couple of them out with me and showed them how the thing operated. They became so enthused about it that they sent the word back to the War Department to try to get the same thing for themselves, added onto the navy contract. They had some kind of a new bombsight in development, which they wouldn't see for a couple of years.

One officer over there—the gunnery officer of a bombardment squadron—was a pretty good friend of mine. He asked me if as a favor, after we finished our night formation practice, we would let him have one of our bombsights to install in a Keystone bomber, by his own people—a completely assembled sight—in order to put an added boost behind their push for getting our sight in the Army Air Corps. I agreed to that on my own. I wouldn't ask for higher authority because if I'd asked I knew the answer would have been no. I said that if he would take good care of it and let me have it back on demand, he could have it to test, but that I'd bring my people over to install it for him.

So I did. He went out with it and took everybody around there in the air corps with him. He had results similar to ours. But he didn't return it when he said he was going to return it. I kept calling him and calling him, and finally when we had another practice coming up that required bombsights in all six planes and we only had five bombsights, I called him up and said, "Look, I've got to have that sight."

He said, "Well, we're doing this, that, and the other; we'll let you have it next week."

"No, I must have it by tomorrow."

He said, "Well, I'll do my best."

Tomorrow came, but the bombsight didn't. So I got my squadron truck and drove around on the other side of the island. I went down to his squadron gunnery shop to get that bombsight and bring it back. When I got in there, I saw about eight people working on it. They had taken that bombsight apart completely to see how it worked, to learn all about it, and they couldn't get it together again. Parts of that bombsight were all over the ordnance and gunnery shop. I died a thousand deaths because we had to use it in a couple of days, and it was going to take more than a little bit of putting together.

I got all my best men over there right away and said to the others, "Leave us alone; we'll take it as it is." And so, with about thirty hours of exhausting work, we finally got that thing put back together and back in commission in one of our airplanes. We operated it in the practice. Nobody but my crew ever knew about that. I never breathed a word. Beauty Martin didn't know a thing about it. That was the first air corps experience with a Norden bombsight—one that I let them have on a cumshaw basis!

II

FROM A NOBODY
TO A SOMEBODY

Lt. Comdr. Robert E. Carl

Robert E. Carl *was born on 30 July 1914 in Jeromesville, Ohio, son of Irene and Clarence Carl. He graduated from Jeromesville High School and enlisted in the navy on 12 June 1934 as an apprentice seaman. He progressed through the ranks to retire in 1956 in the rank of lieutenant commander. His early years were spent as a yeoman on the carrier USS* Saratoga *(CV-3), after which he became a communications specialist. Most of his career was spent with the U.S. Naval Security Group and under the Director, Naval Communications, performing duties as a traffic analyst, cryptanalyst, and electronics officer, among many others.*

After his retirement in 1956, Lieutenant Commander Carl worked for RCA and then seventeen years for Communications Satellite Corp. He retired again in 1978 and later took up residence in Lake Columbia, Brooklyn, Michigan.

I grew up during the depression in a real strict church-going family. We weren't rich, but we weren't poor either. My father owned a hardware store in Jeromesville, Ohio, and on some days he was lucky to sell twenty dollars worth of hardware. He also used to clerk sales of farmers who were either selling out or being sold out by the bank. I never saw him so depressed as he was after he came home from one of the foreclosure sales of people he had known back into the early 1900s. I would hear him tell my mother that many of these foreclosed farmers had no where to go if relatives did not take them in or the local church coffers were too empty to help them out. Even the collection plate suffered from the depression.

So each summer I'd work away from home at farmwork for my room and board. The small town of Jeromesville is about sixty miles south of Cleveland on Lincoln Highway, and there would be sailors hitchhiking through town, so I'd interview them about the navy. I always liked the navy, and I thought I'd want to be an aviator—until my experiences on the carrier *Saratoga* changed my mind.

When I finished high school, where I learned typing and shorthand and a few useful things like that, there were no jobs. They wouldn't even consider a single man for any kind of a job. The married men needed the work for their families worse than the single people, and there was just nothing to do but farmwork and going to work for your room and board. I worked on a farm in Mansfield, Ohio, where most of the work was for relatives. Sometimes that wasn't too good, but every summer I'd come back home the day before school started.

After high school, I would have liked to have gone to college, but no one could afford it. With seven children in the family, each about a year or so apart, that would have been real rough. I just gave that up and left home to join the navy. I hitchhiked up in my overalls and shirt and one pair of shoes and got on the waiting list. While I was waiting, I did farmwork. At one place they gave me a pair of shoes, and at another they gave me a pair of overalls. I ran the tractor, plowed corn; it was very discouraging to get out of high school and not find anything to do other than that.

In a year and a half the navy sent me a card to show up at Cleveland, in June 1934. So I hitchhiked back up again. They were building the navy up to seventy-five thousand people, they told me, at that time. Eight or nine of us showed up, and they took three of us because we each had a high school education. They could afford to be very selective in that kind of an environment. So when I was accepted in the navy they gave us meal tickets to get on the train without having to buy our own chow on the way to Norfolk, Virginia. I thought that was really living high on the hog. A kid named Scharfenstein from Chicago was my buddy, and when we got off the train in Washington to take another train for Norfolk, he called up some relatives, and they came and took us around. We were flabbergasted at that.

After we arrived in Norfolk, we reported in for training. My buddy and I were in the same platoon, and I got to be the company clerk. The chief saw that I was carrying a portable typewriter, so he said, "You want the job of company clerk?" So I had a little office with a bunk in it, and I did the chief's typing, made up watch lists, etc., and went through all the drills.

The fleet was around on the East Coast in 1934, and they really wanted people to break up training early if they wanted to get a ship going back to the West Coast. So we broke up early, and they gave everybody a week's leave. You could take it, or you couldn't take it, or you could go home for two or three days, hop on the bus, and come back. They gave us bus tickets, which I did use. I wanted to make the *Saratoga,* so this chief petty officer said, "I'll help you get the *Saratoga."* I figured I'd be an aviator and be flying since Lindbergh was my hero and I built model planes.

So in September I went home for two or three days. Scharfenstein and I agreed to come back, and we'd both go to the *Saratoga.* So we got back, got our sea bags and everything, and went to see the chief. He said, "I'll get you on the detail. There's some recruits going off to the *Saratoga* this evening." So we got our gear, went down to the dock, got in the *Saratoga's* boat, motored out—and I never saw anything that big in my life!

I finally got up the gangway with the damn sea bag, and we were all standing on the hangar deck. All the different ship's company people who wanted to pick up people were down there looking to see whom they wanted for their department—communications, deck force, air, and so on—and 90 percent of us ended up in the deck force. But they happened to be looking for a yeoman striker for the air office. They had only one guy in the air office, and he was down there, saw my typewriter, and wanted to know how I'd like to be a yeoman and work in the air office. That was a good deal; I got out of the deck force on that one!

The home port of the *Saratoga* was Long Beach, California. The ship came around from the East Coast with a stop at Gonaives Bay, Haiti, in September 1934. What an awful place that was! That was my first introduction to how the other half lived—people with sores on them, the smell of the place. We went over to play baseball, and the natives snuck through the cactus and stuff and stole a lot of the sailors' clothes, the jumpers they'd taken off. That was a poverty-stricken place.

When we got to Panama in October, we went on liberty in Panama City, and it was one step lower than Haiti, it seemed to me. The trip through the canal was quite an experience. We had a pilot suspended from a crane in a little pilot house in the middle of the ship with a phone to guide the ship through. The ship was so wide that one of my jobs was to stand at a porthole with a stick and report by phone how much clearance there was between the side of the ship and the lock walls. There were only two feet of clearance on each side of the ship. My porthole was just at the edge where we'd scrape along the dock. A lot of the portholes were brass, and they got all banged and scraped off. They'd go along for a long stretch there, scraping the whole side of the ship. It was the overhang of the flight deck that knocked over the lampposts.

When I went on the *Saratoga*, I lived in a hammock for a while. Then, for security reasons, they decided they wanted somebody to sleep in the air office, so they rolled a cot in the office. So I got the duty all the time, sleeping in the air office. The air officer at that time was Comdr. G. D. Murray, a prissy old guy—the type you read about, a fancy dresser in civilian clothes. Commander Murray never came up to the office; you had to go up to his room. All he ever did was dictate letters ordering shoes someplace, at $32 a pair. The phone would ring, and he'd say, "This is Commander Murray speaking. I have some papers up here. I also want to dictate another letter." So I'd go up and knock on the door; you'd never go in without knocking. I learned the hard way because you were liable to run into the situation where he had visitors on board. This was the old navy so you had to be careful of that.

Being a yeoman covered all kinds of professional duties. I was privy to writing officers' personal and official correspondence, so I had to keep my mouth shut about the fights with other departments. I had access to classified stuff. Later, when I worked in communications, I had access to some classified publications and that type of thing. It wasn't like it is now, where I had to have a clearance to touch that stuff. I also had to type up the operating orders and flight orders for people to get their four hours flying time a month. This was a big racket back then. These were the ship's company officers, not the squadrons, so the big deal was to get the four hours in to get their flight pay, no matter how they did it. Murray always flew to that big fancy hotel in Denver, Colorado. He'd fly there to get his flight time in over the weekend, two hours there and two hours back.

When I reported aboard the *Saratoga* in September 1934, Capt. Kenneth Whiting was the skipper, followed by William F. Halsey in July 1935 and then John Towers in June 1937. Halsey tried to act tough, but I don't think he was really as tough as he tried to act. Later on, during the war when they had a hard time holding Halsey down, I think he was a more flamboyant type. They had problems with him getting off on his own and then screwing up the works. He wasn't too well liked by the crew of the *Saratoga*. He handed out too many summary courts-martial. You had to be careful with him if you ever got up in front of him for captain's mast. The exec, Frederick Sherman, tried to keep as few people going to him as he could. Sherman seemed to be more of the human type. He didn't have too many discipline problems.

The operations officer was Comdr. R. P. McConnell, and he was a very capable officer. The assistant air officer was D. C. Watson, a sort of wild character. McConnell took a liking to me, apparently, and when we came in from one of the fleet problems and he was being transferred from the ship, he let me get in the Grumman JF-2 amphibian and ride in the bottom, and we flew into San Diego with the mail and went on to Long Beach. We landed at Long Beach Airport, and I got home before the *Saratoga* ever arrived in port. Don't think I wasn't scared down in the bottom of that airplane. They hoist you off out in the ocean in the swells, so you have to wait until you get that thing up on the swells to take off. The water would be flying during takeoff, but once we got in the air, it was real nice.

Of course, the lineup of squadron commanders changed frequently during my four years on the *Saratoga*, but in the fall of 1934 I remember Lt. Comdr. Felix B. Stump was the Scouting Squadron 2B (VS-2B) squadron commander. When they spotted the deck, he was the first one off in his Vought SU-2 Corsair. He didn't have much room to get that thing off. They were biplanes, and they put the chocks under him. He would rev up to near full throttle, the chocks would be pulled, and down the flight deck he'd go. He'd dip off the bow, and we weren't sure he was going to make it, and finally he'd make it. Commander Stump had a real good reputation—gutsy, the leader, and a hell of a nice man, too. You could talk to him.

The next one off was Lt. Comdr. Ralph Ofstie, skipper of Fighting 6B (VF-6B), flying Boeing F4B-4s. Then came Allan Flagg, commanding the light bombing squadron VB-2B with Curtiss BFC-2s. Then Herman E. Halland had VT-2B, with Great Lakes TG-2 torpedo planes with folding wings and three people in them. The plane landed like a flying duck; it was a suicide job if there ever was one.

When the planes would come in for a landing, sometimes they would miss a wire and go into the barriers, and the telescope sight nearly went right into their head. One time the sight went right into a pilot, damn near through his head. Then they had a guy in an asbestos suit; when the plane caught on fire, he was to run over there and sacrifice his life to pull the guy out of it. That was no easy job, especially when the top wing folded up on the pilot. When I'd see them hauling these people out of there down to the sick bay, I started to lose my interest in flying somewhat.

They crashed quite often. They'd either catch a late wire and go into the barrier, or they'd miss a wire completely and go into the barrier. The barrier wire, which was real thick cable, would pull the landing gear under and put the prop right into the teak wood deck sometimes. A couple of times the barrier wires broke and cut off a couple of legs of the personnel in the flight deck crew. Once the plane caught a wire, then the guy who would stand at the edge of the flight deck would lower the barrier down. There were three of them, and they'd lower them down so the plane could taxi over them.

Every time any of the ship's company pilots had a crackup, I'd type up the accident report papers. It would be pilot error ½ percent, matériel failure 99 ½ percent. There was never a pilot error in all the time that I was doing this. It was a common joke. One time I kidded Commander McConnell about it, when I got to know him, and he said, "You folks did catch onto that, did you?" Half of these people had to have a safety pilot in the rear seat, and the safety pilot was an aviation pilot (AP). AP Manders was an enlisted pilot, a friend of mine, and he used to fly backup for Captain Halsey, Frederick Sherman, Admiral Butler, and the rest of them. The admiral had a fancy blue biplane. They'd collect the flight pay, but they weren't allowed to fly alone; they had to have the safety pilot. They got their four hours, that was the main thing. This was in the depression, so money counted. The officers didn't have a lot of money to entertain with in Long Beach.

So one time Halsey decided he was going to make a carrier landing with this thing—and he was in the front cockpit, and Manders was in the back cockpit. They got the hook down and made the approach. He was about four feet off and was going to miss the wire by four feet, so Manders threw the throttle to it and off they went. Manders was sure he was going to end up in the barrier, wrecking the thing if he had come in. Manders caught hell out of it.

The communication officer at that time was Commander Wyatt, whose brother, Mathias B. Wyatt, was a pilot on the ship. On 11 May 1935, he took off and apparently hit the slipstream from the preceding airplane and nosedived into the sea. Despite a frantic search by the destroyer

MacLeish, they never recovered Wyatt's body, and two wheels from the plane were all that was spotted. I'll never forget it as long as I live. All they got from that were the two wheels.

Then a year later, in May 1936, a hell of a nice guy named Hugh Boadwee went in, a young fellow. He crashed into the water astern of the *Saratoga.* They never found him, but the wheels of the plane and a flight helmet were recovered. Those guys earned their money.

In another case, we had Lt. L. W. Curtin who had been the landing signal officer (LSO) on the *Saratoga.* His wife was to arrive on a commercial ship coming into Panama. He was stationed at Coco Solo. It appeared that he dove the plane right into the dock where the ship was going to moor. It was in the newspapers back then—on 14 August 1936. He crashed that damn plane right into the dock. So they're sure that was suicide. He was assistant air officer or something at the Coco Solo air station at the time.

My battle station when I worked in the air office was to be the speaker up on the flight bridge, or primary flight control. The air officer was up there controlling the landings, and he had a red and a green light and a flag he'd stick out in the breeze. The landing signal officer was back at the stern. So when the planes were all spotted, my job was to announce, "Man the planes." The next thing was, "Start engines," and after they started up, then nobody could hear me anyway. Once in a while they'd get in a hurry and give you about six different things to say at once. So I finally got a pad, and I'd take it down on this pad. Murray wasn't too bad. Watson had no patience. There would be a little noise, so I'd say, "Could you give it to me again?"

So he'd say, "At 0605, all pilots will report to the ready room. At 0610, get your plotting boards and man the planes. At 0630, we will start engines." He'd give me all this, and he'd be reading it off, but he'd never hand it to me—I was supposed to remember all that stuff to give out over the loudspeaker system. If I screwed up, everybody was going to laugh at me, too, down below. So I got so I'd write it all down and make sure I had what he wanted to say first. So I thought I had a lot of power there to say, "Pilots, man your planes," and "Start engines," etc.

When the pilots got ready to land and the ship turned into the wind, why naturally they were grading the officers on landing, and I got to see some of the first night landings that were made on the *Saratoga* when they first put the lights on. The ship anchored off Long Beach and the pilots made the approach to the ship to see if the lights were going to work or not. Chief Photographer Goodnight was always back there in the wind taking movies of all the landings.

A friend of mine worked for Goodnight in the photo lab. The bureau used to study all the crash pictures. So when we had nothing to do at night or on the weekends, we'd go up and run all these crash movies. It wasn't anything fun, but you could slow them up and see what really happened. We thought that was something great at the time. Watching those movies also helped discourage my ambition to be a pilot, especially when they went over the side and the ship had gone over them, or something like that. Sometimes they'd miss a wire, and then they'd give it the gun and bank off to the left. If the engine didn't pick up quick enough, down they went into the water. The plane guard destroyer would come and try to pick them up. I saw a lot of life go in.

A big Fleet Problem was held each year, and the *Saratoga* participated in her share. One notable exercise was Fleet Problem XIX, in March 1938, when she steamed toward Hawaii from the northwest and sent a reconnaissance plane in to reconnoiter Pearl Harbor. There was no activity around the navy yard, no indication of a patrol up or anything, so the pilot came back to the ship. In those days, to keep from breaking radio silence, the radioman put the message in a small cloth sandbag, and the pilot flew down the side of the ship. The radioman stood up and threw this damn bag onto the flight deck. Whoever got it was supposed to rush it up to the air officer and captain up on the bridge. Since there was no patrol at Pearl Harbor, the *Saratoga* launched planes before dawn, and they went in and attacked Pearl Harbor, Hickam Field, and a radio station, catching them completely off guard.

This was when Rear Adm. Ernie King was commander Aircraft, Battle Force, with his flag on the *Saratoga*. I didn't see too much of him. He was on the wing up above. He yelled down at Halsey from the flag bridge up there once in a while. We could hear this going on. I don't know how well those two got along together, but we heard lots of stories about King. He was supposed to be a big womanizer and all that type of thing.

The living conditions on board weren't too bad. Pay was supposed to have been twenty-one dollars a month. Then President Roosevelt cut the pay to $19.50. Then we had to sign an allotment to send ten dollars home to our parents. So I sent ten dollars home, and once in a while they didn't use it and they'd send it back to me. So they would send me a ten dollar bill back in a letter. That went on for the first year or two I was in, and then they finally stopped that. So that left $9.50. We paid for our own laundry on the *Saratoga*. We had laundry, but we also had to wash our own clothes, too, with saltwater soap. So if your laundry would be thirty cents, something like that, it didn't leave you much money to go on. Of course, three or four or five dollars went a long ways back then.

In those days, the chiefs, warrant officers, and commissioned officers had their own messes. There was a general mess for first class petty officers and below. There was a definite social separation between officers and enlisted on board the ship. The officers were pretty haughty about that. You always had to call them "sir" and everything else. The only pilot I knew in the squadrons was Boadwee; Stump and Ofstie would come to the air office. The pilots kept pretty much to themselves, away from the ship's company. They had all the extra rooms in officers' country reserved for them, and they stayed pretty much in the pilots' ready rooms.

The meals on the *Saratoga* were nothing special. We never saw ready-to-eat cereal that they have nowadays on board ship. Forget assorted fresh fruit—a little green apple you couldn't eat. They talk about chilled fruit juice now; never got that. If we got fried eggs, they were powdered eggs, and they were either green or some other color. Omelettes we never got. For meat, the only thing was that stuff on the shingle. We never got hot griddle cakes or pancakes or maple syrup or buttered grits. If you got pastry, you got cornbread. Beans and cornbread was a standard Saturday breakfast. Who in the hell wants beans for breakfast? "Assorted beverages" was coffee. That's all. Black coffee.

For lunch we might have chicken that hiked all the way from Iowa out to Long Beach to get there—a greenish color. Once in a while they had cold soup. We got some stale bread and some more coffee. For dinner, we might get more green chicken, or we got cold cuts. There were two or three different kinds of cold cuts, and they were horrid, probably the cheapest they could get. Then maybe we got another green apple for dessert and coffee.

The officers ate high on the hog, though. Every time we went to San Clemente, the commercial fishermen were out there catching lobsters and stuff, and the lobster character would come along side, and the officer's country would buy all these lobsters off of these people. They were eating lobsters, shrimp, high on the hog. I got acquainted with a Filipino working in the officer galley, so I'd trade him white helmets and parachute scarfs for shrimp once in a while. He was crazy about that. The parachute riggers would take all the old parachutes and make scarfs out of them. The aviators all wore scarfs, and they were made from this silk. My friend worked as a parachute packer, so he'd give me some of these once in a while, and I'd trade them off for good chow.

I never heard of drugs in those days, and they didn't have many weirdos. Very few. I don't think I ever heard of them catching a weirdo on the *Saratoga* even. If they did, they would have been court-martialed and kicked off. So I'm appalled about the problems that they're having in the service now. They didn't have that. As for drinking, when you're at sea, you go ashore and drink two beers, it hits some people and makes them look worse than they are. We had the usual share of drunks ashore, but it was mostly kids who couldn't handle it. On the other hand, there were some of the old-timers who were perpetual drunks. We had a character on the ship who used to drink Aqua Velva. He'd cut the ends off a loaf of bread and then drain the Aqua Velva through it.

But generally speaking, there was little drinking on board ship by the enlisted. The officers did their share, though. We had a Warrant Officer Larson on there who worked for the air department. I had been up to his cabin when he was entertaining, having a round of drinks. He'd call up and want some papers brought up or something; and once in a while when we were in port I'd get a call at the air office to bring up some helmets and scarves, and there the officers were with dames in the room, having a party. One time I called the parachute loft to have them bring the scarfs up. This kid took them up instead of me, so he went in, and there was this dame sitting on the bunk. She was the madame of some house over at Long Beach, called the "Rex Rooms," where the sailor had been to, and he recognized her. They were supposed to get visitors off the ship at midnight or around that time. They pulled the officer's gig alongside, and the kids who had the watch on the quarterdeck, their job was to make sure the visitors didn't fall in the drink and to help them down the gangway.

When the ship anchored at Lahaina Roads, Hawaii, native hula shows came aboard to entertain the crew. The *Saratoga* had a chaplain on board who was quite a rounder. These female hula dancers came on board, and there would be two nice-looking dames, and the rest would be about three hundred pounds of beef. They'd have a *holuku* dress on, and you'd see a bump on this side of the gown, and you'd see a bump over here, and, oh, they were gyrating under that, but you couldn't tell it. The old chaplain thought that stuff was great, so he brought them out to the ship in the gig for the show. He was actually up on the stage there announcing what they were going to do next and all that. He was like a kid with a new toy. Then he loaded them again into the gig and took them all ashore—but he never got back to the ship until the next morning. The kid down on the quarterdeck said they received a signal from the dock in the morning to send the gig in for somebody, and it was the old chaplain, so he got over there somewhere and got tangled up, I guess. That made the rounds of the ship! The *Officers' Guidebook* in the 1930s stated "officerdom is equivalent to the priesthood." In my experience, that was doubtful in many cases.

When we were in Hawaii, they tried to arrange tours, like the present-day USO, to keep us out of the other places, and the same in Honolulu to take in the sights. But there were so many sailors ashore, the place was flooded with them. As for the West Coast ports, such as San Francisco and Bremerton, everybody hated Bremerton, the climate up there and so forth. Bremerton itself was like Norfolk, the same as Granby Street. That's all it was outside the navy yard gates but much smaller than Norfolk. So you'd have to take the *Kalakala* ferry to go to Seattle, and they had a beer bar on the *Kalakala*. It was an hour trip on there, and it cost you fifty cents, so you'd get a round-trip ticket for one dollar and put one half the ticket in your shoe to make sure you got back. They served Rainier beer in those days on that thing going over, so a lot of the crew would be not feeling too bad by the time the ferry docked in Seattle. The last ferry left around midnight from Seattle coming back to Bremerton, and liberty would be up at 8:00 A.M. on the dock, so you had to be sure you made the last ferry back.

We would be up there for a couple of months in the dry dock, and when we left Long Beach, they'd take up everybody's cars and junk on the hangar deck on the *Saratoga*. There were all these cars tied down up on the hangar deck, and everybody would be doing their car work on the hangar deck, getting anything on the ship they could get to repair and gas them up with aviation gas before they took them off. When we'd get into Bremerton, we'd move into the dry dock. They'd let the water out, and then the whole crew went over the side to scrape off the barnacles. The next day, we'd slap on the red paint before they ran the water back up again.

So we lived on the ship with telephones lines and electricity from the shore. It was a good life for the officers. Watson used to bring his cocktails down in a thermos bottle of some kind and have his drinks on the ship. He sat that thing on the desk in the air office, and once in a while he'd pour himself one there in the office. I never ever saw him loaded or anything; he was just flush of face. Commander Murray would never do a thing like that or McConnell. Murray was too dignified a gentleman.

Back in those days they had short arm inspections, which now would probably be too controversial. But every time we went in port and came back out, everybody had to fall in down on the hangar deck, and down came Commander Agnew, the medical officer, with his flashlight. You had to go through this. Everybody had to line up—except the officers. They were down there making sure everybody showed up. It was the damnedest thing. That's the way it was, indignities or not.

There was counseling before going ashore. They handed you a sanitube, and you had no place to put the stuff except in your jumper pocket. That's all, a sanitube and a damned pack of rubbers. You had to take them before you could get off the ship. So the sailors went around with this stuff sticking out of their pockets. A lot of them threw it overboard on the way in. At that time they published the VD list, and by the time they left Seattle they had four hundred on the list. The damnedest thing I ever heard of. They restricted those sailors, and they lost pay at that time. It was called SKMC—Sick Misconduct. You got your pay docked and everything else for that. When you went ashore and you had any activity and came back, you had to sign the book and take a shot and all that kind of junk. If you didn't sign the book and got it, then you got a summary court-martial. People got courts-martial out of it, lost their pay and that type of thing. They would have been better off if they had told you some of these things back when you were a kid in high school. They had some lectures, but not like they have published for the kids nowadays on TV.

The navy tried to discourage tattoos, and the ship's medical people put out the word about tattooing and the possibility of getting infections from that, but it certainly didn't stop some people. I don't have any tattoos, but I got in line for one down in Panama. I was going to get a flag with this gal's initials from back home. But the liberty was up at six o'clock on the dock, and that saved me. I was third or fourth in line from getting in. The horrible scabs they got on those things were awful. The guys really suffered. I don't think they were as good at it then as they are now, maybe. Everybody got their dragons and their flags and their dames' initials on their arms. My buddy got a flag and his girl's initials; about a month later he got a "Dear John" letter or something after that, so he was trying to figure out how to get it off, which is hard to do. The old-timers had the tattoos—the characters who had been in for ten or fifteen years and were still third class petty officer. There were a lot of people back then who got busted all the time and had been up and down the ladder three or four times—the boatswain's mate types. It was more of the deck outfit who were the tough ones, the ones that went up and down the scale.

For entertainment we had boxing tournaments and "Class Z" movies. Of course, if they made a movie on the ship, then the ship got a free copy of it. When Pat O'Brien made his movie on the *Saratoga* with Joe Brown, the ship received a free copy. Movies were shown on the hangar deck. The movie didn't start until the captain came, and the crew had to stand up. When he sat down, we sat down, then the movies would start. When the movie was over, we had to wait until the captain left. How he could sit through some of that stuff, I wouldn't know—but he was game. Looking back on it, even in the thirties, they were old, corny movies—Tom Mix and that type of stuff. I guess everybody thought they were great then, though.

It didn't do much good to complain about a sailor's life on board ship. There wasn't any place else to eat, to sleep, or relax. You were just hoping you'd go ashore and get a good meal or something like that. I don't think it was due to the depression; there was just that much difference between the way the officers lived and the way we lived.

I have always wanted to write a book on my life and experiences while serving on the USS *Saratoga* from 1934 through 1939. Then, dreaming along, I would also tell the story of my experiences in the Combat Intelligence Unit at Pearl Harbor during and after World War II. Since I was eventually commissioned as an officer, in August 1945, I figured the title of this book on my experiences from chief petty officer to commissioned rank would be *Going From a Nobody to a Somebody*.

SEARCHING FOR AMELIA

Rear Adm. Francis D. Foley

FRANCIS DRAKE FOLEY *was born on 4 July 1910 in Dorchester, Massachusetts. On 2 June 1932 he graduated from the U.S. Naval Academy, and after designation as a naval aviator on 1 February 1936, he served in various squadrons ashore and afloat until the summer of 1942, when he joined the USS* Hornet *(CV-8) as air operations officer. After the* Hornet *was lost in the Battle of the Santa Cruz Islands, he was ordered to duty as assistant operations officer on the staff of commander, Task Force 65. He later served at Guadalcanal on the staffs of commander, Air Solomons, and commander, Fleet Air, South Pacific. Between 1943 and 1945 he was head of the Officer Flying Section, Office of the Chief of Naval Operations.*

After World War II, Admiral Foley served on board the carrier Franklin D. Roosevelt *(CVB–42) and on the staff of the chief of Naval Air Training, Pensacola, Florida; he assumed command of Helicopter Squadron 2 (HU-2) in July 1949. Following tours of staff duty ashore, he commanded the seaplane tender USS* Salisbury Sound *(AV-13), flagship of the commander, U.S. Taiwan Patrol Force, from August 1955 until October 1956, and took command of the attack carrier* Shangri-La *(CVA-38) in November 1956. Subsequent tours of duty included staff of commander in chief, Pacific; commander, Carrier Division 1; assistant chief for Program Management of the Bureau of Naval Weapons; deputy assistant chief of staff, Plans and Policy Division, Supreme Headquarters, Allied Powers, Europe; assistant chief of naval operations (Fleet Operations and Readiness); commandant of the Third Naval District, New York City; and senior member of the United Nations Command Military Armistice Commission, Seoul, Korea. He was placed on the retired list on 1 July 1972.*

Admiral Foley's awards include the Legion of Merit, the Bronze Star with Combat "V," the Navy Commendation Medal with Combat "V," the Joint Services Commendation Medal, and the Chou Cross of South Korea.

My first duty assignment after I was designated a naval aviator at Pensacola on 1 February 1936 was to Scouting Squadron 41 (VS-41), flying Vought SBUs from the aircraft carrier USS *Ranger* (CV-4). The commanding officer of the ship was Capt. Patrick N. L. Bellinger (naval aviator no. 8), certainly a famous name in aviation, and also a friend of my father's, which was nice. He knew who I was right away and sent for me to get to know me. So he was nice to have as a skipper, sort of keeping his eye on me.

In those days, we were based a good deal of the time at North Island in Coronado, California. When the ship was in port, the squadron was ashore so we could do our flying. But when the ship went to sea, we were normally aboard ship unless there was something that was just purely a ship exercise, like short-range battle practice. The *Ranger* had four squadrons in it at that time—two scouting squadrons, a bombing squadron, and a fighter squadron, and all were eighteen-plane squadrons. We were there, along with the *Langley* (CV-1), *Lexington* (CV-2), and the *Saratoga* (CV-3), with all four air groups. They didn't call them air groups in those days, as such, but while I was in the *Ranger,* we had what became the first carrier air group in the navy with an air group commander.

The *Ranger* was the first carrier built from the keel up as a carrier and was the only ship of her kind that was ever built. She was a light carrier in the sense that she was not heavily built and armored and heavily gunned, as were the *Lexington* and the *Saratoga,* which were really converted battle cruisers. But her aviation configuration was more flexible than the *Lexington* and *Saratoga,* although the ship herself was not nearly as capable. She had her engines and machinery spaces all the way aft in the ship and had six smokestacks that swiveled, three on each side.

When we were conducting flight operations, the stacks were horizontal and when the ship was steaming normally without flight operations, they were vertical. One of the problems with the stacks being way aft like that and at the same level practically as the flight deck, just ten feet below, was the stack gases, even when the stacks were horizontal. In fact, that made it worse because they were right at the same level as a pilot was when he was coming in for landing on his final approach.

The *Ranger* had two catapults on the hangar deck, in addition to those on the flight deck. I made one catapult shot from the hangar deck and that was enough for me! Those catapults were athwartships, and you went out of an opening to starboard or port and suddenly there you were, having to make a turn into the wind without burying a wing tip into the sea. The ship steamed across the wind to some extent, but you still weren't going to get a direct head wind. And furthermore, the ship would only fire one plane out on the starboard side and then had to turn to place the wind correctly to operate the catapult to the port side. That was a pretty slow procedure, but it was a move in desperation in case nothing else worked. If the flight deck was completely out of commission, it was still possible to get airplanes in the air. You might not get them off with a full bomb load, but you could get them in the air and save them.

The *Ranger* was regarded, and had been built, as what they called a "battle line carrier." She was supposed to operate with the battleships and the heavy cruisers but primarily the battleships. She was supposed to provide the scouting for the battleships to find the enemy fleet, and at the same time she was supposed to provide the fighter protection for the battle line. But we found during the two and a half years that I was in the squadron that she was seldom used in such a role. She was used in support of the battleships, but only on rare occasions did she operate with them as part of the formation. But when she did, she would be right in the middle of the formation. Although she wasn't the flagship, she would be the guide.

So that concept was quite interesting, but it really never did take hold, and it was abandoned. I know that during my last year in the squadron, she was being used just like the *Lex* and *Sara* were. She was very light and had few damage control features. She couldn't have taken the punishment that the battleship or the *Lex* and *Sara* could have. She was just a very light ship. She needed to be out of harm's way, and she was going to be the weak link if she were damaged.

In those days, whenever the whole air group of a ship was operating, the senior squadron commander directed the operation. My squadron commander was Lt. Comdr. Vernon F. "Jimmy" Grant, who was very senior, very experienced, and very professional. He'd been flying for a long time, was absolutely fearless, and was very exacting. We would often take off in eighteen-plane formation and land in nine-plane formations. We were using the whole field at North Island, so we could almost always get lined up into the wind and have enough room for an eighteen-plane takeoff.

Jimmy Grant used to take the whole squadron up for squadron tactics, with the idea of playing "chicken." He would put the squadron into a climb, with all eighteen SBUs closely packed, and beat on the sides of the fuselage, which was the signal to close up. He had two rearview mirrors so he could look back at both sides and see how they were lined up in back of him. When we were as close as he thought we could get, he'd start pulling the nose up and start climbing. Then he'd start easing the throttle back. He'd get the planes just above stalling speed, which was about 70 knots, and he'd watch to see who was the first to spin out. Usually somebody spun out because he was sloppy in his formation flying, catching the wing wash of another airplane. As soon as somebody spun out, Jimmy put the nose down, and we'd do something else.

Another stunt of his was to put everybody in an echelon and head for a mountain, like Palomar. Everybody in the echelon had to be looking at him, not at the mountain out of the other side of his eye; but he would watch and see who fudged and got out of this echelon because they were watching out of the corner of their eye for the mountain. He was just waiting to see who was going to chicken out. Toward the end of his tour in the squadron, when he knew that he was going to be transferred, he decided that he would have some fun. He said, "By God, I'm the senior one around here, and I'm going to have some fun before I get out of this business." So every time we came back from any kind of an exercise, the whole damn outfit, however many planes he had with him—six planes, nine planes, twelve planes, or the whole squadron—would buzz the whole goddamn fleet in San Diego Bay. We'd just give them a mock strafing attack right at mast level, right down the bay from the destroyer base, almost as far as Point Loma, come back, break up, and land. Jimmy just loved to do that, and he said he didn't give a damn if they put him on report or not, he was going to have some fun.

He just liked to test people. It's a funny thing. The people who chickened out were the people who sooner or later gave up their wings. I know at least two who turned in their wings, not because of this but because of other things. I really can't explain it. But it strikes me that they are the people who said they'd had enough. I heard that Jimmy Thach once kept a little black book in which he listed the names of the guys in his squadron he thought would be killed first. It turned out to be prophetic, so he threw his book away.

The Vought SBU was a scout-bomber primarily used as a scout. The idea was that the SBU went out and found the enemy for the bomber people, who followed, or came after the scout found the enemy. In the meantime, the scout pilot went back and got loaded up with bombs and went out as a bomber. But sometimes, when we went out as scouts, we were loaded with bombs, too, although not normally because you wanted the maximum range of your airplane. I liked the scouting squadron because you had so damn much navigation to do, which was demanding, and then you were off usually with just two planes or three planes in a scouting section.

The very first flight I made from the *Ranger* on fleet exercise was a scouting flight. A fellow named Bill Miller was my flight leader, and I was a wing man. We went out on this flight, and we were in a sector all by ourselves. I noticed that when we started out, we had plotted our navigation to go out on sort of a pie-shaped sector and come back. We had compared our navigation solutions to the problem before we left the ready room, and we both agreed on what the courses were to be to fly our assigned sector. I guess we went out about 175 miles or so from the ship, then we did the dogleg for about 20 miles or so and then headed back.

I noticed when we were going out, Bill was about 3 or 4 degrees off course, so I flew up alongside him and signaled to him that the course was no good, it was 3 degrees off. And he shook his head, "Don't worry about it." He kept right on course. So finally we got out to the end of the leg, and we turned on our 90-degree dogleg, and he was right on. So I thought, "Well, it's okay now." And then we headed back, and he was 3 degrees off in the opposite direction. We got back to where the ship was supposed to be—and there was no ship. It was clear as a bell. You could see for miles, and there was no ship!

So we started doing what we called an expanding square search, flying a box with each leg a specified distance longer than the preceding leg. In the meantime, we broke radio silence, and asked for what they call "MOs," the signal that they gave you so you could get a bearing with a direction finder. So the ship started sending "MOs" in Morse code and we turned in that direction, but we still didn't see any ship. However, the ship started making heavy black smoke skyward, which we saw and headed for. Well, we got back to the ship, and Bill signaled for me to land first. I landed and was able to taxi out of the arresting gear, and my engine quit when I taxied up the deck! He landed and his engine quit sitting there in the arresting gear!

Boy, we went to general quarters about what the hell had happened, and we found that Bill's compass had not been properly calibrated. His deviation curve had been reversed, so his compass was off. We were 3 degrees off for 175 miles in one direction and then 3 degrees off coming back. In the meantime, the ship had been recovering all the other aircraft, and she'd been steaming away from her PIM (position of intended movement) when we were due back, so the combination of the two compounded the problem. Fortunately we were able to find the trouble, which was very difficult to do accurately aboard ship. We found by lining his airplane up with other airplanes and turning them around together that his compass headings didn't match anybody else's. His deviation readings were reversed.

We were designated as a scout-bomber squadron, but I'm sure that we did just as much bombing as the bombing squadrons. We couldn't carry quite the load that they could. A five hundred–pound bomb was the best that we could do. The bombers could do a one thousand–pounder in those days. But as far as the training was concerned, both bombing and gunnery, I could see no difference between what they did and what we did, as far as the amount of time we devoted to it. I'm proud to say that my last year in the squadron I had an "E" in gunnery and an "E" in bombing. The last bomb that I dropped in the SBU in VS-41 was a one hundred–pound water-filled bomb, and I dropped it right down the stack of the *Utah* (AG-16), an ex-battleship. There was an enormous cloud of vapor and steam and everything that came out, which marked the hit. The *Utah* was then used as a mobile target, and she was steaming out there doing violent turns and one thing and another, and my last bomb was right down the stack. I thought, well, I'd better quit while I'm ahead.

Our bombing techniques varied. With the *Utah*, we would start our runs at about 18,000 feet, which was about as high as we could go without oxygen—which we didn't use very much. We started off by climbing up to about 18,000 feet, getting the squadron in a long echelon, peeling off, and diving down. But the ship would start violent turns, and she could turn so much that you would have to squirm all around and ruin your dive, which was about a 60-degree angle on the ship. So they could fool you; you'd just miss. We found that by splitting a nine-plane outfit into three sections of three planes each and spreading them out about a mile between them, we could then approach the ship and watch which way she turned. We could then time and coordinate our attacks to compensate for the ship's turns, and our accuracy got to be pretty damn good using that tactic.

All we had was a telescopic sight. After you once started in your dive, you aimed the plane and put your cross hairs in the telescope on the target. The terminal velocity of the SBU was about 365 knots, and gosh, boy, I'll tell you, we got up to terminal velocity a lot of times. The plane was a good, rugged airplane, and I remember that Jimmy Grant's airplane had some phenomenal number of terminal velocity dives on it—in the hundreds.

A lot of our tactics and doctrine in that period were disseminated just by people getting together and sitting around a cup of coffee. We didn't have all the tactical publications and so forth that came into being later on, although they were beginning to. There was a constant exchange of information between squadrons on both coasts. I think that one of the things that contributed to it was the rivalry with the marines because every time the navy did something that they thought was pretty good, then the marines would go out and do it better. So it was a constant interchange there. There wasn't anything secret about it. It was just everyone trying to outdo everyone else.

In April–May 1937 the *Ranger* participated in Fleet Problem XVIII out in Hawaiian waters, during which we conducted two attacks on Pearl Harbor using our whole air group plus those from the *Lexington* and/or *Saratoga*. We conducted two mock attacks on Pearl Harbor that later were credited with giving the Japanese the idea of how best to do it. They would have known how to do it, but the point was that I'm sure that the Japanese agents around Hawaii were observing what was going on and that the rest of the fleet were just sitting ducks in Pearl Harbor taking this beating.

We got back from that cruise in late May 1937. Back in those days, in the thirties, the month of June was sort of a stand-down for squadrons, certainly out on the West Coast. There were a lot of personnel changes, a lot of new people coming in, old-timers leaving, so there was a turnover of maybe 25 to 35 percent of people in a squadron. June was used to indoctrinate the new pilots who came into the squadron, get reorganized, have a squadron shakedown right at home base. The aviation cadets were starting to get into the squadrons; we were skeptical at first, but we were soon convinced that they could do the job, too. I think that they were very good. The early ones were really handpicked people that had a great deal on the ball.

So, we were getting ourselves regrouped for the coming year when Amelia Earhart was lost in the Pacific, in July 1937, during her attempt to fly around the world. She and her navigator, Fred Noonan—who was probably the most accomplished aerial navigator of his time—got as far as Lae, New Guinea, which is on the eastern tip of the island; they were going to fly to Hawaii, via Howland Island. Howland Island was about 2,550 nautical miles from Lae. It's fairly near the Gilbert Islands and just a tiny bit north of the equator and just across the international date line. This was the longest single leg of their flight, from Lae to Howland.

They started out flying with a weather forecast that apparently they had received from Hawaii, which was really a long-range forecast. The radio facilities in the Pacific were mostly due to the work that Pan Am had been doing down there. There was apparently a powerful radio station at an island called Nauru, which was about halfway along their trip. The trip was almost right along the equator, from one side of the equator to the other. There was this powerful radio equipment at Nauru, and then there was, I think, some radio equipment at Howland Island where they were going, and that was supplemented by equipment put ashore by the Coast Guard. There was a Coast Guard cutter down there, the *Itasca*. The Coast Guard had put some radio equipment, I think a direction finder, on Howland. And there was also a fleet tug out there in the area to provide support, a plane guard support.

When George Putnam put so much pressure on the navy to do something, they decided to order a search. The most available carrier was the *Lexington*, up in Long Beach. The *Lex* steamed down to the vicinity of San Diego, and we flew out fourteen planes from VS-41 and joined planes from other squadrons, all of them two-place airplanes. We landed aboard the *Lex*, and all of us thought we would just go out to sea, and the ship would steam out a thousand miles or so. Then they'd call the whole thing off because we had so far to go, two-thirds the way across the Pacific. So none of us took anything but a change of skivvies and some socks and one clean uniform, and that was it.

But the *Lexington* started out at 28 knots, and she never deviated. They had two new destroyer plane guards with us; they couldn't even keep up with her. They slowed down to about 20 knots or so, and we kept on. The ship didn't go to Pearl; she went to Lahaina Roads; there we rendezvoused with an oiler, and they replenished the *Lex* and topped her off to 100 percent. We didn't know when we were going to get any more oil, and we were going to have to support the destroyers when they finally caught up with us after refueling at Pearl Harbor.

They rejoined in about a day later or so, and we started out and went down to the vicinity of Howland and Baker islands. We had been working on our search plan the whole way out there, figuring precisely how we were going to search an area the size of the state of Texas. The search was done in a very interesting way. We went out in small groups, four to six airplanes in a group, and took station about five miles astern of the ship; then there was another group ten miles astern of the ship, one five miles ahead and another one ten miles ahead, all at 500 feet altitude. At a given signal, we all formed two scouting lines, with a mile separation between airplanes, and went out starboard and port perpendicular to the base course of the ship. We would fly out approximately 125 to 150 miles, and then all turn at the same time and fly up parallel to the ship's base course for about 25 miles or so, and then turn and fly back in again and meet the ship at the point along the PIM.

Fortunately, the weather was just beautiful—crystal clear, a few little scattered clouds and maybe about 10 knots of wind—so if there was anything there, we would have seen it—a life raft, for instance, or a life jacket. I know we could have seen it. We saw other debris, one thing and another, from time to time. We were flying about 500 feet above the water. It was absolutely fantastic how well people learned how to fly abreast in a scouting line twenty-five miles long. Planes extended well over the horizon on either side of you. We got very, very expert at this thing. The man in the back seat was searching with binoculars, while the pilot was flying the plane and looking to preserve his position in the line and also searching.

We had agreement on who was going to look to which side in each airplane so that nothing would be overlooked.

Those flight operations extended over a period of six days. We flew two flights apiece one day, and then one flight the following day, with forty-eight airplanes on each flight. Aircraft availability was absolutely fantastic. My God, there were very few downed airplanes, and in those days, for availability to be so high was really remarkable. But, of course, we weren't beating up the airplanes; we were just flying them at cruising speed, not dive-bombing and all that kind of business.

We played a lot of volleyball and did calisthenics and things like that to work out the kinks when we weren't flying. It was hotter than hell right on the equator. I think the morale was awfully high. One of the big problems was lack of clothes. We had to buy clothes because everybody thought we were going to go for a couple of nights and that would be it; that turned out to be a big error.

But after ten days of this thing, we were getting kind of low on aviation fuel and had to think about how the heck we'd get back to San Diego or Pearl Harbor when we finished. We didn't have the tremendous logistic support out there that we would get during a fleet exercise or something, just too darn far away. So the last thing that we did was to make one flight where everybody in the air group went up and flew back and forth across the equator on the international date line, so that we could put a little insignia of a turtle with wings on it, a flying turtle, on all the airplanes. But we never did, of course, find Amelia Earhart, and she's never been found to this day. We gave it the old college try, but it didn't quite work. I'm pretty sure she just ran out of fuel and crashed in the ocean.

When we finally finished, we had to steam home at 10 knots! We thought we would never get there. We only had two movies on board. Every night we would have one movie or the other, and they'd show them over and over and over again. One of them was a movie with Rin Tin Tin, the police dog, and every time that dog barked, the whole ship's company barked with him. We knew everything that was going to happen. It got to be a riot to go up to those movies. One thing that we didn't run out of was steak. I don't know how they ever managed to store so much steak in a ship, but we had steak out the gazoo. Every time we turned around, we had steak. We almost felt as though we should stop and catch some fish or something. I remember that the night I finally got home, we had steak for dinner. I thought, "Oh, no!"

When VS-41 returned from searching for Amelia Earhart, we embarked once again on the *Ranger* for a trip to South America. By this time Capt. John S. McCain was the commanding officer. They sent the *Ranger* down to Peru with her whole air group to participate in the Inter-American Technical Aviation Conference. Messerschmitt and Junkers from Germany and the Caproni people from Italy were all trying to sell the Peruvian Air Force airplanes, and we were determined to sell them on American products if we could.

So the *Ranger* was sent down there to put on a real aerial demonstration for them. We crossed the equator on 12 September, and the entire *Ranger* air group and the utility aircraft were launched to give all pilots and plane crews the opportunity to fly over the line. As a result, all the airplanes on the *Ranger* were decorated with the insignia of the "Flying Turtle." We arrived at Callao, the seaport for Lima, on 15 September and immediately launched into a strenuous social routine, with the days and evenings filled with cocktail parties, dinners, receptions, and balls.

After consulting with the ambassador and the local people, including the Peruvian government, we decided to take the president and his cabinet and all the top military and civilian people out for a day at sea to really show them a firepower demonstration. We towed a target that everybody dive-bombed and strafed and showed them the catapult launchings and all the deck business and the landings. Then we came on back, and they were, of course, really quite impressed because it was a spectacular show. Everything just worked great, and we had no mishaps or anything. We got a lot of compliments about this thing.

The competitive atmosphere between the various countries that were represented at the conference was very obvious. The Germans and Italians each had a couple of squadrons of airplanes there, operating out of the brand-new international airport called Lima Tamba, which was being inaugurated while this whole air show business was going on. On the occasion of the dedication of the airport, the captain decided to take the ship to sea and send the whole damn air group back into the airport, and I want to tell you that we really did an air show at that thing. We cruised serenely overhead at about 5,000 feet so they could see some decent mass formations. Then we went down to about 2,000 feet or 1,000 feet, then down to about 100 feet right over the ground, right down the field at full gun. And then the fighters put on a little acrobatics for them.

Then finally we landed. Unfortunately it was a very small and dusty field, so my God, the clouds of dust and everything were simply horrible. But we landed the entire air group in less than twenty minutes and took off again in less than twenty-eight minutes. We all took off in as compact formations as we could, but we couldn't do our eighteen-plane formations; it just didn't permit that. I really don't know how that all turned out, except that I think that we very definitely impressed the Peruvians, and they were certainly very pleasant with us. From the impression this made, I wonder what those observers would have thought had they seen our normal operations at North Island!

We were there ten days, and when the day finally came to leave, we were aghast to find that the officers' motorboat was missing. We were hoisting in all the boats, preparatory to leaving, and there was no officers' motorboat—and boy, nobody could figure it out. Finally the officer of the deck said that he had heard a boat engine start in the middle of the night, but he thought that somebody was just testing a boat or something. But what had happened was that a marine and a fireman had jumped ship about two o'clock in the morning, climbed down into the officers' motorboat, cast off and drifted back from the ship a few hundred yards, then started it up. The fireman could run the engine, and the marine managed to steer the damn thing, and off they went. They got about thirty miles or so up the coast in this damn boat, no lights or anything.

By that time, the boat had been discovered missing. We had two amphibians in the ship that we hoisted over. They took off; one flew south, the other north, looking for the damn boat. And sure enough, they found it. The boat was close inshore, and when the plane buzzed the boat, the two people jumped overboard and swam ashore with life jackets on. So there was the boat adrift on the coast. Well, the airplanes really couldn't do anything about it. They could land on the water, but they still couldn't get into the boat safely without damaging the airplane.

So by that time, some Peruvians in a fishing boat picked up the boat and said, by God, it was theirs—salvage. They had found it abandoned at sea. They knew enough about maritime law to know it was theirs. Well, the Peruvian navy came along, and I think they were sort of sympathetic with these fishermen; but they persuaded them, for good relations with the U.S. Navy and everything, to return the boat.

They towed the boat back to the ship because it was out of gas. We hoisted the boat aboard, got the fishermen off their fishing boat, and they came aboard ship. They took them up to the captain's cabin. Captain McCain settled with them for one carton of cigarettes and a couple of skivvy shirts and pants for each of them. The whole business didn't cost twenty bucks, and we got our $35,000 officers' motorboat back!

Then we were all ready to get under way. Thank God, we got the boat back, but we were missing two men. Just then we got a message from the shore saying that the president wanted to see Captain McCain. So they hoisted the gig out again, the captain got in, went ashore to the palace or wherever the president stayed, and the president decorated him for the tremendous things that the U.S. Navy had done for the city of Lima and for Peru.

So the captain came back to the ship, and we got under way for San Diego on 24 September, and it was a long way—three thousand miles to Lima from San Diego—so it was about a ten-day trip back. Captain McCain decided we would try out our bow arresting gear. The *Lex,* the *Sara,* and the *Ranger* all had bow arresting gear. The arresting gear on the after part of the ship pulled in one direction, while the arresting gear on the front of the ship pulled to the opposite direction. The only time they'd ever used the bow arresting gear was when the ship first went into commission and was being tested. The idea of the bow arresting gear was in case part of the flight deck was damaged, there was an alternative available. What they didn't realize was that you never, never, never stop a man-of-war at sea in wartime if you can possibly avoid it—and you had to stop the damn thing to back down. The minute you stop, you're a dead duck if an enemy submarine is anywhere around.

We conducted several days of flight operations going home, during which we practiced landing the whole air group over the bow. It was quite an operation. The ship could make about 18 knots backing down; she could only make about 29 knots going ahead. Well, we had a little wind, and we'd just back her into the wind to get a little more. Waveoffs were to the right instead of left because of the island structure to port. Unfortunately, we had two mishaps on the way back. On 2 October, an F3F-1 skidded over the port side on landing and hung suspended between the number 4 and 6 stacks, but the pilot managed to scramble free. Two days later an SBU from VS-42 spun into the water during an attempted landing over the bow. Again, the crew was rescued, but the plane was lost.

I stayed in VS-41 another year, and it was during that period, on 1 July 1938, that they formalized the role of air group commander. I think that it recognized the role that Jimmy Grant had been playing. People saw a need for that. You needed someone who could go up and talk to the skipper, for instance, or the admiral, right away, about things that affected the air group as a whole. Just send the air group commander and let him settle it. It was a natural evolution. You needed the representation on up the line with someone who could talk at the head of department level or even higher than that, really, because after all, he is epitomizing what the damn ship is there for, and once they get in the air, he is it. He's in command of the main battery.

====== 13 ======

WILLIWAWS, GIG 'EMS, AND ST. ELMO'S FIRE

Adm. John S. Thach

JOHN SMITH THACH *was born in Pine Bluff, Arkansas, on 19 April 1905.*
He was appointed to the U.S. Naval Academy in 1923, was graduated and com-
missioned ensign on 2 June 1927, and was designated naval aviator on 4 Jan-
uary 1930. He served in a wide variety of carrier-based, patrol, and experi-
mental squadrons, and had numerous command tours ashore and afloat as he
advanced to the rank of admiral, to date from March 1965. Admiral Thach was
commander in chief, U.S. Naval Forces, Europe, from 25 March 1965 until his
retirement on 1 May 1967.

During World War II, Admiral Thach participated in twelve major engage-
ments or campaigns, operating from seven different aircraft carriers. He was twice
awarded the Navy Cross for extraordinary heroism in aerial combat with Japan-
ese forces. He later went to the Fast Carrier Task Force in the Pacific as air oper-
ations officer, where he developed the system of blanketing enemy airfields with
a continuous patrol of carrier-based fighters and planned and directed the navy's
final offensive blows against the Japanese homeland. During the Korean War
Admiral Thach commanded the carrier USS Sicily *(CVE-118), from which*
marine aircraft provided close air support during many crucial battles.

Admiral Thach's decorations include the Navy Cross with Gold Star, the Distinguished Service Medal, the Silver Star, and the Legion of Merit with two Gold Stars.

In June 1934, after two years as an experimental test pilot at the Naval Air Base Hampton Roads, Virginia, I was assigned to Patrol Squadron 9 (VP-9) based on the USS *Wright* (AV-1). We were scheduled in 1935 to fly up to the Aleutian Islands in Martin PM-1 open-cockpit, twin-engine biplane flying boats. The purpose of the trip was to exercise and test the squadron in deployment to various out-of-the-way places for advance base exercises, in case we had to operate there sometime in the future.

This was a fascinating flight we made up there with two squadrons of patrol planes. At that time there were very few navigational aids along the coastline of Alaska and the Aleutians. In fact, we didn't know where the coastline was, and our charts had a dotted line, which, according to the cartographer, meant the coastline is about here, but we're not sure. Furthermore, there were certain small peaklike islands sticking up that were not on the chart. When one of these suddenly loomed up ahead in a fog, it became a very interesting sort of thing. We found that the best thing to do when we ran into a fog, which we did often, was to fly right down a few feet over the beach. We could see white water when we couldn't see anything else.

We had to make short flights. For instance, we flew from San Diego to San Francisco, from San Francisco to Bremerton, Washington, then to Seattle. And then on various short hops until we finally got out to the vicinity of Dutch Harbor. We not only had very few navigational aids but weather forecasting was also not very good. We had a little bird-class tender, the USS *Sandpiper* (AVP-9). They were very small things, almost like ocean tugs, but they could carry food and gasoline, and you could hoist one of these PM-1s aboard the stern. The airplane stuck out all over both sides of the little ship.

We were up there in the latter part of June and July 1935. We kept hearing from the salmon cannery people everywhere we went, "If you don't get out of here by such-and-such a date, you might as well wait till next year." That's the way they felt about it, and they were natives. This disturbed us somewhat. Another thing that was quite a surprise was the very high tide. We went into Kodiak, for example, one of our first stops in the Aleutian

Island chain, and the tender had planted buoys with a five hundred–pound anchor attached to each one. So we just landed and tied up to a line of buoys, one for each airplane. Then we went aboard the tender, and the next morning we came out and looked, and all the airplanes were high and dry up on the rocks. The tide there was twenty or thirty feet. But it didn't seem to damage the planes much because it was inside a protected harbor, and the wind wasn't blowing. So, as the tide came up, they just moved the buoys into deeper water, so that with the next low tide, the aircraft didn't end up on the rocks.

Our next stop was at a little anchorage in the Shumagin Islands. There wasn't any settlement there, but that was the last stop before Dutch Harbor. We took off on a nice, sunshiny day and started flying along, and we passed by an island that was near the tip end of Unimak Island. We went on a few minutes more, and all of a sudden we were in the worst looking blizzard I've ever seen. You could just dimly make out the plane ahead of you in this formation of six aircraft. We held our course for about an hour hoping to run out of this thing, and then the skipper decided we'd better turn around and go back.

The last place we had seen before going into this storm was a kind of clay-looking cliff that was a different color than the rest of the rocks. We turned around, and in about seven minutes there we were right back again at this cliff! The wind had come up to about 60 or 70 knots, and our cruising speed was 80, so we had just been almost standing still in that blizzard. I didn't realize how strong the wind was blowing until we took only seven minutes to return to a spot we had left sixty minutes before. You couldn't see anything but snow. It was bitter cold, but we had very heavy bearskin flying suits, with gloves, which kept us pretty warm, although your face got cold in an open cockpit.

We finally wound up finding a landing place in Morzori Bay, now called Cold Bay, on the northern side of the Aleutians. The wind was blowing hard and, of course, the tender was nowhere near us because they didn't expect that we were going to land there. Although we were sort of in the lee of this land, we were still getting 50 knots on the air speed meter, and each one of the planes was dragging its anchor. We had lightweight anchors in the plane that would hold in a light breeze in good mud, but with these rocks that we were anchored over we found ourselves drifting; when we pulled the anchor up, the flukes were bent back. We decided this was an unsatisfactory situation because we had to crank and crank the engines to start them up before we drifted clear across the bay onto the rocks on the other side. The skipper, Henry T. Stanley, decided that we'd better get the hell out of there. Looking at the chart, we figured we might find some kind of a sandy beach if we followed the coastline.

Well, I had an engine I couldn't get started, so everybody went off and left me. I knew where they were going, and we had sent a message saying what we planned to do. I gave up trying to start that engine. We were all exhausted from cranking the flywheel starter up to speed, and we were soaking wet. When those bearskin coats got wet, they were not only heavy but they didn't smell very good and might even make you sick to your stomach.

We got one engine going and decided that we would drag a bucket in the water on that side, and that would keep us from going around in circles. If you have just one engine going, you give it throttle to make some progress, and when you start to turn too much off the desired course, you slack off on the throttle. The bucket drags in the water and straightens you back out again. So we went on like this, in kind of a zigzag, until we finally saw the other planes at just about dusk. They all had their noses up on what looked like a beach. There wasn't any sand in that vicinity, just jagged rocks or round rocks.

Well, they'd found some round rocks, anywhere from the size of a football to the size of a baseball or a golf ball, and they had left one small opening for me. It was a very short little beach. There was just nothing else but cliffs. So I was supposed to get into that little opening, or else spend the night going around and around. I decided I could make it and approached parallel to the beach, with it on the dead engine side, going close along the tails of the other planes. When I got to my slot, I gave it full gun, and it just swung me right around into my spot. Then they all grabbed the plane to hold it while we took the anchor over a little hill, buried it, and put logs on top of it.

That night, all of the planes, one after another, dragged and pulled their anchors right out of the ground, and each of us had to crank up again several times. We were still in this bad storm and couldn't take off. There was nowhere we could go. We didn't have the instruments to do very well with instrument flying, certainly not precise enough to avoid mountain peaks and jagged islands and so forth. There were no landing approach aids whatsoever. So it was the better part of valor to stay put until the storm blew over. And after all that, we thought half of us were going to be sick with pneumonia and everything else, but not a single person even caught a bad cold. The tender *Sandpiper* finally arrived, we got some hot food, and the weather cleared up. We moored to the buoys laid by the tender and went aboard the ship to get some much needed rest.

Anyone up there can tell you what the weather is going to be in the Aleutian Island chain—it is going to be unpredictable. We had a rude introduction to how suddenly the weather can change from nice to violent. It was about midnight, and I was in the after bunkroom of the tender when the word was passed, "Flight crews man your planes; a williwaw is building up." I had never seen a williwaw but thought it couldn't be very bad because I had been out on deck fifteen minutes earlier and there was no wind, the bay was like a millpond, and all the stars were out.

But what a change in fifteen minutes! Now there was a strong wind, and the water was being whipped into a frenzy of white caps. We hurried into the motor whaleboat and headed for the airplanes. My plane was shackled to the fifth buoy in line; by the time we got to the fourth the wind had increased much more and the planes were dancing around, almost flying like kites tied to the buoys. My plane appeared to have broken loose from the buoy and was drifting rapidly down wind. We chased it and scrambled aboard over the nose. I wondered how many minutes we would have before being blown onto the rocks on the opposite side of the bay. We would have to get those engines started and soon!

Fortunately, each one caught on the first try, and we started to taxi back up wind. We were out of sight of the ship's lights but soon saw them and the searchlight that was being used to illuminate the line of seaplanes moored to the buoys. My plane was the only one that had broken away. I taxied toward the gap in the line of planes where my assigned buoy was supposed to be, but we couldn't see it. I reduced the throttle to let the plane drift back for another approach in case we had already passed it. All of a sudden the buoy appeared right alongside the nose. I yelled at the man in the nose, "Grab it, grab it!" He put a boat hook through the ring on the buoy, pulled it up close, and secured us.

Soon the wind died down to a flat calm, and the stars came out again. It was difficult to realize that this williwaw took only about an hour from beginning to end, and yet at its peak gusts to 75 knots were registered on the ship's anemometer. I do not need to see another williwaw!

I left VP-9 after two years and spent a year in command of the aviation unit on the light cruiser USS *Cincinnati* (CL-6), flying Curtiss SOC seaplanes. Following that tour, I was once again ordered back to the patrol plane navy, this time to Patrol Squadron 5F (VP-5F), based at the Fleet Air Base, Coco Solo, Canal Zone. I thought, "Oh, boy, they're sending me to Siberia." I wasn't very happy with those orders. I didn't want to go for two reasons. I didn't particularly want to go to Panama, and I was hoping to get back into fighter-type aircraft. But the policy in those days was a good one. It was to give officers well-rounded experience when they were young so that, later, if they were promoted enough to get a large command with various types of aircraft and ships, they'd know something about them, having been there themselves. This was a good policy, but I did object to it at the time. I didn't make any official objection. I just griped to some of my friends, and they said, "You'd better just go and keep quiet," which I did; this turned out to be one of the most interesting and valuable tours of duty I had at that point in my career, both professionally and otherwise.

We had some interesting experimental work to do in that squadron. We were given the job of developing the tactics and procedures for illuminating a ship or a group of ships with flares so that they could be bombed at night. We had to work out the coordination between a bombing group and the illumination group. The tactics became pretty complex when there was a wind blowing. The flares hung on little parachutes during descent, and enough of them had to be dropped at just the right place at the right time, so that when the bombers arrive at the dropping point, they had the maximum illumination of the target. This took a lot of trial and error and experimentation, so the squadron devoted itself to actually working at night instead of in the daytime—so we didn't fly very much in the daytime for the first six months that I was in the squadron.

There were some aviation cadets who reported to the squadron. At that time, the aviation cadet students who finished the course of flight training at Pensacola weren't commissioned; they were still aviation cadets when they reported to the fleet squadron, and then, if they were successful, they were promoted to ensigns from aviation cadets. This was one of the first groups of aviation cadets we had in the navy, and they were really top-notch people. They were good pilots, and they were very fine young men in all respects. The interesting thing about their experience in the squadron was the fact that they had never seen Consolidated P2Y-3 aircraft before, yet they had to qualify to fly them as copilots—so we had to do it at night. They were flying and became qualified to take off and land in the harbor there at night, and they had never flown in the daytime. I will never forget the horror stories that they all told when they had to make a day landing. They said they didn't realize they were coming so close to this or that obstruction to get into this little bay right in Coco Solo.

We went through the usual gunnery competition program and most of our training was scouting, search, and horizontal bombing. A number of us qualified for "E" scores in bombing and were given an opportunity to attempt to qualify as Master Bombers, a title that only a very few people in the whole navy qualified for. I think the only ones that existed were at Dahlgren, Virginia, the ordnance proving grounds, and they were testing equipment and would drop hundreds of bombs every day. They did nothing else, and they got really good, of course.

To get an "E" score, you had to drop four bombs separately, with separate runs, inside of a ten-mil circle. A mil is one in one thousand; if you're a thousand feet up, a mil is one foot. If you're ten thousand feet up, you have a ten-foot radius that you can play with. But to qualify as a Master Bomber, you had to get within six mils, and you had to have four different practices on different days so that the weather conditions would be sure to be different. You had to contend with different kinds of weather conditions, and if you failed on any one of those four qualification efforts to get the bombs inside of six mils, you were finished.

On two qualification attempts I was successful, but on the third one I failed to get all the bombs close enough. I was disappointed because I thought I could do it. But my skipper said, "You know what would happen to you if you got to be a Master Bomber? You'd get detached and be sent to Dahlgren and spend the rest of your life dropping bombs and testing bomb sights!" So there was a silver lining in this failure.

Being based at the Fleet Air Base, Coco Solo, periodically we would go up to Guantánamo Bay, Cuba, for advanced base exercises, and other times we'd go to some small protected harbor and simply live off of the seaplane tender. This kept us mobile and ready to move with all of our equipment and the things we needed to maintain the aircraft. Guantánamo, of course, was not quite as austere as a truly advanced base because we had some buildings we could live in, and we didn't need a tender there. There was a long flat building we used as a BOQ, a kind of a barracks. We had a difficult time sleeping at night because of "gig 'ems," little gnats that could fly right through a small screen and stung like the very devil when they bit you. Some people were very allergic to this, and I've seen people who have been bitten on the legs, and their legs just swelled up and got infected.

We didn't have very modern facilities. We had an outhouse that was really a masterpiece, unique because it was constructed hanging over a cliff about five hundred feet above the Atlantic Ocean! Whoever had constructed this had taken some old ship anchor chains, huge chains, anchored them in the ground and used them as a kind of a suspension bridge construction to support this thing that was simply sitting out beyond the cliff. If anybody had ever fallen through there they would go right into the Atlantic Ocean. This was quite sanitary, but it was a strange one.

One night we heard a great commotion outside the BOQ on the pathway to this place. Several of us ran out in time to see our Chinese cook running up the path with his pants still down. I've heard stories that a man can't run with his pants down. Well, it was disproved. This fellow was really running, and he was terribly excited and frightened. Lt. Cam Briggs was the first one that got to him and said, "What's the matter?" He said he was sitting out there reading a funny paper, and he thought there was a bug on his ear, and he slapped at it—he had slapped a great big snake in the face—the snake was looking over his shoulder.

So Cam said, "Well, now, pull up your pants and tell us about it." So he described this snake, and I went and got a nine iron. There was one overhead bulb in this place so we got some more flashlights and went out there and, sure enough, here was this big snake still reading the funny papers. So, I killed him with the golf club. It was a type of moccasin that was native to Cuba.

The squadron had been assigned Consolidated P2Y-3 aircraft since 1935, and the time finally came to get new airplanes. The PBY Catalina had been developed by Consolidated, so the squadron was ordered to turn their old aircraft in at Norfolk, then go to San Diego and pick up new PBYs, which we did. It took quite a few weeks there installing bomb sights and new equipment that enabled the airplane to fly its bombing run through an automatic pilot arrangement.

Before we departed San Diego for our home base at Coco Solo, the commanding officer, Warren K. Berner, asked me to work out a procedure for foul weather deployment in case we ran into bad weather while we were in formation. I worked out a system so that the leader (the skipper) would hold his course and altitude while the other aircraft—starting with the ones that were farthest out in the formation—would turn out, fly for a certain specified time, then climb up a certain assigned number of feet above the pilot's former position. Then each pilot was supposed to go back to his original course and hold his new altitude. I figured it out so that we could spread the formation very quickly in case we were all suddenly in the soup, and we would have lateral as well as altitude separation.

One day we finally took off with fourteen aircraft and headed for Panama from San Diego on a nonstop flight. Near the Gulf of Tehuantepec, about midnight, we ran into a pretty husky front, and the captain ordered the foul weather spread, and everybody started going to his newly assigned position. But this weather got real bad, and the captain then called me and said, "You climb up as high as you can and see whether we can get over the top of it or not." I didn't like this very much because I knew there were other planes wandering around up there where I might butt into them as I was going up, but of course I had to do it. So I went on up. I was the leader of the second section of three planes. We had five sections flying a vee of vees. I climbed and climbed and climbed and finally got up to around 22,000 feet and couldn't get over it. I looked out and saw the instrument lights reflected on a big strut that looked like it was coming right down into the side of this seaplane hull—and we didn't have any strut that was anywhere near there. I wondered if something had gotten loose from the aeroplane and was swirling around and stuck in the side. I just couldn't understand, so I asked the copilot to get a light and shine on it and look at it up and down. It looked about as big as your arm.

He said, "It's ice. It's the antenna all iced up!" I looked at my altimeter, and we were beginning to lose altitude; I called my skipper, but I couldn't get him. We went on down a little, and the ice fell off. I finally got the skipper on the radio and told him my experience. By this time, we were getting very turbulent air and lightning struck my aircraft and burned my radioman's fingers; his fingers were all blackened, and he had little black spots on his hand.

And then a strange thing happened—blue balls, about as big as a baseball, were drifting around in the cockpit, kind of roaming around, like St. Elmo's fire. I slapped at one of them, and it just stood still and looked at me. So I decided that I might be beginning to lose my mind, and I'd better pay attention to my instruments because we didn't want to turn upside down as well as being struck by lightning. It turned out that thirteen out of the fourteen aircraft were struck by lightning, some of them a little worse than others, but most of them without too much damage.

But those balls of blue fire were frightening—also sort of eerie! I thought we were going to another world, for more reasons than one. A little bit later, when we were still on instruments and I was back down supposedly in my position, a light in the rear of the aircraft, back in the hull somewhere, started bothering me. It was reflecting on the glass in the cockpit, and it irritated me a little bit, so I called the crew on the intercom and told them to put out the light back there. There was no answer for a while, and I called specifically to the radioman. He said, "Captain, I don't see any light back here. I'll check with the other people."

So there wasn't any light back there. I looked back, and I noticed it was outside the aircraft, not in it, and it was so close it was reflected and bothered me. It turned out it was one of my wing men! I called him and told him to go away, get back on his station, and he said, "Well, I can see you all right. I've been with you all the time." He had never left his position on my wing!

This whole episode lasted until about daybreak. We began to come out into clearer weather just before dawn, and I know we went into the thing at midnight. So, we finally came out of it, and I saw two aircraft ahead of me that looked like they were about where the skipper was supposed to be; I joined up on them, and my wing man came on. We finally established communications with everyone else and eventually rendezvoused over the coastline nearest San Salvador, the country of El Salvador, and then headed on down over Nicaragua.

About late morning, a huge black cloud appeared in front of us, stretching almost half of the horizon over Nicaragua. So the captain said, "Now, let's have this foul weather spread and do it right this time." So, in we went. This wasn't as severe as the Tehuantepec storm, but it was heavy rain, zero-zero visibility at 8,000 feet or whatever it was. When we came out of that storm, everybody was exactly in the right position. You could see everybody just as soon as we came out. So we had learned a lesson. We finally landed at Coco Solo after about twenty-four hours' flying time, nonstop.

I would say that the flight was somewhat hairy, but after an aviator has had enough experience, he's tired, of course, but he has been conditioned to it. By that time we had flown many twelve-hour patrols, six hours out in the ocean and six hours back, for example, to an unlighted coast down in Central America during fleet problems, and flying in Alaska. There are some flights, such as that one, you're glad they're over and you hope you never run into a thing like that again, but since you handled it once, why can't you handle it again?

GODDAMN, I'M A MARINER

CWO Cecil St. Clair King Jr.

Cecil St. Clair King, Jr. *grew up in a series of small Texas towns and enlisted in the navy in 1934, shortly after graduating from high school. Following boot camp training at San Diego, he plunged enthusiastically into the life of a sailor, serving first on board the heavy cruiser USS* Portland *(CA-33). It was there that he began striking for yeoman and thus laid the foundation for his entire naval career. He advanced to chief petty officer in that rating and eventually became a warrant ship's clerk.*

King first put on the rating badge of a petty officer when he was serving at Fleet Air Base, Coco Solo, Panama. He then served for a time in destroyers before volunteering for duty in the Asiatic Fleet in 1940. In late December 1941, following the onset of World War II, he managed to escape from the Philippines on board the four-stack destroyer USS Peary *(DD-226). After the* Peary *reached the Dutch East Indies, King was evacuated to Australia for a time before returning to duty with the fleet. Subsequent wartime assignments included the carrier USS* Hornet *(CV-12) during the Battle of the Philippine Sea and other actions during the Central Pacific campaign.*

At war's end he was in the commissioning crew of the new carrier USS

Princeton (CV-37) and later served on the staff of commander, Air Force, Pacific Fleet and chief of Naval Air Training. In the 1950s, as a warrant officer, King was in the crew of the carriers USS Midway (CVB-41) and USS Franklin D. Roosevelt (CVA-42). He then served in the office of three successive chiefs of naval operations in the 1950s: Adm. William M. Fechteler, Adm. Robert B. Carney, and Adm. Arleigh A. Burke.

Chief Warrant Officer King retired from the navy in 1957 and subsequently served as the assistant to two successive chairmen of the Atomic Energy Commission, John McCone and Glenn Seaborg, and then as assistant to the AEC assistant general manager, retiring from government service in 1972.

As I was growing up in Aransas Pass, Texas, during the depression, I had very little awareness of the navy, although I always had a kind of an affinity for salt water. I spent a lot of time in and around the water in Aransas Pass, working on shrimp boats in the summertime and that kind of thing. When my high school class graduated in 1934, we received a form letter from the naval recruiter over at Corpus Christi. That just put it all together for me. I thought, "This is it; I'm going to have to do this." There was no hope of my going to college, none whatsoever. There was no work in Aransas Pass; it was really a hard, grinding economic time in a small town. It wasn't a hardship, but I was pragmatic enough to know that there was nothing for me in Aransas Pass, nor would there be.

So when I got that letter, I hitchhiked over to Corpus the very next day. There was a waiting list of several months, they told us at that time, but my number came up very quickly, in July. I did this on my own; I didn't consult with my folks. I just thought it was a good thing to do. The navy was very selective during that time because it was a small force, and I was terribly surprised that my number came up. But, I did pretty well on the test and was a high school graduate. It wasn't a rarity, but I think high school graduates had a certain amount of prestige in that part of Texas in those days.

The main point that the recruiter made in the letter was the security— that I could do twenty years and come out with $62.00 a month, or something like that. I never dreamed of such wealth in such a short period. I thought, "Twenty years! I'll be thirty-seven years old and will have sixty-some-odd dollars a month." That was enough to get along on in those days. I told my dad, and he almost fell out of his chair. He said, "Great goodness alive, thirty-seven years old and you can retire." He was all for it. Also, I had somewhat of a patriotic frame of mind. I think most kids did in those days. So there was something about serving my country that appealed to me. I think there was also a certain flavor of travel, see the world and that sort of thing. But this was 1934, and war was not even thought of. It was just mainly, "Join the navy and see the world."

So, along with thirty or forty other kids, I took a train to Houston, where I was sworn into the navy on 17 July 1934. Then we were put on a train to go to San Diego. They put one kid in charge of all of us, and the reason he was in charge was because he had been in the National Guard at one time. We gave him a lot of respect. I thought that was really something, that the guy was in charge of all us troops. But we just had a good time on the train. I'd never been away from home before in my whole life, never been far at all from wherever we lived.

I failed my preliminary physical because my pulse was high. I guess I was excited; there were several of us, and they put us off to one side. I was scared to death that I wouldn't pass. But I settled down after a while, and my pulse was normal. Then we went through the line to get our clothes and gear. It was just a great, brand-new, wonderful world to me. I enjoyed every second of it. I had a few pangs of homesickness after several days, when it finally dawned on me that I was away from home. It had some impact on me, but it was transient. I was so wrapped up in being in the navy, and I just loved everything about it.

Our company commander was a chief torpedoman named Adams. Chief Adams was kind of a fatherly type, a no-nonsense guy, as they all were. In barracks conversation at night, we would say about these chiefs, "You know, those guys, they're thirty-eight, they're forty years old. They're really old." I couldn't imagine a guy that old that had been in the navy that long. They just seemed like old, wrinkled men to me. I remember this tremendous impact—how old these fellows were.

We slept in hammocks that were six feet or so above the concrete deck. There was a certain amount of trepidation in climbing up and getting into a hammock over a concrete deck. The navy was a little cavalier about our well-being. I detected no note of sympathy or concern about falling out of our hammocks—you just didn't fall out of your hammock. If you did, you suffered the consequences. Getting in the hammocks was kind of an adventure, but once you got the hang of it, it was fine.

We trained and were out on the grinder—the drill field—every day. I liked the drilling and the discipline part of it. We were on the grinder every morning at eight o'clock, complete with leggings, whites, and neckerchiefs. Tucked in our leggings we had little semaphore flags. We would drill with semaphore flags, through the alphabet and everything. The little navy white hats that we wore were no protection from the California sun. We had some severe cases of sunburn. Some kids got burnt just terribly bad. I was not at the time impressed in a negative way about the navy, but I remember the terrible cases of kids burnt to a crisp. But we stayed out on the grinder, and the sunburn eventually cleared up.

I got the impression that the navy was a no-nonsense organization, and I'd better get along in it. It was up to me. I wasn't going to get any free rides, and none of us dared ask why things were done the way they were. I wouldn't have asked why for a million dollars. I was so wrapped up in that transition that it never occurred to me to question anything. I just did exactly what I was told, the minute I was told to do it. There were a couple of kids that did get in trouble because of various minor infractions. That made an impression on me. That wasn't going to happen to me.

But it was kind of a grinding routine, a rough routine. We had field day every Friday, up at four o'clock to scrub our hammocks. There was a great emphasis on uniforms and personal appearance—haircut inspection much more often than it was needed, just for the effect; bag inspection every day—lay our bags out, roll our clothes up, and tie them up with clothes stops. We got quite a heavy dose of that.

The first three weeks we were in detention to see if we had any communicable diseases, I suppose. After that we had weekend liberty but had to be in by midnight. Most of us would just go around wide-eyed at San Diego and California. It was a brand-new world to us. They had a YMCA there. I didn't hang out there, but usually you would just go there because that was the kind of place where you spent a few minutes before you decided where to go in town—to go here or go there. We were strictly on our own. I drank a little beer and "smoke-stacked" when I got back. Smoke-stacking's when you act like you had more beer than you really had. I wanted to be a real salty sailor.

We went to some of those places along Broadway that particularly catered to sailors, like the "Pot O' Gold," where they had a 26-ounce mug of beer for ten cents. San Diego was a 100 percent navy town. I enjoyed being in that atmosphere with sailors everywhere; there were no civilian clothes in those days. The kind of places I went, where civilians were, they treated us very fine—cafes, dance halls, and that sort of thing. I didn't notice any negative feeling. But we heard stories in those days about Norfolk. We were told, "Boy, don't ever go to Norfolk. They have 'Dogs and sailors, keep off the grass' signs." I don't know how true that was, but I liked San Diego very much, and I just immersed myself and enjoyed it.

There were a lot of dance halls, and in the 1930s a dance hall was not a bad place to go. It was really *the* place to go. Music was big in those days—the big band sort of thing, and I liked dancing. I liked the popular music, and I danced a lot. I don't remember any one particular girl; I didn't have any serious affairs of the heart there. As a matter of fact, none of my peers—oh, one or two guys would come back and tell these tremendous stories about how they met this girl with a Cadillac, and she had a white bearskin rug, or something like that. But we didn't really believe it. That was like another version of smoke-stacking!

I just have pleasant memories of boot camp, and also, I sensed the maturing process in myself. I could feel that going on, and I thought that was good, too. I didn't write home, I was so busy being a sailor. My mother wrote to the chaplain. I was hauled up before the chaplain—which scared the bejesus out of me because he was a commander. So I went up to see him, and he wanted to know why I hadn't written home. I didn't have any good reason, so he had me sit down in his office and write a letter home that he mailed. He told me I'd better write home, which I did fairly often after that.

I made an allotment out to my folks of ten dollars a month. Our pay was $19.75 a month because that was still during the pay cut era, a 5 percent pay cut. Twenty-one dollars a month less 5 percent made it $19.75, which left me $9.75—and I was rich beyond my wildest dreams! I started smoking when I was thirteen or fourteen years old, so I felt as long as I had enough money for cigarettes and a dollar or two for liberty from time to time, that was all I asked out of life.

So my boot camp passed very quickly; we went in July and got out in October, and it was great. When I did get home I felt like I was about nine feet tall. My dad was very proud of me, and my mother cried a lot. She thought I'd gotten too old, too quick. I was anxious to get back and go to sea duty. We were allowed to indicate our preference, but we really didn't know what we were asking for. Some kids asked for battleships because they were big. But most of our education about that was just word of mouth at night. We talked about, "What are you going to get on?"

"I'm going to get on a heavy cruiser. How about you?"

"I'm going to get on a light cruiser."

We didn't know what a heavy cruiser or light cruiser was. I didn't know what a battleship or a destroyer was, so I put in for a heavy cruiser because it sounded kind of glamorous to me. Kids would say, "Well, a heavy cruiser's not as big as a battleship, but it's bigger than a destroyer."

When we got back to San Diego, we were put at the naval base there, on board a receiving ship, the destroyer tender USS *Rigel* (AD-13). Then we were gradually sorted out—battleships, cruisers, destroyers, whatever—and were placed on the hospital ship USS *Relief* (AH-1) for transfer to Long Beach where the fleet was. While we were on the ship, I had an interesting experience that made a lasting impression on me. There was an aviator who had been killed and was in the morgue, and we lined up to see him. That was such a momentous thing to us.

"There's a dead aviator in the morgue."

"Really?"

"You can see him if you go down this deck there and look through the porthole."

So we lined up, and we went down this deck and looked through the porthole. There was this body on the slab and I just thought, "My God, there is this dead aviator." That was a tremendous experience for me. Apparently, the plane crash had broken up a lot of his bones. His body had sort of flattened out; it was just about three or four inches thick. There was a pharmacist's mate in there on guard with him. He would look up at us with a blasé look on his face. But I had dreams about that for a couple of days, about this body on the slab. That was my first experience with the real life in the navy.

We went to Long Beach and went aboard the USS *Houston* (CA-30), the cruiser flagship and also the ship that President Franklin D. Roosevelt was very fond of. It had quite a name in the navy, the *Houston*. I'd always thought it'd be kind of nice to be on the *Houston* because I was from Texas. So they lined us all up in the mess hall. The fleet athletic officer came around with three or four officers who just looked at us as though we were cattle. They were looking for big fellows because fleet athletics were big in those days—the fleet rowing teams, fleet boxing, fleet this, and fleet that. *Houston* had quite a name for having a lot of good athletic teams.

So these officers just lined us all up: "You're on the *Houston*. You're on the *Houston*." Anybody over six feet tall, or with any athletic ability, was going to the *Houston*. I was small, five-eight or five-nine, something like that, and I was skinny. But this annoyed me. I felt discriminated against. So, after they picked all the big jocks for the *Houston*, they said, "Now, who else wants to be on the *Houston*?" They had that kind of latitude. So a lot of guys from Texas stepped out.

But I thought, "I'll be damned if I will. By God, I don't care what I get. I'm not going to be on that *Houston*." So I sat back, and then they just divided up all these cruisers: the *Chester* (CA-27), the *Indianapolis* (CA-35), and the *Portland* (CA-33), for instance. They each had ten or twelve, and they were alphabetical. They got to the Ks, and the Ks were the *Portland*. That's how I got the *Portland*. I was pleased about that. I thought, "That's great. That's the luck of the draw."

So I went aboard the *Portland,* which was a fairly new ship at that time. She and the *Indianapolis* were near sister ships. They were beautiful ships to me. They had that flared bow. The *Indianapolis,* commissioned in November 1932, had two even stacks, and the *Portland,* commissioned in February 1933, had a stack-and-a-half. I thought, "Boy, that's a good-looking ship." I really thought that the *Portland* was beautiful. When I got on there, I thought, "Now, it kind of worked out. I got the best ship in the navy."

On the *Portland,* duty assignment was a hit-or-miss thing. The chief engineer came up and tried to make a pitch to some of these kids: "You want to be in the black gang, down below deck, no weather, and wear dungarees," and this great stuff. Then the gunnery officer said, "Now think about the deck force. You're up there in the open. You get a battle station; you get a gun; you're up topside and see what's going on." So I chose the deck force. I thought that would be good, and I got the fourth division, which had the boat deck, with 5-inch deck guns.

When you first went aboard a ship in those days as a seaman in the deck division, there was a strict pecking order. I had a leading seaman in charge of my group; he might as well have been an admiral. I really thought he was great. It was a good routine. We had the boat deck—a teak deck—and every morning, in the morning watch, we got up and scrubbed the deck down with brushes, and holystoned it on Fridays. We used salt water with a fire hose to wash it down. We'd roll up our undress blues and be barefooted. I'd stand there in that ice-cold salt water and scrub that deck down. I remember how good I felt physically those days, just feeling like I could whip my weight in wildcats.

After morning watch, we'd have breakfast, chow down. We had mess tables that were on racks in the overhead—wooden mess tables that folded up. There was red linoleum on the mess deck. I got very familiar with that linoleum when I was a mess cook. In the deck force, you did your turn. You were a mess cook for three months, and you were a side cleaner for three months—and if you weren't careful, you were captain of the head for three months. I was somewhere in the middle. I wasn't captain of the head, but I was a side cleaner for a while, and I was a mess cook for three months.

The mess cooks would take the mess tables down out of the metal overhead racks and set them up for each meal, then spread oilcloth on them. We, the mess cooks, would go up to the galley and get these metal tureens in a rack and rush back down and put the tureens up on the table. The mess cooks would set up a table, put the silverware out, and so on. We ate off crockery—white GI coffee cups and white crockery. Each mess had a mess captain, who sat at the head of the table. He was the bull of the woods for that particular table, called all the shots.

The guys at each table would tip their mess cook on payday—a moderate amount, a dime or a quarter, something like that. But that was big money, so we worked our tails off for these tips. The food was excellent. There was a lot of competition amongst the mess cooks to curry favor with the galley to get good chow for your particular mess because the better you fed your mess, the more tips you got. There was a certain amount of jockeying that went on. The cooks were aware of this, and they'd play favorites, too. If you got along with the cooks, you'd probably get better steaks and so on.

What power those cooks had over the mess cooks! You had really better get along with the cooks, or your name was mud. During the time that I was mess cook, we drew a week's duty with the "jack-of-the-dust," who was in charge, in effect, of dry stores. The jack-of-the-dust was a guy that I kind of had a little bit of a rapport with. We would sit up and drink coffee and smoke cigarettes at night after taps in the mess hall, which was kind of devilish. It was all right. Nobody ever bothered anybody; a lot of kids did that. Smoking cigarettes was not really fostered; it was certainly not only condoned, but everybody was expected to smoke. I smoked like a stove. In fact, I didn't know anybody that didn't smoke amongst my friends there on the ship. Cigarettes were pretty cheap, too—four cents a pack for sea stores.

When we were involved in a Fleet Problem, with all the battleships, with their big clocks on the after mast, the destroyers, and what have you, I felt like it was Hollywood. One time the USS *Macon* (ZRS-5), the airship, was taking part in the fleet maneuvers, and the *Macon* had planes on board. During the course of this particular fleet maneuver, the *Macon* was very close to the *Portland,* and she launched her planes. That meant a lot to me, too, to actually see that.

Later on, when I was in the captain's office, the postal clerk on the ship was a great collector of first day covers and cachets and what not. One day in February 1935, the *Macon* went down, crashed off Point Sur. This guy came down and got me out of my bunk and took me up to the captain's office, and he made a quick rubber stamp that said, "USS *Macon* down off Point Sur." He asked me to stamp it with the ship's date-and-time stamp machine in the captain's office. I hesitated at first, but then it seemed legitimate, so I went ahead and did it. So I did twenty-five or thirty of them, and he gave me some of the covers. I guess he figured the special stamp and the date and time also marked on the envelopes would make them collector's items. He was right.

One time we had a night battle practice in which the whole fleet was involved. There were star shells—illumination rounds fired by 5-inch guns—and lots of light and noise, and it was just really great. My battle station was a sound-powered telephone talker from the bridge to a gun station. This one night there came a very critical point involving searchlights. We had done this before as drill but not the real McCoy. This was a real battle practice. Our skipper, Capt. David M. LeBreton, was on the bridge and some enemy—blue force or red force—came into view. I was all wrapped up in it, and I sort of forgot my duties as talker. So the critical moment came, and Captain LeBreton said, "Illuminate."

The OOD said, "Illuminate."

And I was supposed to say, "Illuminate"—but I didn't say, "Illuminate." I was too busy watching what was going on.

So LeBreton said it a second time: "Goddamn it, I said 'Illuminate.'"

Then it dawned on me. "Illuminate," I said. But we missed the opportunity. So, gee, that was terrible.

The captain said, "I want to find out who didn't pass the word."

So it finally got down to me. I lied like a trooper. I said, "I passed it. I certainly did."

It was a lie, but I thought, "I'm going to get the firing squad here." So I swore that I said, "Illuminate."

After I served my time on the deck force on the *Portland,* I had an opportunity to be a yeoman striker because I took shorthand and typing in high school. A striker undergoes training in a particular rating specialty as preparation for becoming a petty officer in that rating. The only reason I took typing and shorthand was because of all the girls in the class; I didn't take it because of any motivation. But those two courses that I took did me more good than anything else in the navy. I wound up in the captain's office as a yeoman striker.

The chief yeoman was a guy that smoked cigars. I thought that was an awesome thing, being a chief yeoman. He had an eccentricity, which was that he never used carbon paper twice. Back in those days when you did an official letter, you had a lot of copies. You'd put together your carbons, your bonds, your yellows, your greens, and so on. He'd put a fresh set of carbons in his typewriter and do the letter, yank it out, and throw the carbons in the wastepaper basket. The next batch was a brand new set of carbons again. That's just the way he did it. His basket was always full of carbon paper. He would smoke cigars and would sometimes tap his cigar. The hot ash would fall in the carbon paper, and the basket would flare up. So it was my job to always pull out the carbon paper in the chief's wastepaper basket before something happened. It was a rather extravagant way of using the carbon paper, but that was just the mark of the authority and responsibility of a chief petty officer. If he wanted to use fresh carbons, he could use them. I thought that was wonderful.

There was a little bit of association between the officers and the enlisted men but not much. It was mainly enlisted to enlisted. Up above me, up in the petty officers and chiefs, I guess, there certainly was. But the only one I was much in contact with was the ship's secretary, a lieutenant. When I was in the captain's office, I reported to him. He was the first officer that I ever spoke much to or had much contact with. That also made a big impression on me. His name was Arthur D. Ayrault, a rather aristocratic guy. I would have to go to him with a requisition for anything: a pencil, piece of paper, or whatever.

One day this bright idea occurred to me. I went to Lieutenant Ayrault, and I said, "You know, if I brought you several requisitions, and you just signed them all, when I needed something I would just go ahead and fill it in. Then I'd go down and get it, and I wouldn't have to bother you."

He looked at me for a moment. I mean, I'm sure he didn't think I was serious at first. He finally saw that I was serious. It never dawned on me that anyone would do that and use those requisitions for anything unorthodox. I was such a straight arrow that I just thought that would be a good way to do business. He was shocked when I asked him, and it finally dawned on him that I was serious. So then he explained to me that maybe it's better each time that I bring them to him, so he could sign and he would know what it was all about.

The ships were kept immaculate. We just kept on painting, like painting the Golden Gate Bridge. We were always painting somewhere on the ship. There was a lot of competition with other ships as far as appearance and so forth, and that was a great mark of pride, to have your ship in top-notch shape. If we passed by a train ship—auxiliary ships that provided services to combatants like fuel, repair parts, medical care, and so forth—like an old, beat-up tanker, I would think to myself, "What a terrible thing to be on a ship like that." Early in my naval career, I thought I would never serve on a train ship. I'd always be on a warship because there was just something about them I liked.

There was also competition between the various divisions on board the ship. The first division had the quarterdeck, and the fourth division had the boat deck, although that was not a clear line of demarcation. There were elite groups on there like the fire controlmen, who operated the equipment that aimed the ship's guns. They were just kind of a cut above, probably because of the equipment they used. The quartermasters, the people up on the bridge, were kind of an elite group, too—more head work than back work. The deck apes—and I was a full-fledged deck ape for most of my time on the *Portland*—we just worked.

They'd pass the word from time to time, "Now send one hand from the first, second, third, and fourth divisions. Report to the boatswain's mate of the watch for a working party." I used to say that they'd pass the word,

"One hand from the first, second, third, and King from the fourth division, report to the boatswain's mate of the watch." I drew every working party that came along, it seemed like. But we did have a great respect for petty officers, and particularly for elite petty officers like fire controlmen, quartermasters, signalmen, radiomen, and communicators.

We went out to Hawaii, and that was my first "foreign" liberty—a magical moment for me. There was the usual thing on the dock, girls and hula skirts and the ukuleles and all. I went ashore every chance I got. I was very much impressed with being in a foreign port. That was the sort of thing I hadn't even dreamed of when I was in Texas. We also went to Alaska, and that was also a great adventure for me—Nome, Juneau, Unalaska. The captain took the ship up very close to the Columbia glacier, and when we fired the ship's signal guns, great chunks of ice fell off the glacier. We went ashore in Alaska, although there was not much in the way of liberty there. It was really a sort of primitive place at that time, very primitive.

We got to San Francisco, and I remember very well passing Alcatraz, still an active prison at that time. I thought of all the Alcatraz movies I'd seen and the poor devils on Alcatraz. It was cold in San Francisco. My God, it was cold. It was in the summertime, but, boy, when the sun went down it was really bitter cold. I wasn't dressed for it the first time; I almost froze to death. But San Francisco was kind of a glamorous place, had a lot going on in there—night life and the restaurants. In fact, I thought it was more glamorous to me, by Aransas Pass standards, than Honolulu was.

Discipline wasn't a big problem on the *Portland*—mostly petty violations of ship's regulations, like sleeping late, being late for muster, and so on. The master-at-arms (MAA) would make the reveille rounds every morning and take names of late sleepers. One morning, he stopped at a bunk, shook the guy, and said, "What's your name?"

The guy said, "Smith."

The MAA wrote it down and said, "Smith, you're on report."

Same with the next guy. "Okay, Jones, you're on report."

The MAA came to the next guy and said, ""What's your name?"

The guy said "Przystovski."

The MAA put his pencil back and said, "Watch it, Ski. Don't let this happen again!"

From 2–23 October 1935, the *Portland* and the *Houston*, with President Roosevelt on board the *Houston*, took a leisurely cruise from the West

Coast through the Panama Canal and up to Charleston, South Carolina, where President Roosevelt disembarked and proceeded on to Washington, D.C., by train. Along the way, the ships stopped almost every day so that President Roosevelt could go fishing. One of his favorite fishing spots was the Cocos Islands off the west coast of Costa Rica. It was a big thing to me to have the president of the United States on the ship next to us. One day he went out fishing and had good luck, caught several big fish, and had the coxswain of his boat come over to the *Portland* and circle our ship. When he circled the *Portland,* he held a big fish up as he went by. We just manned the rail and cheered and hollered and yelled like nothing you ever saw; we just thought that was great. He had that old straw hat of his on and that cigarette holder.

President Roosevelt came over to the *Portland* to visit. I had morning watch and was shining bright work with a friend of mine named Johnson from Denver. The president was in a wheelchair, but it was not a big deal. He didn't seem disabled. He could walk with a cane or ride in a wheelchair, either one. He had a certain charisma about him such that when he would look at a group of people, I guess everybody in the group felt like he was talking or looking at them. He came over to where Johnson and I were. I was standing at attention so much that I was almost paralyzed.

He said, "Where are you from?"

I said, "Aransas Pass, Texas, sir."

He said, "Oh, I know it well. Good fishing down there, great fishing. You know so and so?" I didn't know him.

Then he went to Johnson, and he said, "Where are you from?"

He said, "Denver, sir."

"Oh," he said, "that's a great place. I've done so and so there. You remember so and so?"

Every person he had contact with, he could personalize it, and I felt for the longest time like that was a great encounter with the president of the United States, to say something like that. He was a tremendous politician. He really had that gift.

There's a great sense of loyalty in the navy, generally speaking—ship loyalty. Every ship I was ever on I thought was about the best ship I was ever on. I liked the *Portland* very much, and I really was very proud to be on there. But, when we came back through the Panama Canal after the cruise with the president and a short visit to the Norfolk Navy Yard, an opportunity was presented for several seamen to get off and be assigned to duty at the Panama Canal. I don't know why I did it. I just thought it'd be a good thing to do, so I put in for it and got it.

So, I went to Panama as a yeoman striker at the Fleet Air Base, Coco Solo. My duty station was in a little, green wooden frame building at one end of the base, the administration building. In this administration building were the radiomen, the captain's office, and the base administration office. The base itself was really old and in bad shape. There were no new buildings there except for the barracks, which were cement, with screened sides. There were a lot of bedbugs in the bunks. At the end of the bunk were the spring ends sticking out, about six inches long. We would borrow a blowtorch and run the flame on the spring end, and the springs would be just alive with bedbugs. You did this from time to time; whenever you noticed you had a little bit of a problem, you'd take off your mattress and burn your bunk. It was awful.

The routine there was great because we had 7:00 A.M. to 1:00 P.M. working hours, with a break at 10:00 A.M. for soup and a sandwich. And then at 1:00 P.M., we were off for the day because of the heat. Ships would come through and would marvel at this. The routine was such that a lot of guys just spent most of their time on the base because it had a big swimming pool, and there were a lot of activities on the base. We had our beer parties out in the jungle, and the liberty was unusual. It was Panamanian liberty—off the streets in uniform at 11:00 P.M. You had to wear civilian clothes after eleven o'clock. Most sailors couldn't afford civilian clothes. They had rental places down there that would rent clothes. For fifty cents you could rent an aloha shirt and a pair of pants. We called the garb "sliders." So at 11:00 P.M. if you're going to stay over for a while, you go down to Sam's Locker Club and put your clothes in a locker—put on your aloha shirt, your pants and navy shoes, and then you were okay.

There were three seaplane squadrons—Patrol Squadron 2 (VP-2), Patrol Squadron 3 (VP-3), and Patrol Squadron 5 (VP-5). When I got there in '35, VP-3 had old Douglas P2Ds, patrol planes with two pontoon floats suspended beneath the wings. The P2Ds in VP-3 were replaced in 1937 by PBYs. One squadron had Martin PM-2 flying boats; they called them "motor boats" because they had trouble taking off. There were also some P2Ys, the forerunner of the PBY.

I used to spend a lot of time bumming rides down there. They were very good about it. I flew in all those old planes they had. As a matter of fact, they had a daily guard mail plane trip from Coco Solo over to Balboa. My boss, Lt. L. H. Hunte, was an aviator, and I would go with him from time to time in a Vought O2U, a biplane observation aircraft. It had a hand crank inertia starter, and as hot as it was down there, the guy in the other seat—which would be me, of course—would crank it. I would take this inertia starter and engage it and stand up on the wing, with one foot in a foothole there and one on the edge of the wing. I'd crank the starter—very slow at first because it was stiff, and then it would pick up momentum. I would go faster and faster, disengage it, run back, and get in the rear seat, and Hunte would fire the thing off and take off. During those flights from Coco Solo to Balboa, he would sometime get a fair amount of altitude, such that we could see both the Atlantic and Pacific oceans at one time.

One time there was a Pan American Grace "Panagra" plane crash that killed several people. The pilot of that plane was a former naval aviator; he had some connection with the Naval Reserve or something, so they had a naval court of inquiry into this crash. I was the navy court reporter in Panama. A chief yeoman and I took the court of inquiry for this plane crash. The chief would take the morning, and I would take the afternoon or vice versa, and the other guy would transcribe what we took in the morning. At one time Igor I. Sikorsky himself came down—it was a Sikorsky plane—and testified. I remember being very impressed by him and his thick Russian accent.

At one point I was trying to make third class petty officer any way I could, so I took the exam for radioman and yeoman. At that time I was assigned to VP-5 for purposes of studying at night for radioman and taking the exam. When my yeoman rating came back, I went back on the ship's company at the base. It was really tough to make petty officer in that era. For example, they used to post the pay list every payday in seniority order. I was number one seaman at the airbase for quite some little time because I'd been seaman for such a long time. My pay number was 5-1, which made me the bull seaman first class on the base.

Promotion was awfully tough. In fact, when it finally opened up a little bit in '37 and '38, they had fleet-wide exams, even for third class. You'd take the exam and wait and wait and wait until the results came out. You didn't expect to make third class on your first cruise. And you could pass and still not make it. It was how high you scored on the test that would determine whether or not you made it.

Of all the aviators with whom I came in contact in Panama, I remember Capt. John S. McCain the best, probably because of an incident that involved both of us. One of my duties at the base was editor of the ship's paper. We had daily press news, which the radiomen would copy. They were so good that they could copy it right on the stencil. Then part of my job was to run the stencils off and staple them together, and that was our newspaper.

We had a kid down there named Almour; his father was a navy chief warrant officer. Almour was a little strange. He was not dense; he was just sort of eccentric. Almour loved anything connected with the possibility of war; anything that had to do with war he got very excited about. So a radioman friend of mine named Stevens and I cooked up a little scheme. Almour was a messenger and had a bicycle on which he went around the whole base every hour or so. One time, while he was out on his bike, I wrote some phony press items, and Steve sandwiched them in between regular items. The first one said, "Flash, flash, Japanese Bomb Hits U.S. Embassy in Shanghai." Then stock market items, then three or four more items. "Death Toll High In Embassy Bombing," then some more stuff. We embellished it with "British Ambassador Missing." And then "U.S. Declares State of Alert."

When Almour came back, he would always look over Steve's shoulders to see what the hot news was. When he saw this, he went absolutely bonkers. He was trying to pull it out of the typewriter. But Steve played the game and said, "Go on, Almour, leave us alone. We've got stuff to do that's important." So we had as much fun as we thought we should, and then Steve and I were going to lunch. So Steve just tore the stencils up and threw the pieces in this one great big barrel for used stencils and stencil ink. It was an awful looking thing—full of soggy, inky used stencils.

Well, we went to lunch and took our time. After about an hour, we came back. As we got close to the ad building, something told me that things weren't right. I had this terrible premonition that something bad was going to happen. In fact, I looked up, and there was a big black limousine in front of the ad building. I went in the building, and it was high excitement, people running around. Almour had retrieved those stencils, had taken them out, pieced them together, and had run off a copy of it!

Captain McCain was our skipper then. He was commander, Aircraft Squadrons and Attending Craft, Fleet Air Base, Coco Solo, as well as commanding officer, Fleet Air Base, Coco Solo. He was trying to get at the bottom of this foolishness. I looked up, and there was Lieutenant McKillip, my boss, dashing up and down the hall looking all unglued. So I went up and tried to catch him. He said, "Don't bother me now, don't bother me."

I said, "I've got to. I think there's something wrong with this press news." That brought him to a halt, so I told him the whole thing then.

He said, "I'm not going to tell the skipper. You're going to tell him. You're going to go in there."

So he went in and closed the door. After a while he said, "Okay."

So I went in. McCain was a little, wizened guy, physically, but such a great man. He smoked Bull Durham cigarettes and didn't wear shoes at all at the office. He was walking around in his stocking feet, rolling Bull Durham cigarettes. So I walked in. He had the story, I guess, from Lieutenant McKillip.

He said, "I'm not going to do anything right now. I'm too mad. I'm really mad. That was dumb. What you guys did—you're in trouble. You're really in bad trouble.

"Just get out of here. I want to think about this for a while. I don't know what I'm going to do to you—general court-martial or what."

Oh, my God, I walked out of there, and I was really shaken. I considered desertion, the French Foreign Legion, anything you could think of. I knew I was in the worst trouble I'd ever been in in my whole life. I don't believe I slept that night. The next day I went back to the ad building and saw McKillip, who said, "The captain wants to see you."

I went in and by that time, I guess, perspective had set in. So McCain just chewed me out, and I mean he chewed me out. He said, "I hope you've learned your lesson." When he said that, I thought I might be home free. He said, "You can cause terrible trouble by things like that. Don't ever fool with official dispatches." He just gave me a hell of a lecture.

The sequel to that story was that I was on Manus Island in New Guinea when I got rotated off the *Hornet* in 1944. I was a chief petty officer then, and a bunch of us were at the receiving unit there at Manus waiting for a ride home to the United States. Three or four of us chiefs were walking down a very muddy road going back to our barracks. Up toward us came three or four officers. This was the height of the war, and everybody was in khaki. Rank was really not very distinguishable from outward appearances. They got closer, and one of them had all sorts of stars on his collar. So one of us said, "Admiral!" So we all lined up, and as he came down the road, we gave him a real tremendous salute. It was McCain, who at that time was commander Task Force 38, the fast carrier task force. They went right on by and went walking down the road. We started walking away, and then I heard this, "Hey!" I looked around, and it was Admiral McCain, pointing his finger at me.

"You're the son-of-a-bitch that almost started World War II all by yourself." He laughed and said, "I've told that story many a time since then."

So I laughed and he laughed, and he went on down the road. And I thought, "What a memory."

Every skipper is a legend to his people. He was a legend to us—the fact that he smoked Bull Durham cigarettes, rolled them himself; the fact that he didn't wear shoes; the fact that he was just really a hell of a sailor, just a giant of a guy. Everything he did was first class. It was the unanimous opinion of the people down there that he was a hell of a skipper, and the aviators thought awfully highly of him. I was so struck by his compassion and understanding. The common conception was that he would go the last mile and some more too. He had qualified as an aviator late in his career. He didn't fly an awful lot. It was said the base prayed for his safe return each time he flew. But he did put in his time.

There was a real war in progress at this point—actually, there were two: the Chinese-Japanese War and the Spanish Civil War. The Chinese-Japanese War seemed closer to home because of the naval involvement—the sinking of the Yangtze River gunboat *Panay* (PR-5) by Japanese aircraft near Nanking, China, in December 1937. I just had the feeling that someday I would be involved, if anything ever happened. We talked about that a lot, the sailors did. We drew these scenarios, probably something happening someday, but not very specific. I think all of us saw it as something that we'd hear more about before we heard less.

There was a guy called the "pantless gunner of *Panay*." His name was Swede Mahlmann—chief boatswain's mate Ernest R. Mahlmann. There was a poem written about him by Kansas City poet Vaun Al Arnold. Mahlmann was on the *Panay* when it was sunk by the Japanese. He was in his bunk and came up in his skivvy shorts and manned his machine gun. He was nationally known, the "pantless gunner of *Panay*." About a year later, after I left Coco Solo, I was in New York, and he was at the receiving station there. To me he was a legendary figure. I spent some time around him, just to sort of say I shook the hand of the "pantless gunner of *Panay*."

I got one leave during the three years that I was in Panama, so I took that occasion to ride the USS *Wright* (AV-1) back to San Diego. The *Wright* was the flagship of commander, Aircraft Base Force, Rear Adm. Ernest J. King, who later served as chief of naval operations and commander in chief U.S. Fleet during World War II. While the ship was on its way back, we were in Acapulco Bay, Mexico, one morning when Admiral King was supposed to take off in an experimental four-engine seaplane. The pilot was chief boatswain Albert E. Baker, a flying boatswain, who was a kind of legendary figure in naval aviation. Boatswain Baker had done it all.

I was looking out a porthole of the *Wright* that morning, and the plane took off and headed away from the *Wright,* toward the mouth of the channel. There was no wind at all; the water was just like a mirror. Apparently Baker couldn't get it up on the step. When the plane hit the entrance to the channel, the wind was coming down the coast, so he turned around a little bit, and somehow the right wingtip—I think it had a pontoon on it—hit the water. The plane spun around a couple times and pancaked—panic, pandemonium, the admiral's in the water.

The only boat that wouldn't start was the crash boat. The coxswain flooded the engine in his haste, so they finally had to chug-chug out in a motorboat or motor launch to pick up the people from the plane. The plane hadn't sunk. It was in the water, and they were in the water hanging on. The boat came back with Admiral King, and he came up the gangway. The OOD was a young jg or ensign, who just said something like, "Oh, Admiral, I'm so glad you're alive," or whatever. King, who was a very stern, formidable figure with a volcanic temper, just roasted him, just ate him alive, on how to properly bring an admiral aboard ship. He just ate him up, to the amusement of quite a few people who were gathered around—but not to the ensign.

King also had this thing about uniforms. During the time I was in Panama, at different times, he would prescribe variations on the standard uniform—for example, white tops and blue bottoms; white jumpers and blue trousers one day, and the next day, blue jumpers and white trousers for officers and crew. It just looked so funny. They weren't designed to go together. To see a guy with a potbelly with about four inches of skin between the top of his pants and the bottom of his jumper walking around the ship trying to pull them down—it was ludicrous. We were all saying, "Well, the next thing will be mattress covers and peacoats." Later on, during World War II, he instituted the gray uniform for officers.

To a young kid like me, Panama was sort of glamorous. The town of Colón was our liberty port. There wasn't any organized entertainment in Panama; it was just kind of a cabaret town. There were no laws to speak of. The barrooms and cabarets didn't close up; they had no doors. A lot of the bartenders in all the gin mills and cabarets were retired navy. There weren't many Panamanians in that line of work. There were some foreigners; a guy named Chris ran the Lighthouse Bar, one of the most popular places down there. I think he was German or Czechoslovakian.

We did a lot of things out in the jungle. We would have a jungle party: get a keg of beer, go out in the jungle somewhere, and shoot iguanas and drink beer. We had fishing expeditions, but most of the activity was base oriented. It was a hell of a nice base for creature comfort. With tropical working hours, your time was generally your own. There were free movies every night. The average sailor went to the movies as much as he did anything else. He might go ashore only once a week, something like that because it was expensive. There was never any inexorable pull to go ashore. As a matter of fact, we didn't go ashore at all when a navy ship was in. Every time a ship came, we wouldn't go near the beach—pandemonium!

I wound up my enlistment there in Panama. I was on what they called a kiddie cruise, a minority cruise, until the day before I was twenty-one. So when the time came, May 1938, I went home on leave. I didn't know what I wanted to do really. I guess in the back of my mind I knew that I was staying in the navy, but it was something we talked about: to do your time and go home. So I went home, and I looked around for a job a little bit. My heart wasn't really in it. I spent some time there just hanging around town. I just renewed my acquaintance in Aransas Pass with all my high school friends. I took up with a girl from my high school class and just had a real good time.

All of a sudden, it began to really eat on me about shipping over. In those days, if you didn't ship over inside of ninety days, you'd had it. You couldn't get back in. I began to get very worried about that ninety-day period. So I anticipated a little bit, I guess, and I decided that I'd better get back where I knew I should be. I hitchhiked to Houston and went in to ship over. I was a third class yeoman then, and they said, "Well, you can ship yourself over," and they just handed me the forms. So I shipped myself over.

When I came to the shipping articles, there was a line in there for "occupation." I asked this first class yeoman what to put on there, and he said, "Put down 'mariner.'" So I did, and that was one of the proudest moments of my life when I put that in.

I thought, "Goddamn, I'm a mariner."

IT HELPS TO BE A SAILOR

Rear Adm. Francis D. Foley

I N JUNE 1939, I wound up my tour of flying small observation float-planes in VO-4 off the battleship USS *Maryland* (BB-46) and made a complete transition into patrol aviation. I was assigned to Patrol Squadron 31 (VP-31), which was part of Patrol Wing 3. There were three twelve-plane squadrons homeported and based in Coco Solo, Panama, flying Consolidated PBY-2 and -3 Catalina flying boats. It took me a month or so to get qualified as patrol plane commander (PPC), and I flew with an aviation cadet who was already a patrol plane commander; he was a good instructor, I thought, because I had no trouble. You could do a lot of dumb things in a PBY, but it had enough power, stability, and good aerodynamic qualities that really stood you in good stead. The fore and aft trim in the thing was a lot better than other seaplanes I had flown at Pensacola. It was more tolerant, maybe because it was bigger. And it had very good single-engine characteristics, with enough power on one engine to sustain flight with almost a maximum load at lower altitudes. Then it had an enormous cruising range—a little over two thousand miles in a PBY-2, which was pretty good. Certainly it was amazingly strong, and its capability in rough water was very, very good. I'm sure there were sea-planes that were better later on, but it was pretty damn good for its time.

Since we were a patrol-bomber squadron and also equipped with machine guns, we did a lot of bombing and gunnery practice. We had a couple of bombing targets down on the Pacific side of the Panama Canal that we used, way out in the reefs. My bombardier, Lt. Comdr. Frank M. Beck, was rated as a master of the art. He had been brought up at 10,000 feet in the South American Andes and was not happy until we got to such an altitude. We called him "Bomber Beck." We also went to Guantánamo periodically with the whole squadron to go on more or less advanced base operations for a month or so and do nothing but bombing.

When it came around to air-to-air gunnery, we had .50-caliber waist mounts, a .30-caliber in the bow, and a .30-caliber in the tunnel (in the tail). The target aircraft that we used for our gunnery business were Grumman F2F fighters, and they had a couple of them down at Coco Solo. There was no field, just sort of a parade ground. Lt. Edward A. Hannegan, Ned Hannegan, and I—I'd been with Ned in the *Ranger* (CV-4) when he was the landing signal officer—were the only ones in our squadron with recent carrier experience. They asked me if I was a fighter pilot, and I said, "Yes," which was not quite so. Like everyone else, I had my fighter pilot training at Pensacola, so they let me fly the F2F.

This was particularly fun for me because I would go and get my PBY and do a gunnery flight with that, and then come back and I'd go over to the field and get in the F2F and take that up and just have a ball against my own squadron. It was really great. Ned Hannegan, who was a protegé of Jimmy Thach's, tried to impart a lot of his knowledge and technique to me, so I really appreciated that. I got some A-number-one instruction from a real ace. But the contrast between the PBY and the F2F in suc-cessive flights was really remarkable.

I had a plane captain named Watson, who was one of the handsomest men I've ever seen. He looked like a movie actor, and he was a first class aviation machinist's mate. He was well educated, with a couple of years of college, and very, very sharp. He was a big man, lean but big, and he got me an "E" in gunnery in the airplane because he was a crack shot with a .50-caliber machine gun. The PBY-2s didn't have the side blis-ters that the PBY-3s and later airplanes had for the waist .50-caliber guns. The guns were just free; you swung them out, and they were in the clear with no wind screens or blisters over them.

Watson manned one of these guns and sometimes each of them in turn, and he could get hits when no one else could. I found out by pure chance how he did it. He had a special safety belt about eight or ten feet long attached to another safety belt around his waist and up over his shoulders. When we made a gunnery run, he wouldn't stay inside the hull of the airplane; he would get out on the fuselage with that safety belt attached so that he could get behind the gun at any angle, particularly when he had to shoot down and the breech of the gun had to be up high. He would be out there in the breeze, the airplane making 130, 140 knots or so, but with that belt on. I couldn't see him from the cockpit, but when I found out he was doing it, I told him, "Unh-unh, we cannot do that anymore."

"Mr. Foley," he said, "Look. You want an 'E' on this airplane, don't you?"

"I certainly do."

"Let me get it for you. You fly the airplane. I'll get the 'E.'"

"Okay, Watson, but I warned you now. You stay inside the airplane."

A lot of that prewar training was pretty unrealistic. But we also used camera guns, and I was on the other end of this thing many times because I was flying the fighters against the PBYs. They would use camera guns against the fighters, and that was much more realistic. But, in the final analysis, you had to let the people fire the guns to know what it felt like and to be able to clear jams and things like that. You could give them the basics on the ground, but they had to do it in the air to get the real feel for it.

The squadron was doing an aerial survey of Ecuador, and I went down there with two airplanes. We were to be gone a month, and it was going to be an advance base situation, where we were to be moored at buoys in the ocean the whole time. There was a little tender down there, an ex-minesweeper, the USS *Sandpiper* (AVP-9), that was going to take care of us for fuel, lodging, and subsistence.

Lt. (jg) James R. Reedy was the pilot in command of the other airplane. Jim was one year junior to me, a very interesting fellow as a matter of fact, and he had a plane captain who was even more interesting—Ferrero, who was Italian and probably the most popular man in our squadron. He was an absolutely delightful individual, a tremendous musician—a one-man band who could play a harmonica, a drum, and a banjo at the same time.

He had the harmonica strapped around his head, the banjo in his hand, the drums operated with his feet. Ferrero was a second class aviation machinist's mate and a crackerjack, but he could not even sign his own name. He had to write "X" on his pay receipts. He was long overdue to be a first class petty officer, but he couldn't pass the exam. So we got permission from the Bureau of Navigation to give him an oral exam for first class, and we passed him and made him first class petty officer!

So, we were flying down—I guess we were at about 10,000 feet—and I had crossed the equator several times in the *Ranger* and in the *Lexington* (CV-2) so I was a shellback, but Jim was a pollywog—never crossed the line before. There were a lot of other people in those two PBY plane crews who were also pollywogs. We were flying down over the west coast of South America, very close to the equator, when Jim called me on the radio and said, "Thirty-one prep two from three. What is that strange white line I see ahead running east and west?"

I called back and said, "Thirty-two prep three from two. Check your pollywog navigation. We already crossed that strange white line five minutes ago."

Well, about the time we crossed the equator, Jim Reedy was sitting in the cockpit on the left side, flying along, fat, dumb, and happy, and Ferrero, who was a shellback, went back in the galley of the plane and got a quart can of strawberry jam. He took the whole top out of the can, and he came up and got in the navigator's compartment, sat on the desk there, and reached in and dumped the whole quart of strawberry jam over Jim Reedy while he was sitting at the controls. This strawberry jam just went all over Jim. Oh, my God, the stuff was all over his face, his hands, the seat, all over the airplane, down in the bilges. It was simply a God-awful mess. Then Jim looked around at this guy—and Ferrero just laughed.

Ferrero left the navigator's compartment and went back into the after part of the aircraft, where he got a pillow, which he cut and ripped open. Jim Reedy was still trying to get the strawberry jam off his face and hands and the controls and whatnot, when Ferrero again sat on the navigator's table, reached through the aperture, and dumped all of the feathers out of this pillow on top of Jim, to sort of tar and feather him. Poor Jim could have killed that fellow Ferrero, but he had to take it with a laugh, which he did. After we arrived in Ecuador, it took days and days to clean that airplane up because we had no means of hosing down, since we were anchored out at buoys. So it was poor Ferrero, the plane captain, who had his hands full getting that mess cleaned up later on.

We landed down in a place called Salinas, Ecuador, where the tender was, and we went to our buoys and made fast to them. Some of the tender crew came out in a motor whaleboat and took the plane crews off, all except the security watch. We went over to the tender, and they had the Neptune party all ready for us! They didn't even wait to find out whether you were a shellback or not. We all went through the crossing-the-line ceremony over again, and the last thing that they did was to shave your head at a barber's chair that was on hinges and tip the barber chair upside down and dump you in the ocean over the fantail. They did have a couple of people in wet suits in the water there in case you had any trouble. I had it all over again. I even had my shellback card with me, but I never even got a chance to show it.

When I got to Ecuador, the survey was going very, very slowly. We had to fly at exactly 10,000 feet during a survey run, and you couldn't deviate more than 50 feet from that altitude because they wanted everything to be exactly the same scale in the photographs. So we were just glued to 10,000 feet all the time we were in the air. Each aircraft had a special camera that was built for the aerial survey. It was mounted so that the lens was horizontal over the tunnel hatch in the after part of the airplane. During a run, the camera just simply kept cranking out pictures; as long as you kept feeding the film into the thing, it would take picture after picture. I think there were only about three or four such cameras in the whole navy inventory, so we had to be very, very careful.

We found the cloud cover would just absolutely drive us out of our minds—cloud cover that we couldn't normally penetrate with the cameras. What we were trying to do was run three parallel lines, one about five miles inland, and one about maybe a mile inland, and then one right off the coast so that it would encompass reefs and shallows and things like that. We had hundreds of miles of coastline to do.

We found during the first few days that we were only taking pictures every fifteen or twenty minutes or so, going where the aerologists said to go. We decided that was for the birds. We decided to take off, one aircraft going south and the other going north at 10,000 feet, and we would just stay up there all day to wait for the low clouds to disappear, not wait for the aerologist to tell us where to go. From above we could detect clearing as it occurred. By using this procedure in that month I was there, we finished 70 percent of what remained of the project.

We found that the planes, while moored to buoys out in the ocean, began to accumulate little barnacles on their hulls that covered the entire underwater body of the airplane, and it made our takeoffs kind of hairy. We had to use a hell of a lot of power and a long takeoff run, which was pretty damn hard on the engines. We were always going with a full load of fuel, anyway, because we had to stay up all day. The only way that we had of taking care of this was to put side wheels on the airplane as if we were going to take it up on a ramp, then taxi the airplane up on a sand-bar, wait for the tide to drop, and get out there with scrubbers and scrub like hell to get those damn barnacles off. Boy, that took a lot of doing because it had to be done so quickly, and you had to do it while it was all still wet or otherwise you'd just keep splashing water up on it and that took more time. Furthermore, we weren't really prepared for this. We were using all the scrubbers the ship had to take care of it as it was.

On one occasion the tender had to go off to a place called Guayaquil, a big city on the Guayas River. It was 150 or so miles from where we were on the coast at Salinas. The tender had to go to Guayaquil to establish additional moorings for us there and replenish her fuel oil, aviation gas, and other supplies, so she shoved off and left us at the ocean buoys, anchored out in the ocean in an exposed, crescent-shaped beach area. There we were, all by ourselves, just the two planes sitting on the water. We had established a radio watch with the tender every two hours to main-tain contact. When the tender got to Guayaquil she put down the buoys in the river, close aboard, and then we flew over to Guayaquil and the Guayas River, which is a freshwater river.

While we were in Guayaquil for several days, we slept in the airplanes and refueled both airplanes from the tender right there in the river. It was quite an interesting operation. Fortunately the current was so swift that it was easy to do because we could keep some power on the airplane until we got it right snug to the stern of the ship before we had to cut our engines. So the swiftness of the current actually gave us a lot of control and takeoffs were greatly assisted.

The other thing that we did was clean the bottoms of the airplane. The current in the Guayas River, which was fresh water, ran very, very swiftly— 5 to 8 knots, pretty darn strong. That current cleaned those bottoms like dishes out of the dishwasher. They were pristine. But we did have a lot of problem with debris floating down the river, and the debris would look like a little island, maybe about the size of a desk—a little clump of dirt and foliage that had broken loose from the embankment further upstream and was carried down. The only problem was that some of these things would get tangled in our mooring or in our wingtip float—and we saw an awful lot of snakes in them!

One thing that we found during the aerial survey of Ecuador was that the people who were most interested in it, besides the hydrographic office, were the oil companies because those pictures revealed promising areas for drilling. As a matter of fact, I think the navy did cooperate with the American oil companies in letting a consortium of them look over the photographs. They did a lot of drilling down in that area where we had surveyed, and they did hit oil. On the side, we were taking radio bearings of clandestine Nazi radio stations that were being constructed in that area of Latin America.

Shortly after I returned from the Ecuador survey, I was sent with just my own airplane up to the Gulf of Fonseca, on the west coast of Central America, surrounded by Nicaragua, Honduras, and Guatemala. The purpose of the trip up to the gulf was to survey an alternate route for a new Panama Canal, a new transoceanic canal. The route most favored by the engineers ran from the east coast across Nicaragua to Lake Nicaragua and then turned northward up to the Gulf of Fonseca. So I had my same camera crews and everything that I had in Ecuador on board, and we made the aerial survey just flying up there. We did it in one pass. It was fantastic. It was just a strip that we had to fly up and get pictures of, then land in the Gulf of Fonseca. We all thought it was going to take several days to do this, but the weather was perfect. And one of the nice things was, we even had a wind sock in the form of a volcano, with a slight emission coming from the top. The volcano was about 4,000 or 5,000 feet high and gave us a perfect wind sock.

They had sent a destroyer up there to act as a tender for me, the USS *Tattnall* (DD-125), one of the old four-stackers from the Special Service Squadron. We landed in Fonseca, and the destroyer laid out a buoy for us; we didn't even need any fuel. The engineers, quartermasters, signalmen, communicators, and everybody else on the destroyer were navy except for the deck force; they were marines because they were a landing force for the Special Service Squadron. They had a few sailors, boatswain's mates and people like that in the deck force, but almost 90 percent of the deck force were marines, about a hundred of them.

So the second lieutenant who had this outfit wanted to exercise his marines ashore. One of the things that we had surveyed before we landed was a site that had been picked out for a seaplane base at the southwest corner of the Gulf of Fonseca. This was one of the spots that had been chosen by the Hepburn board, which went around and located strategic base sites in the southern part of the United States, the Caribbean, Central America, and South America. This site was covered with jungle growth. The marines decided that they would make an assault on the beach at the proposed seaplane base, and at the same time, we would take all the quartermasters and equipment from the ship and do a topographical survey of the terrain.

So we really were getting quite a bit accomplished, and we had all the equipment, all the theodolites and the transits and so forth to do this survey with. We got the ship's boats all over the side, the marines embarked with their combat gear, each one of them armed with a machete, which you needed for that jungle growth. We got to the beach, which extended several hundred yards long but only ran about maybe twenty yards inland before you were in jungle. Well, the marines assaulted the place, and I went along to watch what was happening—and they couldn't get through the jungle. They were hacking away with the damn machetes and this jungle growth was just so thick that after about an hour or so of wielding these darn things, they had calluses on their hands and were getting tired—and they weren't making a dent on this damn jungle growth, not really. They did manage to cut a couple of lanes inland for about maybe fifty or a hundred yards so we could do the survey.

Well, we thought, "Okay, we've had our drill, we've captured the place and so forth, we'll retire." So we all reembarked in the boats and started back for the ship about maybe a mile or two from the beach. As we started back, we saw a dark cloud up to the north end of Fonseca, which is a pretty big bay—bigger than San Francisco Bay. We thought, "Gosh, that's a funny looking thing," but, as we started back to the ship, we realized that the cloud was getting closer to us. Then suddenly we began to realize that it wasn't a cloud at all; it was a flock of locusts—and it was huge.

There was a ship leaving Fonseca, and we thought it looked like an old tramp steamer that had just been blowing tubes or something and made a big puff of black smoke. But the first thing you know, locusts started dropping, and they were the forerunners of the cloud. By the time we got back to the *Tattnall* she was absolutely covered with locusts and so was my airplane, and I thought to myself, "Oh, God, there goes the fabric on the ailerons and the horizontal stabilizer, the rudders." They were all over the ship, and the ship had gone to General Quarters just to batten down the hatches and everything because the damn locusts were getting down below.

When we arrived at the ship, they told us to lay off. The captain and exec had gotten up on the bridge and started blowing the whistle and the siren, and those damn locusts took off. They couldn't stand that sound. I was worried about my airplane. I thought I would be stuck up there for days; the security watch on the airplane had closed her up but didn't know what else to do. When they blew the whistle and siren on the ship, the locusts left the airplane, too, and fortunately they didn't hurt it. But the locusts went over and landed at the prospective seaplane base that we had surveyed. We stayed overnight on the ship, and by the next day, that place was clear. We couldn't hack our way through, but the locusts ate their way through that seaplane base. It was fantastic!

In September 1939, President Roosevelt proclaimed the neutrality of the United States in the European war and directed the navy to organize a neutrality patrol. The chief of naval operations ordered the commander of the Atlantic Squadron to establish combined air and ship reconnaissance of the sea approaches to the United States and West Indies for the purpose of reporting and tracking any belligerent air, surface, or underwater units in the area. Soon, all of the patrol squadrons on the Atlantic Coast were engaged in the neutrality patrols from Nova Scotia all the way to Mexico and across the Caribbean to Trinidad and all around through the West Indies as well. It was a massive operation, where we kept the shipping lanes under constant daytime surveillance, with spasmodic patrols at night just to keep the submarines down, if there were any.

We patrolled the shipping lanes at an altitude of between about 300 and 500 feet. I don't think I ever got above 500 feet, so we had to be very alert to what we were doing. The traffic was pretty well confined to the shipping lanes, although occasionally we'd find somebody out of them. When we would spot a ship, we would make a pass. Usually, in one pass, we could decide whether it was a tanker or freighter or what have you, noting the position of the ship, her name, the nationality—if possible, from the flags that were flying—the course and the speed and an estimate of the tonnage of the ship, and whether she was laden or empty.

As part of the overall effort, my squadron sent three planes to San Juan to augment a six-plane Norfolk squadron there and three planes to Key West to augment another six-plane squadron there, leaving six planes in Guantánamo. I went up with a section of three planes to Key West. The senior aviator was Lt. Eugene E. "Pooch" Davis, who was quite an interesting character, a very experienced naval aviator. We did a patrol from the Tortugas to Canaveral, including the northwest coast of Cuba in the Havana area, and, of course, including the whole Florida Straits, and occasionally all the way to Yucatan, if we were suspicious about something, although we didn't see many German ships.

The patrol was very demanding, and we flew hundreds and hundreds of hours. Usually when we got to about ninety or a hundred hours, we quit and went swimming and one thing and another. But we had enough spare pilots to keep it up. The patrols were more precautionary than anything else, and also informative because you knew precisely what was going on, and of course, it had its payoff with reporting ships in distress occasionally. I made many trips over to Havana to check on the shipping in port. We'd go close enough aboard to see what was there, and what was coming and going, so I got many, many views of Havana, which was a beautiful city, of course.

I had one traumatic experience in Key West. They discovered a corrosion problem in the fuel tanks of the PBYs. The fuel tanks were in the wings, extending out from the center line of the plane about ten or twelve feet on either side. They held 1,750 gallons of gas. The corrosion had been discovered somewhere in some PBY going through overhaul and was in the outer bulkhead of the fuel tank on either side. The only way to inspect these airplanes was for someone to crawl into the wing and to crawl through a scuttle about ten or fifteen feet from the end of the wing. The wingspan was 104 feet, so it was approximately 20 or 30 feet to go from this scuttle, all the way back to the bulkhead on the wing tank through a labyrinth of frames and supports. The opening was maybe a foot and a half in diameter, at the most. Of course, as you got closer to the tank, the wing became thicker, which was good.

I was the smallest officer in the outfit, so I had the dubious distinction of inspecting the wings of nine airplanes—eighteen wings, starboard and port. I wore a gym suit, and they put men with axes and hacksaws up on the wing in case something happened to me while I was inside—they were to hack the wing off! I didn't wear a breathing apparatus, but if it were very hot, they would pump air in through the air holes to the manhole. But I would go in with a flashlight and worm my way. Oh, boy, that was tough work!

Then it was very difficult to turn around once I got in there, but I found a way to do it, then wormed my way out again. And the worst of it was, when my tour in Key West was over, I went back to Guantánamo where they still hadn't conducted the inspection of all the airplanes. I had to do a couple more after I got there. I didn't find any corrosion at all, fortunately, but boy, I was sure looking.

While we were in Key West, Pooch Davis was detached, and they sent him back on the "honeymoon special" back to Coco Solo. So I became the senior aviator of VP-31 at Key West. Well, the first available government transportation that was leaving Coco Solo for the States was an old S-boat, a submarine. Pooch had always wanted to go to sea in a submarine and had never been able to do it. They were sending this S-boat to New London, Connecticut, where she was going out of commission, and he said, "My orders say first government transportation leaving Coco Solo. I'm going in the S-boat."

Well, the S-boat was so questionable that they wouldn't, or couldn't, submerge it. They sent a destroyer along to escort it to New London. As Pooch told the story later, he said that they got out in the Caribbean, and it was pretty rough; this damn submarine was on the surface, and she was rolling and pitching badly. He said, "The skipper and I were using his bunk. It was a hot bunk idea. He would sleep in it for eight hours, then I'd sleep in it for eight hours, and then we'd be seasick the rest of the time."

The bunk had a drawer that extended the whole length of the bunk, under the bunk. He said. "I went down to the cabin once and turned in. The sub gave a violent lurch to port, and the drawer broke open and rolled out. I rolled out of the bunk and into the drawer, and the ship rolled back the other way, and the drawer closed. They didn't find me for two days!"

When the time came for me to go back to the squadron at Guantánamo, I got a personal message from the naval station at Guantánamo addressed to the senior naval aviator, VP-31, at Key West, and it said, "Can you pick up one thousand baby chicks from Biscayne Hatcheries, Miami, and return them to Guantánamo for replenishment of station poultry farm?" And then it was added, "Agnew sends." Well, Agnew was Dwight Agnew, then a lieutenant, who was later the chief of naval communications, as an admiral.

So I thought about this, and I sent back a message to Lieutenant Agnew, a personal message, saying, "Your so-and-so, affirmative. Have chicks delivered Pan Am ramp, Biscayne Bay without delay. Cannot guarantee safe delivery because of possible high altitude return flight." And then I added, "Question: are chicks safe for solo?" That means—can you let them fly by themselves? And then I said, "Foley sends."

The next day I flew up to Biscayne Bay, Miami, went to the Pan Am ramp, and sure enough, the Biscayne Hatcheries truck was there. They delivered these cartons that had 144 chickens in a carton, each chick in a little cubicle of its own, safe and sound and snug. We stacked all the cartons in the waist compartment of the airplane and took off and flew back to Guantánamo, which was six or seven hundred miles away.

We got there, and I was taxiing in to the ramp, and they put the side wheels on the airplane, and the skipper, Joe Dunn, was there waiting for me. He was shaking his head sadly at me and pointing his finger at me and saying, "You've done something naughty."

I thought, "What the heck is this all about?" I hadn't done anything.

He said, "A motor whaleboat is standing by right here. I want you to go immediately out to the aircraft carrier in the bay. Vice Adm. Ernest J. King, commander, Aircraft Battle Force, wants to see you as soon as possible."

I said, "Well, skipper, let me go and get some fresh clothes on if I'm going to see the admiral."

He said, "The admiral said as soon as possible. Get in the boat and go."

So I went out to the carrier and was met at the accommodation ladder by the staff duty officer, who took me up to the admiral's cabin. I waited a couple of minutes, and then the admiral told the orderly to send me in. I went in there and reported, "Lieutenant Foley, sir. You sent for me?"

"Sit down, young man. Are you one of Paul Foley's sons?"

"Yes, sir."

"Which one are you?"

"I'm the younger one.

"Well, I'm a great admirer of your father. He and I were at the Naval Academy together. I think highly of him, a fine naval officer. Have you ever been to Havana?"

"Yes, sir, I've been there once on the United Fruit Line when I was going to Coco Solo. I've flown over it many times since, close aboard."

"Well, I want you to go to Havana immediately and go to the Pan Am ramp, and they'll have somebody there from the embassy, probably the naval attaché, who will give you instructions. It's a party of people that you have to bring back. I need them as quickly as possible. How soon can you go?"

"My plane is ready now, sir. We always refuel them immediately with nothing on the yellow sheet. I'm ready to go right now."

"Well, get going. And by the way, young man. Hereafter, don't send any more facetious dispatches. That's my prerogative!"

He had read this damn message that I had sent to Agnew about "Are chicks safe for solo?" I think somebody probably found it and brought it to his attention to give him a laugh—but it didn't seem to have had that effect!

So I flew up to Havana, and it was just about dark when I got up there. Sure enough, the party of about six or eight people, a whole bunch of engineers were there. It turned out the carrier was having some trouble on her shakedown cruise; she was actually out of commission at the moment for some minor thing, and they needed all this expertise on board as quickly as possible. So everything ended up well, but I had thought my naval career was coming to a grinding halt when I walked into Admiral King's cabin.

I left VP-31 in November 1940 to become chief flight instructor with Training Squadron 15 at the Naval Air Station Jacksonville, Florida, where I was again heavily involved in flying the PBY. By that time, I had become a real lover of seaplanes. To me they were a great challenge because in the air, although they were slower than comparable land planes, they acted just like any other airplane, they responded in the same way. But the challenge that they presented on the water was so far different from the challenge that is presented to you by landing a plane on a field, that there was no comparison—particularly in those days when we did not have reversible props, and we had to do with things like sea anchors and putting a man out on the wing and stuff like that to be able to turn the airplane or slow the airplane down. And all the advance base operations, the anchoring, getting under way, going to buoys, making beach approaches, takeoffs in restricted areas, landings at sea to pick up someone, or in the case of a forced landing—all presented problems that a land plane pilot didn't face.

There was an awful lot of seamanship involved with a big patrol plane, even more, it seems to me, than there was with the little observation planes. People who had had some sailing experience seemed to catch on quicker in handling a seaplane on the water than people who hadn't had any sail training—it was both an airplane and a boat. The wind on the water was such a big factor in what you were trying to do, and then, of course, you had to cope with current and depth of water, too, in various places such as going up a river.

I loved everything about the PBY; it was certainly a kindly airplane in the air, forgiving as could be, and I enjoyed every day of the almost four years I spent in that old airplane.

═══ 16 ═══
THE END OF AN ERA

Adm. Thomas H. Moorer

Thomas Hinman Moorer *was born in Mount Willing, Alabama, on 9 February 1912, son of Dr. R. R. Moorer and Mrs. Hulda Hill Hinson Moorer. On 10 June 1929 he entered the U.S. Naval Academy, was graduated and commissioned ensign on 1 June 1933, and through subsequent promotions attained the rank of admiral, to date from 26 June 1964.*

After graduation in June 1933, he served in various sea duty assignments until reporting to the Naval Air Station, Pensacola, Florida, for flight training. He was designated a naval aviator in July 1936, after which he served in carrier-based fighter squadrons and patrol squadrons. Moorer's PBY squadron was sent to the Southwest Pacific after the Japanese attack on Pearl Harbor on 7 December 1941, and during the Dutch East Indies Campaign, he was shot down on 19 February 1942. He was rescued by a ship that was sunk by enemy action later that same day.

Following subsequent combat action with Patrol Squadron 100 in the South Pacific, Moorer was temporarily assigned from August 1942 to March 1943 in the United Kingdom as a mining observer for the commander in chief, U.S. Fleet. He then commanded Bombing Squadron 132, operating in Cuba and

Africa; served on the staff of commander, Air Force, Atlantic, from March 1944 to July 1945; and from August 1945 until May 1946, he was assigned to the Strategic Bombing Survey-Japan and was engaged in the interrogation of Japanese officials. Subsequent service included extensive command and staff duties ashore and afloat, including commanding officer of the USS Salisbury Sound (AV-13).

Admiral Moorer served as special assistant, Strategic Plans Division, Office of the Chief of Naval Operations, following his selection for flag rank in July 1957. He then went on to serve as assistant chief of naval operations (war gaming matters), commander, Carrier Division 6; director of the Long Range Objectives Group; and in October 1962, he assumed command of the Seventh Fleet. In June 1964 he became commander in chief, Pacific Fleet, and assumed command of NATO's Allied Command, Atlantic, the U.S. Unified Atlantic Command, and the U.S. Atlantic Fleet on 30 April 1965.

On 1 August 1967, Admiral Moorer became the eighteenth chief of naval operations, and was reappointed for a second term by President Richard M. Nixon on 12 June 1969. He was then nominated by President Nixon on 14 April 1970 to serve as chairman of the Joint Chiefs of Staff, a position that he held until he was transferred to the retired list of the U.S. Navy on 1 July 1974.

Admiral Moorer's decorations include the Defense Distinguished Service Medal with one Gold Star, Army Distinguished Service Medal, Air Force Distinguished Service Medal, and the Navy Distinguished Service Medal with four Gold Stars, Silver Star Medal, Legion of Merit, Distinguished Flying Cross, Purple Heart Medal, and the Ribbon for the Presidential Unit Citation to Patrol Squadron 22. He has also been decorated by thirteen foreign governments. His many special awards include the Stephen Decatur Award for Operational Competence from the Navy League; Honorary Doctor of Laws Degree awarded by Auburn University; General William Mitchell Award, Wings Club of New York City; Member, Alabama Academy of Honor; Honorary Doctor of Humanities Degree awarded by Samford University; Frank M. Hawks Award for Outstanding Contributions to the Development of Aviation by the American Legion Air Service Post 501, New York City; the Gray Eagle of the United States Navy Award; member, National Aviation Hall of Fame and the Naval Aviation Hall of Honor.

In the mid-1930s, when I completed flight training at Pensacola, the idea was that you would go through a fighter squadron and then transfer to a flying boat squadron. Some of the fighter pilots thought that was going from the sublime to the ridiculous, but the real purpose was to train leaders of the future. They considered the fighter at the top of the heap. After fighters, some would go to scouting planes. The intent was to give everyone a cross section of experience, which of course is not done today. Now the policy is to designate people as carrier pilots, multi-engine pilots, or helicopter pilots. I think that I can honestly say that I went along with the concept, and I wanted to get as much variety as possible.

The whole idea was to train commanders in what it was all about, as much as anything else. It was intended that there be coordination and mutual understanding among and between the various types of aviation activity in the fleet. Of course, the young officers wanted to think their unit was best, so there was rivalry between the fighters and the bombers, and the carrier people and the patrol plane people and so on. The patrol pilots would say, "You guys go out for two hours and then get back in here, and we go out for fifteen hours." Or they'd say, "You can't navigate between Coronado and San Diego, and we navigate all the way to Hawaii."

So in July 1936, when I completed flight training and was designated a naval aviator, I chose fighters and was happy with that assignment. My first tour was with Fighter Squadron 1B (VF-1B) on the *Langley* (CV-1). Shortly thereafter the *Langley* was converted to a seaplane tender. She was the first carrier, and she simply just wasn't suitable for that purpose anymore, although she made a good seaplane tender. When the navy inactivated the *Langley* to convert her, they split the two *Langley* squadrons and put the scouting squadron on the *Saratoga* (CV-3) and the fighter squadron on the *Lexington* (CV-2) as an additional squadron. Normally they had four squadrons on the ship—fighter, bombing, torpedo, and scouting squadrons.

The *Lexington* was a rare ship in every sense of the word because the admiral on board was Rear Adm. Ernest J. King and the captain was John H. Hoover, "Genial John" Hoover, some people called him. The air officer was J. J. "Jocko" Clark, and the two landing signal officers were Sperry Clark and Thurston B. Clark. So there were three Clarks.

Although we were only assigned to the *Lexington* about six months, that period with Admiral King and Captain Hoover was interesting, to say the least. Of course, at that time I was an ensign, and I didn't confer with Admiral King too often. I think the people on the ship were more concerned about Hoover than they were about King. Hoover had the habit of lining up all the junior officers in his cabin and walking back and forth about two or three minutes. All of a sudden he'd stop and stick his fingers in front of you and say, "What have you done for the navy lately?" Hell, when it's the first time you've ever been in a captain's cabin in the first place and particularly Hoover's cabin, you couldn't think of anything you had done for the navy!

The air wing commander was Andrew J. Crinkley, who was an old-time World War I aviator and who also had command of the squadron, which was manned with chief petty officers. These chief petty officers were the wing men in each section of aircraft. They were awfully, awfully good because they stayed in the squadron for ten or twelve years, while the officers were rotated. So they could outgun you or outdo you in most anything.

Andy Crinkley was a little slow in accommodating to some of the advances in technology that we were experiencing in those days. Normally, when we were flying within sight of the carrier, the ship would send us messages by flashing light. But on one particular occasion they sent out a flight equipped with new radios, which was a first for Andy Crinkley. In those days, the ship never talked in plain language. It was always some kind of code, which could mean "proceed on mission" or "return to ship" or "land aboard" or "attack enemy to the east." We carried a legend of these things on our kneepad. But the first time Crinkley was flying with a new radio, he received a signal and didn't know what it meant. So he *whispered* to his wingman over the radio: "Two Fox Two from Two Fox One. What does Charlie Dog [or whatever the signal was] mean?" He whispered, thinking if he whispered that Ernie King wouldn't hear it down on the ship. And of course, Ernie King heard everything and had a few choice comments to make to Andy after we got back to the ship!

In those days, we had what they called an annual Fleet Problem. It would be associated with some strategic goal that was part and parcel of the war plans, namely, either the defense of Panama or the defense of Hawaii, which in this case, in 1937, was defense of Hawaii. These fleet exercises, which normally lasted about five or six weeks, were always very interesting, and we'd prep for them for quite a while. For the fleet exercise off Hawaii, we divided the fleet into two separate forces, one of which was the Japanese, called the Black Fleet. They approached from the west, and the idea was for the defending forces to locate them and try to destroy them before they could attack Hawaii. It was a typical operation, and it wasn't unlike what actually happened eventually in 1941.

The rest of the time at sea we generally operated along the coast to places like Seattle and San Francisco. For instance, I participated in the opening of both the Golden Gate Bridge and the Oakland Bay Bridge. The carriers had a major fly-over of every plane we could get in the air as part of the ceremonies associated with the openings.

After our six months on the *Lexington*, we were then ordered from San Diego to Norfolk to put the *Enterprise* (CV-6) in commission. She and the *Yorktown* (CV-5), her sister ship, were constructed by the Newport News Shipbuilding & Drydock Company. Now these were a considerable improvement over the *Lexington*. They were designed from the keel up as aircraft carriers and had far better facilities in terms of aircraft fuel supply, shop space, and things of that kind than those in the *Lexington* and *Saratoga*, which were simply conversions. Of course, we had learned quite a bit from those two ships. There were improvements in the arresting gear on *Enterprise* and *Yorktown*, but, on the other hand, they had hydraulic, high-speed elevators that turned out to be no good. They incorporated a very long piston and cylinder arrangement, with the elevator sitting on the piston—and it moved awfully fast. But they found when the *Enterprise* got hit by a bomb during World War II that this alignment was easily distorted by shock and that's why all the carriers today have cables—block-and-tackle is what it amounts to—to raise and lower the elevators, so that they are not as sensitive to misalignment.

They had arresting gear forward so that you could actually come aboard while the ship was backing down. The idea was that it would be possible to launch the fighters, which were always up on the bow, then back the ship down and get them back on board without pushing all the planes forward. That was the idea, but it didn't work out too well because as time went on there were other changes made, and it wasn't used too much in the war.

For years the navy had been buying reduction gears from one company. Apparently there were two or three skilled workmen who used to cut these gears; but, on a closed bid arrangement, another company got the contract for gears in both the *Yorktown* and the *Enterprise*. When they went out for trials, they were so noisy that they were totally unacceptable. They had to take the ships back and buy the other gears and discard the original ones. Consequently there was a delay in commissioning these two ships.

The ships did finally get into commission—the *Yorktown* on 30 September 1937 and the *Enterprise* on 12 May 1938. By this time, I was in Fighting 6 (VF-6), and the squadron was equipped with the Grumman F3F-2, which had the first 1,000-horsepower engine on-board carriers. Finally all the squadrons were equipped on both ships, and this carrier division—*Enterprise* and *Yorktown*—was given to Rear Adm. William F. Halsey. It was his first sea command after he had received his wings and had made admiral.

During the period that the ships were working up, there was some spare time so far as the air group was concerned, so in the big drill hall there at the Naval Training Station at Norfolk, Admiral Halsey would assemble the pilots, particularly in bad weather when they couldn't fly, and we'd get around in a circle. We'd have war games—tactical games was what they were—wherein we examined different kinds of formations, how the carrier would operate with the other types of ships, where you had the option of either turning the entire force into the wind or let the carrier go off on its own and come back and rejoin the force. How would we provide for antisubmarine support for the carrier while it was involved in launch and recovery?

All these things were examined, and it was there that the circular formation—as opposed to a line formation that was used by the surface ships—was developed. In the decades following the war, generally speaking, the formations were spread even further. But in those days—again bearing in mind that everything we were doing was based on the assumption that we didn't have radar—we were still thinking in terms of eyeball. As a junior grade lieutenant, I found all this very interesting, and I gave it a lot of thought. It was important when you launched from a carrier to know what was planned and generally what kind of formation you were going to find the fleet in when you returned after you had been out a couple hundred miles and were flying back.

During the course of these discussions and tactical games, Capt. Miles Browning, who was chief of staff to Halsey, began one of his lectures with the statement, "If you are so fortunate as to be in the navy when we encounter the Japanese, you should know these particular tactical factors"; Halsey succeeded in injecting some of his fighting spirit into the assembly. Everybody was crazy about Admiral Halsey, I think, because he could kind of get with it; there wasn't too much of a separation between the junior officers and the admiral. He had a knack of involving everybody in the discussion. You can only describe him one way—he was a leader. That's what leadership is all about. He was an example of an officer who demonstrated the characteristics in peacetime as well as in wartime. Quite often it doesn't happen that way. People perform extremely well in peacetime and then are not too effective in wartime—and it happens the other way, too.

That happened to Miles Browning, who later became Adm. Raymond Spruance's chief of staff during the Battle of Midway in 1942. The Miles Browning problem, as seen from my lowly station, was that he was absolutely and totally inconsiderate of people, some said with the disposition of a snapping turtle. As I've said many times, it's been my experience that it's the people that work for you that make you look good, not the people you work for. If young officers would just remember that point, they wouldn't try to butter up the boss. Instead of that, they would butter up the guys that are working for them—make it quite clear that you are aware of their presence, you know what they are doing, you appreciate their contribution, and you are looking out for their welfare. It works. I guarantee that. It's the only thing that got me through—the people working for me. I didn't do it; they did it.

The *Enterprise* took a shakedown cruise down to Rio and had several operations getting our squadrons in shape, doing routine things like gunnery and bombing. Then in the spring of 1939 Fleet Problem XX, a very large fleet exercise, was planned. This time it was associated with the Panama Canal. Admiral King brought the Pacific Fleet carriers through the Canal—the *Saratoga* and the *Lexington*—to join *Enterprise, Yorktown*, and *Ranger* (CV-4), so we had all the carriers in the Atlantic. The exercise in defense of the Panama Canal was not too much unlike the Hawaiian operation in the sense the fleet was divided; one group was the United States defending, and the other group was the enemy attacking. The exercise involved submarine scouting lines set up in such a way that the defense would initiate all kinds of searches with patrol planes and bring about contact.

I was in the defensive force along with John Hyland, who many years later would become commander in chief of the Pacific Fleet during the Vietnam War, and we were ordered by Admiral King to strafe the "enemy" battleships. We strafed the hell out of them. We flew right down between the masts. Adm. Claude C. Bloch, commander in chief of the

U.S. Fleet, took a dim view of this, so he sent over a scathing blast at us, and Admiral King, in turn, sent a scathing blast back. He stuck up for us, saying we were doing just what we were told to do.

I was viewing this battle problem from a junior grade lieutenant's point of view and wasn't too involved in the overall strategy, although everyone was briefed on the full nature of the exercise. But they generally followed the pattern of separation, followed by scouting by all means—submarines, patrol planes, and scouting planes from the carrier—then contact, and attack, just like things actually occurred in the war. The name of the game was to attack the other guy before he launched aircraft and attacked you. Then they would always arrange for the battleships to go out against one another. They had to have that. Finally, there would be a critique of some kind where everybody met in a big auditorium and talked it over.

After the final operation was completed there would be a replenishment, and we'd go into some port. In this case, we went into Norfolk and expected to go to New York to the World's Fair, but while we were in Norfolk the radio began blaring out, "All hands return to ship immediately." So we didn't get to New York; the whole fleet, with minor exceptions—the *Ranger* was left in the Atlantic—went to the Pacific. Then we formed what was called the HAWDET—the Hawaiian Detachment. That's when the argument began between Adm. James O. Richardson, who commanded the Pacific Fleet, and President Roosevelt about whether that was the proper place to keep the fleet.

At that point, in 1939, I had been in that squadron three years so I was transferred to Patrol Squadron 4 (VP-4), later redesignated Patrol Squadron 22 (VP-22), and I started flying the Consolidated PBY Catalina flying boat. My wife and I moved to Hawaii, and I was fortunate enough to go out aboard the *Matsonia*, one of the Matson Line ships. Once in Hawaii, I found the squadron working pretty hard, working a seven-day week many, many months before the war. We had patrols about every day; we'd go out a thousand miles—an eighteen-hour patrol.

Since there was no radar, everyone was flying a pie-shaped sector, based on the idea that you could only separate two tracks by double the visibility. To search adequately in all directions, we required about forty airplanes, and we didn't have that many available all the time. So, there'd usually be six aircraft at a time, flying sectors at random—sometimes northwest, sometimes southwest, sometimes some other direction. The weather was never any problem on the patrols, but the visibility was. Even on a clear day, we had people posted with binoculars, each man searching a certain sector.

The mechanics in those days were superb—the enlisted men in the flight crews and the maintenance crews. They could make just about every repair themselves. For instance, I had a very interesting flight with my commanding officer at the time, Frank O'Beirne. The decision had been made to send Boeing B-17s to the Philippines. At that time there were no airstrips on Midway, Wake, or Guam that were suitable for these aircraft. So the only way they could get to the Philippines was to go from Hawaii down to Rabaul, then to Port Moresby, to Australia, and then turn and go back up to the Philippines. It was necessary to survey the route, so Frank O'Beirne and I were ordered to take the air force officers on this flight so they could make logistics arrangements. They had something new called 100 octane fuel, which was very rare, and they were going to consume just about every gallon in all of Australia to get these aircraft through to the Philippines.

This was very, very secret, and the entire flight was done under complete radio silence, with all the navigation being celestial. When we left Hawaii we had one of every kind of spare part—a generator, a starter, an air speed meter, an altimeter, a vacuum pump, an oil pump, etc. All the accessories for normal repairs were aboard these planes plus six hundred pounds of food. We made this whole circuit, which was about 120 flight hours, without any problem at all because those mechanics and radiomen were so good. The radioman, Thomas, could listen to the radio, and if it wasn't working right he just knew by instinct that he should change such and such a vacuum tube, and he had a spare. These boys could repair anything right on the spot.

We had five or six squadrons in Hawaii, but then we began to send them to the Philippines. We sent two of the squadrons out—Patrol Wing 10, they called it. Everyone knew that things were getting tense. The B-17s and the PBYs were going out to the Philippines, as were the submarines. It wasn't as if everybody was oblivious to the fact that the Japanese existed. There was a tremendous amount of concern about it, and we were fairly certain that there was going to be a war. The only question was how and when it would start.

But there wasn't any lack of attention, and it wasn't a matter of any-one being asleep before Pearl Harbor because with the information they had the main concern was that the ships would be attacked by either sabotage or by submarines. So the idea was to get them inside Pearl Harbor behind the nets. That was a mistake in one sense but on the other hand, if the ships had been out at sea those that were sunk would have been gone forever when in fact we recovered practically everyone of them except the *Oklahoma* (BB-37) and the *Arizona* (BB-39). But there wasn't just "business as usual" as one might think from what he would normally read about Pearl Harbor.

The press is always making somebody out a dolt. Gen. Walter C. Short and Adm. Husband E. Kimmel were described as stupid to let this happen. Of course, Admiral Kimmel took a very unfair rap. Somebody has to be a scapegoat, and I'm not too much opposed to this in the sense that I think the president of the country should stay aloof from operations so that he can make a move like that in order to restore public confidence. But when presidents get involved—such as Johnson did through McNamara in telling the services how many bombs to put on bomb racks in Vietnam and when to come and go, whether you can do this or that in a tactical situation—what that does is leave them no out. It's far better for the president not to get involved in those things because then he can fire the military man or fire his own people and start all over.

The marines began to fortify the islands with units called Defense Battalions—one on Wake, one on Midway, and there had been one in Guam for some time. The construction companies built an airstrip on Wake to refuel B-17s being flown to the Philippines and as a base for marine fighters from Hawaii to participate in the defense of Wake. The fighters were put aboard *Enterprise*, and Admiral Halsey took them within a few hundred miles of the island. Meanwhile, my squadron had been located at Midway, and we had been patrolling around Midway since early November 1941. We were ordered suddenly to go to Wake Island, which was farther west, for what purpose we didn't exactly know.

After we got there, we were asked to go out and do two things: scout the operating area of the *Enterprise* so she wouldn't be observed by the Japanese and send one plane to escort and navigate this squadron into the island. That happened to be my assignment. I went out about four hundred miles in my PBY, picked up the carrier, and then turned around, with the fighters following me back to Wake. The idea was that if one of them went into the water I'd pick them up, and I also could do all the navigating for them, using celestial means.

There wasn't any way the *Enterprise* could be observed because we were sweeping out the area she was moving into. But I think that Admiral Halsey would have attacked if they had been observed because his aircraft were carrying bombs all the time. He wasn't going to get surprised; he was ready to go to war right then and there. That's how tense things were, and this was a few days before Pearl Harbor.

After the marines arrived, we were ordered back to Midway and then directed to return to Hawaii. We arrived at Hawaii after our two-month deployment to Midway late at night on Friday the 5th of December. The squadron was scheduled to fly every day of the week, so I was all dressed on the way out to go take my regular flight that Sunday. My patrol mission would have been headed southwest, toward the Japanese islands. I was leaving home when I saw the Japanese planes of the first wave striking Hickham Field and Pearl Harbor. It wasn't long before I was airborne that night in one of the two serviceable aircraft left in the squadron, flying to the southwest on a fruitless search for the Japanese strike group.

Pearl Harbor marked the end of two wonderful decades for U.S. naval aviation—the "golden age," if you will—and the beginning of a new age that changed naval aviation forever. As much as we have progressed technologically during the past fifty years with the introduction of jet aircraft, missiles, and nuclear weapons, I still have many fond memories of those years between the wars, when there seemed to be more room, more tolerance for the individual, for creativity, and for freedom of expression. Every day on board ship, or flying long distances over the ocean, brought new challenges and adventures the likes of which we will never experience again.

29. Adm. Joseph Mason Reeves, known alternatively as "Bull" or "Billygoat," was a non-aviator who became a convert to naval aviation and subsequently revolutionized carrier warfare tactics in the 1920s and '30s. *(Courtesy Special Collections, Nimitz Library, U.S. Naval Academy)*

30. Lt. Alfred M. Pride (*second from right*), with other *Lexington* aviators, poses before the ship's Martin T3M-2, c. 1927–28.

31. Reminders of a by-gone era: The USS *Lexington* (CV-2), identified by the horizontal black band on her funnel and her distinctive 8-inch guns, which were retained for defensive

purposes if she were unable to conduct air operations. The USS *Los Angeles* (ZR-3), the "eyes of the fleet," hovers overhead.

32. The seaplane tender USS *Jason* (AV-2), with Vought O2U-3s of Scouting Squadron 8A (VS-8A) on board, is shown at anchor in Manila Harbor, the Philippines, in February 1932.

33. The Heavier-than-Air (HTA) Unit of the USS *Akron* (ZRS-4) was photographed in the fall of 1932. Aviators in the second row (*from left to right*) are: Lt. (jg) Frederick N. Kivette, Lt. (jg) Harold B. Miller, Lt. D. Ward Harrigan, Lt. Frederick M. Trapnell, Lt. Howard L. Young, and Lt. (jg) Robert W. Larson. (*Courtesy Rear Adm. D. W. Harrigan, USN [Ret.]*)

34. A Curtiss F9C-2 Sparrowhawk from the *Macon* (ZRS-5) engages the trapeze prior to being hoisted aboard the airship.

35. A Vought O3U-1 is seen here during flight operations, probably from the USS *West Virginia* (BB-48), c. 1933.

36. The USS *Richmond* (CL-9) with Curtiss SOCs on board, c. mid-1930s.

37. Her flight deck lined with aircraft two and three abreast, the USS *Saratoga* (CV-3) recovers her air group during operations on 2 March 1932.

38. The heavy cruiser USS *Portland* (CA-33) leads the fleet review on 31 May 1934.

39. Consolidated P2Ys from Patrol Squadron 10F (VP-10F), Mokapu Point, Oahu, in early 1934. Six VP-10F P2Ys flew nonstop from San Francisco to Pearl Harbor in January 1934 in twenty-four hours, thirty-five minutes.

40. A Vought SBU-1 of VS-41 is spotted on the flight deck of the USS *Lexington* (CV-2) during the search for Amelia Earhart and Fred Noonan, July 1937.

41. Martin PM-1, assigned to Patrol Squadron 9 (VP-9), c. 1934. *(Courtesy National Air and Space Museum)*

42. A Douglas P2D-1 patrol bomber from Patrol Squadron 3 (VP-3) at NAS Coco Solo flies over Miraflores Locks, Panama Canal, on 1 February 1936. The land-based T2D torpedo bomber was redesignated as a patrol bomber to avoid army criticism of the navy's operating land-based bombers. *(Courtesy National Air and Space Museum)*

43. The best known of any navy flying boats, PBYs became famous for their long range, versatility, and rugged construction. In June 1937, these PBY-1s from Patrol Squadron 3F (VP-3F) were flown nonstop from San Diego to the Canal Zone in a little less than twenty-eight hours.

44. Fighter Squadron 6 (VF-6), assigned to the USS *Enterprise* (CV-6), parade their Grumman F3Fs in a typical squadron display of the era.

45. Lt. (jg) Thomas H. Moorer (*third from left*), with his PBY crew, in a snapshot taken at Ford Island, Hawaii, in 1940. Admiral Moorer (chairman of the Joint Chiefs of Staff from 1970 to 1974) and Adm. Arthur W. Radford (JCS chairman from 1953 to 1957) were the only two naval aviators of the "golden age" to attain the nation's highest military office.

A Selected Chronology of U.S. Naval Aviation, 1910–1941

1910

SEPTEMBER

26—The secretary of the navy reported that Capt. W. I. Chambers had been designated as the officer to whom all correspondence on aviation should be referred. This is the first recorded reference to a provision for aviation in Navy Department organization.

OCTOBER

13—The secretary of the navy approved the recommendation of the chief constructor that an officer from the Bureau of Construction and Repair and another from the Bureau of Steam Engineering be appointed to investigate the subject of aviation and gain technical knowledge of airplanes; he directed that these officers keep Capt. W. I. Chambers fully informed of work contemplated and the results of all experiments.

NOVEMBER

14—Eugene Ely, a civilian pilot, took off in a 50-horsepower Curtiss plane from a wooden platform built on the bow of the USS *Birmingham* (CL-2). The ship was at anchor in Hampton Roads, Norfolk, Virginia, and Ely landed safely on Willoughby Spit.

29—Glenn H. Curtiss wrote to the secretary of the navy offering flight instruction without charge for one naval officer as one means of assisting "in developing the adaptability of the aeroplane to military purposes."

DECEMBER

23—The first naval officer to undergo flight training, Lt. T. G. Ellyson, was ordered to report to the Glenn Curtiss Aviation Camp at North Island, San Diego.

1911

JANUARY

18—At 11:01 A.M., Eugene Ely, flying a Curtiss pusher, landed on a specially built platform aboard the armored cruiser USS *Pennsylvania* (ACR-4) at anchor in San Francisco Bay. At 11:58 A.M. he took off and returned to Selfridge Field, San Francisco, completing the earliest demonstration of the adaptability of aircraft to shipboard operations.

26—The first successful hydroaeroplane flight was made by Glenn Curtiss at North Island, San Diego.

FEBRUARY

17—Glenn H. Curtiss taxied his hydroaeroplane alongside the USS *Pennsylvania* (ACR-4) at anchor in San Diego Harbor, was hoisted aboard and off again by ship's crane, and then returned to base.

MARCH

4—The first funds for naval aviation were appropriated, providing $25,000 to the Bureau of Navigation for "experimental work in the development of aviation for naval purposes."

9—The Wright Company made a formal offer to train one pilot for the navy contingent upon the purchase of one airplane for the sum of $5,000. This offer was later made unconditional, and Lt. John Rodgers was ordered to Dayton for flight training.

APRIL

14—The embryo office of naval aviation was transferred from the General Board and established in the Bureau of Navigation.

MAY

8—Capt. W. I. Chambers prepared requisitions for two Curtiss biplanes. One, the Triad, was to be equipped for arising from or alighting on land or water. The Triad became the navy's first airplane, the A-1. This event on 8 May 1911 has been officially proclaimed to be the birthday of naval aviation.

JUNE

27—Lt. (jg) J. H. Towers, who became naval aviator no. 3, reported for duty and instruction in flying at the Curtiss School, Hammondsport, New York.

JULY

1—At 6:50 P.M., Glenn Curtiss demonstrated the A-1, first aircraft built for the navy, taking off from and alighting on Lake Keuka at Hammondsport, New York.

3—Lt. T. G. Ellyson flew the A-1 from Keuka to Hammondsport, N.Y., on the first night flight by a naval aviator, landing successfully on the water without the aid of lights.

6—Capt. W. I. Chambers was ordered to temporary duty at the Naval Academy in connection with the establishment of an aviation experimental station on Greenbury Point, making it the first base for naval aviation.

13—The navy's second aircraft, the A-2, was set up and flown at Hammondsport, New York.

SEPTEMBER

7—A memorable experiment in the navy's search for a shipboard launching device was completed at Hammondsport when Lt. T. G. Ellyson made a successful take-off from an inclined wire rigged from the beach down to the water.

OCTOBER

10—Assistant naval constructor Holden C. Richardson reported to aviation at the Washington Navy Yard, becoming the navy's first engineering and maintenance officer for aviation.

DECEMBER

29—The aviators at Annapolis were ordered to transfer with their equipment to North Island, San Diego, to set up an aviation camp on land offered for the purpose by Glenn H. Curtiss.

1912

MAY

22—1st Lt. Alfred A. Cunningham, USMC, the first U.S. Marine Corps officer assigned to flight instruction and later designated naval aviator no. 5, reported to the superintendent of the Naval Academy for "duty in connection with aviation." This date is recognized as the birthday of Marine Corps aviation.

OCTOBER

6—Lt. J. H. Towers took off from the water at Annapolis at 6:50 A.M. and remained in the air six hours, ten minutes, thirty-five seconds, setting a new U.S. endurance record for planes of any type.

NOVEMBER

12—The navy's first successful launching of an airplane by catapult was made at the Washington Navy Yard by Lt. T. G. Ellyson in the A-3.

30—The C-1, the navy's first flying boat, was tested at Hammondsport, New York, by Lt. T. G. Ellyson.

1913

JANUARY

6—The entire aviation element of the navy arrived at Guantánamo Bay, Cuba, and set up the aviation camp on Fisherman's Point for its first operations with the fleet.

FEBRUARY

8—Lt. J. H. Towers reported on experimental work under way at Guantánamo, including bombing, aerial photography, and wireless transmission.

MARCH

4—The Navy Appropriations Act for fiscal year 1914 provided an increase of

35 percent in pay and allowances for officers detailed to duty as flyers of heavier-than-air craft, limited to thirty the number of officers that could be so assigned, and further provided that no naval officer above the rank of lieutenant commander, or major in the Marine Corps, could be detailed to duty involving flying.

13—Capt. W. I. Chambers was awarded the medal of the Aeronautical Society for the year 1912 and cited for "his unusual achievements in being the first to demonstrate the usefulness of the aeroplane in navies, in developing a practical catapult for the launching of aeroplanes from ships, in assisting in the practical solution of the hydroaeroplane by the production in association with others of the flying boat...."

JUNE

12—Secretary of the navy approved detailing assistant naval constructor J. C. Hunsaker to the Massachusetts Institute of Technology to develop "a course of lectures and experiments on the design of aeroplanes and dirigibles, and to undertake research in that field."

20—Ens. W. D. Billingsley, piloting the B-2 at 1,600 feet over the water near Annapolis, was thrown from the plane and fell to his death—the first fatality of naval aviation. Lt. J. H. Towers, riding as passenger, was also unseated but clung to the plane and fell with it into the water, receiving serious injuries.

OCTOBER

7—The secretary of the navy appointed a board of officers, with Capt. W. I. Chambers as senior member, to draw up "a comprehensive plan for the organization of a Naval Aeronautic Service." Its report was in all respects the first comprehensive program for an orderly development of naval aviation.

DECEMBER

17—Capt. Mark L. Bristol reported to the Navy Department for special duty as officer in charge of aviation, thereby relieving Capt. W. I. Chambers of that duty.

1914

JANUARY

10—The secretary of the navy, Josephus Daniels, announced that "the science of aerial navigation has reached that point where aircraft must form a large part of our naval force for offensive and defensive operations."

20—The aviation unit from Annapolis, consisting of nine officers, twenty-three men, seven aircraft, portable hangars, and other gear, under Lt. J. H. Towers as officer in charge, arrived at Pensacola, Florida, on board the USS *Mississippi* (BB-41) and USS *Orion* (AC-11) to set up a flying school. Lt. Comdr. Henry C. Mustin, in command of the station ship *Mississippi*, was also in command of the aeronautic station.

APRIL

20—In less than twenty-four hours after receiving orders, an aviation detachment of three pilots, twelve enlisted men, and three aircraft, under command of Lt. John H. Towers, sailed from Pensacola on board the USS *Birmingham* (CL-2) to join Atlantic Fleet forces operating off Tampico in the Mexican crisis.

21—A second aviation detachment from Pensacola of one pilot, three student pilots, and two aircraft, commanded by Lt. (jg) P. N. L. Bellinger, embarked in the USS

Mississippi (BB-41) and sailed for Mexican waters to assist in military operations at Vera Cruz.

MAY

2—The AH-3 hydroaeroplane, piloted by Lt. (jg) P. N. L. Bellinger with Ens. W. D. LaMont as observer, flew the first mission in direct support of ground troops as the marines, encamped near Tejar, reported being under attack and requested the aviation unit at Vera Cruz to locate the attackers.

JULY

1—Aviation was formally recognized with the establishment of an Office of Naval Aeronautics in the Division of Operations under the secretary of the navy.

NOVEMBER

23—The title "director of naval aeronautics" was established to designate the officer in charge of naval aviation, and Capt. Mark L. Bristol, already serving in that capacity, was ordered to report to the secretary of the navy under the new title.

1915

MARCH

3—A rider to the Naval Appropriations Act created the National Advisory Committee for Aeronautics. Navy members in the original organization were Capt. Mark L. Bristol and naval constructor Holden C. Richardson, secretary.

3—The Naval Appropriations Act, 1916, added enlisted men and student aviators to those eligible for increased pay and allowances while on duty involving flying.

22—The title "naval aviator" replaced the former "navy air pilot" designation for naval officers qualified as aviators.

APRIL

16—The Curtiss AB-2 flying boat was catapulted successfully from a barge by Lt. P. N. L. Bellinger at Pensacola. The success of this and subsequent launchings led to installation of the catapult aboard ship.

23—Lt. P. N. L. Bellinger, in the Burgess Dunne AH-10, established an American altitude record for seaplanes by ascending to 10,000 feet over Pensacola.

OCTOBER

12—A directive was issued establishing an officer in charge of Naval Aeronautics under the newly created chief of naval operations and giving authority for aviation programs in the Navy Department to the chief of naval operations and to the bureaus, in effect abolishing the Office of the Director of Naval Aeronautics.

NOVEMBER

5—Lt. Comdr. H. C. Mustin, in the Curtiss AB-2 flying boat, made the first catapult launching from a ship, flying off the stern of the USS *North Carolina* (ACR-12) in Pensacola Bay.

1916

MARCH

4—Capt. Mark L. Bristol was detached as director of naval aeronautics and both the title and the office ceased to exist. Captain Bristol was assigned to command the USS *North Carolina* (ACR-12) and, under a new title of commander of the Air Service, assumed operational supervision over all aircraft, air stations, and the further development of aviation in the navy. Such aviation duties as remained in the office of the chief of naval operations were assumed by Lt. C. K. Bronson.

JUNE

3—Formal instruction in free and captive balloons was instituted at Pensacola.

9—Lt. R. C. Saufley, on an endurance flight in the Curtiss AH-9 over Santa Rosa Island off Pensacola, crashed to his death after being in the air eight hours and fifty-one minutes.

JULY

12—The Curtiss AB-3 flying boat, piloted by Lt. G. de. C. Chevalier, was catapulted from the USS *North Carolina* (ACR-12) while under way in Pensacola Bay. The launch completed calibration of the first catapult designed for shipboard use and by it the *North Carolina* became the first ship of the U.S. Navy equipped to carry and operate aircraft.

1917

JANUARY

6—A board of army and navy officers recommended to the secretaries of the war and navy departments that an airship of the Zeppelin type be designed and constructed under the direction of the chief constructor of the navy with funds provided equally by the army and the navy.

FEBRUARY

13—At Pensacola, Capt. Francis T. Evans, USMC, performed the first loop with a seaplane, a Curtiss N-9 floatplane, at 3,000 feet and then forced it into a spin and successfully recovered.

MARCH

24—The First Yale Unit of twenty-nine men enlisted in the Naval Reserve Flying Corps and four days later left college to begin war training at West Palm Beach. This was the first of several college groups to join up as a unit for war service.

APRIL

6—The United States declared a state of war with Germany. The strength of naval aviation, the navy, and the marines combined, was 48 officers and 239 enlisted men, 54 airplanes, 1 airship, 3 balloons, and 1 air station.

7—By Executive Order the president directed that the Coast Guard be transferred from the Treasury Department to operate as a part of the navy until further orders.

MAY

30—The navy's first successful dirigible, the Goodyear B-1, landed in a meadow ten miles from Akron, Ohio, completing an overnight test flight from Chicago.

JUNE

5—The first military unit sent to France in World War I, the First Aeronautic Detachment, arrived in Pauillac, France, aboard the USS *Jupiter* (AC-3). The detachment, consisting of seven officers and 122 enlisted men, including the element aboard the USS *Neptune* (AC-8) (which arrived at St. Nazaire on 8 June), was commanded by Lt. Kenneth Whiting. Offloading was completed by 10 June.

22—Enlisted men of the First Aeronautic Detachment began preliminary flight training in Caudron land planes under French instructors at the Military Aviation School, Tours, France. At about the same time, fifty men of the detachment were sent to St. Raphael for training as mechanics.

JULY

7—Lt. Kenneth Whiting, commanding the First Aeronautic Detachment, cabled the secretary of the navy reporting the results of his negotiations with the French in regard to training and establishment of air stations and requested departmental approval. Under the terms of the agreement, the French agreed to train personnel of the detachment at existing French Army aviation schools and to start construction of three patrol stations for American use.

23—Ground instruction for prospective pilots and for aviation ground officers began at the Massachusetts Institute of Technology with a class of forty-three students comprising the Naval Air Detachment under command of Lt. E. H. McKitterick.

27—An Act of Congress authorized the president to take possession of North Island, San Diego, for use by the army and navy in establishing permanent aviation stations and aviation schools. The arrival of Lt. E. W. Spencer Jr. on 8 November 1917, marked the beginning of the present Naval Air Station, North Island.

27—Construction of the Naval Aircraft Factory (NAF) at the Navy Yard, Philadelphia, was authorized for the purposes of constructing aircraft, undertaking aeronautical developments, and providing aircraft construction cost data.

AUGUST

8—The approval by the secretary of the navy of plans to establish one training and three coastal patrol stations in France was the first of several dealing with an overseas base construction program that was expanded successively and ultimately provided twenty-seven locations in France, England, Ireland, and Italy from which naval air units were operating at the close of the war.

25—The NC flying boat development was initiated by chief constructor D. W. Taylor in a memo that outlined certain general requirements of an airplane needed in war and directed his staff to investigate the subject further.

SEPTEMBER

7—A winged foul anchor was adopted as an official device to be worn on the left breast by all qualified naval aviators. The design adopted was essentially that of the wings worn today.

26—Lt. L. H. Maxfield, commanding the Naval Air Detachment at Akron, Ohio, reported the qualification of eleven students, including himself, as lighter-than-air pilots, the first trained specifically as dirigible pilots.

OCTOBER

21—The 12-cylinder Liberty engine was successfully flown for the first time in a Curtiss HS-1 flying boat at Buffalo, New York. This flight and other successful demonstrations led to the adoption of both the engine and the airplane as standard service types.

24—The first organization of U.S. Naval Aviation Forces, Foreign Service, which had evolved from the First Aeronautic Detachment, was put into operation as Capt. H. I. Cone relieved Lt. Comdr. Kenneth Whiting of command over all naval aviation forces abroad.

NOVEMBER

18—U.S. aerial coastal patrols in European waters began with Tellier seaplanes from LeCroisic at the mouth of the Loire River.

DECEMBER

7—The Naval Aeronautic Station Pensacola was redesignated a naval air station.

1918

JANUARY

21—The First Marine Aeronautic Company, Capt. F. T. Evans, USMC, commanding, arrived at Naval Base 13, Ponta Delgada, to fly antisubmarine patrols over convoy lanes in the Azores area.

MARCH

7—The office of the director of naval aviation was established in the Office of the Chief of Naval Operations, and the aviation section became a division.

27—The first aircraft built at the NAF, the H-16, was flown for the first time. The H-16 was used in antisubmarine patrol from U.S. and European stations.

APRIL

15—The First Marine Aviation Force, commanded by Capt. A. A. Cunningham, USMC, was formed at Naval Air Station, Miami, and it later transferred overseas to operate as the Day Wing of the Northern Bombing Group.

30—The secretary of the navy approved a plan for air operations to be undertaken in the Dunkirk-Zeebrugge region against German submarine support facilities by a specially organized unit later designated the Northern Bombing Group.

SEPTEMBER

24—Lt. (jg) David S. Ingalls scored his fifth aerial victory in six weeks to become the navy's first ace.

NOVEMBER

11—An armistice was signed ending the hostilities of World War I. In the nineteen months of U.S. participation, the strength of naval aviation had grown to a force of 6,716 officers and 30,693 men in navy units, and 282 officers and 2,180 men in Marine Corps units, with 2,107 aircraft, 15 dirigibles, and 215 kite and free balloons on hand. Of these numbers, 18,000 officers and men and 570 aircraft had been sent abroad.

DECEMBER

30—Lt. T. C. Rodman, piloting a Curtiss H-16 flying boat at Pensacola, scored the navy's first win in the Curtiss Marine Trophy Race, an annual competition set up by Glenn H. Curtiss in 1915 to encourage seaplane development.

1919

MARCH

9—Lt. Comdr. E. O. McDonnell, piloting a Sopwith Camel, made the first flight from a turret platform on a U.S. Navy battleship as he successfully took off from no. 2 turret of the USS *Texas* (BB-35), lying at anchor at Guantánamo.

13—The chief of naval operations issued a preliminary program for postwar naval airplane development. Specialized types desired were fighters, torpedo carriers, and bombers for fleet use; single-engine, twin-engine, and long-distance patrol and bomber planes for station use; and a combination of land planes and seaplanes for Marine Corps use.

MAY

8—Seaplane Division 1, comprised of three Navy/Curtiss NC flying boats, took off from NAS Rockaway, New York, at 10:00 A.M. for Halifax, Nova Scotia, on the first leg of a projected transatlantic flight. Commanding the division, and the NC-3, was Comdr. John H. Towers. The NC-4 was commanded by Lt. Comdr. A. C. Read. The NC-1 was commanded by Lt. Comdr. P. N. L. Bellinger.

27—At 8:01 P.M. the NC-4 landed in the harbor at Lisbon, Portugal, completing the first crossing of the Atlantic Ocean by air. The only one of three NC boats to reach the Azores by air, the NC-4 arrived the afternoon of the seventeenth, and after a layover of ten days, covered the last leg of the crossing to Lisbon. The NC-4 flight terminated at Plymouth, England, on 31 May.

JULY

1—The secretary of the navy authorized installation of launching platforms on two main turrets in each of eight battleships.

1920

SEPTEMBER

17—The site of the naval aviation activities on Ford Island was officially designated Naval Air Station, Pearl Harbor.

NOVEMBER

4—The third of a series of tests to determine the effectiveness of aerial bombs against ships was completed, using the old battleship *Indiana* (ex-BB-58) as a target at Tangier Sound in the Chesapeake Bay.

1921

MARCH

7—Capt. William A. Moffett relieved Capt. T. T. Craven as director of naval aviation.

JULY

12—An Act of Congress created a Bureau of Aeronautics, charged with matters pertaining to naval aeronautics as prescribed by the secretary of the navy.

21—The German battleship *Ostfriesland* was sunk by heavy bombs dropped by army bombers in the last of a series of tests to determine the effectiveness of air weapons against combatant ships and the means by which ship design and construction might counter their destructive capability. The tests, in which the army participated at the invitation of the navy, were carried out off the Virginia capes beginning 21 June. The significance of the tests was hotly debated and became a bone of contention between generations of army and navy air officers. The one firm conclusion that could be drawn was that aircraft, in unopposed attack, could sink capital ships.

AUGUST

11—Practical development of carrier arresting gear was initiated at Hampton Roads as Lt. A. M. Pride taxied an Aeromarine 39-B onto the dummy deck and engaged arresting wires. These tests resulted in the development of arresting gear for the USS *Langley* (CV-1), consisting essentially of both athwartship wires attached to weights and fore-and-aft wires.

SEPTEMBER

1—The Bureau of Aeronautics, under its chief, Rear Adm. W. A. Moffett, began functioning as an organizational unit of the Navy Department.

OCTOBER

26—A compressed-air, turntable catapult, in its first successful test, launched a Curtiss N-9 seaplane piloted by Comdr. H. C. Richardson from a pier at Philadelphia Navy Yard.

NOVEMBER

3—A Curtiss-Navy racer, powered by a 400-horsepower Curtiss engine, on loan to the builder and piloted by Bert Acosta, won the Pulitzer Race at Omaha with a world record speed of 176.7 mph.

1922

FEBRUARY

6—The Washington Treaty, limiting naval armament, was signed at Washington, D.C., by representatives of the British Empire, France, Italy, Japan, and the United States. The treaty established a tonnage ratio of 5-5-3 for capital ships of Great Britain, the United States, and Japan, respectively, and a lesser figure for France and Italy. The same ratio for aircraft carrier tonnage set overall limits at 135,000-135,000-81,000 tons. The treaty also limited any new carrier to 27,000 tons with a provision that, if total carrier tonnage were not exceeded thereby, nations could build two carriers of not more than 33,000 tons each or obtain them by converting existing or partially constructed ships that would otherwise be scrapped by this treaty.

MARCH

2—Experimental investigation and development of catapults using gunpowder were initiated, eventually producing a new type of catapult for use in launching aircraft from capital ships.

20—The USS *Langley* (CV-1), converted from the collier *Jupiter* (AC-3), was placed in commission at Norfolk as the first carrier of the U.S. Navy, under command of her executive officer, Comdr. Kenneth Whiting.

MAY

24—Routine operation of catapults aboard ship commenced with the successful launching of a Vought VE-7 piloted by Lt. Andrew C. McFall, with Lt. D. C. Ramsey as passenger, from the battleship USS *Maryland* (BB-46), off Yorktown, Virginia. A compressed-air catapult was used.

JULY

1—Congress authorized conversion of two unfinished battle cruisers to aircraft carriers, the *Lexington* (CV-2) and the *Saratoga* (CV-3), as permitted under the terms of the Washington Treaty.

3—Class 16, the first class of student naval aviators to be trained in land planes, began training at Pensacola.

OCTOBER

8—The Curtiss Marine Trophy Race for seaplanes, held at Detroit as an event of the National Air Races, was won by Lt. A. W. Gorton, flying a Naval Aircraft Factory TR-1.

14—Lts. H. J. Brow and A. J. Williams, flying CR-2 and CR-1 Curtiss Racers, finished third and fourth in the Pulitzer Trophy Race at Detroit, making speeds of 193 and 187 mph respectively.

17—The first carrier takeoff in the U.S. Navy was made by Lt. V. C. Griffin in a Vought VE-7SF from the USS *Langley* (CV-1), at anchor in the York River.

26—Lt. Comdr. Godfrey De C. Chevalier, flying an Aeromarine 39-B, made the first landing aboard the carrier USS *Langley* (CV-1) while under way off Cape Henry.

NOVEMBER

14—Lt. Comdr. Godfrey de C. Chevalier, naval aviator no. 7, died in the Naval Hospital, Portsmouth, Virginia, of injuries received in a plane crash two days before at Lochaven, near Norfolk.

18—Comdr. Kenneth Whiting, piloting a Naval Aircraft Factory PT seaplane, made the first catapult launching from the carrier USS *Langley* (CV-1) while at anchor in the York River.

1923

FEBRUARY

18–22—Aviation was employed in a U.S. Fleet Problem for the first time as Fleet Problem I tested the defenses of the Panama Canal against air attack. Blue Fleet and army coastal and air units defending the Canal were assisted by the operations of eighteen patrol planes of Scouting Plane Squadron 1 (VS-1) based on the tenders *Wright* (AV-1), *Sandpiper* (AVP-9), and *Teal* (AVP-5). During the exercises, a single plane representing an air group flew in undetected and, without air opposition or antiaircraft fire, theoretically destroyed Gatun Spillway with ten miniature bombs.

JUNE

6–13—At San Diego, California, planes and pilots of Aircraft Squadrons, Battle Fleet, established twenty world records for Class C seaplanes for various performance categories including speed, distance, duration, and altitude.

SEPTEMBER

4—The USS *Shenandoah* (ZR-1) made its first flight at Naval Air Station, Lakehurst, Capt. F. R. McCrary commanding.

28—U.S. Navy aircraft won first and second places in the international seaplane race for the Schneider Cup at Cowes, England, and in winning established a new world record for seaplanes with a speed of 169.89 mph for 200 kilometers. Lt. David Rittenhouse, the new record holder, marked up 177.38 mph for the race, and Lt. Rutledge Irvine placed second with 173.46 mph.

trimotor named the *Josephine Ford*, made the first flight over the North Pole. After circling the pole, they returned to base at Kings Bay, Spitzbergen, completing the round trip in fifteen and a half hours.

14—The Curtiss Marine Trophy Race, held off Haines Point over the Potomac River, was won by Lt. T. P. Jeter in a Curtiss F6C-1 Hawk with a speed of 130.94 mph.

JUNE

6—The last elements of the Alaskan Aerial Survey Expedition, under command of Lt. B. H. Wyatt, departed Seattle for Alaska to conduct an aerial mapping survey.

24—An Act of Congress, implementing the recommendations of the Morrow Board of 1925, provided that command of aviation stations, schools, and tactical flight units be assigned to naval aviators; that command of aircraft carriers and tenders be assigned to either naval aviators or naval aviation observers; that the office of an assistant secretary of the navy be created to foster naval aeronautics; and that a five-year aircraft program be set up under which the number on hand would be increased to reach one thousand useful airplanes.

AUGUST

9—In a day of tests to determine the speed with which aircraft could be operated at sea, pilots of Fighter Squadron 1 (VF-1) completed 127 landings aboard USS *Langley* (CV-1). As a result of the experience gained, the same squadron later landed twelve airplanes in twenty-one minutes under the emergency conditions created when the ship ran into a heavy mist.

27—Comdr. John Rodgers, naval aviator no. 2, on a flight from Anacostia, crashed in the Delaware River near the Naval Aircraft Factory dock at Philadelphia and received injuries from which he died on the same day.

NOVEMBER

13—Lt. C. F. Schilt, USMC, flying a Curtiss R3C-2, took second in the Schneider Cup Race at Hampton Roads, Virginia, with an average speed of 231.363 mph. This was the last navy participation in international racing competition.

1927

JANUARY

1—A flight test section was established as a separate department at Naval Air Station, Anacostia, with Lt. G. R. Henderson in charge.

1—To test the feasibility of using enlisted pilots in fleet squadrons, Fighter Squadron 2 (VF-2), manned with four naval aviators and ten aviation pilots, was put into commission at San Diego, Lt. Comdr. J. M. Shoemaker commanding.

MAY

27—Dive-bombing came under official study as the chief of naval operations ordered the commander in chief, Battle Fleet, to conduct tests to evaluate its effectiveness against moving targets. Carried out by Fighter Squadron 5S (VF-5S) in late summer and early fall, the results of these tests led directly to the development of equipment and adoption of the tactic as a standard method of attack.

JULY

4—Lt. C. C. Champion, flying a Wright Apache, reached 37,995 feet over

Anacostia, thereby breaking his own world altitude record for Class C seaplanes. This height exceeded any previously reached by heavier-than-air craft.

17—Maj. Ross E. Rowell, USMC, led a flight of five de Havilland DH aircraft in a strafing and dive-bombing attack against bandit forces surrounding a garrison of U.S. Marines at Ocotal, Nicaragua. Although instances of diving attacks had occurred during World War I and Marine Corps pilots had used the same technique in Haiti in 1919, this attack was made according to doctrine developed in training and is generally considered to be the first organized dive-bombing attack in combat.

25—Three weeks after breaking the seaplane altitude record, Lt. C. C. Champion took off from Anacostia in a Wright Apache rigged as a land plane and reached 38,419 feet, establishing a new world record that stood for two years.

NOVEMBER

16—The USS *Saratoga* (CV-3), first carrier and fifth ship of the navy to bear the name, was placed in commission at Camden, New Jersey, Capt. H. E. Yarnell commanding.

DECEMBER

14—The USS *Lexington* (CV-2), first carrier and fourth ship of the navy to carry the name, was commissioned at Quincy, Massachusetts, Capt. A. W. Marshall commanding.

1928

JANUARY

5—The first takeoff and landing on the USS *Lexington* (CV-2) was made by Lt. A. M. Pride in a Vought UO-1 as the ship moved from the Fore River Plant to the Boston Navy Yard.

11—The first takeoff and landing on the USS *Saratoga* (CV-3) was made by her air officer, Comdr. Marc A. Mitscher, in a Vought UO-1.

FEBRUARY

27—Comdr T. G. Ellyson, naval aviator no. 1, Lt. Comdr. Hugo Schmidt, and Lt. Rogers Ransehounsen, crashed to their deaths in a Loening amphibian in Chesapeake Bay while on a night flight from Norfolk to Annapolis.

JUNE

12—The USS *Lexington* (CV-2) anchored in Lahaina Roads at the end of a speed run from San Pedro to Honolulu that broke all existing records for the distance with an elapsed time of seventy-two hours, thirty-four minutes.

JULY

11–12—A Naval Aircraft Factory PN-12 piloted by Lt. A. W. Gorton and Chief Boatswain E. E. Reber, in a flight out of Philadelphia, set five world records for Class C seaplanes.

1929

JANUARY

23–27—The carriers *Lexington* (CV-2) and *Saratoga* (CV-3) appeared in fleet

1932
MARCH

24—The Army Air Corps, in response to enthusiastic reports from its observers who had witnessed the performance of the MK XV Norden bombsight in navy trials, requested the navy to provide it with twenty-five MK XV sights. This was the army's first commitment for the navy-developed sight that was to become essential to the high altitude precision bombing of World War II.

APRIL

2—Torpedo Squadron 5A (VT-5A, ex-VT-20) sailed from the Philippines on board the USS *Jason* (AV-2). When Scouting Squadron 8A (VS-8A), the only squadron remaining in the area, was decommissioned the following June, aviation in the Asiatic Fleet was reduced to the observation aircraft on board cruisers.

JUNE

30—The USS *Los Angeles* (ZR-3) was decommissioned for economy reasons at Naval Air Station, Lakehurst, after eight years of service and more than five thousand hours in the air.

1933
FEBRUARY

16—The president presented to Col. Nathan D. Ely, USA (Ret.), the Distinguished Flying Cross, awarded posthumously to Colonel Ely's son, Eugene B. Ely, for extraordinary achievement as a pioneer aviator and for significant contribution as a civilian to the development of aviation in the navy when, in 1910 and 1911, he demonstrated the feasibility of operating aircraft from ships.

APRIL

4—The rigid airship USS *Akron* (ZRS-4) crashed in a severe storm off Barnegat Light, New Jersey. Among the seventy-three fatalities were Rear Adm. William A. Moffett, chief, Bureau of Aeronautics, and Comdr. Frank C. McCord, commanding officer of the *Akron*.

JUNE

16—Under the terms of the National Industrial Recovery Act, the president allotted $238 million to the navy for the construction of new ships, including two aircraft carriers. In less than two months, contracts were awarded for two carriers, eventually commissioned as the *Yorktown* (CV-5) and *Enterprise* (CV-6).

23—The USS *Macon* (ZRS-5), having made its first flight on 21 April, was commissioned at Akron, Ohio, with Comdr. Alger H. Dressel as commanding officer.

AUGUST

8—Commander Aircraft, Battle Force, requested authority to use variable-pitch propellers during forthcoming exercises on six Boeing F4B-4s of Fighter Squadron 3 (VF-3), based on board the *Langley* (CV-1), and on one F4B-4 of Fighter Squadron 1 (VF-1), based on board the *Saratoga* (CV-3). This request marked the initial service acceptance of the variable-pitch propeller.

SEPTEMBER

7–8—Six Consolidated P2Y-1 flying boats of Patrol Squadron 5F (VP-5F), under the command of Lt. Comdr. H. E. Halland, flew nonstop from Norfolk, Virginia, to Coco Solo, C.Z., making a record distance formation flight of 2,059 miles in twenty-five hours, nineteen minutes.

OCTOBER

28—A contract was issued to Consolidated for the XP3Y-1 flying boat, marking the initiation of navy-sponsored development of the PBY Catalina series of flying boats that were used throughout World War II.

NOVEMBER

17—The sum of $7.5 million was allotted to the navy from funds provided under the National Industrial Recovery Act of 16 June 1933, for the procurement of new aircraft and equipment, thereby permitting the Bureau of Aeronautics to maintain its thousand-plane program, to equip operating aircraft with modern navigation instruments and radios, and to make other improvements in naval aircraft and their accessories that were not possible under the annual appropriation.

1934

JANUARY

10–11—Six Consolidated P2Y-1s of Patrol Squadron 10F (VP-10F), Lt. Comdr. K. McGinnis commanding, made a nonstop formation flight from San Francisco to Pearl Harbor in twenty-four hours, thirty-five minutes, thereby bettering the best previous time for the crossing.

MARCH

27—An Act of Congress, approved by the president and popularly known as the Vinson-Trammell Act, established the composition of the navy at the limit prescribed by the Washington and London Naval Treaties. Among other things, the act authorized construction of a number of ships, including one aircraft carrier of about 15,000 tons. Under the authorization, the *Wasp* (CV-7) was laid down in 1936.

APRIL

28—The equipment and techniques of alongside recovery by plane net had developed to the point that commander Cruisers, Battle Force, issued a directive describing the method that would be used by all ships of his command, and underway recovery of seaplanes by battleships and cruisers soon became routine.

JUNE

4—The USS *Ranger* (CV-4) was placed in commission at Norfolk, Virginia, Capt. A. L. Bristol commanding.

21—First landings and takeoffs were made aboard the USS *Ranger* (CV-4) by the ship's aviators led by Lt. Comdr. A.C. Davis. After completing normal operations, the ship went full speed astern and aircraft were landed into the bow arresting gear.

JULY

19—Lt. H. B. Miller and Lt. (jg) F. N. Kivette, flying Curtiss F9C-2s without their landing gear, dropped from the trapeze of the USS *Macon* (ZRS-5) to scout for the USS *Houston* (CA-30) returning from a cruise in the Pacific with President

F. D. Roosevelt on board. Because of the improved performance of the aircraft on this first flight without landing gear, it became standard operating procedure to fly *Macon* planes from the trapeze in this configuration.

1935
FEBRUARY

12—After encountering a severe gust of wind that caused a structural failure, the rigid airship USS *Macon* (ZRS-5) crashed off Point Sur, California, with two fatalities.

JULY

20—The first class of aviation cadets to report for flight training convened at NAS Pensacola.

30—The first blind landing aboard a carrier was made by Lt. Frank Akers, who took off from NAS San Diego in a Berliner Joyce OJ-2 with hooded cockpit, located the USS *Langley* (CV-1) under way in an unknown position, and landed aboard.

NOVEMBER

15—The chief, Bureau of Aeronautics, approved recommendations from a fighter design competition and thereby initiated development of the Grumman XF4F-1 biplane and the Brewster XF2A-1 monoplane. The developmental sequence thus set in motion provided prototypes of the navy's first-line fighters in use when the United States entered World War II.

1936
MAY

6—Construction of the facility, which was later named the David W. Taylor Model Basin, was authorized by legislation, providing buildings and appliances for use by the Bureau of Construction and Repair in investigating and determining shapes and forms to be adopted for U.S. vessels, including aircraft.

SEPTEMBER

15—The USS *Langley* (CV-1) was detached from Battle Force and assigned to commander Aircraft, Base Force, for duty as a seaplane tender. After a brief period of operation, she went into the yard for conversion, from which she emerged early in 1937 with the forward part of her flight deck removed.

1937
JUNE

30—A contract was issued to the Martin Company for the XPBM-1 twin-engine flying boat patrol plane. The aircraft was the initial prototype in the PBM Mariner series of flying boats used during World War II.

SEPTEMBER

30—The USS *Yorktown* (CV-5) was placed in commission at Norfolk, Virginia, Capt. E. D. McWhorter commanding.

1938

MAY

12—The USS *Enterprise* (CV-6) was commissioned at Newport News, Virginia, Capt. N. H. White commanding.

JULY

1—New command billets titled commander, carrier air group, were authorized, and carrier squadrons were organized into groups, each designated by the name of the carrier to which it was assigned.

AUGUST

23—A contract was issued to Martin for the XPB2M-1 four-engine flying boat. Initially intended as a patrol plane, this craft was later converted to the PB2M-1R Mars transport and served as a prototype for the JRM series of flying boats.

1939

APRIL

7—An amphibian version of the PBY Catalina flying boat was ordered from Consolidated. This aircraft, the first successful amphibian patrol plane procured by the navy, was the prototype for the PBY-5A, which was widely used in World War II.

JUNE

13—The USS *Saratoga* (CV-3) and the tanker USS *Kanawha* (AO-1) completed a two-day underway refueling test off the coast of southern California, thereby demonstrating the feasibility of refueling carriers at sea.

AUGUST

4—The USS *Yorktown* (CV-5) and USS *Enterprise* (CV-6) made successful launchings of Curtiss SBC-3 and Vought O3U-3 aircraft from flight deck and hangar deck catapults in the first practical demonstration of launching aircraft from carriers by means of a hydraulic flush-deck catapult and in the first demonstrations of catapulting aircraft from the hangar deck.

30—Lt. Comdr. Thurston B. Clark, flying a twin-engine Lockheed XJO-3 equipped with tricycle landing gear, made eleven landings aboard and takeoffs from the *Lexington* (CV-2) off Coronado Roads, thereby demonstrating the basic adaptability of twin-engine aircraft and of tricycle landing gear to carrier operations.

SEPTEMBER

5—The president proclaimed the neutrality of the United States in the European War and directed that the navy organize a Neutrality Patrol. In complying therewith, the chief of naval operations ordered the commander of the Atlantic Squadron to establish combined air and ship reconnaissance of the sea approaches to the United States and West Indies for the purpose of reporting and tracking any belligerent air, surface, or underwater units in the area.

8—The president proclaimed the existence of a limited national emergency and directed measures for strengthening national defenses within the limits of peacetime authorizations.

11—In the first redeployment of patrol squadrons on the Neutrality Patrol, Patrol Squadron 33 (VP-33), equipped with Catalinas, transferred from the Canal Zone to Guantánamo, Cuba, for operations over the Caribbean. Two days later, the Catalinas of Patrol Squadron 51 (VP-51) arrived at San Juan, Puerto Rico, from Norfolk to patrol the southern approaches to the Caribbean through the Lesser Antilles.

21—Patrol Squadron 21 (VP-21), with fourteen PBY aircraft, took off from Pearl Harbor for the Philippines via Midway, Wake, and Guam, to become the first patrol unit in the Asiatic Fleet since 1932.

DECEMBER

20—A contract was issued to Consolidated for two hundred PBY aircraft to support an increase in patrol plane squadrons growing out of Neutrality Patrol requirements. This was the largest single order for naval aircraft since the end of World War I.

1940

FEBRUARY

29—The Bureau of Aeronautics initiated action that led to a contract with Professor H. O. Croft, University of Iowa, to investigate the possibilities of a turbojet propulsion unit for aircraft.

MARCH

22—Development of guided missiles was initiated at the Naval Aircraft Factory with the establishment of a project for adapting radio controls to a torpedo-carrying Great Lakes TG-2 airplane.

APRIL

25—The USS *Wasp* (CV-7) was commissioned at Boston, Capt. J. W. Reeves, Jr., commanding.

JUNE

14—The Naval Expansion Act included authorization for an increase in aircraft carrier tonnage of 79,500 tons over the limits set 17 May 1938, and a revision of authorized aircraft strength to 4,500 useful airplanes.

15—Congress revised its previous action and set the aircraft ceiling at 10,000 useful airplanes, including 850 for the Naval Reserve, and not more than 48 useful airships.

JULY

19—Authorization for a further expansion of the navy provided an increase of two hundred thousand tons in the aircraft carrier limits set the previous month, and a new aircraft ceiling of fifteen thousand useful planes. The act also allowed further increases in aircraft strength on presidential approval.

AUGUST

25—A contract was issued by the National Defense Research Committee to the Department of Terrestrial Magnetism, Carnegie Institution of Washington, for research that culminated in the radio VT fuze for antiaircraft guns and both radio and photoelectric VT fuzes for bombs and rockets.

SEPTEMBER

2—In exchange for fifty four-stack destroyers, Great Britain ceded to the United States, for a period of ninety-nine years, sites for naval and air bases in the Bahamas, Jamaica, St. Lucia, Trinidad, Antigua, and British Guiana, and extended similar rights freely and without consideration for bases in Bermuda and Newfoundland.

OCTOBER

5—The secretary of the navy placed all divisions and aviation squadrons of the Organized Reserve on short notice for call to active duty and granted authority to call Fleet Reservists as necessary. On the 24th the Bureau of Navigation announced plans for mobilizing the aviation squadrons, which called for one-third to be ordered to active duty by 7 November and all by 1 January 1941.

28—The chief of naval operations reported that aircraft with some form of armor and fuel protection were beginning to go into service use, and that within a year practically all fleet aircraft would have such protection.

1941

MARCH

11—The president was empowered by an act of Congress to provide goods and services to those nations whose defense he deemed vital to the defense of the United States, thus initiating a lend-lease program under which large quantities of the munitions and implements of war were delivered to U.S. allies. The USS *Archer* (BAVG-1), transferred on 17 November 1941, was the first of thirty-eight escort carriers transferred to the United Kingdom during World War II.

28—The commanding officer of the *Yorktown* (CV-5), after five months of operational experience with the CXAM radar, reported that aircraft had been tracked at a distance of one hundred miles and recommended that friendly aircraft be equipped with electronic identification devices and carriers be equipped with separate and complete facilities for tracking and plotting all radar targets.

MAY

21—The Bureau of Aeronautics requested the Engineering Experiment Station, Annapolis, Maryland, to undertake development of a liquid-fueled assisted take-off unit for use on patrol planes, marking the navy's entry into the field that later came to be called JATO.

27—The president proclaimed that an unlimited national emergency confronted the country, requiring that its military, naval, air, and civilian defenses be put on the basis of readiness to repel any and all acts or threats of aggression directed toward any part of the Western Hemisphere.

JUNE

2—The USS *Long Island* (AVG-1), first escort carrier of the U.S. Navy, was commissioned at Newport News, Virginia, Comdr. D. B. Duncan commanding. The *Long Island* was a flush-deck carrier converted in sixty-seven working days from the cargo ship *Mormacmail*.

30—Turboprop engine development was initiated as a joint army-navy project, with a navy contract to Northrop Aircraft for the design of an aircraft gas turbine developing 2,500 horsepower.

JULY

7—The First Marine Aircraft Wing, composed of a Headquarters Squadron and Marine Air Group I, was organized at Quantico, the first of its type in the Marine Corps and the first of five wings organized during World War II.

18—Patrol Wing 7 squadrons became the first operational units of the U.S. Navy to be supplied with radar-equipped aircraft.

AUGUST

6—In recognition of the radical change that radar was causing in the method of using fighters to protect the fleet, the chief of naval operations issued a "Tentative Doctrine for Fighter Direction from Aircraft Carriers" and directed that carriers and other ships equipped with radar immediately organize fighter direction centers.

OCTOBER

20—The USS *Hornet* (CV-8) was commissioned at Norfolk, Capt. Marc A. Mitscher commanding.

21—In tests with MAD gear (Magnetic Airborne Detector), a PBY located the submarine *S-48*.

29—Patrol Squadron 82 (VP-82) received the first of a planned full complement of Lockheed PBO-1s at NAS Norfolk, marking the beginning of what became an extensive use of land planes by patrol squadrons during World War II.

NOVEMBER

1—By Executive Order the president directed that, until further orders, the Coast Guard operate as a part of the U.S. Navy subject to the orders of the secretary of the navy.

DECEMBER

7—Japanese carrier aircraft launched a devastating attack on ships at Pearl Harbor and on the military and air installations in the area. The three aircraft carriers of the Pacific Fleet were not present. The *Saratoga* (CV-3) was moored at San Diego. The *Lexington* (CV-2) was at sea about 425 miles southeast of Midway toward which she was headed to deliver a marine scout bombing squadron. The *Enterprise* (CV-6) was also at sea about two hundred miles west of Pearl Harbor, returning from Wake Island after delivering a marine fighter squadron there.

8—The United States Congress declared a state of war with Japan.

The source for this appendix was the Department of the Navy's "United States Naval Aviation, 1910–1995," prepared in 1997.

Glossary of Terms and Abbreviations

Air officer: ship's officer responsible for aviation matters in an aircraft carrier

AP: aviation pilot; enlisted naval aviator

Arresting gear: arrangement of wires on a carrier flight deck that stops an airplane after airplane's tailhook has engaged it

ASW: antisubmarine warfare

Barograph: a recording barometer; an instrument for measuring atmospheric pressure, used in weather forecasting and in determining elevation

Barricade: a collapsible arrangement of vertical webbing rigged on an aircraft carrier in an emergency to arrest airplanes unable to make a normal arrested landing

Barrier: collapsible fences on a carrier flight deck that stop those airplanes whose hooks have missed the arresting gear; before the advent of the angled deck

Big Bertha: a large cannon used by the Germans in World War I

Blackshoes: surface or ship personnel; brownshoes refer to aviators

BOQ: Bachelor Officers Quarters

BuAer: Bureau of Aeronautics

Bungee: an elasticized cord used as a fastening or shock absorbing device, especially for airplanes on the deck of a carrier

CAA: Civil Aeronautics Administration

Captain's mast: a formal meeting at which the commanding officer either awards punishment, listens to requests, or commends men for special services

Carrier air group: aircraft of a carrier, made up of squadrons

Cat: catapult; steam-actuated mechanism used to hurl (launch) aircraft from the deck of an aircraft carrier

Chief of staff: captain or admiral who assists an admiral, as his second in command, especially in supervising his staff

CNO: Chief of Naval Operations; top uniformed officer in the navy

CO: commanding officer

Cocarde: a distinguishing mark on an airplane to indicate special military status

Collier: a coal ship

ComCarDiv: Commander, Carrier Division

Continuous wave (CW): radio waves that continue with unchanging intensity or amplitude without modulation and that are used in telegraphy in which the wave is turned on and off with a key to form the dots and dashes of a code, as in Morse code

Cruise: a tour of sea duty

Cumshaw: a tip; gratuity; present

Cut: a mandatory signal from LSO for pilot to land on the carrier

CV: aircraft carrier

CVA: attack aircraft carrier

CVAN/CVN: attack aircraft carrier, nuclear-powered

CVE: escort carrier

CVL: light carrier

DCNO (Air): Deputy Chief of Naval Operations for Air

Dead reckoning (DR) navigation: method of navigation using direction and amount of progress from the last well-determined position to a new DR position

Division: basic administrative unit into which men are divided on board ship, in aircraft squadrons, or at shore activities; also, a tactical subdivision of a squadron of ships or aircraft (four)

Dolly: a low mobile platform that rolls on castors, used for moving heavy loads

E (battle efficiency award): an award by CNO to ships and aircraft squadrons of the fleet

F.A.I.: Federation Aeronautique Internationale

Fiddle bridge: on early aircraft carriers, upright pieces of wood used to support arresting wires above the flight deck to facilitate engagement of the wire by the tailhook of an airplane; eventually replaced by metal strips, or yielding elements

Fire wall: a fire-resistant transverse bulkhead separating the engine compartment from the other parts of an aircraft structure

Flag: admiral rank

Flag bridge: bridge of a ship used by a flag officer and his staff

Flag lieutenant: personal aide to a flag officer

General quarters: condition of maximum readiness for combat with the crew at battle stations

G-suit: anti-G suit worn by pilots; a system of air bladders that compress legs and abdomen so the blood does not pool in the lower extremities during high performance maneuvers; prevents loss of blood to the brain

JO: junior officer, lieutenant and below

Landing signal officer (LSO): landing signal officer; man stationed on a platform at the aft end of a carrier who assists pilots in carrier landings

Leadline: The lead with attached line, used for taking soundings; also called a hand lead

Longerons: the fore-and-aft member of the framing of an airplane fuselage

Magnetic anomoly detector (MAD): detects submerged submarines by the slight change in the earth's magnetic field caused by the presence of a submarine in the area; the MAD "stinger" protrudes from the tail of modern maritime-reconnaissance aircraft

Makeylearn: one with little formal training in a particular field of expertise assigned to a billet in which he must learn through experience and "on-the-job" training

Master-at-arms (MAA): ship's police, headed by chief MAA who reports to the executive officer

Mustang: an officer who has risen from the ranks

N.A.C.A.: National Advisory Committee for Aeronautics

Nacelle: generally applied to the engine housing, or engine nacelle; correctly refers to any small construction on an aircraft, even including the fuselage, or crew nacelle

NAS: Naval Air Station

Omnirange: radio beacon, omnidirectional; a radio directive device employing a rotating radio beam which gives an indication of the relative bearing of the radio transmitting station

OOD/SDO: Officer of the Deck/Squadron Duty Officer; the officer who is responsible for handling the daily routine of the ship/squadron

OpNav: Office of the Chief of Naval Operations; Op-O5 (DCNO for Air) is a division within OpNav

PIM: position of intended movement; the anticipated position of a ship at a specified time

Plebe: freshman at the U.S. Naval Academy

Pollywog: one who has not crossed the equator

PPC: patrol plane commander

Quarters: an assembly, as *quarters for inspection* or a gathering on stations as *fire quarters;* government-owned houses or apartments assigned to naval personnel; living spaces on board ship

Ready room: compartment on a carrier where air crew gather for flight briefing, training, etc.

Roger: LSO signal with arms (paddles) extended horizontally to either side meaning landing approach is satisfactory

Rotary engine: an engine having revolving cylinders arranged radially around a common fixed crankshaft

Scuttlebutt: a shipboard drinking fountain; also, rumor or gossip

Section: with aircraft, generally a unit of two planes

Shakedown: period of adjustment, clean up, and training for a ship after commissioning or a major overhaul; after commissioning, a ship makes a *shakedown cruise*

Shellback: one who has crossed the equator

Short arm inspection: slang for a venereal, medical inspection of enlisted men

Sled: net trailed behind a ship in which a hook on a seaplane's pontoon engages as the seaplane is recovered with the ship under way

SOS: international distress signal; Save Our Ship

Squadron: with aircraft, a unit of twelve to twenty-four airplanes

Squirrel cage (loops): an endless, repetitive series of loops, frequently with a formation of airplanes

Star man: midshipman at the U.S. Naval Academy who excels academically

Tail skid: a skid attached to the rear underside of certain airplanes to act as a runner

Tandem: one behind the other

Tin can: slang for destroyer

Touch-and-go landing: landing during which pilot applies full takeoff power after touching down, with the intent of taking off, rather than coming to a full stop

Waveoff: mandatory signal from LSO to pilot not to land

XO (exec): executive officer

Zouave: a member of a French infantry unit, formerly composed of Algerian recruits, characterized by colorful oriental uniforms and precision drilling

APPENDIX C

Selected Bibliography

ORAL HISTORIES

Note: Unless otherwise indicated, all oral histories were conducted by John T. Mason Jr. and are a part of the U.S. Naval Institute Oral History Collection.

Barnaby, Capt. Ralph Stanton. 1969.
Carl, Lt. Comdr. Robert E. 1986. Interviewed by Paul Stillwell.
Cline, Ens. Joseph Charles. 1969. Interviewed by Comdr. Etta-Belle Kitchen.
Foley, Rear Adm. Francis D. 1985. Interviewed by Paul Stillwell.
King, CWO Cecil St. Clair. 1989. Interviewed by Paul Stillwell.
Miller, Rear Adm. Harold Blaine. 1981.
Moorer, Adm. Thomas H. 1975.
Pride, Adm. Alfred Melville. 1970. Interviewed by Peter Spectre.
Riley, Vice Adm. Herbert D. 1971.
Thach, Adm. John S. 1970. Interviewed by Comdr. Etta-Belle Kitchen.
Tomlinson, Capt. Daniel Webb IV. 1985. Interviewed by Barrett Tillman.
Van Deurs, Rear Adm. George. 1969. Interviewed by Comdr. Etta-Belle Kitchen.
Warren, Aldred K. 1970.

SECONDARY SOURCES

Althoff, William F. *Sky Ships: A History of the Airship in the United States Navy.* New York: Orion Books, 1990.

Arthur, Reginald Wright. *Contact: Careers of Naval Aviators, Assigned Numbers 1–2000.* Washington, D.C.: Naval Aviation Register, 1967.

Barker, Ralph. *The Schneider Trophy Races.* London: Chatto and Windus, 1971.

Byrd, Richard E. *Discovery: The Story of the Second Byrd Antarctic Expedition.* New York: Putnam, 1935.

———. *Little America, Aerial Exploration in the Antarctic, the Flight to the South Pole.* New York: Putnam, 1930.

Caidin, Martin. *Golden Wings: A Pictorial History of the United States Navy and Marine Corps in the Air.* New York: Random House, 1960.

Chesneau, Roger. *Aircraft Carriers of the World, 1914 to the Present: An Illustrated Encyclopedia.* Annapolis, Md.: Naval Institute Press, 1984.

Coletta, Paolo E. *Patrick N. L. Bellinger and U.S. Naval Aviation.* Lanham, Md: University Press of America, 1987.

Creed, Roscoe. *PBY: The Catalina Flying Boat.* Annapolis, Md.: Naval Institute Press, 1986.

Davis, Burke. *The Billy Mitchell Affair.* New York: Random House, 1967.

Dickey, Philip S. III. *The Liberty Engine, 1918–1942.* Washington, D.C.: Smithsonian Institution Press, 1968.

Elliott, John M. *The Official Monogram U.S. Navy and Marine Corps Aircraft Color Guide.* Boylston, Mass.: Monogram Aviation Publications, 1987.

Foxworth, Thomas G. *The Speed Seekers.* Newberry Park, Calif.: Haynes Publications, 1989.

Friedman, Norman. *U.S. Aircraft Carriers: An Illustrated Design History.* Annapolis, Md.: Naval Institute Press, 1985.

Frothingham, Thomas G. *The Naval History of the World War.* Cambridge, Mass.: Harvard University Press, 1924–26. 3 vols.

Fry, John. *USS* Saratoga, *CV-3: An Illustrated History of the Legendary Aircraft Carrier, 1927–1946.* Atglen, Pa.: Schiffer Publishing, 1996.

Gibson, Richard H., and Maurice Predergast. *The German Submarine War, 1914–1918.* New York: Richard Smith, 1931.

Grant, Robert M. *U-Boats Destroyed: The Effect of Anti-Submarine Warfare, 1914–1918.* London: Putnam, 1964.

Grossnick, Roy A., et al. *United States Naval Aviation, 1910–1995.* Washington, D. C.: Naval History Center, 1997.

Halsey, William F., and Bryan J. Halsey III. *Admiral Halsey's Story.* New York: McGraw-Hill, 1947.

Hezlet, Sir Arthur R. *Aircraft and Sea Power.* London: P. Davies, 1970.

Hook, Thom. *Shenandoah Saga.* Annapolis, Md.: Air Show Publishers, 1973.

Knott, Richard C. *The American Flying Boat: An Illustrated History.* Annapolis, Md.: Naval Institute Press, 1979.

Knox, Dudley W. *The Eclipse of American Sea Power.* New York: Army & Navy Journal, 1922.

Larkins, William T. *Battleship and Cruiser Aircraft of the United States Navy, 1910–1949.* Atglen, Pa.: Schiffer Publishing, 1996.

Layman, R. D. *Before the Aircraft Carrier: The Development of Aviation Vessels, 1849–1922.* Annapolis, Md.: Naval Institute Press, 1989.

MacLeish, Kenneth. *The Price of Honor: The World War I Letters of Naval Aviator Kenneth MacLeish.* Geoffrey L. Rossano, ed. Annapolis, Md.: Naval Institute Press, 1991.

Melhorn, Charles M. *Two-Block Fox: The Rise of the Aircraft Carrier, 1911–1929.* Annapolis, Md.: Naval Institute Press, 1974.

Messimer, Dwight R. *No Margin for Error: The U.S. Navy's Transpacific Flight of 1925.* Annapolis, Md.: Naval Institute Press, 1981.

Miller, Edward S. *War Plan Orange: The U.S. Strategy to Defeat Japan, 1897–1945.* Annapolis, Md.: Naval Institute Press, 1991.

Moffat, Alexander W. *Maverick Navy.* Middletown, Conn.: Wesleyan University Press, 1976.

Naval Aviation War Book Committee. *Flying Officers of the U.S. Navy, 1917–1919.* Washington, D.C.: National Capital Press Inc., 1919.

Paine, Ralph D. *The First Yale Unit: A Story of Naval Aviation, 1916–1919.* Vol. 2. Cambridge, Mass.: Riverside Press, 1925.

Pelz, Stephen E. *Race to Pearl Harbor: The Failure of the Second London Naval Conference and Onset of World War II.* Cambridge: Harvard University Press, 1974.

Polmar, Norman. *Aircraft Carriers: A Graphic History of Carrier Aviation and Its Influence on World Events.* New York: Doubleday, 1969.

Potter, E. B., and Chester W. Nimitz, eds. *Sea Power: A Naval History.* Englewood Cliffs, N.J.: Prentice-Hall, 1960.

Reynolds, Clark G. *Admiral John H. Towers: The Struggle for Naval Air Supremacy.* Annapolis, Md.: Naval Institute Press, 1991.

———. *The Fast Carriers: The Forging of an Air Navy.* Huntington, N.Y.: Robert E. Krieger Publishing, 1978.

Robinson, Douglas H., and Charles L. Keller. *Up Ship: U.S. Navy Airships, 1919–1935.* Annapolis, Md.: Naval Institute Press, 1982.

Roseberry, C. R. *Glenn Curtiss: Pioneer of Flight.* Garden City, N.Y.: Doubleday & Company, 1972.

Roscoe, Theodore. *On the Seas and in the Skies: A History of the U.S. Navy's Air Power.* New York: Hawthorne Books, 1970.

Scharff, Robert, and Walter S. Taylor. *Over Land and Sea: A Biography of Glenn Hammond Curtiss.* New York: David McKay Company, 1968.

Shipman, Richard. *Wings at the Ready: 75 Years of the Naval Air Reserve.* Annapolis, Md.: Naval Institute Press, 1991.

Smith, Peter C. *The History of Dive Bombing.* Annapolis, Md.: Nautical & Aviation Publishing, 1982.

Smith, Richard K. *First Across: The U.S. Navy's Transatlantic Flight of 1919.* Annapolis, Md.: Naval Institute Press, 1973.

———. *The Airships Akron & Macon: Flying Aircraft Carriers of the United States Navy.* Annapolis, Md.: Naval Institute Press, 1965.

Swanborough, Gordon, and Peter Bowers. *United States Navy Aircraft since 1911.* Annapolis, Md.: Naval Institute Press, 1990.

Sweetman, Jack. *The Landing at Veracruz, 1914: The First Complete Chronicle of a Strange Encounter in April, 1914, When the United States Navy Captured and Occupied the City of Veracruz, Mexico.* Annapolis, Md.: Naval Institute Press, 1968.

Tate, Jackson R. "We Rode the Covered Wagon." U.S. Naval Institute *Proceedings* 104, no. 10 (Oct. 1978): 62–69.

———. "Moonlighters." *Naval Aviation News* (March 1972): 35–36.

Taylor, Theodore. *The Magnificent Mitscher.* New York: W. W. Norton, 1985.

Terzibaschitsch, Stefan. *Aircraft Carriers of the U.S. Navy.* 2d ed. Annapolis, Md.: Naval Institute Press, 1989.

Trimble, William F. *Admiral William A. Moffett: Architect of Naval Aviation.* Washington, D.C.: Smithsonian Institution Press, 1994.

———. *Wings for the Navy: A History of the Naval Aircraft Factory.* Annapolis, Md.: Naval Institute Press, 1990.

Turnbull, Archibald D., and Clifford L. Lord. *History of United States Naval Aviation.* New Haven: Yale University Press, 1950.

U.S. Naval History Division. *Dictionary of American Naval Fighting Ships.* (8 volumes.) Washington, D.C.: Naval History Division, 1959–1991.

Vaeth, J. Gordon. *Blimps and U-Boats.* Annapolis, Md.: Naval Institute Press, 1992.

Van Deurs, George. *Anchors in the Sky: Spuds Ellyson, the First Naval Aviator.* San Rafael, Calif.: Presidio Press, 1978.

———. *Wings for the Fleet: A Narrative of Naval Aviation's Early Development, 1910–1916.* Annapolis, Md.: Naval Institute Press, 1966.

Van Wyen, Adrian O. *Naval Aviation in World War I.* Washington, D.C.: The Chief of Naval Operations, Government Printing Office, 1969.

Westervelt, George C., et al. *The Triumph of the NCs.* Garden City, N.Y.: Doubleday, 1920.

Wheeler, Gerald E. *Prelude to Pearl Harbor: The United States Navy and the Far East, 1921–1931.* Columbia: University of Missouri Press, 1963.

Woodhouse, Henry. *Textbook of Naval Aeronautics.* New York: The Century Co., 1917.

Wooldridge, E. T., ed. *Carrier Warfare in the Pacific: An Oral History Collection.* Washington, D.C.: Smithsonian Institution Press, 1993.

Index

About the Author

●

A graduate of the U.S. Naval Academy's class of 1950, Capt. E. T. "Tim" Wooldridge was designated a naval aviator in April 1952. As a test pilot at the Naval Air Test Center, Patuxent River, Maryland, he flew every type of aircraft in the U.S. Navy in the late 1950s. He later became commanding officer of a carrier-based fighter squadron and executive officer of the aircraft carrier USS *Forrestal*. Captain Wooldridge also attended the National War College and served several tours of duty on the strategic plans and policy staffs of the Navy Department and Joint Chiefs of Staff.

Captain Wooldridge joined the National Air and Space Museum in 1976 as a curator of naval aviation and eventually became Assistant Director for Museum Operations. In 1990 he was appointed Ramsey Fellow and Aviation Historian for the National Air and Space Museum and served in that post until December 1994. During that time, Captain Wooldridge wrote a number of books for the Smithsonian Institution Press, including *Images of Flight* (1983), *Focus on Flight* (1985), and a companion volume to this one, titled *Carrier Warfare in the Pacific: An Oral History Collection*.

Captain Wooldridge has written for the U.S. Naval Institute's *Naval History* bimonthly magazine, and he has edited another companion volume to *The Golden Age Remembered* titled *Into the Jet Age: Conflict and Change in Naval Aviation, 1945–1975*, which was published by the Naval Institute Press in 1995.